I0886795

Harnessing Human Capital Analytics for Competitive Advantage

Mohit Yadav
BML Munjal University, India

Shrawan Kumar Trivedi
Indian Institute of Management Sirmaur, India

Anil Kumar
BML Munjal University, India

Santosh Rangnekar
Indian Institute of Technology Roorkee, India

A volume in the Advances in Business Information Systems and Analytics (ABISA) Book Series

IGI Global
DISSEMINATOR OF KNOWLEDGE

Published in the United States of America by
IGI Global
Business Science Reference (an imprint of IGI Global)
701 E. Chocolate Avenue
Hershey PA, USA 17033
Tel: 717-533-8845
Fax: 717-533-8661
E-mail: cust@igi-global.com
Web site: http://www.igi-global.com

Copyright © 2018 by IGI Global. All rights reserved. No part of this publication may be reproduced, stored or distributed in any form or by any means, electronic or mechanical, including photocopying, without written permission from the publisher.
Product or company names used in this set are for identification purposes only. Inclusion of the names of the products or companies does not indicate a claim of ownership by IGI Global of the trademark or registered trademark.

Library of Congress Cataloging-in-Publication Data

Names: Yadav, Mohit, 1985- editor. | Trivedi, Shrawan Kumar, 1985- editor. | Kumar, Anil, 1980- editor.
Title: Harnessing human capital analytics for competitive advantage / Mohit Yadav, Shrawan Kumar Trivedi, Anil Kumar, and Santosh Rangnekar, editors.
Description: Hershey : Business Science Reference, [2018]
Identifiers: LCCN 2017027630| ISBN 9781522540380 (hardcover) | ISBN 9781522540397 (ebook)
Subjects: LCSH: Human capital. | Personnel management. | Competition.
Classification: LCC HD4904.7 .H325 2018 | DDC 658.3/06--dc23 LC record available at https://lccn.loc.gov/2017027630

This book is published in the IGI Global book series Advances in Business Information Systems and Analytics (ABISA) (ISSN: 2327-3275; eISSN: 2327-3283)

British Cataloguing in Publication Data
A Cataloguing in Publication record for this book is available from the British Library.

All work contributed to this book is new, previously-unpublished material.
The views expressed in this book are those of the authors, but not necessarily of the publisher.

For electronic access to this publication, please contact: eresources@igi-global.com.

Advances in Business Information Systems and Analytics (ABISA) Book Series

ISSN:2327-3275
EISSN:2327-3283

Editor-in-Chief: Madjid Tavana, La Salle University, USA

MISSION

The successful development and management of information systems and business analytics is crucial to the success of an organization. New technological developments and methods for data analysis have allowed organizations to not only improve their processes and allow for greater productivity, but have also provided businesses with a venue through which to cut costs, plan for the future, and maintain competitive advantage in the information age.

The **Advances in Business Information Systems and Analytics (ABISA) Book Series** aims to present diverse and timely research in the development, deployment, and management of business information systems and business analytics for continued organizational development and improved business value.

COVERAGE

- Data Analytics
- Big Data
- Legal information systems
- Strategic Information Systems
- Geo-BIS
- Information Logistics
- Data Strategy
- Performance Metrics
- Data Management
- Data Governance

IGI Global is currently accepting manuscripts for publication within this series. To submit a proposal for a volume in this series, please contact our Acquisition Editors at Acquisitions@igi-global.com or visit: http://www.igi-global.com/publish/.

The Advances in Business Information Systems and Analytics (ABISA) Book Series (ISSN 2327-3275) is published by IGI Global, 701 E. Chocolate Avenue, Hershey, PA 17033-1240, USA, www.igi-global.com. This series is composed of titles available for purchase individually; each title is edited to be contextually exclusive from any other title within the series. For pricing and ordering information please visit http://www.igi-global.com/book-series/advances-business-information-systems-analytics/37155. Postmaster: Send all address changes to above address. ©© 2018 IGI Global. All rights, including translation in other languages reserved by the publisher. No part of this series may be reproduced or used in any form or by any means – graphics, electronic, or mechanical, including photocopying, recording, taping, or information and retrieval systems – without written permission from the publisher, except for non commercial, educational use, including classroom teaching purposes. The views expressed in this series are those of the authors, but not necessarily of IGI Global.

Titles in this Series

For a list of additional titles in this series, please visit:
https://www.igi-global.com/book-series/advances-business-information-systems-analytics/37155

Business Architectures for Risk Assessment and Strategic Planning...
James McKee (Wollongong University, Australia)
Business Science Reference • ©2018 • 118pp • H/C (ISBN: 9781522533924) • US $155.00

Handbook of Research on Emergent Applications of Optimization Algorithms
Pandian Vasant (Universiti Teknologi Petronas, Malaysia) Sirma Zeynep Alparslan-Gok (Suleyman Demirel University, Turkey) and Gerhard-Wilhelm Weber (Middle East Technical University, Turkey)
Business Science Reference • ©2018 • 812pp • H/C (ISBN: 9781522529903) • US $445.00

Cloud Computing Technologies for Green Enterprises
Kashif Munir (University of Hafr Al-Batin, Saudi Arabia)
Business Science Reference • ©2018 • 424pp • H/C (ISBN: 9781522530381) • US $215.00

Smart Technology Applications in Business Environments
Tomayess Issa (Curtin University, Australia) Piet Kommers (University of Twente, The Netherlands) Theodora Issa (Curtin University, Australia) Pedro Isaías (Portuguese Open University, Portugal) and Touma B. Issa (Murdoch University, Australia)
Business Science Reference • ©2017 • 429pp • H/C (ISBN: 9781522524922) • US $210.00

Advanced Fashion Technology and Operations Management
Alessandra Vecchi (London College of Fashion, University of London Arts, UK)
Business Science Reference • ©2017 • 443pp • H/C (ISBN: 9781522518655) • US $200.00

Maximizing Business Performance and Efficiency Through Intelligent Systems
Om Prakash Rishi (University of Kota, India) and Anukrati Sharma (University of Kota, India)
Business Science Reference • ©2017 • 269pp • H/C (ISBN: 9781522522348) • US $175.00

For an entire list of titles in this series, please visit:
https://www.igi-global.com/book-series/advances-business-information-systems-analytics/37155

IGI Global
DISSEMINATOR OF KNOWLEDGE

701 East Chocolate Avenue, Hershey, PA 17033, USA
Tel: 717-533-8845 x100 • Fax: 717-533-8661
E-Mail: cust@igi-global.com • www.igi-global.com

Editorial Advisory Board

Umesh Bamel, *Institute of Management Technology Ghaziabad, India*
B. S. Bodla, *Kurukshetra University, India*
Benu Chaudhry, *Ansal Properties and Infrastructure Ltd, India*
Manoj Kumar Dash, *ABV-Indian Institute of Information Technology and Management, India*
S. G. Deshmukh, *ABV-Indian Institute of Information Technology and Management, India*
Ramjiwari, *Thapar Univerity, India*
Parshant Singh Rana, *Indian Institute of Technology New Delhi, India*
Mukesh Kumar Sarsawat, *Motilal Nehru National Institute of Technology, India*

Table of Contents

Detailed Table of Contents

In this chapter, the results of an empirical case carried out in 2014 in a thermal centre in Spain are exposed. The aim of this study is to identify/evaluate current labour satisfaction of the employees to analyse strengths and weaknesses of the labour conditions that will allow the suggestion of some improvement actions to the managers and test whether the proposed scale based on the EFQM model is a valid measurement scale for measuring job satisfaction in organizations. A descriptive analysis was used as methodology, and a questionnaire was sent to 55 employees of the thermal centre with the aim to collect data; the response rate was of a 76.36%. The obtained results show that the employees are satisfied with the organizational climate, 4.09 points in average, and the measuring instrument was tested and validated. Furthermore, it shows areas with possibilities of improvement are training, internal communication, knowledge and identification of objectives, and organization and change management, on the other hand, the areas that need to improve are the work conditions, the perception of the executives and salary. The Originality this paper is detect the dimension's strengths and weaknesses of the labour.

Are your employees happy? How happy are they? Does happiness really matter? It is well said that when people are monetarily capitalized, they want a return, and when people are emotionally devoted, they want to contribute. In organisations, emotions are imperative. Emotions, whether positive or negative, drive our behaviour, especially at the workplace where the contribution of each employee is an asset to the organisation. So, the query arises, Can organisations employ positive emotional contagion to change the behaviour of individuals to do what they want? This chapter emphasizes a new ground that happiness is having critical importance in today's parlance to both employees and employers. This chapter presents a snapshot of various definitions, theories, findings of various studies, causes, and consequences of happiness and unhappiness in the organisation and how the happiness can be nurtured or improved at the workplace.

At the time of this writing, 2017, there is noticeable reduction in the perceived ability of people to think critically. Both the popular press and the scientific/professional literature recognize this worldwide drop. This chapter presents the use of experimental design of ideas, conjoint measurement, originally a tool used in marketing, as a tool to inspire creative thinking. The chapter presents the approach and application of conjoint measurement as a tool for discovery, and then delineates a new computer APP, Big Mind, as user friendly to enhance critical thinking. Big Mind embodies conjoint measurement to help researchers study topics, uncover new substantive findings, and learn to think critically as an outcome from the process.

A company cannot be successful if it fails to retain talent in the organization. They have to manage effectively their resources, comprising financial, psychical, and human resources. This is important because higher attrition rate can have various consequences that an attrition incident can cause. It can affect profitability, customer loyalty, revenue, and market image. This chapter aims to identify the antecedents and precedents of attrition in different sectors and evaluates the data received to understand the actual scenarios and its implication on future. This aspect is very important as employee attrition and retention strategies influence the trajectory of the organization.

The corporate world in the present times pays special heed to the skills, knowledge, and attitude of an employee as these characteristics plays a crucial part in the success of the organization where the employee works. In this chapter, the authors map the various aspects that are completely indispensable for the learning and development of the employee given by the leader ultimately transforming the employee into a more efficient and responsible professional. Pervading the relevant knowledge to the employee and the organization by a leader can cause tremendous change in the behavior and performance of the employee. This exchange of knowledge results in a more focused approach and instills a sense of belief within the employee, and this creates a camaraderie that leads to smooth working and creates a milieu of trust and confidence in turn benefiting the organization in the long run.

This chapter creates a place in which TQM (total quality management) differs from business sustainability. Management can focus themselves more accurately when they understand the missing link between these two aspects. It also helps to reduce and eliminate certain wastes related to cost and efficiency and helps to produce better quality with minimum waste. In this study, a TQM framework is developed according to a comprehensive literature review: primary data collection through a structured questionnaire and interview of performers/nonperformers at various levels in different organizations. Analysis of data is used to establish the relationship between attributes of TQM and business sustainability. TQM enhances the cost effectiveness while helping suppliers to produce enhanced quality to their customers and with minimum efforts and lesser rejection. Analysis of data is used to establish the relationship between attributes of TQM and cost effectiveness in an organization.

Relationships are an unavoidable part of life, and yet can be a prospective source of pressure at workplace or organizations. In organisations, performance, delivery, and efficiency are required, often from mere acquaintances. To perform better, individuals need to work on trust and a strong establishment of noble working connections. The fundamental interpersonal relations orientation-behavior (FIRO-B) instrument focuses on these needs, distinguishing the drivers basic to the practices that shape connections for people inside an association. This chapter, therefore, deals with various aspects of the interpersonal relationship and why there is a need to emphasize on these particular areas.

The chapter examines various viewpoints in regards to Reliance Jio and Bharti Airtel. This includes the entry of Jio in the telecom space along with the difference in the market Jio bought right after its introduction of the services for public. The focus area for the research has been the secondary sources. A complete understanding of both these companies has been taken into account for this study to pick up the points that both Jio and Bharti have been lacking upon and areas in which one has surpassed the other by attracting a new set of consumers into their family. The chapter as recorded by the facts presented through the Telecom Regulatory Authority of India Analytics Portal witnessed that Jio proved to have an upper hand in terms of the quality of service, which included data speed and tariffs. The other side of the story shows Bharti Airtel's lack of dominance in 4G experience delivery after Jio's entrance.

This chapter explores the influence of empowering leadership on organizational commitment of Indian millennials. Also, the mediating effect of trust in the leader is examined. Primary data were collected from the sample of 440 IT employees working in Delhi/NCR. Structural equation modeling (SEM) was used to test the proposed relationships based on model fit and standard path coefficients. Findings indicate that empowering leadership has a significant positive effect on organizational commitment and trust in the leader, which also has a significant positive effect on organizational commitment, and trust in the leader has shown to have a partial mediating effect on the relationship between empowering leadership and organizational commitment of millennials. The chapter contributes to the limited empirical literature on the linkage between empowering leadership and organizational commitment in a generational context, specifically millennials in Indian context. The chapter provides a leadership-based approach to bolster organizational commitment of millennials.

This chapter empirically investigates the decision of small and medium-sized enterprises of wooden handicraft located in Saharanpur, India to adopt ecommerce. The study is motivated by the fact that even though the handicraft sector plays a vital role in the Indian economy in terms of exports and employment, it has not adopted ecommerce as one of the prominent sales channels for their products. Most of the studies in the literature focus on consumers, but here the focus is on the executives and the managers of SMEs. The study was done by surveying 163 sampled SMEs and the findings reveal that initial e-commerce adoption is mainly determined by organizational awareness and technological readiness. This chapter suggests training providers should focus on recipient and situation specific training to SMEs while designing programmes. Philosophy of one-size-fits-all is not suitable for handicraft training. Post-understanding determinants of initial and institutionalized ecommerce adoption require customized context-specific programmes with special focus are needed to be implemented.

This chapter is an attempt to explore the factors affecting high employee turnover (ET) in the Indian manufacturing sector. The study shows the association between meaningful work (MWF), organizational information and communication (OIC), and organizational trust (OT). The authors have chosen convenience sampling method and 211 respondents' data was collected from the five Indian manufacturing organizations located in Uttarakhand state. Reliability and validity (convergent and divergent) were also checked and found high. They used conditional process modeling to check the mediation effect of OIC. Findings suggest that MWF positively impacts OT and OIC positively impacts OT. Partial mediation effect of OIC was also captured on the relationship of MWF and OT. The managerial implications, limitations, and future scope were also discussed in detail. These implications provide the good insights to all the employers who are constantly seeking the solution to resolve the issues of attrition and high ET in their respective organizations.

The role of HR has become like that of a firefighter, remembered only in emergencies. Their presence is felt only in their absence. HR is seen as a reactive staff function and a cost centre. The message is clear. Despite its best effort to keep organization together with uniform policy, norms, and values, HR is compelled to prove its financial worth to the organization. HR is under constant pressure for showing their results in quantifiable and financially measurable terms. Introducing Six Sigma in processes of HRM functions seems to be a solution to this problem. However, in some of "Total Six Sigma Organizations," the human resources department has been practically untouched by Six Sigma. The main reason being the difficulty in quantifying and measuring the financial returns of HR processes. But, some others feel that this is as easy as identifying the gaps and using the right formula. The real problem therefore lies in the perception of an individual HR professional. It takes an HR manager to think statistically and analyze how a process can be quantified.

The topic of self-disclosure has been explored significantly and considered to greatly impact employees' relationships. Thus, this chapter explores the association between

Foreword

In today's competitive environment, where businesses are on constant pressure to perform or perish; what makes a business sustain is Human Capital. Human capital, which is aggregate of knowledge, skills and intelligence of the entire workforce need to always increase. Therefore, it becomes utmost important for the management to manage and develop the human capital. HR Analytics is one of the emergent tool to realize this dream. Using the power of Data Analytics to make informed decisions makes businesses grow and employees happy. HR Analytics has huge implications on both micro as well as macro level. Individually, it empowers employees to develop his/her skills and expand knowledge and at collective level, helps organizations to predict and prepare for present and future challenges.

This book compiles various research chapters which are contributed by eminent researchers globally. The book has range a chapter on topics from Personality, critical thinking, interpersonal relationships to Total Quality Management (TQM), Six Sigma. It also touches upon soft issues like employee happiness, attrition, and knowledge sharing, leadership and service innovation. This type of project will open new windows of research and applications. I sincerely think that these issues are of paramount importance and have been pretty well researched and commented in the form of research chapter in the book.

It is my pleasure to write a short and a simple "Foreword" to this Edited Book Volume Titled: *Harnessing Human Capital Analytics for Competitive Advantage,* published by IGI Global-USA, under the able editorship of Dr. Mohit Yadav and his colleagues. I congratulate the editors and the contributors who had put in a lot of effort and time in bringing out this book.

Manoj Kumar Dash
ABV-Indian Institute of Information Technology and Management, India

Preface

The complete work of this book is divided into fourteen chapters. The brief description of each chapter is follows.

Chapter 1 is titled "Total Quality Management Practices and Employees' Satisfaction"; in this chapter, the authors José Álvarez-García, María de la Cruz Del Río-Rama, Evaristo Galeana-Figueroa and Dora Aguilasocho-Montoya exposes the results of the results of an empirical case carried out in 2014 in a Thermal Centre in Spain. The aim of this study is to identify/to evaluate current labour satisfaction of the employees to analyse strengths and weaknesses of the labour conditions that will allow us to suggest some improvement actions to the managers and testing whether the proposed scale based on the EFQM model is a valid measurement scale for measuring job satisfaction in organizations. A descriptive analysis was used as methodology, and a questionnaire was sent to 55 employees of the Thermal Centre with the aim to collect data; the response rate was of a 76.36%. The obtained results show that the employees are satisfied with the organizational climate, 4.09 points in average and the measuring instrument was tested and validated. Furthermore, it shows areas with possibilities of improvement are training, internal communication, knowledge and identification of objectives and organization and change management.

Chapter 2 is titled "Employee Happiness: A Valuable Tool to Drive Organisations". In this chapter, the authors Rinki Dahiya and Santosh Rangnekar from IIT Roorkee, India tries to answer the questions like- are your employees happy? How happy are they? Does happiness really matter? It is well said that when people are monetarily capitalized, they want a return and when people are emotionally devoted, they want to contribute. In organisations, emotions are imperative. Emotions whether positive or negative drives our behaviour and especially at the workplace where the contribution of each employee is an asset to the organisation. So, the query arises can organisations employ positive emotional contagion to change the behaviour of individuals to do what they want? This chapter has emphasized on a new ground that happiness is having critical importance in today's parlance to both employees and employers. This chapter has presented snapshot of various definitions, theories, findings of various studies, causes and consequences of happiness and unhappiness in the organisation and how the happiness can be nurtured or improved at the workplace.

Chapter 3 is titled "I'd Like to Teach the World to Think: Mind Genomics, Big Mind, and Encouraging Youth". In this chapter, the authors Howard Moskowitz, Jyotsna, Andi Sciacca and Andrew Lester discusses the utility of App Big Mind in helping to think critically. At the time of this writing, 2017, there is noticeable reduction in the perceived ability to people to think 'critically.' Both the popular press and the scientific/professional literature recognize that world-wide drop. This chapter presents the use of experimental design of ideas, conjoint measurement, originally a tool used in marketing, as a tool to inspire creative thinking. The chapter presents the approach and application of conjoint measurement as a tool for discovery, and then delineates a new computer APP, Big Mind, as a user-friendly too enhance critical thinking. Big Mind embodies conjoint measurement to help researchers study topics, uncover new substantive findings, and learn to think critically as an outcome from the process.

Chapter 4 is titled "Attrition Risk Management". In this chapter author Anugamini Priya Srivastava from SIBM Pune, India discusses the value of Attrition risk management. A company cannot stand successful if it fails to retain talents in their organization. They have to manage effectively their resources comprising financial, psychical and human resources. This is important because higher attrition rate can have various consequences that an attrition incident can cause. It can affect profitability, customer loyalty, revenue and market image. This chapter aims to identify the antecedents and precedents of attrition in different sectors and evaluates the data received to understand the actual scenarios and its implication on future. This aspect is very important as employee's attrition and retention strategies influence the trajectory of the organization.

Chapter 5 is titled "Service Innovation and Its Consequences: The Growing Imperative of Knowledge Sharing and Donating on Quality of Service Innovation Techniques". In this chapter, the authors Mrinal Tyagi, Hrishikesh Hulyalkar, Harshvardhan Kothari, Amrita Kapoor, Aishwarya Bhatia and Alisha Vij from BML Munjal University discusses how knowledge sharing and donating influences service quality. The corporate world in the present times pays special heed to the skills, knowledge and attitude of an employee as these characteristics plays a crucial part in the success of the organization where the employee works. In this study, we would be mapping the various aspect that are completely indispensable for the learning and development of the employee given by the leader ultimately transforming the employee into a more efficient and responsible professional. Pervading the relevant knowledge to the employee and the organization by a leader can cause tremendous change in the behavior and performance of the employee. This exchange of knowledge results in more focus approach and instills a sense of belief within the employee and the creates a camaraderie that leads to smooth working and creates a milieu of trust and confidence in turn benefiting the organization in the long run.

Chapter 6 is titled "Role of TQM in Sustained Business Performance in Indian Automotive Supply Chain". In this chapter, the authors Sanjiv Narula, Satwinder Pal, Vinay Saini, Prabhat Saxena, Ajay Goyal and Mohit Yadav tries to create a place in which TQM (total quality management) differs from Business sustainability in the real life management can focus themselves more accurately when they understand the missing link between these two aspects, it also helps to reduce and eliminate certain wastes related to cost, and efficiency and helps to produce better quality with minimum wastages. In this study, a TQM framework is developed according to a comprehensive literature review, Primary data collection through a structured questionnaire and interview of performers/nonperformers at various levels in different organizations. Analysis of data is used to establish the relationship between attributes of TQM & Business Sustainability. TQM enhances the cost effectiveness while helping suppliers to produce enhanced quality to their customers and with minimum efforts and lesser rejection. Analysis of data is used to establish the relationship between attributes of TQM & cost effectiveness in an organization.

Chapter 7 is titled "People Need People: A Study of Instrument FIRO-B". In this chapter, the authors Teena Bharti and Santosh Rangnekar focuses on interpersonal relationship between people. Relationships are an unavoidable part of life, and yet can be a prospective source of pressure at workplace or organizations. In organisations, performance, delivery, and efficiency are required, often from mere acquaintances. To perform better, individuals need to work on trust and a strong establishment of noble working connections. The Fundamental Interpersonal Relations Orientation–Behavior (FIRO-B) instrument focuses on these needs, distinguishing the drivers basic to the practices that shape connections for people inside an association. This chapter, therefore, deals with various aspects of the interpersonal relationship and why there is a need to emphasize on these particular areas.

Chapter 8 is titled "Jio-Bharti Airtel Data War and Strategy". In this chapter, the authors Anil Kumar, Mohan Balaji, Ujjwal Krishna and Mohit Yadav tries to examine various view point in regards to Reliance Jio and Bharti Airtel. This includes the entry of Jio in the Telecom Space along with the difference in the market Jio bought right after its introduction of the services for public. The focus area for the research has been the secondary sources. A complete understanding of both these companies has been taken into account for this study to pick up the points which both Jio and Bharti has been lacking upon and areas which one has surpassed others by attracting new set of consumers into their family. The study as recorded by the facts presented through the Telecom Regulatory Authority of India Analytics Portal witnessed that Jio had proved to be have an upper hand till date in terms of the Quality of Service which included Data Speed, Tariffs. Although the other side of the story which shows Bharti Airtel presence and lack of dominance in 4G experience delivery after Jio entrance.

Chapter 9 is titled "How Does Empowering Leadership Contribute to Organizational Commitment of Millennials? An Indian Perspective". In this chapter, the author Mohammad Faraz Naim aims to explore the influence of empowering leadership on organizational commitment of Indian Millennials. Also, the mediating effect of trust in the leader is examined. Primary data were collected from the sample of 440 IT employees working in Delhi/NCR. Structural equation modeling (SEM) was used to test the proposed relationships based on model fit and standard path coefficients. Findings indicate that empowering leadership has a significant positive effect on organizational commitment and trust in the leader, which also has a significant positive effect on organizational commitment, and trust in the leader has shown to have a partial mediating effect on the relationship between empowering leadership and organizational commitment of Millennials. The study contributes to the limited empirical literature on the linkage between empowering leadership and organizational commitment in a generational context, specifically Millennials in Indian context. The study provides a leadership-based approach to bolster organizational commitment of Millennials.

Chapter 10 is titled "Training for Ecommerce Adoption: Macro Assessment of Determinants". In this chapter, the authors Rohit Yadav and Tripti mahara empirically investigates the decision of small and medium-sized enterprises of wooden handicraft located in Saharanpur, India to adopt ecommerce. The study is motivated by the fact, that even though handicraft sector plays a vital role in the Indian economy in terms of exports and employment, it has not adopted ecommerce as one of the prominent sales channels for their products. Most of the studies in the literature focus on consumers, but here the focus is on the executives and the managers of SMEs. The study was done by surveying 163 sampled SMEs and the findings reveal that initial e-commerce adoption is mainly determined by organizational awareness and technological readiness. This study suggests training providers should focus on recipient and situation specific training to SMEs while designing programmes. Philosophy of one-size-fits-all is not suitable for handicraft training. Post understanding determinants of initial and institutionalized ecommerce adoption require customized context-specific programmes with special focus are needed to be implemented.

Chapter 11 is titled "Factors Affecting High Employee Turnover in Indian Manufacturing Sector". In this chapter, the authors Nishant Singh and Santosh Rangnekar attempts to explore the factors, affecting high employee turnover (ET) in the Indian manufacturing sector. The study shows the association between meaningful work (MWF), organizational information and communication (OIC), and organizational trust (OT). We have chosen convenience sampling method and 211 respondents' data was collected from the five Indian manufacturing organizations located in Uttarakhand state. Reliability and validity (convergent and divergent) were also checked and found high. We used conditional process modeling (Hayes, 2013) to check the mediation effect of OIC. Findings suggest that MWF positively impacts OT and OIC positively impacts OT. Partial mediation effect of OIC was also captured on the relationship of MWF and OT. The managerial implications, limitations and future scope were also discussed in detail. These implications provide the good insights to all the employers who are constantly seeking the solution to resolve the issues of attrition and high ET in their respective organizations.

Chapter 12 is titled "Applicability of Six Sigma in Human Resource Management". In this chapter, the author Nagaraj Shenoy examines applicability of Six Sigma in HRM. The role of HR has become like that of firefighter, remembered only in emergencies. Their presence is felt only in their absence. HR is seen as reactive, staff function and a cost centre. The message is clear. Despite its best effort to keep organization together with uniform policy, norms, and values, HR is compelled to prove its financial worth to the organization. HR is under constant pressure for showing their results in quantifiable and financially measurable terms. Introducing Six Sigma in processes of HRM functions seems to be a solution to this problem. However, in some of 'Total Six Sigma Organizations' too, the Human Resources Department, has been practically untouched by Six Sigma. The main reason being the difficulty in quantifying and measuring the financial returns of HR processes. But, some others feel that this is as easy as identifying the gaps and using the right formula. The real problem therefore lies in the perception of an individual HR professional. It takes an HR manager to think statistically, analyze how a process can be quantified.

Chapter 13 is titled "Does Locus of Control Mediate the Relationship Between Personality Integration and Self-Disclosure? Personality Integration, Self-Disclosure, Locus of Control". In this chapter, the authors Nagendra Singh Nehra and Santosh Rangnekar explores the association between personality integration and self-disclosure considering locus of control acts as a mediator. Sample collected from public and private sector organizations in Uttarakhand. The data collected through a cross–sectional survey-based research design and a convenience sampling method was used. Thus, total 192 questionnaires were distributed during office hours. In the final analysis, only 189 responses were considered; the rest were discarded due to missing data. We use correlation and four-step hierarchical multiple regression analyses were employed. Results show that internal locus of control partially mediates said association. Further, it was found that personality integration positively associated with self-disclosure through the internal locus of control. Additionally, external locus of control has a positive effect on self-disclosure. Implications and scope for future research are highlighted.

Chapter 14 is titled "Employee Retention: Important Factors to Be Considered by Human Resource Professionals While Creating Retention". In this chapter, the authors Karteek Ramalinga Ponnuru and Rashik Gupta focuses on the measures to be taken to retain employees. Attrition is a major problem in many Indian IT firms. On an average attrition stands at around 14.5% in many major IT firms making it a major problem. Attrition is not only a result of poor HR policies it is also because of the many aspirations and need for career development for many young professionals who come with big aspirations. This gap between fulfilling the aspirations of the new entrants and the scope of development at any organization is the result of attrition. From the study it has also been concluded that recognition, valuing one's individual opinion and also the aspect of broadening and the scope of an organization to provide enough career development prospects in terms of training, executive education and salary etc. are also factors because of which many young professionals leave their respective organizations. Therefore, there is a need to amend the existing employee practices in order to meet the ever-changing momentum across the organizations and reduce the cost which happen due to attrition.

Acknowledgment

The editors would like to acknowledge the help of all the people involved in this project and, more specifically, to the authors and reviewers that took part in the review process. Without their support, this book would not have become a reality.

We would like to extend special thanks and gratitude towards Mrs. Shubhi Yadav and Dr. Benu Chaudhry for constant support in this long and tiresome journey.

We would like to thank each one of the authors for their contributions. The editors wish to acknowledge the valuable contributions of the reviewers regarding the improvement of quality, coherence, and content presentation of chapters. Most of the authors also served as referees; we highly appreciate their double task.

We are grateful to all members of IGI publishing house for their assistance and timely motivation in producing this volume.

We hope the readers will share our excitement with this important scientific contribution the body of knowledge about various applications of predictive analytics within the service sector.

Mohit Yadav
BML Munjal University, India

Shrawan Kumar Trivedi
Indian Institute of Management Sirmaur, India

Anil Kumar
BML Munjal University, India

Santosh Rangnekar
Indian Institute of Technology Roorkee, India

Chapter 1
Total Quality Management Practices and Employees' Satisfaction

José Álvarez-García
University of Extremadura, Spain

María de la Cruz Del Río-Rama
University of Vigo, Spain

Evaristo Galeana-Figueroa
Universidad Michoacana San Nicolás de Hidalgo, Mexico

Dora Aguilasocho-Montoya
Universidad Michoacana de San Nicolás de Hidalgo, Mexico

ABSTRACT

In this chapter, the results of an empirical case carried out in 2014 in a thermal centre in Spain are exposed. The aim of this study is to identify/evaluate current labour satisfaction of the employees to analyse strengths and weaknesses of the labour conditions that will allow the suggestion of some improvement actions to the managers and test whether the proposed scale based on the EFQM model is a valid measurement scale for measuring job satisfaction in organizations. A descriptive analysis was used as methodology, and a questionnaire was sent to 55 employees of the thermal centre with the aim to collect data; the response rate was of a 76.36%. The obtained results show that the employees are satisfied with the organizational climate, 4.09 points in average, and the measuring instrument was tested and validated. Furthermore, it shows areas with possibilities of improvement are training, internal communication, knowledge and identification of objectives, and organization and change management, on the other hand, the areas that need to improve are the work conditions, the perception of the executives and salary. The Originality this paper is detect the dimension's strengths and weaknesses of the labour.

DOI: 10.4018/978-1-5225-4038-0.ch001

Copyright © 2018, IGI Global. Copying or distributing in print or electronic forms without written permission of IGI Global is prohibited.

INTRODUCTION

Labour satisfaction of the employees with their job and their labour environment, called Organizational Climate, is a very important aspect that must be managed by the enterprises' executives. It is defined as a number of features that determine a company, that differentiate it from others, and that affect in many cases the employees' behavior, as well as their motivation or satisfaction. Several researches have shown that satisfaction affects productivity, level of absenteeism and employees' rotation (Clegg 1983; Akerlof et al. 1988), aspects that also affect quality of a service that is provided to a client (Flynn 2005). Therefore, organizational climate is a key for a company's success, and its regular analysis can help to improve those aspects where the organization is not so effective.

Considering all this, it is highly important to measure labour satisfaction in enterprises, because it helps to understand experiences or expectations of an employee that affect in an indirect way a client and, as a consequence, the quality of services that are provided to them. Therefore, measuring of satisfaction with job's conditions allows to find out which aspects should be worked out to improve labour environment.

Taking into account all these points, the aim of this research is to determine the level of current labour satisfaction of the employees of a Thermal Centre[1], so strengths and weaknesses of labour conditions can be analyzed, and it will allow to suggest some ways of improvement to the executives and determine whether the proposed scale based on the EFQM model is a valid measurement scale for measuring job satisfaction in organizations.

The chosen for this research Thermal Centre is managed with a quality management system (QMS) based on a standard UNE 186001:2009 (Thermal resorts) and UNE 182001:2008 (Tourist hotels and apartments), so it has a Q Mark for Tourist Quality. Therefore, we have decided to use a quality approach to analyse labour satisfaction, basing on a tool of the Total Quality Management (EFQM Model) that allows an enterprise to evaluate itself regarding 9 criteria, being human resources management and results on persons two of them. The first criterion, human resources management, evaluates the way an enterprise manages and use knowledge and potential of its employees, and the second one, results on persons, measures the results that have been got in relation to its staff. According to Robles-García et al. (2005, p.127), to measure these results, "*it is necessary to have some measures of perception that could show aspects related to motivation and satisfaction. In short, measuring of organizational climate*". Definitively, this model is considered as very suitable for measuring the labor satisfaction as it includes all the aspects that in the literature are related to job satisfaction (working conditions, training, promotion and career development, recognition,remuneration, command-partner relationship, participation, organization and change management, work environment, communication, knowledge and identification with objectives and perception of direction).

To reach this objective, the article has been organized in five parts. After the introduction where the theme is set in a context and the objective is laid out, the second part develops a theoretical framework where a concept of labour satisfaction, the factors that form it and its consequences, relation between both satisfaction and quality and satisfaction and productivity, and the way to measure it are explained. Empirical research that allows us to achieve the article's goal is set out in the third part. In the fourth one, the collected data are analysed, and finally the most important conclusions originated by this analysis are introduced.

LITERATURE REVIEW

Labour Satisfaction

Empiric literature has been gone through to demarcate a concept of labour satisfaction, and we can determine that it is "*a quite wide term, and there are many definitions of it and many variables that are included in it*" (Castro et al. 2009, p.107). In this revision, we have been verified that there are two groups of labour satisfaction: the one that is focused on emotional state and feelings and the other one that is considered to be a generalized attitude towards a job (Chiang 2013, p. 42-43). So, Barraza and Ortega (2009, p.1) define it as "*an attitude that an employee shows towards its job, and this attitude is based on beliefs and values that the employee develops doing its job, and that will influence in a significant way on his behavior and his results*", Andresen et al. (2007, p. 719): "*an emotional pleasant or positive state produced by the work experience; this state can be achieved by satisfying some individual requirements through a job*", and for Lee and Chang (2008, p. 733) it is "*a general attitude that an individual has towards his job*".

Considering the literature revised for this research, labour satisfaction is a negative or positive attitude that an employee has doing his work (Feldman and Arnold 1995; Robbins 2004). The attitude that depends on a number of factors as an economic one, academic training, relationship with the colleagues, work conditions, labour climate, etc., that according to the theory by Herberg (1968) can be grouped in two factors: intrinsic factors or motivational ones, and extrinsic ones or those of hygiene.

The first one includes "*personal development, responsibility, recognition, the work itself, strengths and aims*" meanwhile the second one refers to "company's policy, salary, interpersonal relationships, private life, status and safety" (Herbert 1968).

The theory of two factors or the theory by Herzberg (1959) is one of the main explanatory theories of the labour satisfaction, and it forms part of the so called

"*Theories of content and cause*" together with the theories by Maslow (1954), the ERG theory by Alderfer (1969) and the one by McClelland (1961) called the learned needs theory. These theories are in charge of analyzing both the motivations that lead people to work and the factors and elements that influence and impact on their interest on working. Another aspect of explanatory theories on labour satisfaction is formed by the "*Process Theories*" that "*pretend to show the way the labour behaviour is strengthened, managed and carried out*" Campbell et al. (1970).

Consequences of Labour Satisfaction

Labour satisfaction is closely related to people's behavior in their workplace that basically affects the employee and the company. In this way, Gamero (2003, p. 9-13) makes a recompilation of consequences originated from labour satisfaction according to an individual scale (physical and mental health, longevity, escape or retreat attitudes, life satisfaction) and an organizational one (neglect, absenteeism, protest activities, productivity, civic behavior in the company, counterproductive work).

Many researchers corroborate these consequences, in other words, a relationship between labour satisfaction and behaviour of an employee. Álvarez (2004, p. 105) affirms "*there are many researches that have confirmed that loyalty of an employee towards his enterprise, his productivity, his level of absenteeism and his labour rotation depend a lot on the level of his labour satisfaction*". Other researchers as Mangione and Quinn (1975) and Clegg (1983) claim that there is a positive relationship between labour satisfaction and productivity and a negative one between satisfaction and labour absenteeism, and McEvoy and Cascio (1985) and Akerlof et al. (1988) say that there is a negative relationship between labour satisfaction of an employee and his neglect. On the other hand, Rogers et al., (1994) and Fosam et al. (1998) say that there is a positive relationship between the employees' satisfaction and the clients' satisfaction in the service sector.

Productivity is highly related to labour satisfaction. Productivity is defined as "*a way that a system of operations or proceedings of an enterprise function*" (Chiang, 2013, p. 44). The researches carried out between the 50th and the 60th claim that there is a positive relationship between productivity and labour satisfaction through the following phrase: "*A happy employee is a productive employee*", meanwhile 30 years later they still define it positive but not so much. Other studies say that productivity leads to satisfaction, but not vice versa; a higher productivity leads to economic, social and psychological rewards that produces higher level of satisfaction for an employee, if he considers these awards to be appropriate (Chiang and Ojeda 2013, p. 45).

However, not all the employees are satisfied with their job or the enterprise where they work, so their dissatisfaction must be taken into account as well. In this sense, according to Locke (1976), labour dissatisfaction is defined as a negative emotional response towards the job that finally affects labour values of the employee, frustrating or ignoring them.

Labour Satisfaction Versus Quality

Labour satisfaction and quality are two related concepts. In this sense, a model of the European Foundation for Quality Management (EFQM) considers people to be one of the most essential points for the development of an enterprise, so it belongs to the second and the seventh criteria of the nine that exist grouped in two categories: Facilitating agents and Results. This model refers to the employees in the following sense:

excellent enterprises value the persons that work for them and create a culture that allows to get all the personal goals and those of the enterprise in the most profitable for both parts way. They develop people's abilities and encourage justice and equality. They care about the employees, communicate with them, reward and appreciate them, so the employees are motivated, their commitment with the company increases, and they use their abilities and knowledge for the enterprise's benefit.. (Guide Review of managing people, p. 8)

Given the fact that people's behavior is basic for providing of services of high quality, because they have a direct contact with clients, it can be said that the service's quality and the image of the enterprise depends on the employees. In addition, if we consider the previous paragraph that say that the employees' behavior depends on their labour satisfaction, it becomes a highly important aspect to be taken into account by the managers of any enterprise that would like to provide a quality service. According to Yee et al. (2008) the satisfied employees work better and try to provide a service of higher quality (Loveman 1998; Silvestro and Cross 2000).

In this sense, an argument that "*the employee's satisfaction improves the quality of a service*" is based on the theory of the equity of social exchanges (Blau 1964; Organ 1977); this theory makes reference to the fact that when managers of an enterprise offer appropriate work conditions that make the employees feel more satisfied, they tend to "correspond" appropriately through their efforts doing their work, a reciprocal fact between a company and an employee that leads to the quality of services; it means that the employees' satisfaction has a positive effect on the quality of services (Wayne et al. 1997; Flynn 2005).

According to Snipes et al. (2005), the researches on labour satisfaction and quality of services are the most studied phenomenon in the literature on organizational behavior. Several researches find out that labour satisfaction influences positively on the quality of services (Yoon et al. 2001; Hartline and Ferrell 1996). According to Heskett et al. (1994) quoted by (Snipes et al. 2005, p. 1331), "*financial efficiency of an enterprise arises from the clients' satisfaction that in turn arises from the employees' efficiency that in turn arises from the employees' satisfaction*".

Taking into account everything told previously, labour satisfaction and quality of services are closely related. An employee works better and provides a higher level of quality to the services, if he is motivated and rewarded by his supervisors that makes him feel more satisfied in the company. According to Zeithaml and Bitner (2000), quality of services depends directly on the impression that the employees cause to the clients.

Tools to Measure Labour Satisfaction

There are several ways to measure labour satisfaction, for example, those quoted by Meliá and Peiró (1989). On one hand, there are global measures and on the other hand, there are specific aspects.

According to Harpaz (1983), there are other ways of measuring of labour satisfaction, as, for example, direct and indirect methods. The direct ones, or those based on the European model of EFQM management (Osakidetza/ Servicio Vasco de Salud, 2001:33) are to facilitate the process of the EFQM self-evaluation. These methods allow to collect information on attitudes of the interviewed people in relation to the work dimensions; the interviewed persons answer according to a scale offered for each item of the questionnaire.

The indirect, or traditional, methods are based on the information of the attitudes of the interviewed people that is more precise that the one of the direct methods; they have a number of disadvantages as subjectivity of interpretation and difficulty of quantification of the answers. There are several kinds of indirect methods, as:

- **Minessota Satisfaction Questionnaire:** MSQ (Weiss et al. 1967) that has as its basis the theory of adaptation to work.
- **Job Diagnostic Survey:** JDS (Hackman and Oldham 1979) that was developed to observe the effects of different characteristics of work on individuals.
- **Job Satisfaction Survey:** JSS (Mueller and McCloskey 1990) tries to measure satisfaction through nine subscales apart from global satisfaction.
- **Job Descriptive Index:** JDI (Smith et al. 1969) tries to measure work through five dimensions related with it.

- Questionnaire S4/82 (Meliá et al. 1986) allows to evaluate satisfaction with supervision and involvement in the enterprise; with physical environment; with material service; with remuneration, basic service and job safety; with interpersonal relationships and intrinsic satisfaction with a job.
- **Job in General Scale:** JIG (Ironson et al. 1989) allows to evaluate general satisfaction of an employee, being its second goal to measure some dimensions of job.
- Multidimensional scale of job satisfaction (Shouksmith et al. 1990) contains salary, opportunity of promotion, relationship with the colleagues and job conditions.
- Overall Job Satisfaction (Warr et al. 1979).

METHODOLOGY

Universe and Field of Study

The employees of a Thermal Centre in Spain have formed population of this study. The Thermal Centre has facilities where treatments are performed with mineral hot spring water and in the same building there is a 4 stars hotel with 105 rooms that also has a restaurant, a coffee-shop and an 18 whole golf course. The Thermal Centre has 55 employees both permanent and seasonal that belong to eight departments. It is the only one Spanish Thermal Centre that has three Q (hotel, thermal resort and golf course) awarded by the Spanish Tourist Quality Institute of the Tourism Ministry.

Questionnaire and Measurement

The questionnaire has two different parts. The first one gets the information that allows us to define the profile of the interviewed persons (socio-demographic and labour), and the second one evaluates the labour satisfaction of the employees. A measuring tool is an adaptation of the questionnaire used by Osakidetza/ Servicio Vasco de Salud (2001, p. 10), that deals with areas recommended by the EFQM Model and that takes into account all the aspects included in the personal criterion (Facilitative Agents) and in the criterion of the personal results. The employees were also asked about environmental policy and impact.

All the employees of the Thermal Centre have marked their level of satisfaction with 13 dimensions identified in the EFQM model linked with the employees' satisfaction plus environmental aspect. These aspects are labour conditions, training, promotion and professional development, recognition, payment, organization and change management, labour climate, internal communication, knowledge and identification with objectives, perception of the executives and environmental policy and impact. A question on general perception of the level of satisfaction has been also made, so the questionnaire has 38 items. A Liker scale has been used, being 1 very unsatisfied and 5 very satisfied.

For the distribution of the questionnaire among the employees, an HR department of the Thermal Centre has been got in touch with asking for their collaboration and their permission to hand over the questionnaire to all the employees. The questionnaire was collected guaranteeing the anonymity of the respondent to avoid the bias the answers. It was handed over the 6th of March, and it was picked up 20 days later. The response index is a 76.36% that means 42 of the 55 employees. The sampling error is 7.50 for the level of confidence of 95% Z= 1.96 p=q=0.5.

Validation of the Measurement Scale

The current study used SPSS 19.0 to validation of the measurement scale using exploratory factor analysis (EFA). The psychometric properties of the scales (reliability, validity and dimensionality) are analyzed (Anderson and Gerbing, 1988); the item-total correlation of each of the proposed scales is observed (recommended minimum value 0.3 by Nurosis, 1993) and Cronbach´s Alpha was verified (greater than 0.7 according to Nunnally, 1979). To check the unidimensionality, an EFA was conducted with varimax rotation (Bagozi and Baumgartner, 1994) that allows us to determine which observable variables loaded on which latent variables: explained variance (must be greater than 50%) and factor loading (loadings lower than 0.3 are considered significant according to Hair et al, 1999).

The results show that measuring instrument of reliability shows that all items have an item-total correlation above the recommended 0.3 minimum and the Cronbach Alpha in all scales is greater than 0.7, which indicates adequate internal consistency (table 1). With regard to unidimensionality analysis, their results did not lead to removal of any item; in all cases the factor loadings are greater than 0.5 and the accumulated percentage of explained variance is greater than 50% in each of the scales.

With regard to the content validity of the scales it is based on the literature review for the design of the scales; they were taken as reference the EFQM Model and the work performed by Osakidetza/ Servicio Vasco de Salud (2001), García-Pozo et al. (2010), Pérez-Ciordia et al. (2012), Robles-García et al. (2015). Convergent validity implies that the same measured phenomenon of several independent forms leads to similar results and the reliability of the measurement scale through the coefficient Cronbach's alpha reflects the degree of cohesion among the items on the scale and is therefore an indirect indicator of convergent validity.

Table 1. Results of the Exploratory Factor Analysis (EFA)

Factors Identified and Number of Items	Cronbrach´s Alpha	Items Eliminated	% Explained Information
Relationship with supervisors (6 items)-RS	0.920	Do not delete any item	71.75%
Involvement (2 items)-I	0.780		82.00%
Received recognition (1 items)-RR	---		---
Environmental policy and impact (3 items)-EPI	0.974		95.13%
Promotion and professional development (3 items)-PPD	0.879		80.77%
Labour climate (2 items)-LC	0.601		71.45%
Training (3 items)-T	0.949		90.91%
Internal communication (3 items)-IC	0.899		83.52%
Knowledge and identification of objectives (2 items)-KIO	0.954		95.63%
Organization and change management (3 items)-OCM	0.770		70.23%
Work conditions (4 items)-WC	0.907		79.33%
Perception of executives (2 items)-PE	0.958		96.10%
Salary (2 items)-S	0.773		81.63%
General perception (2 items)-GP	0.699		77.33%

Source: Authors' own data

We analyze the correlations between different scales and particularly with general perception (table 2). In all cases there is correlation, but it not significant in the relationship between relationship with supervisors with knowledge and identification of objectives and labour climate; involvement with labour climate. We can see that there is a correlation between all the scales used to measure job satisfaction with general perception.

DATA ANALYSIS

We have started to analyze the data observing the profile of the employees who answered the questionnaire. They belong to all the departments of the Thermal Centre, having the cleaning department the highest rate of answers (26.19% of the total), being 62% women and 38% men. Regarding the educational level, a 16.67% of them are licensed, and a 9.52% have professional training. An 81% of them (34 employees) are permanent, and a 19% are seasonal; the shifts are rotating. The data show that a 40% of the employees have been working in the enterprise for 5-8 years, and a 15% - for more than 8 years.

Table 2. Pearson correlation between scales

		RS	I	EPI	PPD	LC	T	IC	KIO	OCM	WC	PE	S
RS	r	1	.685**	.315*	.355*	.265	.421**	.450**	.277	.546**	.402**	.367*	.388*
I	r	.685**	1	.315*	.514**	.297	.529**	.615**	.480**	.599**	.465**	589**	.444**
EPI	r	.315*	.413**	1	.738**	.593**	.799**	.746**	.592**	.597**	.759**	.678**	.573**
PPD	r	.355*	.514**	.738**	1	.659**	.841**	.886**	.676**	.739**	.814**	.816**	.743**
LC	r	**.265**	**.297**	.593**	.659**	1	.735**	.788**	.540**	.749**	.805**	.800**	.806**
T	r	.421**	.529**	.799**	.841**	.735**	1	.867**	.725**	.789**	.913**	.864**	.770**
IC	r	.450**	.615**	.746**	.886**	.788**	.867**	1	.654**	.815*	.815**	.874**	.791**
KIO	r	**.277**	.480**	.592**	.676**	.540**	.725**	.654**	1	.813**	.802**	.751**	.654**
OCM	r	.546**	.599**	.597**	.739**	.749**	.789**	.815**	.813**	1	.842**	.859**	.774**
WC	r	.402**	.465**	.759**	.814**	.805**	.913**	.815**	.802**	.842**	1	859**	.801**
PE	r	.367*	.589**	.678**	.816**	.800**	.864**	.874**	.751**	.859**	.859**	1	.815**
S	r	.388*	.444**	.573**	.743**	.806**	.770**	.791**	.654**	.774**	.801**	.815**	1
GP	r	.323*	.482**	.752**	.875**	.703**	.862**	.840**	.770**	.779**	.810**	.829**	.719**

r = Pearson correlation; ** correlation significant at 0.01; * correlation significant at 0.05

Source: Authors' own data

To analyse labour satisfaction of the interviewed employees we have measured their level of labour satisfaction with all the job dimensions that we have taken into account, and it has been compared with the level of general perception. The table 3 shows the average and standard deviation of each dimension. An analysis of reliability has been done as well; it studies internal consistency of each tool of measuring. For this aim a Cronbach's alpha has been used that evaluates internal consistency of the scale through an average correlation of each variable with the rest of the scale. All the scales are over the minimum recommended value of 0.7 (Nunnally 1979).

The best valued dimensions, it means, those where the employees have a higher level of satisfaction, are: their relationship with supervisors, possibility to participate in the improvement process and decision making in their work area that the company gives them, and recognition of their work that the employees receive from their supervisors; all of them are the dimensions that have obtained an average of more than 4 points (being 4 "satisfied"). To the contrary, the less valued dimensions are the level of satisfaction with the salary, with perception of the executives related to the decision making and receptivity to the employees' demands and the work conditions; all of them valued with more than 3,70 in average (being 3 not satisfied neither unsatisfied).

The employees have been asked to value "*a general perception of the level of satisfaction*" that allows to compare the deviation between the valued level of satisfaction taking into account each dimension and general perception valued in

Table 3. Studied aspects

Level of Satisfaction With	Average*	Standard Deviation	Cronbach's α
Relationship with supervisors	4.50	0.10	0.920
Involvement	4.45	0.00	0.780
Received recognition	4.31	0.00	--
Environmental policy and impact	4.17	0.10	0.974
Promotion and professional development	4.13	0.10	0.879
Labour climate	4.11	0.36	0.601
Training	4.08	0.05	0.949
Internal communication	4.02	0.05	0.899
Knowledge and identification of objectives	4.01	0.08	0.954
Organization and change management	3.94	0.36	0.770
Work conditions	3.86	0.22	0.907
Perception of executives	3.79	0.07	0.958
Salary	3.75	0.05	0.773
All the previous dimensions	4.09	0.12	---
Level of satisfaction general perception	4.26	0.10	0.699

* 1: Very unsatisfied; 2: unsatisfied; 3: Not satisfied neither unsatisfied; 4: Satisfied; 5: Very satisfied
Source: Authors' own data

a general way. An average of 4.09 has been obtained, if we take into account an addition of the averages obtained from each of the 13 valued aspects and an average of 4.26 in the case of general perception, the deviation is 0.15 in favour of general perception. As a conclusion, we can say that the employees are satisfied with the company.

Taking into account standard deviation, we can conclude that both average standard deviation of the studied aspects and the one of general perception are practically the same: 0.12 and 0.10. Therefore, variability between the collected data in general is uniform.

Regarding general perception of labour satisfaction (Figure 1), a 57.14% said that they were very satisfied both with the quality of services that they offer to their clients and with the way they feel working in this company.

With the aim to determine the areas to be improved, each studied work aspect is analysed to evaluate labour satisfaction separately, taking into account the items that are used to measure the level of satisfaction.

Figure 1. Level of satisfaction general perception
Source: Authors' own data

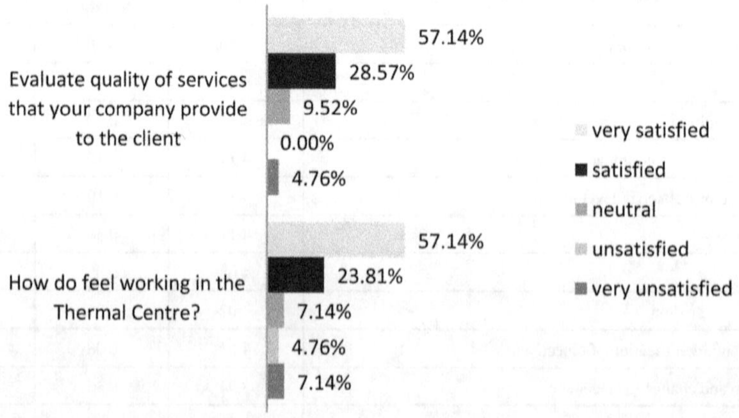

Level of Satisfaction With Work Conditions and Training

The employees are not satisfied neither unsatisfied with their work conditions with an average of 3.86 in general terms, being the best valued item safety conditions (4.05) and the less valued with an average of 3.55 is the way their company obey the agreement/regulations/labour laws. We can also see that a 76.19% of the employees are satisfied or very satisfied, being only a 7.04% those who are not.

Regarding the dimension of training, we can say that the employees are satisfied with it with the average of 4.08. The Table 4 shows the averages of the items that we have used to measure the training aspect; the scoring is very homogeneous being more than 4 points (satisfied) for all the items.

Level of Satisfaction With Promotion and Professional Development, Received Recognition and Salary

The level of satisfaction with promotion and professional development has an average of 4.13 and has more than 4 points in three items used for measuring. As we can see in the table 5, an 83.33% of the employees are very satisfied or satisfied with their job and the level of use of their professional abilities; a 76.19% of them are very satisfied or satisfied with the expectations of promotion or professional development. In this last item, a percentage of the employees that say that are unsatisfied is the highest one (23.81%).

Speaking about the recognition of the employees by the superiors for a well-done job, the average is 4.31, so they are satisfied. An 83.33% of the interviewed

Table 4. Work conditions and training

	Average	Satisfied or very satisfied	Neutral	Unsatisfied or very unsatisfied
Level of Satisfaction WORK CONDITIONS				
Safety conditions	4.05	76.19%	16.67%	7.04%
Physical and environmental conditions	3.95	73.81%	16.67%	9.52%
Working timetable	3.90	64.28%	28.57%	35.72%
The way their company obey the agreement/ regulations/labour laws	3.55	59.52%	16.67%	23.81%
Level of Satisfaction with TRAINING				
Opportunities of training for professional development	4.12	83.34%	9.52%	7.14%
Received training for professional development	4.10	80.96%	11.9%	7.14%
Response to requests for training	4.02	78.90%	14.29%	6.81%

Source: Authors' own data

Table 5. Promotion and professional development, received recognition and salary

	Average	Satisfied or very satisfied	Neutral	Unsatisfied or very unsatisfied
Level of Satisfaction With Promotion and Professional Development				
Satisfaction with their job	4.21	83.33%	7.14%	16.77%
Level of use of professional abilities	4.17	83.43%	9.52%	16.57%
Satisfaction with the expectations of promotion or professional development	4.02	76.19%	14.29%	23.81%
Level of Satisfaction With Received Recognition				
Recognition of well done job by the supervisors	4.31	83.33%	14.29%	2.38%
Level of Satisfaction With Salary				
Salary in relation to the rest of aspects	3.79	64.28%	21.43%	35.72%
Salary in relation with the done job	3.71	66.67%	16.67%	33.33%

Source: Authors' own data

employees are very satisfied or satisfied and only 2.38% of them say that they are unsatisfied with this recognition.

Salary is one of the lowest valued aspects by the employees of this company with an average of 3.75 points; it is very close to 4 points that means "satisfied". Both the salary paid to the employee and the rest of the aspects have an average of 3.71 and 3.79 points respectively. It means neutral labour satisfaction, not satisfied neither unsatisfied with the mentioned items (Table 5). A percentage of the employees who say that they are unsatisfied or very unsatisfied is very high (35.72% and 33.33% respectively).

Level of Satisfaction With Supervisors and Involvement

Relationship with supervisors is the best-valued dimension having 4.50 points as an average (Table 6). If we observe valuation of the items separately, the employees have a higher level of satisfaction with supervision by their bosses and with an ability of their direct supervisor to practice their organizational functions with an average of 4.60 in both cases; none of the employees said that they were unsatisfied with this relationship. Observing the percentage of the collected data, we can see that a 90% of the interviewed employees are very satisfied or satisfied with the relationship with their supervisors taking into account all the analyzed items but an item that

Table 6. Relationship with supervisors, involvement, and organization and change management

	Average	Satisfied or very satisfied	Neutral	Unsatisfied or very unsatisfied
Level of Satisfaction With the Relationship With Supervisors				
Supervision exercised over you	4.60	95.24%	4.76%	---
Ability of your direct supervisor to practice his organizational functions	4.60	95.24%	4.76%	---
Evaluation of professional relationship with your direct supervisor	4.57	90.48%	9.52%	---
Personal treatment received by your direct supervisor	4.48	90.48%	9.52%	---
The way your direct supervisor judges your tasks	4.40	95.24%	9.52%	---
Orientation and support received by your direct supervisor for your work practice	4.38	83.33%	16.67%	---
Level of Satisfaction With Involvement				
Possibilities to be involved in the process of improvement of your job	4.45	90.48%	9.52%	---
Frequency of request by your supervisor to take part in decision making that can affect your labour area	4.45	88.09%	11.90%	---
Level of Satisfaction With Organization and Change Management				
Work organization in your labour area	4.36	90.48%	9.52%	---
Level of knowledge on structure, functional areas and activities of the Thermal Centre	3.81	61.90%	28.57%	9.53%
Coordination between several areas	3.67	52.38%	35.71%	11.91%

Source: Authors' own data

measures orientation and support received from their direct supervisor for a work practice (83.33%).

The dimension of involvement as well as relationship with the supervisors is highly valued by the employees with an average of 4.45 points. The Table 6 shows that the employees are very satisfied both with the frequency of requests by their supervisors to take part in decision making about projects that affect their job and possibilities to take part in the process of improvement of functioning of their job; speaking about percentages, 88.09% and 90.48% of the employees respectively.

Organization and change management with an average of 3.94 points allow us to say that the employees are not satisfied neither unsatisfied with job organization in their area (4.36), but not with coordination between other work areas (3.67) neither with a level of knowledge on functional areas, activities of the Thermal Centre and its structure with an average of 3.81 points (Table 6). In both items a percentage of satisfied or very satisfied employees is of 61.90% and 52.38% respectively.

Level of Satisfaction With Labour Climate, Internal Communications, and Knowledge and Identification of Objectives

Average evaluation of labour climate is 4.11, so it allows us to say that the employees are satisfied. They are satisfied with relationship between the colleagues of the same area (4.48), and they are neutral (not satisfied neither unsatisfied) valuating relationships between the colleagues in different areas; in this case a percentage of unsatisfied employees is high (15.06% - Table 7).

Global average in internal communication is 4.02 points. The main part of the interviewed employees says that they are very satisfied or satisfied with internal communication in the company, especially with the fact that they are informed about decisions made by the executives of the Thermal Centre and that they have information enough to develop their job in a correct way; speaking about percentages, a 78.59% and 73.81% of the employees respectively. An 80.95% of them say that they are satisfied or very satisfies with repercussion of suggestions/contributions done to improve their labor area (Table 7).

Achievement of goals is an essential point for any company that basically depends on the employees, so they have to be informed about them and about the result as well, either positive or negative. Table 7 shows that the employees of the Thermal Centre are satisfied with their level of knowledge of objectives, projects and results (73.91%), but they are neutral (3.95 in average) speaking about the level of adjunction of plans and projects to each labour area, so a percentage of satisfied or very satisfied employees decreases (69.04%). A 26.19% of the employees are not sure about the effectiveness of the projects and plans, and 4.77% shows clearly their dissatisfaction.

Table 7. Labour climate, internal communications, and knowledge and identification of objectives

	Average	Satisfied or very satisfied	Neutral	Unsatisfied or very unsatisfied
Level of Satisfaction With Labour Climate				
Relationship between the colleagues and labour atmosphere in your labour area	4.48	88.01%	7.14%	4.76%
Relationship between the colleagues and labour atmosphere between different areas	3.74	75.42%	9.52%	15.06%
Level of Satisfaction With Internal Communication				
Information about decisions made by the executives that affect an employee	4.07	78.57%	9.52%	11.91%
Repercussion of suggestions/contributions done for the labour area improvement	4.00	80.95%	11.90%	7.15%
Information received for a correct work practice	3,98	73.81%	16.67%	9.52%
Level of Satisfaction With Knowledge and Identification of Objectives				
Level of knowledge about objectives, projects and results	4.07	73,81%	23.81%	2.38%
Appropriateness of goals and plans of your labour area	3.95	69.04%	26.19%	4.77%

Source: Authors' own data

Level of Satisfaction With Perception of the Executives and Environmental Policy and Impact

The executives of the company have a very important role for the enterprise, because they decide which kind of work has to be done, when and in which way. There is a number of the employees that are not satisfied neither with the decisions that are made by the executives nor with receptiveness of them towards the problems of the employees. A percentage of these employees is 11.91 and 16.66 respectively.

Environmental policy exists in the Thermal Centre as well. It is executed through the managers that promise to have a responsible attitude towards the environment, and to require other employees and companies and/or persons working for it to have it as well. Taking into account the answers of the interviewed employees (4 points in average), we can say that the employees are satisfied with environmental policy and impact of the company with an average higher than 4 in three analyzed items (Table 8).

Finally, we want to find out is there are any difference between the level of satisfaction of the employees dependent on the employees' sex (16 men and 26 women) and kind of contract (34 permanent employees and 8 seasonal). A t-test has been done; it has helped us to compare the averages of both groups at the same

Table 8. Perception of executives, policy and environmental impact

	Average	Satisfied or very satisfied	Neutral	Unsatisfied or very unsatisfied
Level of Satisfaction With Perception of the Executives				
Receptiveness of the executive towards problems/ demands of the employees	3.83	69.04%	19.05%	11.91%
Appropriateness of decisions made by the executives	3.74	69.05%	14.29%	16.66%
Level of Satisfaction With Environmental Policy and Impact				
Importance of program of environmental management	4.24	78.57%	14.29%	7.14%
Level of implication with the program of environmental management	4.21	83.33%	9.52%	7.15%
Adequacy of environmental policy	4.05	76.19%	16.67%	7.14%

Source: Authors' own data

time (table 9). First of all, we have proved the equality of variances using Levene's test, because these two groups have different size so we could do a normality test.

As for the Levene's test, we can observe that there are several dimensions that do not have homogeneity of variances, so finally the Kruskal-Wallis test is applied. In the sex analysis we can see that the hypothesis of equality is denied in several dimensions (sig. <0.05) because there are significant differences, and we can say that there is an association between a dependent variable (sex) and the independent one (dimension). In the contract analysis, we cannot deny the hypothesis of equality of the variances with the exception of "*level of satisfaction with knowledge and identification of objectives*" where we can say that there are significant differences between permanent and seasonal employees.

We have also analyzed a matrix of correlations of the dimension of labour satisfaction that belong to a quality of service questions. The data reveal that there is a significant Pearson product-moment correlation (r) between satisfaction and quality of service dimensions in exception with "*relationship with your supervisors*" dimension (r=0.237, sig. 0.130) and "involvement" (r=0.280, sig. 0.073).

CONCLUSION

The main contribution of this study is the validation of the proposed scale, the results show that the scale is reliable and valid for use by the thermal centers as a tool to measure job satisfaction. This scale basis using the EFQM model is very new and has been used in health services (Osakidetza/ Servicio Vasco de Salud, 2001;

Table 9. Statistic tests of comparison of the averages according to sex and kind of contract

Level of Satisfaction With	Levene's test		t-test		Sig	Levene's test		t-test		Sig.
	F	Sig.	t	Sig.		F	Sig.	t	Sig.	
Relationship with the superiors	0.371	0.546	-0.986	0.330	>0.05	2.926	0.095	0.022	0.982	>0.05
Involvement	0.001	0.981	-1.973	0.055	>0.05	3.081	0.087	1.022	0.313	>0.05
Received recognition	0.533	0.470	-0.761	0.451	>0.05	0.204	0.654	0.228	0.821	>0.05
Environmental policy and impact	10.397	0.003*	-2.161	0.044	**<0.05**	6.846	0.012*	1.562	0.0157	>0.05
Promotion and professional development	15.400	0.000*	-2.644	0.016	**<0.05**	6.695	0.013*	0.764	0.467	>0.05
Labour climate	42.947	0.000*	3.670	0.002	**<0.05**	1.408	0.242	0.824	0.415	>0.05
Training	4.174	0.048*	-3.416	0.003	**<0.05**	5.934	0.019*	1.138	0.287	>0.05
Internal communication	6.693	0.013*	-3.077	0.006	**<0.05**	4.191	0.047*	0.812	0.439	>0.05
Knowledge and identification of objectives	1.039	0.314	-2.038	0.048	**<0.05**	3.047	0.089	2.284	0.028	**<0.05**
Organization and change management	1.549	0.221	-3.821	0.000	**<0.05**	1.178	0.284	1.527	0.135	>0.05
Work conditions	0,097	0.347	-2.934	0,006	**<0.05**	5.600	0.023*	0.977	0.357	>0.05
Perception of the executives	7.508	0.009*	-4.081	0.001	**<0.05**	0.955	0.334	1.092	0.281	>0.05
Salary	4.320	0.044*	-3.896	0.001	**<0.05**	0.425	0.518	1.251	0.218	>0.05
General perception	11.887	0.001*	-2.406	0.027	**<0.05**	22.303	0.000*	1.398	0.202	>0.05

* As there are some differences of variances, a Kruskal-Wallis test has been used (a chi-squared test). Sig. <0,05 means that the differences are significant.

Sig. > 0,05 means that the differences are not significant.

Source: Authors' own data

García-Pozo et al., 2010; Pérez-Ciordia et al., 2012; Robles-García et al., 2015) but it had not been validated statistically.

A second contribution of this work and not least important, on one hand, to obtain a global evaluation of satisfaction of the employees, and on the other hand, to detect weaknesses of each dimension or factors belonging to it; it would help us to give to the executive manager of the Thermal Centre the dimensions that he has to take into account and to work with them, that are the weaknesses detected by this research, so he could improve labour climate that in an indirect way influence on clients through the quality of services.

Speaking about labour satisfaction, if we take into account the results of this research we can say that the employees of this enterprise are satisfied with their organizational climate with an average of 4.09 (average of dimensions) and 4.26 (general perception) respectively. Following the strategy offered in the book of evaluation and improvement of satisfaction of personas working in enterprises that provide services (Osakidetza/ Servicio Vasco de Salud 2001), considering that excellent areas have more than 43% of satisfied employees, strong ones (41-43%), with possibilities of improvement (39-41%) and those that have to be improved (< 39%), the final results are:

- **Excellent Areas:** Relationship with supervisors, involvement and received recognition.
- **Strong Areas:** Environmental policy and impact, promotion and professional development and labour climate.
- **Areas with Possibilities of Improvement:** Training, internal communication, knowledge and identification of objectives and organization and change management.
- Finally, the areas that need to improve their work conditions are perception of the executives and salary.

To make improvements in the company, the executives have to delete the weaknesses where the employee feels himself less satisfied; it means, to improve work conditions, perception of the executives and salary, and to keep relationship with supervisors, level of satisfaction with their involvement and with received recognition.

As regards the limitations, the first relates to the study population is restricted to a single company, which prevents comparisons with other environments and situations, or to generalize the findings. A second limitation is related to the cross section thereof; it has been performed in a specific moment in time.

REFERENCES

Akerlof, G. A., Rose, A. K., Yellen, J. L., Ball, L., & Hall, R. E. (1988). Job switching and job satisfaction in the U.S. labor market. *Brookings Papers on Economic Activity*, *0*(2), 495–582. doi:10.2307/2534536

Alderfer, C. P. (1969). An empirical test of a new theory of human needs. *Organizational Behavior and Human Performance*, *4*(2), 142–175. doi:10.1016/0030-5073(69)90004-X

Álvarez Llorente, G. (2004). Análisis empírico de los determinantes de la satisfacción laboral en España. *Revista de Economía y Empresa*, *21*(52-53), 105–118.

Anderson, J. C., & Gerbing, D. W. (1988). Structural equation modeling in practice: A review and recommended two-step approach. *Psychological Bulletin*, *103*(3), 411–423. doi:10.1037/0033-2909.103.3.411

Andresen, M., Domsch, M., & Cascorbi, A. (2007). Working unusual hours and its relationship to job satisfaction: A study of European maritime pilots. *Journal of Labor Research, 28*(4), 714–734. doi:10.1007/s12122-007-9010-5

Bagozzi, R. P., & Yi, Y. (1988). On the Evaluation of Structural Equation Models. *Journal of the Academy of Marketing Science, 16*(1), 74–94. doi:10.1007/BF02723327

Blau, P. M. (1964). *Exchange and Power in Social Life*. New York: Wiley.

Campbell, J. P., Dunnette, M. D., Lawler, E. E., & Weick, K. E. (1970). *Managerial behavior, performance, and effectiveness*. New York: McGraw-Hill.

Castro, M. G. A., Padilla, J. M. C., & Ramírez, S. M. (2009). Grado de satisfacción laboral y condiciones de trabajo: Una exploración cualitativa. *Enseñanza e Investigación en Psicología, 14*(1), 105–118.

Chiang, M. M., & Ojeda, J. F. (2013). Estudio de la relación entre satisfacción laboral y el desempeño de los trabajadores de las ferias libres. *Contaduría y Administración, 58*(2), 39–60.

Clegg, C. V. (1983). Psychology of employee lateness, absence and turnover: A methodological critical and an empirical study. *The Journal of Applied Psychology, 68*(1), 88–101. doi:10.1037/0021-9010.68.1.88

Feldman, D. C., & Arnold, H. J. (1995). Personality types and career patterns: Some empirical evidence on Holland's Model. *Canadian Journal of Administrative Sciences, 35*(2), 192–210.

Flynn, F. J. (2005). Identity orientations and forms of social exchange in organizations. *Academy of Management Review, 30*(4), 737–750. doi:10.5465/AMR.2005.18378875

Fosam, E. G., Grimsley, M. F. J., & Wisher, S. J. (1998). Exploring models for employee satisfaction with particular reference to a police force. *Total Quality Management, 9*(2/3), 235–247. doi:10.1080/0954412989090

Gamero, C. (2003). La satisfacción laboral como variable económica. In C. Gamero (Ed.), *PhD thesis: Análisis económico de la satisfacción laboral* (pp. 7–70). Málaga: Retrieved from http://www.eumed.net/tesis-doctorales/cgb/c1.pdf

Guide Review of managing people. (n.d.). Available in: http://www.centrosdeexcelencia.com/dotnetnuke/Portals/0/Guia_cex_personas_def.pdf

Hackman, J. R., & Oldham, G. R. (1975). Development of the job diagnostic survey. *The Journal of Applied Psychology, 60*(2), 159–170. doi:10.1037/h0076546

Hair, J., Anderson, R., Tathaman, R., & Black, W. (1999). *Análisis Multivariante. 5ª edicción*. Madrid: Prentice Hall.

Harpaz, I. (1983). *Job satisfaction: theoretical perspectives and longitudinal analysis*. Libra.

Hartline, M. D., & Ferrell, O. C. (1996). The management of customer–contact service employees: An empirical investigation. *Journal of Marketing*, *60*(4), 52–70. doi:10.2307/1251901

Herzberg, F., & Mausner, B. S. (1978). BB 1959. The Motivation to work. New York: Academic Press.

Heskett, J. L., Jones, T. O., Loveman, G. W., Sasser, W. E. Jr, & Schlesinger, L. (1994). Putting the service–profit chain to work. *Harvard Business Review*, *72*(2), 164–174.

Ironson, G. H., Smith, P. C., Brannick, M. T., Gibson, W. M., & Paul, K. B. (1989). Construction of a Job in General scale: A comparison of global, composite, and specific measures. *The Journal of Applied Psychology*, *74*(2), 193–200. doi:10.1037/0021-9010.74.2.193

Lee, Y., & Chang, H. (2008). Relations between team work and innovation in organizations and the job satisfaction of employees: A factor analytic study. *International Journal of Management*, *25*(3), 732–739.

Locke, E. A. (1976). The nature and causes of job satisfaction. Handbook of Industrial and Organizational Psychology, 1, 1297-1343.

Lopes Branco Bonfada, P., Henn Bonfada, M. R., Alén Gonzalez, M. E., & Gonçalves Gândara, J. M. (2011). El turismo de salud y el uso terapéutico del agua. *Estudios y Perspectivas en Turismo*, *20*(2), 462–477.

Loveman, G. W. (1998). Employee satisfaction, customer loyalty, and financial performance: An empirical examination of the service profit chain in retail banking. *Journal of Service Research*, *1*(1), 18–31. doi:10.1177/109467059800100103

Mangione, T. W., & Quinn, R. P. (1975). Job satisfaction, counterproductive behaviour and drug use at work. *The Journal of Applied Psychology*, *60*(1), 114–116. doi:10.1037/h0076355 PMID:1110252

Maslow, A. H. (1954). *Motivation and Personality*. Harper & Row.

McClelland, D. C. (1961). *The Achieving Society*. Van Nostrand Reinhold. doi:10.1037/14359-000

McEvoy, G. M., & Cascio, W. F. (1985). Strategies for reducing employee turnover: A meta-analysis. *The Journal of Applied Psychology*, *70*(2), 342–353. doi:10.1037/0021-9010.70.2.342

Meliá, J. L., & Peiró, J. M. (1989). The measurement of job satisfaction in organizational settings: The S20/23 Job Satisfaction Questionnaire. *Psicologemas*, *5*, 59–74.

Meliá, J. L., Peiró, J. M., & Calatayud, C. (1986). El Cuestionario General de Satisfacción en Organizaciones Laborales: Estudios factoriales, fiabilidad y validez [presentación del Cuestionario S4/82]. *Revista de Filosofía. Psicología y Ciencias de la Educación*, *11*, 43–78.

Mueller, C. W., & McCloskey, J. C. (1990). Nurses' job satisfaction: A proposed measure. *Nursing Research*, *39*(2), 113–116. doi:10.1097/00006199-199003000-00014 PMID:2315065

Nunnally, J. (1979). *Psychometric Theory*. New York: McGraw-Hill.

Nurosis, M. J. (1993). *SPSS. Statistical Data Análisis*. SPSS Inc.

Organ, D. W. (1977). A reappraisal and reinterpretation of the satisfaction- causes-performance hypothesis. *Academy of Management Review*, *2*(1), 46–53.

Osakidetza/ Servicio Vasco de Salud. (2001). *Manual de evaluación y mejora de la satisfacción de las personas en las organizaciones de servicios*. Available in: http://www.osakidetza.euskadi.net/r850319/es/contenidos/informacion/organizacion_gestion_osk/es_og/adjuntos/satisfaccion/evaluacion.pdf

Robbins, S. (2004). *Comportamiento Organizacional*. Pearson Educación.

Robles-García, M., Dierssen-Sotos, T., Martínez-Ochoa, E., Herrera-Carral, P., Díaz-Mendi, A., & Llorca-Díaz, J. (2005). Variables relacionadas con la satisfacción laboral: Un estudio transversal a partir del modelo EFQM. *Gaceta Sanitaria*, *19*(2), 127–134. doi:10.1157/13074368 PMID:15860161

Rogers, J. D., Clow, K. E., & Kash, T. J. (1994). Increasing job satisfaction of service personnel. *Journal of Service Management*, *8*, 14–26.

Schlesinger, L. A., & Zornitsky, J. (1991). Job satisfaction, service capability and customer satisfaction: An examination of linkages and management implications. *Human Resource Planning*, *14*(2), 141–149.

Shouksmith, G., Pajo, K., & Jepsen, A. (1990). Construction of a multidimensional scale of job satisfaction. *Psychological Reports*, *67*(2), 355–364. doi:10.2466/pr0.1990.67.2.355 PMID:2263682

Silvestro, R., & Cross, S. (2000). Applying the service-profit chain in a retail environment: Challenging the satisfaction mirror. *International Journal of Service Industry Management, 11*(3), 244–268. doi:10.1108/09564230010340760

Smith, P. C., Kendall, L. M., & Hulin, C. L. (1969). *The measurement of satisfaction in work and retirement*. Chicago: Rand McNally.

Snipes, R. L., Oswald, S. L., LaTour, M., & Armenakis, A. A. (2005). The effects of specific job satisfaction facets on customer perceptions of service quality: An employee-level analysis. *Journal of Business Research, 58*(10), 1330–1339. doi:10.1016/j.jbusres.2004.03.007

Warr, P., Cook, J., & Wall, T. (1979). Scales for the measurement of some work attitudes and aspects of psychological well-being. *Journal of Occupational Psychology, 52*(2), 129–148. doi:10.1111/j.2044-8325.1979.tb00448.x

Wayne, S. J., Shore, L. M., & Linden, R. C. (1997). Perceived organizational support and leader-member exchange: A social Exchange perspective. *Academy of Management Journal, 40*(1), 82–111. doi:10.2307/257021

Weiss, D. J., Dawis, R. V., England, G. W., & Lofquist, L. H. (1967). *Manual for the Minnesota Satisfaction Questionnaire*. Minneapolis, MN: University of Minnesota, Industrial Relation Center.

Yee, R. W., Yeung, A. C., & Cheng, T. C. (2008). The impact of employee satisfaction on quality and profitability in high-contact service industries. *Journal of Operations Management, 26*(5), 651–668. doi:10.1016/j.jom.2008.01.001

Yoon, M. H., Beatty, S. E., & Suh, J. (2001). The effect of work climate on critical employee and customer outcomes: An employee-level analysis. *International Journal of Service Industry Management, 12*(5), 500–521. doi:10.1108/EUM0000000006095

Zeithaml, V.A., & Bitner, M.J. (2000). *Services Marketing*. McGraw-Hill.

ENDNOTE

1 Lopes et al. (2011) defines it as "that installation that has mineral hot springs water declared of public utility, medical care and adequate installation to carry out the treatments prescribed" (p. 127). The Thermal Centre has facilities where treatments are performed with mineral hot spring water and facilities where termalist is housed.

Chapter 2
Employee Happiness a Valuable Tool to Drive Organisations

Rinki Dahiya
Indian Institute of Technology Roorkee, India

Santosh Rangnekar
Indian Institute of Technology Roorkee, India

ABSTRACT

Are your employees happy? How happy are they? Does happiness really matter? It is well said that when people are monetarily capitalized, they want a return, and when people are emotionally devoted, they want to contribute. In organisations, emotions are imperative. Emotions, whether positive or negative, drive our behaviour, especially at the workplace where the contribution of each employee is an asset to the organisation. So, the query arises, Can organisations employ positive emotional contagion to change the behaviour of individuals to do what they want? This chapter emphasizes a new ground that happiness is having critical importance in today's parlance to both employees and employers. This chapter presents a snapshot of various definitions, theories, findings of various studies, causes, and consequences of happiness and unhappiness in the organisation and how the happiness can be nurtured or improved at the workplace.

INTRODUCTION

Countless experts approve that happiness is conceivably the furthermost significant component of a pleasant, synergistic and competent work environment. When we look at the organisations of past and present, those organisations having happiness

DOI: 10.4018/978-1-5225-4038-0.ch002

Copyright © 2018, IGI Global. Copying or distributing in print or electronic forms without written permission of IGI Global is prohibited.

among employees are typically efficacious and have spurred success. To reassure supreme involvement, commitment, proficient mastery organisations need to operate in the contemporary world as a "whole person" but the question arises how to get a "whole person"? It means mind, emotions, body and a spirit of an employee. When we embrace the resentments then we lose a part of ourselves throughout interpersonal transgression which creates an impenetrable veil of separation, disaffection, and uncertainty and generates a spiral downward to the happiness.

Here, the significance of positive psychology is very apparent which shelters the untapped areas of psychology and largely encompasses positive traits, enhancement of happiness, optimism, hope, creativity, wisdom and overall well- being. During the last couple of decades' researchers, academicians, and psychologists have mostly accentuated on distress, anger, anxiety and depression but there has been a gradual focus on capturing the positive facets of human strengths that have become an enduring stream of research in psychology. In the modern world, owing to the economic uncertainty and amplified level of competition, on the one hand, the work has been intensified and on the other hand, sustaining a level of happiness at work has turn out to be more substantial.

The initial findings of positive psychology, propagates that constructs of positive psychology are applicable in the workplace (Field & Buitendach, 2011). Researchers believes that study of positive psychology in the workplace will confer an enhanced understanding of what impulses and reassures employees to flourish and achieve their latent abilities in the working environment and undoubtedly, the positive feelings and characteristics will deliver significant contribution to global happiness in the workplace (Fisher, 2010). With the growing realization, the well-being of employees can't be considered solely either on physical or psychological health because the picture remains vague and lopsided lacking a unified and all-inclusive understanding of human functioning of all the levels. Even though the importance of psychological factors in the progress of employees have been emphasized for a long time but real attention has been paid in recent times.

In economics, the social indicator movement focuses on the most recent progress in happiness research which is the advent of 'Happiness Economics' that throws light on the fit between what we expect from a choice known as "expected utility" that does not constantly fit with the satisfaction, we get from the choice known as "experienced utility" with the rationality of satisfaction. In Happiness Economics, the attention is specifically on happiness with the logic of life-satisfaction. (Veenhoven, 2017)

All mankind is having a common goal of life that is happiness which is also the most difficult one to achieve.

Everyone knows that to make an organisation successful, happy employees are pertinent as the performance and happiness drive together (Fisher, 2003). For the sustainable achievement of pre-established goals and objectives of an organisation both an apt management system with a positive approach is required for the encouragement of employees that increases the happiness.

Based on above, this chapter gives an expelling attempt to unlock the significance of employee happiness to drive the organisation and throws light on the flourishing field of happiness at the workplace. This chapter includes the concept, Indian and western theoretical background, concise psychological research, causes and consequences of happiness and unhappiness in the workplace. Also highlights how the organisations can foster or nurture the happiness at work.

BACKGROUND

Many believes or understands the happiness, as feeling "good" or getting "pleasure" but understanding the meaning of happiness as mere pleasure will be a shallow conceptualization of happiness as it is a much deeper concept. Merriam-Webster's Online Dictionary (2008) defines happiness as a state of well-being and serenity, a satisfying or pleasurable experience of an individual on the other hand, Webster's third International Dictionary defines happiness as a state of well-being which is of relative permanence, with continuous natural desire of deep and intense joy and contentment in living. The renowned book written by Robin Sharma (2003) on "the Monk who sold his Ferrari" conveys that "happiness is a journey not destination. Live for today – there will never be another one quite like it". Thus, it can be supposed that happiness is a lifelong enjoyment which refers to the in love with the living.

Definitions of Happiness

Different authors have given different definitions of happiness. The below table 1 presents some popular definitions of happiness:

From the above, various definitions of happiness, the authors of this chapter came to the consensus that a common factor identified among these definitions is the presence of positive affect, relative absence of negative affect and satisfaction with life is clear meaning of happiness. Therefore, happiness can be understood as having positive affect mainly which includes positive state of mind of individuals trusting that life is good.

Happiness and Related Terms

The terms like well- being, flow-peak, quality of life, psychological and subjective well-being have been used interchangeably with happiness, however, they are different from happiness.

Table 1. Definitions of Happiness

S. No.	Author	Definition
1	Jahoda (1958)	Happiness refers to the notion of positive mental health but the author states that it is in- sufficient criterion, reason being, a person can be happy in inappropriate situations which is a sign or symptom of psychological disturbances.
2	Bradburn (1969) & Diener (1984)	Happiness has been constructed as a judgment or evaluation of one 's life over a period and preponderance of positive affect over negative affect.
3	Tatarkiewicz (1976)	Happiness has been referred to as a lifelong, comprehensive, and justified global satisfaction with life.
4	Veenhoven (1984)	Happiness is the degree of favorable judgement of an individual regarding the overall quality of life.
5	Argyle et al. (1989)	Happiness can be defined as having three components. First, the average level of satisfaction over a specific period, second, the frequency and degree of positive affect manifestations and third, the relative absence of negative affect.
6	Dalai Lama (1998)	Authority on happiness, states that happiness is understood as a state of mind rather than external conditions which is supported by feelings of compassion, peace and contentment towards the others.
7	Diener (2000)	Happiness is affective and cognitive evaluations of life of an individual. On the one hand, affective component covers the actual or perceived hedonic balance which states equilibrium between pleasant and unpleasant affect and on the other hand, the cognitive component includes the life satisfaction.
8	Seligman (2000)	He argued that happiness embraces both the positive activities and emotions of three categories- past, present and future. a) **Past:** feeling of pride, serenity, satisfaction and contentment. b) **Present:** enjoying the current activities and emotions like taste of food, listening to music, reading and working. c) **Future:** feeling of hope, faith, trust, optimism, and confidence.
9	Diener et al. (2002)	emphasize personal well-being as happiness which includes cognitive and affective evaluation which is further encompassed of three main elements: the existence of pleasant emotions, absence of unpleasant emotions and life satisfaction.
10	Kahn & Juster (2002)	define the term happiness that varies between the two side of continuum which means from positive to negative.
11	Uchida et al. (2004)	The happiness is that outcome of feelings or experiences in which positive affect is greater than negative affect.
12	Lyubomirsky (2005b)	states the definition of happiness as subjective well- being approach by developing the six strategies for long term happiness which are cognitive and behavioural volitional in nature: (1) regularly recalling the moments of gratitude, (2) involving oneself in self-regulatory and positive thinking, (3) committed to altruism and practicing compassion, (4) following substantial, and inherent life, (5) relishing positive experiences, and (6) being active in practicing the signature strengths in an innovative way.

Source: (Above mentioned respective research papers)

Natvig et al. (2003) stated that well- being is a wider term than happiness as it includes health, wellness, prosperity, contentment as well as happiness. Flow and peak experiences are also used interchangeably with happiness. Averill & More (2000) points out that flow refers to the match between demands of a task with the person's ability to do a task similarly Maslow's concept of peak experience comes very close to the happiness. Although, flow and peak experiences give much emphasis on the moment rather than happiness which is more long-lasting. Happiness is observed as an attribute rather than as a momentary or temporary emotional state (Lu & Lin, 1998).

Another concept which is used interchangeably with happiness is Quality of Life (QOL), although it is much understood that QOL is a wider concept than happiness. Meeberg (1993) suggested four critical traits of QOL: satisfaction with life in general, the evaluation of life as satisfactory or unsatisfactory depends on the mental ability of an individual otherwise an adequate state of social, physical, and emotional health as understood by the individual, and includes the objective evaluation that the living conditions of an individual are satisfactory and not life threatening. Thus, concept of QOL includes happiness.

Happiness with the perspective of subjective or psychological well-being approach, refers to the state of mind related with achievement of or satisfaction of needs or desires. Life satisfaction has been found having the similarity with happiness but with the absence of having any orientation to a state of mind that means success may be denoted or go together with the positive mental state and the individual who is unable to succeed in any random task is embraced by negative feelings (Kozma et al., 1991). Therefore, an individual can be satisfied or dissatisfied in a single or more domain in life for example work, family, health, housing, friends, finances, etc., but happiness includes all domains of life thus, is a construct of global nature.

The Indian Conceptualization of Happiness

There is abundant theoretical and philosophical literature on happiness in India. The *Vedas*, the *Bhagwad Gita and* the *Upanishads*- ancient manuscripts and scriptures have discovered the nature of happiness, and the insights grown from these literatures are still applicable to Indian people, inducing their origins of happiness and administering them on how to live a happy life (Bhawuk, 2011).

For illustration, many sections in the *Bhagavad-Gita*, majorly commended the attention on the clue of evasion of extremes and preserving a kind of stability or equilibrium to relish a state of happiness. It is stated in *Bhagavad Gita* that who is detached from the external world and matters related to the outside world, and is devoted to the inner self, will reach long-lasting supreme happiness (verse 5.21). On the similar ground, the Vedanta philosophy advocated that in consciousness of all individuals, there is constant existence of pure happiness and peace but we can forgo the fact that the desires, needs and fears may disturb the mind and makes the happiness doubtful or unsure that it exists within us always (Padmanabhan, 2010). Such religious and spiritual concepts are very much prevalent and commonly practised in India to ensure the mental and physical well-being (Rangaswami, 1994 & Kiran Kumar, 2003, 2004).

In general, the Indian tradition has documented that at every stage and aspects of life in all human beings there is natural desire of being happy. As per Jaina philosophy *Jiyo aur jeene do* which means live and let live is emphasized that encourages the feeling of reciprocal growth and interdependent living. The inter-reliant model of happiness converts into the following prayer:

Sarve bhavantu sukhinaha, sarve santu niramaya

Sarve bhadrani pasyantu, ma kaschid dukhabhaga bhavet.

(May all be happy, may all be free from disease,

May all perceive good and may not suffer from sorrow).

Certainly, this prayer showcases the collective mind set of Indian people that further elucidates that the desire for happiness and health is not only for own self but also for everyone. Thus, as per the prevalent themes of Indian thoughts, in psychological experience happiness is having the supreme importance which is considered as a spiritual pursuit and same can attained by oneself by turning towards the inner self rather than finding the happiness in the external world.

Psychological Research Related to Happiness in India

There are numerous psychological studies in India that have studied the indigenous views of happiness (Krishnamohan, 2001; Rastogi, 2005; Dalal & Misra, 2006, 2011; Kiran Kumar, 2004, 2008; Srivastava & Misra, 2011 & Misra, 2013) with most of them highlighting the spiritual association of happiness as enlightened by the Indian tradition.

In the last decade, numerous Indian researchers have investigated happiness through the empirical data (e.g. Lal, 2004; Kulshrestha & Sen, 2006; Jha & Kumari, 2009; Chakrabarti, 2009; Gupta & Kumar, 2010; Dave et al. 2011 and Sharma, 2011 etc.) on many samples of Indian population. A study conducted by Lal (2004) explored the relationship between happiness and demographic variables. Results demonstrated that positive and negative feelings are significantly associated with age, education, income of family, and area of residence, in adolescents except gender. The study conducted by Kulshrestha and Sen (2006) offered an insight that those executives who are having high emotional intelligence but with low internal locus of control showcased high positive affect, in comparison with negative affect, and high level of life satisfaction. These studies are lopsided reason being, most of these studies are conducted on the grounds of western conceptualization of happiness which are further measured by the foreign tools. While it is quite evident among researchers that context and culture has a vast impact on happiness but, it is uncertain that how far the measures adopted from other backgrounds, will provide precise insights on the frequency or degree of happiness in a specific domain or in a particular context.

Happiness: Western Theoretical Perspectives

There are many perspectives on happiness, especially when it comes to the western theoretical and philosophical literature. In the western context, the earliest notions on the happiness can be sketched from early 3rd century BCE from the ancient Greek philosophers. Amid the numerous perspectives, two of them have gained incredible consideration by psychologists namely, *hedonism* and *eudaimonia.*

1. **Hedonism:** It is also known as hedonic well- being which is originated on the concept that happiness is the outcome of more pleasure and less pain. Hedonic ideas are based on the notion of subjective well-being that is implied to denote a happy or good life (Gavin & Mason, 2004). As proposed by Diener (1985), hedonic concept of happiness encompasses affective element which means more positive affect, less negative affect, and satisfaction with life as a cognitive element. Further, it is suggested that people feel happy, if they handle the challenges and developed through experiences (Ryan & Deci, 2001).
2. **Eudaimonia:** The Greek philosopher Aristotle propounded ideal of *eudaimonia* (defined by Aristotle as happiness) that people should learn to be true to one's self (Norton, 1976). It is based on notion of achieving or realising the full potential of one's self, living their life based on some objective social values and some internal virtues such as ethics, knowledge and friendship instead of subjective psychological feelings (Tatarkiewicz, 1976; Waterman, 1990; Taylor, 1998; Ryan & Deci 2001& Kashdan et al., 2008). Instances of *eudaimonia* are such as developing one 's potential, gratitude, kindness, compassion and empathy (Huta & Ryan, 2010).

Undoubtedly, there is a wide-ranging psychological research on happiness and related constructs or variables in the West. As per Veenhoven (2015), 9,525 studies have investigated the construct, recorded in the *World Database of Happiness* out of which 4,808 are experimental studies. From these empirical studies, 14,978 correlational findings derived from 1,406 studies are correlational in nature, while the rest of them demonstrates, distributional findings such as in a specific population, how happy people are. Most surprisingly, this database also includes 1,038 measures on happiness.

Components of Happiness

When it comes to the question that what is comprised in happiness. utmost psychological researches have proven the fact that happiness is sum of cognitive and affective components (Diener, 1984; Diener et al., 1999; Galinha & Pais-Ribeiro, 2011) which encompasses domain satisfaction, global judgement and emotional responses of individuals. Diener (1984) in his research paper which is considered as landmark, proposed three components of happiness (or "subjective well-being" term used by Diener for scientific study of happiness) better called as hallmarks of happiness.

1. **Positive Affect:** Positive affect denotes pleasant moods and emotions, like joy, interest, enthusiasm and affection, and produces a response of an individual for the events experienced that indicates life is going on in a desirable way. The major types of positive affect consist of positive reactions to others, positive responses to activities, and general positive moods. Thus, pleasurable engagement in life of an individual is reflected through positive affect.
2. **Negative Affect:** It broadly encompasses emotions and moods that are cold and unpleasant. This type of affect represents negative responses of people in concern with events, health, varied circumstances and their lives. The unpleasant or negative affect consists of worry, sadness, anger, stress, anxiety, envy, helplessness, frustration, guilt and shame. However, it is well said that some of the negative affect is necessary for functioning but it signalled that the one's life is not going good. Thus, it can be said that negative affect is a common factor of personal agony (Bradburn, 1969; Watson, 1988).
3. **Satisfaction with Life:** Life satisfaction takes the happiness judgement globally which has become a very common perspective conceiving the happiness (Watson, 1988). It covers various domains of life like work, friends, family, peers, social groups, finance, health, housing etc.

This contemporary notion of subjective well-being which embraces all these three components has turn out to be very prevalent amid happiness researchers and is expansively deployed in a diverse correlational study on happiness whether for a highly individualist or collectivist culture, those who connected happiness with the principal or imperative human need which further defined as social relationship, and stated higher happiness (Shin et al., 2017).

Orientations to happiness-

Peterson et al. (2005) produced a unified model for happiness which is developed through the combined effects of hedonic and eudaimonic approaches. The orientations to happiness is indicated in Figure 1.

1. **Pleasure:** It is the first orientation to happiness. An enjoyable life can be made up of much pleasure which is gained via the adoption of positive affect (Peterson et al., 2005). To certain limits, any individuals can intensify their positive affect by refining gratitude and forgiveness, by mindfulness and by building hope and optimism (Seligman, 2002). Growing pleasure as orientation on the way to happiness has its notional foundations in hedonism (Park et al., 2009).
2. **Engagement:** It is the second orientation to happiness. When an individual is engaged in activities whether it is work or play and gets inherent gratification and accomplishment (Peterson et al., 2005). The engagement is derived from state of flow reason being, as the person involves himself or herself in the activity experiences a fit between skills and challenges (Moneta & Csikszentmihalyi, 1996).
3. **Meaning and Purpose in Life:** This third orientation is meaningful life which consists of practicing the strengths and talents of an individual in performing the activities (Peterson et al., 2005) which are associated with exogenous goals and transcendence of self (Park et al., 2009), develops social networks and delivers purpose (Schueller & Seligman, 2010).

Figure 1. Orientations to happiness

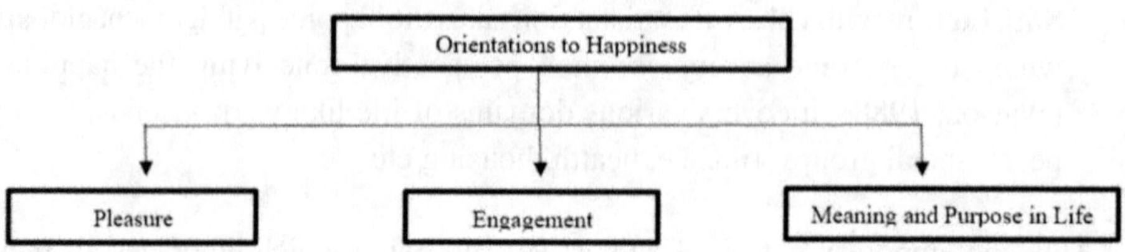

Source: Peterson et al. (2005)

ORGANISATIONAL HAPPINESS

People spend most of their time work, so being happy at workplace is indispensable (Gavin & Mason, 2004; Money et al. 2008; Rego, 2008; VanZyl et al., 2010; Warr, 2009). Happiness has brought many important effects on the employees and the organisation (Fisher, 2010; Van Zyl et al., 2010, Warr, 2009). According to Fisher (2010) organisational happiness can be evidenced on three levels, namely individual level, unit level and transient levels. The chart in figure 2 presents levels of organisational happiness.

When the focus is on the happiness, on personal level it is referred to as individual's happiness and when the focus is on the happiness of whole unit say group or team is referred to as unit level happiness, while transient happiness includes the momentary emotions and moods that employees might experience or go through. However, as per Fisher (2010), construct is related to happiness in over-all, defined and measured at unit level are assumed to be firmer in the long run.

SIGNIFICANCE OF HAPPINESS AT WORKPLACE

The success and survival of the organisations are depended on the employees (Halvorsen, 2005). Undoubtedly, organisations aspire to have success in whatever they do and attain a higher return on the investments. Correspondingly, almost everyone seeks for happiness and it is considered as highly-valued advantage across societies. Happiness is comprehended in every emotion of human being. Feeling and gaining happiness is native function of human experience, and most of the time, majority of people varies from being moderately happy to very happy (Diener, 2000). The construct of happiness is not new but there is gradual increase in the attention of the philosophers (McMahon, 2006), however, the subject has become the central to the psychological research in the recent times. Halvorsen (2005) argued that happy or

Figure 2. Levels of organisational happiness

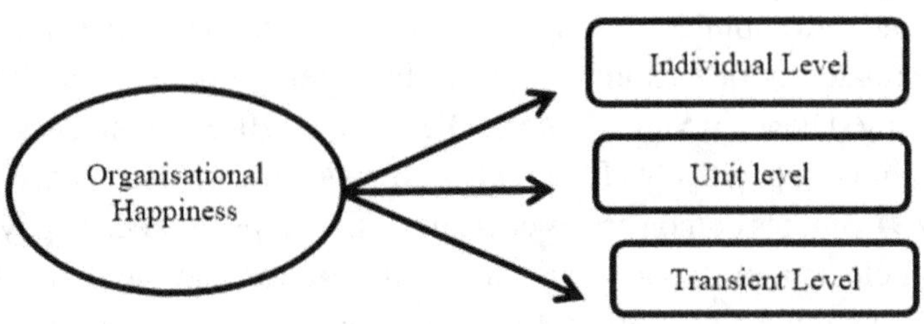

Source: Fisher (2010)

good employees can produce outcomes that are outstanding, while some employees incline to block the path of development of creativity and growth by delaying the completion of tasks at work.

According to Fisher, 2010, happiness is vital in the work environment and research on happiness has been given much consideration throughout the years particularly within the work setting. Rego et al., 2011 contend that contemplating happiness is imperative for the accompanying reasons: happiness is important to society (Diener, 2000); happiness is related with raised execution, and enhanced hierarchical functioning (Fredrickson, 2003); and happiness is a fundamental segment for the great life and for the improvement of society (Diener, 2000). It is likewise advantageous for employers to offer regard for the happiness of their employees. Studies have found that organisations with more employees who have higher levels of employee prosperity additionally tend to report more prominent consumer loyalty and steadfastness, more noteworthy benefit, greater profitability, and lower rates of turnover (Keyes & Magyar-Moe, 2003).

However, as indicated by Weitz (2011), happiness does not come effortlessly, particularly in the workplace and further states that it is especially challenging in most workplaces where due dates, spending plans, and execution issues can bargain with the vast majority's feeling of happiness (p.18). Along these lines happiness in the work environment frequently shows noteworthy exertion from employees. Researches on happiness have demonstrated that happiness is identified with organisational citizenship behaviour (Rego, Ribeiro and Cunha, n.d.). OCBs portray activities in which workers will go beyond their required role necessities (Chien, n.d.). Hence given the foundation to the study and past research findings, the analyst considered that it is vital and indispensable to study about happiness and its association with positive practices in the work environment.

PSYCHOLOGICAL RESAERCH ON HAPPINESS AT WORKPLACE

Considering and advancing the happiness of individuals, particularly in the work place is profoundly applicable. The significance of measuring ideal functioning has been accentuated as of late and happiness has been proposed as a vital marker of ideal working (Diener & Suh, 1997 and Diener et al., 2008). Happiness has different positive results. It positively affects self-acknowledgment, confidence, and morale (Ryff, 1989). Studies demonstrates critical relationships between happy individuals and high inclusion, profound focus, inborn inspiration and the impression of high difficulties coordinated by satisfactory individual aptitude (Vittersø, 2003). Happy employees are more advantageous, keep up better relational connections, appreciate constructed professional achievement, and basically appreciate the happy or great life (Park & Huebner, 2005; Seligman, 2002, 2008). Happy employees are likewise more productive, have higher confidence and are for the most part happy with life (DeNeve & Cooper, 1998).

Working people spend a greater part of their life at work (Wrzesniewski, 2003). Managers have a huge association with organisations (Carson and Lowman, 2002). Further, Kilburg (2000) portrays how managers must mediate as a role model and change specialist of people within teams. The study conducted by Kampa-Kokesch (2001) demonstrated that skilled and happy employees encouraged faster changes in the workplace, diminished individual troubles and added to better leadership in the organisations. Along these lines, considering the happiness at work, and the precursors thereof is very significant.

The happiness of employees can be viewed as an essential research topic for a many reason. Managers spend majority of their working time with people. On the similar ground, Bellah et al., 1985 expressed that the impact of significance of work (which adds to happiness) is more noticeable in a workplace where the people are continually connecting with different social frameworks in an organisation. Besides this, happy employees would be more effective and efficient to fulfil their roles. Managers or top officials are also good examples for happiness in the workplace (Cameron et al., 2003). Lastly, happiness of employees predicts constructive organisational results like low turnover intention, organisational citizenship behaviour, organisational commitment, job satisfaction, and subjective well-being (Harter et al., 2002; Bakker et al., 2003 & Simpson, 2008).

As indicated by May et al. (2004), rewarding co-worker relations, job enrichment, job enlargement, and work-role fit, are forerunners of meaningful work because people connects to the work significantly. There is an alignment between employee's self-concept, work activities and work roles that draws benefit from strengths of employees which results into meaningfulness, further enables them to express their convictions, values and beliefs in their work (Seligman, 2002 & May et al., 2004). Moreover, the researchers of job design (Johns et al., 1992 and Renn & Vandenberg, 1995) have exhibited that job enrichment in the sphere of autonomy, skill variety, task significance, task identity, and feedback prompts psychological meaning. As suggested by Kahn (1990), people should seek more significance in the work place when their interpersonal relations are personal collaborations with their colleagues, when they are approached with dignity, respect, and given importance for their dedicated contributions.

Authentic happiness is also related with different organisational outcomes, including hierarchical responsibility, aim to stay/leave, work fulfilment, and organisational citizenship behaviour. The authentic happiness further explained that job satisfaction is viewed as most important among the other vital indexes of well-being for employees in the workplace (Van & Rothmann, 2010). Generally, job satisfaction is an individual evaluation by the employees for the work given to them. This evaluation can incorporate cognitive evaluations. It is the degree to which an individual experience, being absorbed in work and get a variety of rewards for the good work rendered for example- financial benefits, promotion, and recognition (Bakker & Oerlemans, 2012).

HAPPINESS AND UNHAPPINESS

It is normal to accept that any one cannot be rich *and* poor or tall *and* short at the same time, one cannot be happy *and* unhappy at any given time. A question emerges whether happiness and unhappiness are autonomous of each other, or being happy implies that the individual is not unhappy. It has been realized that positive affect and negative affect are not dependent on each other, thus, accordingly, it is conceivable that an individual high on positive affect may likewise be high on negative effect, and the other way around. Hence, if happiness is evaluated through the measures of positive and negative affect, an individual may score higher on both, and thus on the similar ground, seem to be both happy *and* unhappy in the meantime.

For a positive psychologist, happiness is not only the after effect of absence of negative affect, but also results from presence of many positive states (Seligman, 2002) for example, understanding and deploying the virtues in real life and applying signature strengths of an individual such as humanity, courage, persistence, love, knowledge, wisdom, knowledge, spirituality and transcendence (Snyder & Lopez, 2002, 2007).

Thus, happiness and unhappiness are subjective understanding of the identical objective reality, so the organisations or employers should devise their strategies carefully.

CAUSES OF HAPPINESS AT WORK

Now, an important question arises what are the causes of happiness in the workplace? Fisher (2010) suggested that there are three causes of happiness in the workplace, namely, general causes and organisational causes and combination of causes. On the one hand, the *general causes* are related to the environment like surroundings of the workplace reason being it affect the moods and emotions of the employees. On the other hand, *personal reasons* or causes of happiness are genetics and personality of the employees that impacts the happiness level of an individual and thirdly, there are certain effects which are developed due to the interactive effect of general and personal causes of happiness.

There are other researchers also, who tried to find out causes of happiness in the workplace. The chart in figure 3 presents the causes of happiness at work.

Job Satisfaction

Till date, the most noteworthy reason of happiness in work is job satisfaction. It offers a mix of both positive and negative emotions that employees have for their work. It gives employees a feeling of achievement, and accomplishment of the tasks. It is specifically identified with efficiency and individual well-being. The relationship between subjective well-being (happiness) and job satisfaction is complementary and there is a huge impact or influence of subjective well -being on job satisfaction (Bowling and Wang, 2010).

Figure 3. Causes of happiness at work

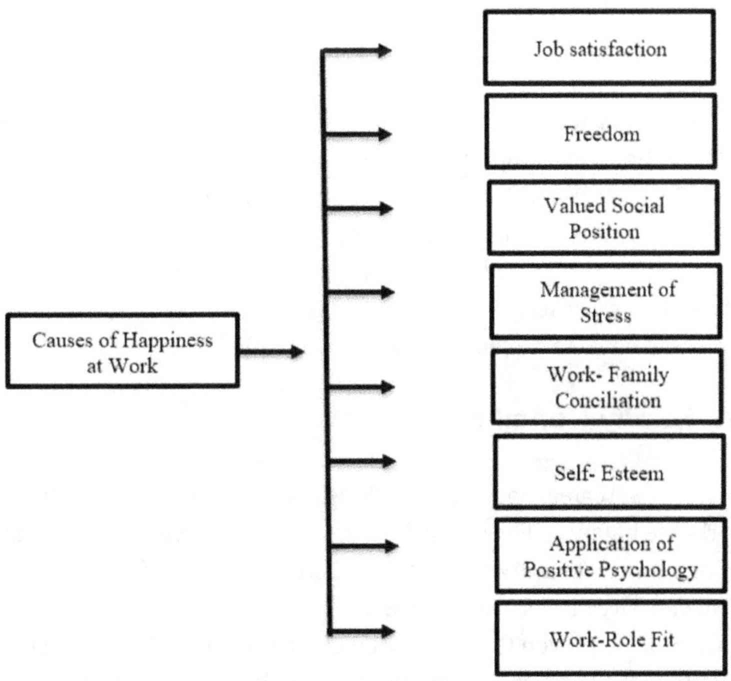

Source: (Tasnim, 2016)

Freedom

An employee derives happiness from ability to take decisions personally or have discretion to take decisions. Those people who like to work on their choice are happier. Therefore, work should be assigned to employees with their consultation by giving due importance to their choices. In comparison to the organisations where employees do not have freedom to exercise their choices while working are less motivated or demotivated, perform less effectively, and efficiently (Gavin and Mason, 2004).

Valued Social Position

As clarified by Warr (2009) that the basic features associated with happiness, includes the externally generated goal, opportunity for personal control, proper utilization of skill use, network at workplace (interpersonal relations), finance, physical security, and a valued social position. He further stated that there is no relation between the happiness and environmental features in a direct manner fashion but there is a noteworthy relationship between the happiness and environment.

Successful Management of Stress

A study conducted by Fairbrother and Warn (2003), emphasised that though work stress is related to the low level of happiness (personal well-being) and lower job satisfaction. But employees who can manage the stress at workplace are less vulnerable to other psychological factors like conflicts, lower confidence, tendency of job hoping, absenteeism, and so on. Thus, employers should give opportunity to the employees to learn how to manage stress and promote open discussion with employees in order to enhance the trust and competency (Rego and Cunha 2008) which contributes to general happiness of employees.

Work Family Conciliation

Mostly, the dual career couples or working couples in the same field faces the problems of work- life balance. These conflicts are bound to occur which reduces the level of positive affect in an individual's life and creates a spiral downward to the happiness such an employee is less productive because they find work meaningless. Similarly, the studies have proven that those who are having work-life balance or work-family conciliation are happier. When they sense balance between work and family, they are more productive, and happy in the workplace (Rego and Cunha (2008).

Self-Esteem

There is a strong relation between happiness and self- esteem. Although the studies have not proved clear cause and effect relationship between them, however, the results advocated that those employees who are having high esteem were happier than those who were having low level of self-esteem. In some situations, those with low self- esteem are more prone to sadness, depression, low efficiency, and shown signs of tardiness hence, resulted into unhappy life (Baumeister et al 2003).

Application of Concepts of Positive Psychology

As the name suggests, the positive psychology helps to gain happiness, and give strengths to the individual for targeting even impossible tasks. Positive psychology is an umbrella term which is having three layers namely, individual's traits, organisational traits, and subjective experiences. In this, the subjective experiences targets to nourish and enrich experiences, well-being and happiness. The concepts of positive psychology, such as hope, optimism, gratitude, psychological contract, psychological ownership, psychological fit helps the employees to develop positive affect or trait, like self- reliance, self- confidence, interpersonal skill, and work ethics, which contributes to happiness.

Work- Role Fit

The work- role fit also influence the happiness in the workplace. The employees who are engaged in the work activities which are goal- directed, showcases the meaningfulness to their life is backed by the self-concept of work-role fit by the organisation which contributes to the satisfaction and happiness to employees (Van Zyl et al., 2010).

CONSEQUENCES OF HAPPINESS AT WORKPLACE

There are different consequences of happiness in the workplace. The studies on happiness have proven that happiness in employees results into successful career (Lyubomirsky et al., 2005; Boehm & Lymbomirsky, 2008; Coetzee & Bergh, 2009; Lumley, 2010, and Ferreira, 2012). Further, improved career success and satisfied employees fruitfully utilises autonomy in performing their duties and taking their responsibilities ((Boehm & Lymbomirsky, 2008). Happy employees have a sense of fulfilment, and able to achieve self- regulation, perform perfectly in whatever they do. This reveals that employee's well-being can be achieved from the workplace easily (Gavin & Mason, 2004) and task significance, role clarity, personal efficacy, work engagement, work commitment and greater awareness of happiness can be developed in the workplace. Besides the consequences discussed, below are some other worth-noting consequences of happiness in the workplace-

Widens Focus of Employees and Expands Thinking

Positive emotions such as, interest, satisfaction, excitement, energy, freedom, enhances a person's capacity to concentrate on anything. When an individual is happy, then his or her thought process speeds up and concentration is also high such a person can think soundly and several ideas are evoked. Thus, creative ideas are generated which can be useful for the progress of the organisation (Tasnim, 2016).

Improves Problem-Solving Ability

While working, employees are encountered with several problems on both the levels, namely, personal and organisational. Point here is that, a happy person is optimistic and can find solutions even in tough circumstances. The positive emotions enhance the problem-solving abilities of employees through which the employees can easily find answers for the difficult challenges of the life (Tasnim, 2016).

Positive Emotions Build Resources

Physical Resources: Happy employees are playful and takes participation in the physical activities. Happy employees do exercise regularly for physical fitness. In comparison to those, who are not happy are more prone to illness. Good health of employees is very important as they are one who runs the organisation and are known as foundation of organisation (Tasnim, 2016).

Intellectual Resources: Employees are known as the intellectual assets of an organisation. Employees can learn better, if they are in a positive attitude. In any company, the most effective and productive employees are those who enjoy the work. Thus, happy employees are intellectual resources for the organisation (Tasnim, 2016).

Social Resources: Good interpersonal relations are very pertinent for the success and survival of the organisations. The studies have proven the fact that those who are happy, also have good interpersonal relations at workplace. It further creates a positive working environment (Tasnim, 2016).

Counteracts Negative Emotions

Happiness is the resolution of negative feelings like anger, distress, doubt, shame, and negative thoughts. At the point when a man 's brain is possessed with positive contemplations, consequently, there is no space for negative considering. The positive emotions counteract, establishes equilibrium, and most of the times negates the negative emotions in the individuals at the workplace. For example, if any negative emotions come to the mind like stress, anger and sadness, it is instantly substituted by the positive emotions (Tasnim, 2016).

IMPROVING OR IMPROVING HAPPINESS OF EMPLOYEES

Fisher (2010) suggests that it is very importance for the organisations to foster or improve the happiness of employees as work is also a main domain of their life and moreover, happy employees brings so many positive organisational outcomes so following are the suggestions (but not limited to) to improve the happiness:

- Formation of such an organisational culture that encourages mutual support and respect.
- Effective leadership at all levels of organisation.
- Ensure organisational justice to employees.
- Provide such roles in the organisations that are engaging, meaningful and independent.
- Encourage target-driven employees.
- Develop interpersonal trust and forgiveness.
- Create such occasions that fosters opportunities for happiness.
- Develop employee-organisational fit.

Diener et al. (1999), suggested another way to promote the happiness in the organisation that rather than focusing on intensity of feeling happy, focus should be given on frequency of feelings of happiness. It means organisations should implement and encourage such measures that prompt the feelings of happiness frequently as opposed to fewer interventions for happiness at big intervals in the organisations. For instance, instead of the big budgeted conference for employees, frequent small budget conferences can be organised throughout the year. From time to time, organisations should make employees understand that their success in work is meaningful to the organisation and this is ultimately, contribute in the happiness of employees (Gavin & Mason, 2004).

Rego (2008) advocated the role of authentizotic psychological environment, through which the organisations can foster happiness in employees and can develop a work culture which is healthy and energetic. Organisations should take note of employee's perceptions by focussing on the following areas:

- Constant learning and development for employees
- Significant and meaningful work.
- Transparency in dealing with subordinates.
- Work Collaboration
- Promoting morale and team cohesiveness.
- System of fair recognition and reward programme.

However, organisation need to consider, that not only exogenous factors can foster employee happiness such as improving the working environment but also the indigenous factors are equally responsible for fostering the happiness, but the big question is here that every effort goes into vein, if the subjective happiness of an individual is very low Graham et al., (2004) hence, the support of employee is also equally required to sustain the organisational happiness.

CONSEQUENCES OF UNHAPPY EMPLOYEES

This unquestionable about the awareness of the organisations regarding the devastating impacts of unhappiness in the workplace as it brings so many negative consequences (Warr 2009). Poor performance, distress, conflicts, burnout, absenteeism, poor health, early attrition, lower efficiency and productivity are majorly derived from the unhappiness in the workplace (Boehm & Lyubomirsky, 2008, and Warr, 2009). In the viewpoint of Wright & Bonett (2007) unhappiness can result into employee turnover.

It is evident that happiness plays an important role in the organisations. While there are various ways of making employees happy at work, organisations need to understand the needs of their employees and build an employee value proposition that addresses these needs.

FUTURE RESEARCH DIRECTIONS

From the above discussion, it is quite evident that it is essential to understand what are the causes and consequences of happiness and unhappiness in the employees in different cultures and sectors. On the similar lines, it is vital to examine and understand the twin aspects of the person and environmental related characteristics. In relation to this context, it is recommended to investigate the existence of direct and indirect mediating- moderating effect of various psychological concepts on relationship between attributes of work and happiness or unhappiness. In this, special focus should be given to the individuals so that proper interventions can be developed in the causal process. But till date, majority of studies have focused on exogenous factors like power, position and wealth. Therefore, there is a huge scope of research to study the interactive effect of both exogenous and indigenous variables of happiness. It will prospect the originations to utilize the signature strength of employees for the benefit of human resource and management in the long-run.

CONCLUSION

Happiness is an umbrella construct that shelters a variety of internal and external factors. Happiness is blend of psychology, philosophy, positive and negative affect. There are various perspective regarding the theories of happiness in different cultures and different contexts. During the last couple of decades' researchers, academicians, and psychologists have mostly accentuated on distress, anger, anxiety and depression but there has been a gradual focus on capturing the positive facets of human strengths that have become an enduring stream of research in psychology. In the modern world, owing to the economic uncertainty and amplified level of competition, on the one hand, the work has been intensified and on the other hand, sustaining a level of happiness at work has turn out to be more substantial. Organisations need to take efforts to nurture or foster the happiness of employees as it is a valuable tool to drive the organisations successfully. A mind set of happiness at work allows employees and their organisations to make the most out of performance and realize their full potential. Happiness comes with a bundle of benefits which embraces faster promotion, more learning and earning, producing more creative ideas, being healthier and reaching greater success.

REFERENCES

Argyle, M. (1987). *The Psychology of Happiness*. London: Routledge.

Argyle, M., Martin, M., & Crossland, J. (1989). Happiness as a Function of Personality and Social Encounters. In J. P. Forgas & J. M. Innes (Eds.), *Recent Advances in Social Psychology: An International Perspective* (pp. 189–203). Elsevier.

Averill, J. R., & More, T. A. (2000). Happiness. In M. Lewis & J. M. Jones (Eds.), *Handbook of Emotions* (pp. 663–676). New York: The Guilford Press.

Bakker, A. B., Demerouti, E., & Schaufeli, W. B. (2003). Dual processes at work in a call centre: An application of the job demands-resources model. *European Journal of Work and Organizational Psychology*, *12*(4), 393–417. doi:10.1080/13594320344000165

Bakker, A. B., Demerouti, E., & Verbeke, W. (2004). Using the job demands-resources model to predict burnout and performance. *Human Resource Management*, *43*(1), 83–104. doi:10.1002/hrm.20004

Bakker, A. B., & Oerlemans, G. M. (2012). Subjective well-being in organisations. In K. S. Cameron & G. M. Spreitzer (Eds.), The Oxford handbook of positive organisational scholarship (pp. 178–189). New York: Oxford.

Bakker, A. B., & Oerlemans, W. G. M. (2010). Subjective well-being in organisations. In K. Cameron & G. Spreitzer (Eds.), *Handbook of Positive Organisational Scholarship* (p. 8). Oxford University Press.

Baumeister, R. F., Campbell, J. D., Krueger, J. I., & Vohs, K. D. (2003). Does high self-esteem cause better performance, interpersonal success, happiness, or healthier lifestyles? *Psychological Science in the Public Interest*, *4*(1), 1–44. doi:10.1111/1529-1006.01431 PMID:26151640

Bellah, R., Madsen, R., Sullivan, W., Swidler, A., & Tipton, S. (1985). *Habits of the heart: Individualism and commitment in American life*. Berkeley, CA: University of California Press.

Bhawuk, D. P. S. (2011). *Spirituality and Indian Psychology: Lessons from the Bhagavad-Gita*. New York: Springer. doi:10.1007/978-1-4419-8110-3

Boehm, J. K., & Lyubomirsky, S. (2008). Does happiness promote career success? *Journal of Career Assessment*, *16*(1), 101–116. doi:10.1177/1069072707308140

Bowling, N. A., Eschleman, K. J., & Wang, Q. (2010). A meta-analytic examination of the relationship between job satisfaction and subjective well-being. *Journal of Occupational and Organizational Psychology*, *84*(4), 915–934. doi:10.1348/096317909X478557

Bradburn, N. (1969). *The Structure of Psychological Well-being*. Chicago: Aldine.

Brickman, P., & Campbell, D. T. (1971). Hedonic Relativism and Planning the Good Society. In M. H. Appley (Ed.), *Adaptation Level Theory: A Symposium*. New York: Academic Press.

Brief, A. P., & Weiss, H. M. (2002). Organisational behaviour: Affect in the workplace'. *Annual Review of Psychology, 53*(1), 279–307. doi:10.1146/annurev.psych.53.100901.135156 PMID:11752487

Cameron, K. S., Dutton, J., & Quinn, R. (2003). Foundations of positive organisational scholarship. In K. S. Cameron, J. E. Dutton, & R. E. Quinn (Eds.), *Positive organisational scholarship* (pp. 1–10). San Francisco, CA: Berrett-Koehler.

Carson, A. D., & Lowman, R. L. (2002). Individual-level variables in organisational consultation. In R. L. Lowman (Ed.), *Handbook of organisational consulting psychology*. San Francisco, CA: Jossey-Bass.

Chakrabarti, D. (2009). Well-being of the elderly residing in old age home vs. those in family setting in Tripura. *Nursing Journal of India, C*(10). Retrieved from http://www.tnaionline.org/oct-09/4.htm PMID:20358676

Chien, M.H. (n.d.). *A study to improve Organisational citizenship behaviours*. Academic Press.

Clark, A. E., Layard, R., & Senik, C. (2012). The causes of happiness and misery. *UN World Happiness Report*, 59-89.

Coetzee, M., & Bergh, Z. (2009). Psychological career resources and subjective work experiences of working adults: An exploratory study. *Southern African Business Review, 13*(2), 1–31.

Coetzer, C. F., & Rothmann, S. (2007). Job demands, job resources, and work engagement of employees in a manufacturing organisation. *Southern African Business Review, 11*(3), 17–32.

Csikszentmihalyi, M. (1990). *Flow: The Psychology of Optimal Experience*. New York: Harper and Row.

Dalai Lama, H. H. (1998). The Art of Happiness. London: Coronet Books.

Dalal, A. K., & Misra, G. (2006). Psychology of health and well-Being: Some emerging perspectives. *Psychological Studies*, 2(2-3).

Dalal, A. K., & Misra, G. (2011). Advances in psychology of health and well-being. In G. Misra (Ed.), *Handbook of Psychology in India*. New Delhi: Oxford University Press.

Dave, R., Tripathi, K. N., Singh, P., & Udainiya, R. (2011). Subjective well-being, locus of control and general self-efficacy among university students. *Amity Journal of Applied Psychology*, 2(1), 151–155.

DeNeve, K. M., & Cooper, H. (1998). The happy personality: A meta-analysis of 137 personality traits and subjective well-being. *Psychological Bulletin, 124*(2), 197–229. doi:10.1037/0033-2909.124.2.197 PMID:9747186

Diener, E. (1984). Subjective Well Being. *Psychological Bulletin, 95*(3), 542–575. doi:10.1037/0033-2909.95.3.542 PMID:6399758

Diener, E. (2000). Subjective well-being: The science of happiness and a proposal for a national index. *The American Psychologist, 55*(1), 34–43. doi:10.1037/0003-066X.55.1.34 PMID:11392863

Diener, E., Kesebir, P., & Lucas, R. (2008). Benefits of accounts of well-being - For societies and for psychological science. *Applied Psychology: An International Journal, 57*(s1), 37–53. doi:10.1111/j.1464-0597.2008.00353.x

Diener, E., Lucas, R., & Oishi, S. (2002). Subjective well-being: The science of happiness and life satisfaction. In C. R. Snyder & S. J. Lopez (Eds.), *The Handbook of Positive Psychology* (pp. 63–73). New York: Oxford University Press.

Diener, E., Lucas, R. E., & Oishi, S. (2005). The science of happiness and life satisfaction. In C. R. Snyder & S. J. Lopez (Eds.), Handbook of positive psychology (pp. 63–73). New York: Oxford.

Diener, E., Lucas, R. E., & Scollon, C. N. (2006). Beyond hedonic adaptation: Revising the adaptation theory of well-being. *The American Psychologist, 61*(4), 305–314. doi:10.1037/0003-066X.61.4.305 PMID:16719675

Diener, E., Nickerson, C., Lucas, R. E., & Sandvik, E. (2002). Dispositional affect and job outcomes. *Social Indicators Research, 59*(3), 229–259. doi:10.1023/A:1019672513984

Diener, E., & Suh, E. (1997). Measuring quality of life: Economic, social and subjective indicators. *Social Indicators Research, 40*(1/2), 189–216. doi:10.1023/A:1006859511756

Diener, E., Suh, E. M., Lucas, R. E., & Smith, H. L. (1999). Subjective well-being: Three decades of progress. *Psychological Bulletin, 125*(2), 276–302. doi:10.1037/0033-2909.125.2.276

Diener, E. D., Sandvik, E. D., & Pavot, W. (1999). Happiness is the frequency not the intensity of positive versus negative affect. *Psychological Science*, 119–139.

Fairbrother, K., & Warn, J. (2003). Workplace dimensions, stress and job satisfaction. *Journal of Managerial Psychology, 18*(1), 8–21. doi:10.1108/02683940310459565

Ferreira, N. (2012). Hardiness in relation to organisational commitment in the human resource management field. *Journal of Human Resource Management, 10*(2), 418–428.

Field, L., & Buitendach, J. H. (2011). Happiness, work engagement and organisational commitment of support staff at a tertiary education institution in South Africa. *SA Journal of Industrial Psychology, 37*(1), 1–10. doi:10.4102/sajip.v37i1.946

Fisher, C. D. (2003). Why do lay people believe that satisfaction and performance are correlated? Possible sources of common sense theory. *Journal of Organizational Behavior, 24*(6), 753–777. doi:10.1002/job.219

Fisher, C. D. (2010). Happiness at work. *International Journal of Management Reviews, 12*(4), 384–412. doi:10.1111/j.1468-2370.2009.00270.x

Fredrickson, B. L. (1998). What good are positive emotions? *Review of General Psychology, 2*(3), 300–319. doi:10.1037/1089-2680.2.3.300 PMID:21850154

Fredrickson, B. L. (1998). What good are positive emotions? *Review of General Psychology, 2*(3), 300–319. doi:10.1037/1089-2680.2.3.300 PMID:21850154

Fredrickson, B. L. (2001). The role of positive emotions in positive psychology: The broaden-and build theory of positive emotions. *The American Psychologist, 56*(3), 218–226. doi:10.1037/0003-066X.56.3.218 PMID:11315248

Fredrickson, B. L. (2003). Positive emotions and upward spirals in organisational settings. In K. Cameron, J. Dutton, & R. Quinn (Eds.), *Positive Organisational Scholarship*. San Francisco: Berrettkoehler.

Fredrickson, B. L., & Brangian, C. (2005). Positive emotions broaden the scope of attention and thought action repertories. *Cognition and Emotion, 79*(3), 313–332. doi:10.1080/02699930441000238 PMID:21852891

Galinha, I. C., & Pais-Ribeiro, J. L. (2011). Cognitive, affective and contextual predictors of subjective wellbeing. *International Journal of Wellbeing, 2*(1), 34–53. doi:10.5502/ijw.v2i1.3

Gavin, J. H., & Mason, R. O. (2004). The Virtuous Organisation: The Value of Happiness in the Workplace. *Organizational Dynamics, 33*(4), 379–392. doi:10.1016/j.orgdyn.2004.09.005

Graham, C., Eggers, A., & Sukhtankar, S. (2004). Does happiness pay? An exploration bases on panel data from Russia. *Journal of Economic Behavior & Organization, 55*, 319–342.

Gupta, S. D., & Kumar, D. (2010). Psychological correlates of happiness. *Indian Journal of Social Science Researches*, *7*(1), 60–64.

Hakanen, J. J., Schaufeli, W. B., & Ahola, K. (2008). The job demands-resources model: A three-year cross-lagged study of burnout, depression, commitment, and work engagement. *Work and Stress*, *22*(3), 224–241. doi:10.1080/02678370802379432

Halvorsen, A. (2005). Incorporating critical thinking skills development into/EFL courses. *The 76 Internet TESL Journal, 12*(3). Retrieved from http://iteslj.org/

Harter, J. K., Schmidt, F. L., & Hayes, T. L. (2002). Business-unit-level relationship between employee satisfaction, employee engagement and business outcomes: A meta-analysis. *The Journal of Applied Psychology*, *87*(2), 268–279. doi:10.1037/0021-9010.87.2.268 PMID:12002955

Hills, P., & Argyle, M. (2002). The Oxford happiness questionnaire: A compact scale for the measurement of psychological well-being. *Personality and Individual Differences*, *33*(7), 1073–1082. doi:10.1016/S0191-8869(01)00213-6

Huta, V., & Ryan, R. M. (2010). Pursuing pleasure or virtue: The differential and overlapping well-being benefits of hedonic and eudaimonic motives. *Journal of Happiness Studies*, *11*(6), 735–762. doi:10.1007/s10902-009-9171-4

Jahoda, M. (1958). *Current conceptions of positive mental health*. New York: Basic Books. doi:10.1037/11258-000

Jha, P. K., & Kumari, U. (2009). Happiness as a function of marital status, locale and caste groups. *Behavioural Scientist*, *10*(2), 91–95.

Johns, G., Xie, J. L., & Fang, Y. (1992). Mediating and moderating effects in job design. *Journal of Management*, *18*(4), 657–676. doi:10.1177/014920639201800404

Kahn, R. L., & Juster, T. F. (2002). Well-being: Concepts and measures. *The Journal of Social Issues*, *58*(4), 627–644. doi:10.1111/1540-4560.00281

Kahn, W. A. (1990). Psychological conditions of personal engagement and disengagement at work. *Academy of Management Journal*, *33*(4), 692–724. doi:10.2307/256287

Kahn, W. A. (1992). ‗To be fully there: Psychological presence at work'. *Human Relations*, *45*(4), 321–349. doi:10.1177/001872679204500402

Kampa-Kokesch, S. (2001). *Executive coaching as an individually tailored consultation intervention: Does it increase leadership?* (Unpublished doctoral dissertation). Western Michigan University.

Kashdan, T. B., Biswas-Diener, R., & King, L. A. (2008). Reconsidering happiness: The costs of distinguishing between hedonics and eudaimonia. *The Journal of Positive Psychology*, *3*(4), 219–233. doi:10.1080/17439760802303044

Keyes, C. L. M., & Magyar-Moe, J. L. (2003). The measurement and utility of adult subjective well-being. In S. J. Lopez & C. R. Snyder (Eds.), *Positive psychological assessment: A handbook of models and measures* (p. 420). Washington, DC: American Psychological Association. doi:10.1037/10612-026

King, L. A., Eells, J. E., & Burton, C. M. (2004). The good life, broadly and narrowly considered. In P. A. Linley & S. Joseph (Eds.), *Positive psychology in practice* (pp. 35–52). Hoboken, NJ: Wiley. doi:10.1002/9780470939338.ch3

Kiran Kumar, S. K. (2003). An Indian conception of well being. In J. Henry (Ed.), *European Positive Psychology Proceedings 2002*. Leicester, UK: British Psychological Society.

Kiran Kumar, S. K. (2004). Perspectives on Well-Being in the Indian Tradition. *Journal of Indian Psychology*, *22*(2), 63–72.

Kiran Kumar, S. K. (2008). Indian Thought and Tradition: A Psychohistorical Perspective. In K. R. Rao, A. C. Paranjpe, & A. K. Dalal (Eds.), *Handbook of Indian Psychology*. New Delhi: Foundation Books. doi:10.1017/UPO9788175968448.003

Kozma, A., Stones, M. J., & McNeil, J. K. (1991). *Psychological Well-Being in Later Life*. Toronto: Butterworths.

Kraut, R. (1979). Two conceptions of happiness. *The Philosophical Review*, *88*(2), 167–197. doi:10.2307/2184505

Krishnamohan, K. (2001). Spirituality and well-being: an overview. In M. Cornelissen (Ed.), *Consciousness and Its Transformation*. Pondicherry: SAICE.

Kulshrestha, U., & Sen, C. (2006). Subjective well being in relation to emotional intelligence and locus of control among executives. *Journal of the Indian Academy of Applied Psychology*, *32*(2), 129–134.

Lal, R. (2004). Demographic correlates of happiness: A study of adolescents. *Indian Journal of Community Psychology*, *1*(2), 267–277.

Lu, L., Gilmour, R., & Kao, S. (2001). Cultural values and happiness: An East-West dialogue. *The Journal of Social Psychology*, *141*(4), 477–493. doi:10.1080/00224540109600566 PMID:11577847

Lu, L., & Lin, Y. Y. (1998). Family roles and happiness in adulthood. *Personality and Individual Differences*, *25*(2), 195–207. doi:10.1016/S0191-8869(98)00009-9

May, D., Gilson, R., & Harter, L. (2004). The psychological conditions of meaningfulness, safety and availability and the engagement of the human spirit at work. *Journal of Occupational and Organizational Psychology*, *77*(1), 11–37. doi:10.1348/096317904322915892

McMahon, D. M. (2006). *Happiness: A history*. New York, NY: Grove Press.

Meeberg, G. A. (1993). Quality of life: A concept analysis. *Journal of Advanced Nursing*, *18*(1), 32–38. doi:10.1046/j.1365-2648.1993.18010032.x PMID:8429165

Merriam-Webster. (2008). *Online Dictionary*. Springfield, MA: Merriam-Webster.

Misra, G. (2013). Happiness. In K. D. Keith (Ed.), *The Encyclopedia of Cross-Cultural Psychology*. John Wiley & Sons, Inc. doi:10.1002/9781118339893.wbeccp259

Moneta, G. B., & Csikszentmihalyi, M. (1996). The effect of perceived challenges and skills on the quality of subjective experience. *Journal of Personality*, *64*(2), 275–310. doi:10.1111/j.1467-6494.1996.tb00512.x PMID:8656320

Money, K., Hillebrand, C., & Da Camara, N. (2008). Putting positive psychology to work in organisations. *Journal of General Management*, *34*(2), 21–36.

Myer, D. G., & Diener, E. (1995). Who is happy? *Psychological Science*, *6*(1), 10–19. doi:10.1111/j.1467-9280.1995.tb00298.x

Natvig, G. K., Albrektsen, G., & Qvarnstrom, U. (2003). Associations between psychosocial factors and happiness among school adolescents. *International Journal of Nursing Practice*, *9*(3), 166–175. doi:10.1046/j.1440-172X.2003.00419.x PMID:12801248

Norton, D. L. (1976). *Personal Destinies: A Philosophy of Ethical Individualism*. Princeton University Press.

Oishi, S., Graham, J., Kesebir, S., & Galinha, I. C. (2013). Concepts of happiness across time and cultures. *Personality and Social Psychology Bulletin*, *39*(5), 559–577. doi:10.1177/0146167213480042 PMID:23599280

Padmanabhan, G. (2010, January 17). An enigma called happiness. *The Hindu*, p. 1.

Paranjpe, A. C. (1996). Some Basic Psychological Concepts from the Intellectual Tradition of India. *Psychology and Developing Societies*, *8*(1), 7–27. doi:10.1177/097133369600800102

Park, N., & Huebner, E. S. (2005). A cross-cultural study of the levels and correlates of life satisfaction among adolescents. *Journal of Cross-Cultural Psychology, 36*(4), 444–456. doi:10.1177/0022022105275961

Park, N., Peterson, C., & Ruch, W. (2009). Orientations to happiness and life satisfaction in twenty-seven nations. *The Journal of Positive Psychology, 4*(4), 273–279. doi:10.1080/17439760902933690

Peterson, C., Park, N., & Seligman, M. E. P. (2005). Orientations to happiness and life satisfaction: The full life versus the empty life. *Journal of Happiness Studies, 6*(1), 25–41. doi:10.1007/s10902-004-1278-z

Rangaswami, K. (1994). Spirituality and psychotherapy. *Indian Journal of Clinical Psychology, 21*, 1–2.

Rastogi, M. R. (2005). Triguna and psychological well Being. *Indian Journal of Community Psychology, 1*(2), 115–124.

Rego, A., & Cunha, M. P. (2008). Authentizotic climates and employee happiness: Pathways to individual performance. *Journal of Business Research, 61*(7), 739–752. doi:10.1016/j.jbusres.2007.08.003

Rego, A., & Cunha, M. P. (2008). Perceptions of authentizoic climates and employee happiness: Pathways to individual performance. *Journal of Business Research, 61*(7), 739–752. doi:10.1016/j.jbusres.2007.08.003

Rego, A., Ribeiro, N., & Cuhna, M.P. (n.d.). *Perceptions of organisational virtuousness and happiness as predictors of organisational citizenship behaviours*. Academic Press.

Renn, R. W., & Vandenberg, R. J. (1995). The critical psychological states: An under-represented component in job characteristics model research. *Journal of Management, 21*(2), 279–304. doi:10.1177/014920639502100206

Rothmann, S., & Joubert, J. H. M. (2007). Job demands, job resources, burnout and work engagement of managers at a platinum mine in the North West Province. *South African Journal of Business Management, 38*(3), 49–61.

Ryan, R. M., & Deci, E. L. (2000). Self-determination theory and the facilitation of intrinsic motivation, social development, and well-being. *The American Psychologist, 55*(1), 68–78. doi:10.1037/0003-066X.55.1.68 PMID:11392867

Ryan, R. M., & Deci, E. L. (2001). On happiness and human potentials: A review of research on hedonic and eudemonic well-being. *Annual Review of Psychology, 52*(1), 141–166. doi:10.1146/annurev.psych.52.1.141 PMID:11148302

Ryff, C. D. (1989). Happiness is everything, or is it? Explorations on the meaning of psychological well-being. *Journal of Personality and Social Psychology*, *57*(6), 1069–1081. doi:10.1037/0022-3514.57.6.1069

Schueller, S. M., & Seligman, M. E. P. (2010). Pursuit of pleasure, engagement, and meaning: Relationships to subjective and objective measures of well-being. *The Journal of Positive Psychology*, *5*(4), 253–263. doi:10.1080/17439761003794130

Seligman, M. E., & Csikszentmihalyi, M. (2000). Positive psychology: An introduction. *The American Psychologist*, *55*(1), 5–14. doi:10.1037/0003-066X.55.1.5 PMID:11392865

Seligman, M. E. P. (2002). *Authentic happiness*. New York: Free Press.

Seligman, M. E. P. (2002). *Authentic happiness: Using the new positive psychology to realize your potential for lasting fulfillment*. New York: Free Press.

Seligman, M. E. P. (2008). Positive health. *Applied Psychology*, *57*(s1), 3–18. doi:10.1111/j.1464-0597.2008.00351.x

Seligman, M. E. P., & Csikszentmihalyi, M. (2000). Positive Psychology: An Introduction. *The American Psychologist*, *55*(1), 5–14. doi:10.1037/0003-066X.55.1.5 PMID:11392865

Sharma, A. (2011). Subjective well-being of retired teachers: The role of psycho-Social factors. *International Journal of Psychological Studies*, *3*(1), 36–42. doi:10.5539/ijps.v3n1p36

Sharma, R. (2003). *The Monk who sold his Ferrari*. Jaico Publishing House.

Shin, J., Suh, E. M., Eom, K., & Kim, H. S. (2017). Article. *Journal of Happiness Studies*, 1–14.

Simpson, M. R. (2008). Engagement at work: A review of the literature. *International Journal of Nursing Studies*, *1*, 1–13. PMID:18701104

Snyder, C. R., & Lopez, S. J. (Eds.). (2002). Handbook of Positive Psychology. New York: Oxford University Press.

Snyder, C. R., & Lopez, S. J. (2007). *Positive Psychology: The Scientific and Practical Explorations of Human Strengths*. Sage.

Srivastava, A. K., & Misra, G. (2011). Happiness and Well Being: An Indian Perspective. In G. Misra (Ed.), *Handbook of Psychology in India*. New Delhi: Oxford University Press.

Tasnim, Z. (2016). Happiness at Workplace: *Building a Conceptual Framework. World. Journal of social Sciences*, *6*(2), 62–70.

Tatarkiewicz, W. (1976). *Analysis of happiness.* The Hague, The Netherlands: Martinus Nijhoff. doi:10.1007/978-94-010-1380-2

Taylor, C. C. W. (1998). Eudaimonia. In E. Craig (Ed.), *Routledge Encyclopedia of Philosophy* (Vol. 3, pp. 450–452). New York: Routledge.

Uchida, Y., Norasakkunkit, V., & Kitayama, S. (2004). Cultural Constructions of Happiness: Theory and Empirical Evidence. *Journal of Happiness Studies*, *5*(3), 223–239. doi:10.1007/s10902-004-8785-9

Van Schalkwyk, L., & Rothmann, S. (2010). Job satisfaction in a chemical factory. *Southern African Business Review*, *14*(3), 108–130.

VanZyl, L. E., Deacon, E., & Rothmann, S. (2010). Towards happiness: Experiences of work-role fit, meaningfulness, and work engagement of industrial/organisational psychologists in South Africa. *SA Journal of Industrial Psychology*, *36*(1), 1–10.

Veenhoven, R. (1984). *Conditions of Happiness.* Dordrecht, The Netherlands: Reidel. doi:10.1007/978-94-009-6432-7

Veenhoven, R. (1991). Is happiness relative? *Social Indicators Research*, *24*(1), 1–34. doi:10.1007/BF00292648

Veenhoven, R. (2003). Happiness. *The Psychologist*, *16*(3), 128–129.

Veenhoven, R. (2015). *Size of the Collections.* World Database of Happiness, Erasmus University of Rotterdam. Accessed on 11-02-2016 at: http://worlddatabaseofhappiness.eur.nl

Veenhoven, R. (2017). Co-development of Happiness Research-Addition to "Fifty Years After the Social Indicator Movement". *Social Indicators Research*, 1–7.

Vittersø, J. (2003). Flow versus life satisfaction: A projective use of cartoons to illustrate the difference between the evaluation approach and the intrinsic motivation approach to subjective quality of life. *Journal of Happiness Studies*, *4*(2), 141–167. doi:10.1023/A:1024413112234

Warr, P. (2009). Work, happiness, and unhappiness. *Cognitive Behavioural Therapy Book Reviews*, *5*(5), 1-3.

Waterman, A. S. (1990). The relevance of Aristotle's conception of eudaimonia for the psychological study of happiness. *Theoretical and Philosophical Psychology*, *10*(1), 39–44. doi:10.1037/h0091489

Watson, D., Clark, L. A., & Tellegen, A. (1988). Development and validation of Brief Measures of Positive and Negative Affect: The PANAS Scales. *Journal of Personality and Social Psychology*, *54*(6), 1063–1070. doi:10.1037/0022-3514.54.6.1063 PMID:3397865

Weitz, K. (2011). *Positivity (happiness) in the workplace and organisational change*. Retrieved from http://libraryofprofessionalcoaching.com/tools/executive-presence/positivity-happiness-in-the-workplace-and-organisational-change/10/

Wright, T. A., & Bonett, D. G. (2007). Job satisfaction and psychological well-being as non- additive predictors of workplace turnover. *Journal of Management*, *33*(2), 141–152. doi:10.1177/0149206306297582

Chapter 3
I'd Like to Teach the World to Think:
Mind Genomics, Big Mind, and Encouraging Youth

Howard Moskowitz
Big Mind Institute of Education and Messaging, USA

Jyotsna
National Skill Development Corporation, India

Andi Sciacca
Big Mind Institute of Education and Messaging, USA

Andrew Lester
Big Mind Institute for Education and Messaging, USA

ABSTRACT

At the time of this writing, 2017, there is noticeable reduction in the perceived ability of people to think critically. Both the popular press and the scientific/professional literature recognize this worldwide drop. This chapter presents the use of experimental design of ideas, conjoint measurement, originally a tool used in marketing, as a tool to inspire creative thinking. The chapter presents the approach and application of conjoint measurement as a tool for discovery, and then delineates a new computer APP, Big Mind, as user friendly to enhance critical thinking. Big Mind embodies conjoint measurement to help researchers study topics, uncover new substantive findings, and learn to think critically as an outcome from the process.

DOI: 10.4018/978-1-5225-4038-0.ch003

Copyright © 2018, IGI Global. Copying or distributing in print or electronic forms without written permission of IGI Global is prohibited.

INTRODUCTION: THE DECLINE OF THINKING IN THE WORLD (ACADEMIC AND POPULAR LITERATURE SEARCH)

A greater percent of the world's population is educated, year after year. At the same time, pundits and professionals alike are lamenting the loss of critical thinking (e.g., Schurman,2013, but many others in the popular, non- academic press). And so, we face a quandary. Our young people today, those of school age, are digital natives, playing increasingly complex, often competitive video games with an enviable ability and with concentration and perseverance, behavior seems not to appear when otherwise needed for schooling. Yet these same young people do not read much, have limited attention span, and worst of all, appear to have lost the ability to think critically, or at least the ability to focus, perhaps because they live in a world of instant messaging and tweeting. The world, filled as it is with increasingly competent 'tech-savviness' is losing that fundamental ability to think through a complex problem, a problem which lacks entertainment value but might be the kind of problem to be later faced in one's life or one's profession.

This chapter is not going to be a eulogy on thinking, but rather will present the authors' approach to encouraging critical thinking by turning the young person into an experimenter, albeit an experimenter with ideas. The chapter is, in fact, a description of an ongoing project begun some years ago, the Mind Genomics project, to create a new science of the mind. The Mind Genomics that was created in the 1990's has evolved into a tool by which to stimulate critical thinking, as well as a tool to create a corpus of knowledge about what we think.

The Digital Age

The past 30-40 years have seen the at first gradual and now rapid emergence of a new age of information and communication, an age many of us call the 'digital age.' The advent of widespread computation, of heretofore unknown computing power, and the nearly universal availability of computation, either in computers or in cell-phones, has changed the way we think. Technologies like the ubiquitous search engine from Google® give us almost immediate access to much of the world's publicly available information. Facebook® lets us stay in contact with people, and send pictures and news of ourselves to distant acquaintances and friends. Twitter® lets us broadcast our news, albeit in 144 or fewer characters. News can be fabricated to the point that we don't know the veracity of what we read.

The foregoing, with the massive increase in information available to people, has also had an effect on the way we think. We are no longer at peace, with little to do but contemplate, finding solace and interest in books. There is not enough time to read, not with the ever-present desire to check in with our friends, about what we are doing, read the bursts of information pushed into our phone, and multi-task, doing several actions simultaneously, switching our attention in a way that, without context, an outside observer would think is a sign of mental aberration, an inability to concentrate.

Lest the foregoing seem to be overstating the case, the reader is invited to observe the behavior of people walking around, and requested to count the number of people who, when walking, running, wheeling a baby carriage, even crossing the street, are seemingly 'glued' to a smart phone, looking, talking, or texting.

The consequence of this described behavior is the gradual loss of our ability to hold concourse with great minds, the loss of free time just to think, the loss of the ability to mentally review what we have learned, either consciously and deliberately, or the loss to fantasize simply because we have free time and ideas flit into our mind, ideas from what we have read. We are too busy, too preoccupied with planning, strategizing, and responding, doing, to think deeply. Unless, of course, our life depends upon something, and we spend the time to think, worry, research, and thoroughly know the topic because the topic is US. If these words are too dire, consider the few items in Exhibit 1 from Google Scholar, obtained on May 22, 2017. When we move out from the academic world, and go to the everyday world, we find literally millions of 'hits' or sites dealing with one or another aspect of critical thinking. Quite a number of these cover the issue of a recent reduction is critical thinking abilities in today's world of computers, Internet, Twitter, and instant messaging.

As the digital age progressed 'gaming' became increasingly popular. The early games, in the 1980's, were relatively mindless, such as PacMan or Donkey Kong. Over time, the games became increasingly complex, calling into play one's ability to think and to plan. Now there are games which require strategy, and are played by hundreds, perhaps thousands of players at the same time. These games require some thinking, of course, often thinking which brings into play strategy. However, the games do not involve the type of thinking which can help a person 'create,' unless, perhaps, we deal with games which require the person to create an alternative reality from the 'bottom up.'

Gaming has occupied a great deal of time, involving young people, and pulling them away from reading and other pursuits. In some ways gaming is addictive, exciting the player, but stealing time and mental energy that would be better spent reading, thinking, and writing. The key notion here is that games are fun, and it is clear that people gravitate to fun. Creative thinking is less fun, less immediately rewarding, but more necessary if a society is to move forward. Society moves forward on the creation of its citizens, not on their score in massive online games.

Figure 1. The first page of 'hits' from a Google Search on "critical thinking" May 22, 2017.Games for fun and Games for the Mind

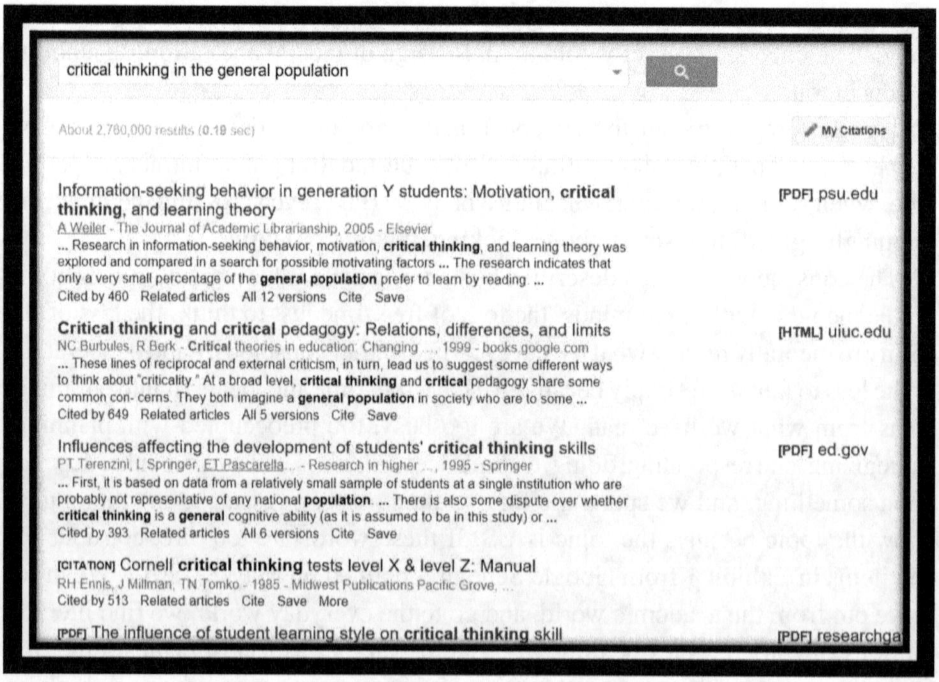

Getting the Student Involved - The Contribution of Psychology and the Social Sciences

In the 1950's, cognitive psychologists began to focus on how people make decision. Although utility theory would suggest that people simply choose 'what's best,' it is often difficult to understand just how a person makes sense of a compound set of variables. For example, many people say that they prefer to work in a business which gives them freedom. But what happens when the business requires a combination of skills, new to the person. Some of these skills may be understanding the product, others may be managing the people in the business, still others may be knowing how to communicate the benefits of the product (or service.

Table 1 presents four descriptions of a business, specifically creating and selling pellets made from agro-waste. The business descriptions come from a project in India, which will be the explicated case history presented here to illustrate the approach to teaching critical thinking necessary for innovation. The question to be answer is which description of the business is interesting, and WHY?

Table 1. Four descriptions of a business for Agro-Pellets

	What does this product do specifically?	Why would I buy this product?	How would I use this product?	What specifically about the product would I tell my friends and family?
1	pellet uses agro-waste or wood residues	cheaper than other forms of energy	use in pellet heaters to heat a house	cheaper than fossil fuels like LPG, coal, kerosene, diesel
2	pellet reduces time used for fuel collection and transportation for domestic purposes	greatly reduces harmful effects because it doesn't burn wood or coal	use in boilers in industry	carbon-neutral -- reduces carbon footprint
3	pellet replaces fossil fuel	environmentally friendly	use in pellet burners to heat air in factories and businesses	reduce problem of waste disposal -- uses agro-waste
4	pellet generates heat (energy) on burning	reduces cooking time for food	use in pellet stove for cooking	makes more jobs for people -- locally manufactured

One way to discover what is important for these different business descriptions asks people to discuss what is important, and infers from the discussion which part of the business description is most important, and which part is least important. This approach is called qualitative research. There aren't any numbers, or in reality not numbers used with statistical analyses to test for the significance of differences across different product description.

Qualitative research is interesting, at least to those people who like asking questions. It would be no surprise to realize that virtually all of us engage in qualitative research when we ask questions. Furthermore, asking enough questions forces a person to think about '*what should I ask,*' and '*how do I interpret what I get.*' The qualitative approach to research makes a person a critical thinker, if the person is well enough disposed, but doesn't typically excite people. There is often no 'ah ha' moment.

When asking questions doesn't excite young people, except a very few who are naturally inquisitive, then how might we make learning and discovery 'fun?' The answer may be that we turn it into experience, in fact hands-on experience. For the biologically oriented student, 'hands-on' may mean working in a zoo, a museum, or a laboratory, learning, and getting excited about watching others learn. For the physics oriented student, hands-on may mean working in a laboratory as a technical aide, seeing how discoveries are made, again a hands-on experience. For the biological and the physical sciences the key to experience is seeing, touching, doing, discovering, and of course sharing in the excitement of scientists nearby, young and old, who become role models.

But what about the social sciences? There are no laboratories where the student can learn. There may be rooms filled with data that the student can analyze, but analyzing reams of data from studies hardly excites most people. One could participate

Table 2. Pellet data, from a simple study based on psychophysical thinking.

Relative weight of the pellets	Relative price of the total	Interest in buying the pellets	Value for the money
145	17	56	60
170	21	62	54
195	25	55	48
210	29	48	39
140	19	56	55
165	23	51	49
190	27	46	45
205	31	39	46

in studies from beginning to end, making measurements, looking for patterns. That's exciting…if the student can conquer the boredom of waiting. If not, then the social and psychological sciences are out.

Psychophysical Thinking … a Gentle Introduction to Experiential Learning in Psychology

Psychophysics is the oldest branch of experimental psychology. Psychophysics may hold a key because it can be real-world and approachable as it discovers the relation between the magnitude or intensity of a stimulus and the intensity of a perception. For example, considering the pellet product, suppose we have different weights of the pellet, and different prices. We can create different variations of weights and prices, all of the other factors held constant. The described product, our AGRO-PELLET, varies in a systematic way. The person, often called the respondent in consumer research or the subject in psychology research, may simply look at the product, and afterwards assign two numbers, first a number to show how 'likely he/she is to buy the pellet, and second the perceived value for the money'. The exercise is lots of fun.

This type of exercise, psychophysical scaling, is a gentle introduction to learning and discovering. It's not only that the people can see the combinations of weights and prices, something they do in everyday life, but there is a discoverable pattern relating weight, price, and interest in buying the product. When students doing this type of experiment discover the 'lawful behavior' of perceived cheesiness versus amount of cheese, there is a sense of awe, as well as giggles of joy at having made a discovery. It's often the discovery of a pattern which excites, a sense of comprehending an aspect of the world, knowing how 'works.'

One of the interesting outcomes of this type of exercise is its ability to excite the young researcher about the joy of discovery. Working with something as familiar as prices and weights makes the science real and interesting. Students begin to ask questions such as 'I see that people can 'track' amount....but ...do they like it?' When the student asks this question, the different between amount of and liking of, we have the beginnings of an excitement with science. Figure 2 shows the two curves, one interest in purchasing, one for value for money, both versus the price.

Figure 2. How purchase intent varies separately with price, and with weight of the pelletsWhen we ask 'what' has happened in this experiment, we would say that the experiment itself ignited the student's interest. The key is that the student suddenly 'sees' how inquiry and simple experiment can reveal how nature works. The key then is create the stimuli, do the measurement, show how nature works, and let the natural excitement of discovery take over.

Moving to the Next Step – the Psychophysics of Ideas

If discovering patterns is exciting, especially when these patterns pertain to something relevant in one's life, such as prices and weights, then perhaps we can take this way of thinking into other topics that can be explored, easily, interestingly and inspiringly. We use these three words deliberately, to convey some messages:

Figure 2. How purchase intent varies separately with price, and with weight of the pellets

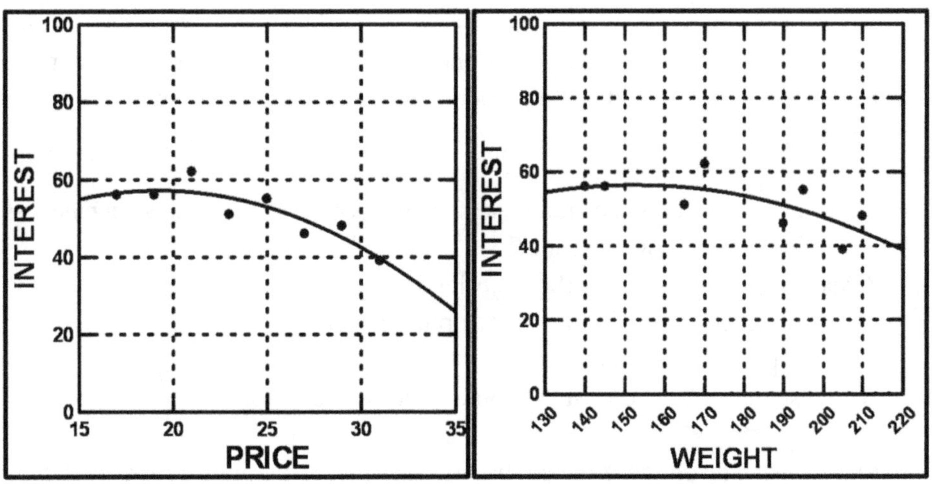

1. **Easy:** It is important that the introduction to thinking be easy, with just a little involvement from the person who is being trained or educated to think. What is easy will likely be done more readily than what is difficult.
2. **Interesting:** It is important that the project maintain the interest of the student. Ideally, the project should lead to more projects, and so forth, rather than simply being one project which is done, reported and that chapter thankfully 'closed.'
3. **Inspire:** The experience must inspire the student, who will then share it with friends, and ideally incorporate the experience into a world view of one's own experience.

Let's review first what we did in the mental psychophysics of economics, the example above. We presented the respondents with different combinations of weight and price, instructing them to rate both interest in purchasing, and perceived value of the offer. We are dealing with simple mental constructs here, weight and price. We could do this experiment either with real combinations, as is done in stores with weights and prices, or we can do it as a purely conceptual analog, with stated weights and prices. In both cases the stimuli are quite simple.

How do we maintain the same involvement when we move from simple ideas to more conceptual ideas, stimuli that can be sensed to ideas that must be evaluated? The question is not particularly easy to answer when our goal is to increase involvement in the task, with the ultimate aim of getting a person to think better, creatively, and critically, respectively.: Keep in mind that we are no longer working with simple stimuli of weights and prices, but rather with stimuli that are evocative, real world, have meaning to the person. To make it more interesting, let's move from weights and prices of pellets to the experience of starting a business selling these kinds of pellets. We move here to the 'experience,' rather than remaining with simple stimuli. It's likely that a study of experience will be even more inspiring. Here is what we might do

1. Follow the same approach but make is applicable to the experience a business involving these AGRO-PELLETS.
2. Create a set of phrases for the experience
3. Ask people to rate the liking of each phrase separately
4. Do the study with 8-15 respondents
5. The results can be shown in a simple table such as Table 3

What we have just done is have our panelists 'scale' the phrases about AGRO-PELLETS in the same way that previously our respondents rated the individual AGRO-PELLETS with different prices and weights. Admittedly, the results may not interest serious researchers, doing this type of exercise for science. We're talking

Table 3. Phrases about the business of making and selling AGRO-PELLETS

What does this product do specifically?	Liking
pellet uses agro-waste or wood residues	68
pellet reduces time used for fuel collection and transportation for domestic purposes	57
pellet replaces fossil fuel	54
pellet generates heat (energy) on burning	40
Why would I buy this product?	
cheaper than other forms of energy	58
greatly reduces harmful effects because it doesn't burn wood or coal	47
environmentally friendly	53
reduces cooking time for food	31
How would I use this product?	
use in pellet heaters to heat a house	56
use in boilers in industry	46
use in pellet burners to heat air in factories and businesses	48
use in pellet stove for cooking	50
What specifically about the product would I tell my friends and family?	
cheaper than fossil fuels like LPG, coal, kerosene, diesel	59
carbon-neutral -- reduces carbon footprint	57
reduce problem of waste disposal -- uses agro-waste	57
makes more jobs for people -- locally manufactured	43

here about exciting a person who is not a scientist, a person who might want an 'epiphany' to understand, to learn, to demonstrate.

1. Asking a person to rate a list of aspects often ends up to be a sterile exercise, both in the way the elements are chosen (what is rated), and how the respondent does the rating.
2. First, the researcher often works with boring statements, 'boiling down' the elements to simple statements, really single minded ideas, without any elegance or tonality of expression. The focus is on the deep idea, the essence of what the element represents, not on how the idea is communicated. Ordinary people find this type of simplistic presentation fairly boring.
3. In order for the element to be 'meaningful' it has to be embedded in a meaningful statement. It doesn't make sense to ask the response to some elements such as price, because price has to be connected with something. Otherwise the

statement of price has to be very general. Here is a comparison of three price statements.

a. The price of a full AGRO-PELLETS is $17.50.
b. The price is $17.50 (but price of what specifically, and how does one measure the value of different prices?).
c. About 15% less expensive than other products of its type (what is less expensive, and how does one measure the value of different relative prices?).

4. Second, the researcher instructs the respondent to read each item in turn, and rate the item on a simple question, such as 'how important is this to you for an AGRO-PELLET?' There's not much imagination left to the respondent who faces a sterile, simple, phrase which communicates an idea. The reality is that to the researcher it is the idea which is of interest, not the expression of that idea. To the respondent, it is the expression of the idea.
5. Third, the result comprises 'good' but 'boring' data, almost like measurement of variables in a clinical test. There may be a picture, but the stimuli themselves tend to be boring, the questions are boring, and the answers are boring. The entire test does not make for involved reading, reading for pleasure. There may be an ***aha*** moment, but not for the 'newbie' in research, the person just beginning the excitement of learning about the world through science.

Is there any way to create a test situation which is 'fun' or at least enchanting? We can always do easy experiments by having a person rate single ideas, but in the memorable words of the songstress, Peggy Lee, '*is that all there is*?' Can we make knowledge discovery more fun?

Experimental Design of Ideas

What if we make the experience of 'evaluating ideas' more fun, inserting in a discovery aspect to it? Can we create a more exciting, dynamic situation, one to inspire? Keep in mind that we are not working with actual physical stimuli, the actual AGRO-PELLETS. Rather, we are working with ideas about the product, ideas whose persuasive and communication powers we want to measure. Our goal is to have the person do the experiment, see the results, and become enthusiastic.

From the authors' experience, one way to excite people, especially young people, is by way of experiment, where the outcome of the experiment is a 'pattern,' bringing new knowledge and insight, as well as that '***aha***' response from the person who is doing the experiment.

The particular experiment, mixing together ideas, is the subject of the rest of this chapter. The chapter continues with a history of this type of experiment, often called 'conjoint analysis,' and how the experiment has evolved from an almost arcane, impossible-to-execute project into a computer APP starting to be used around the world to stimulate experiential learning and critical thinking (Box, Hunter & Hunter, 1978; Moskowitz, Porretta & Silcher, 2005).

What is Conjoint Measurement and why is it so Important for Critical Thinking?

Conjoint measurement (also called conjoint analysis, as well as functional measurement) is a procedure by which the researcher mixes together ideas, presents the mixture(s) of ideas to a respondent, obtains a rating of the mixture, and through statistic such as OLS (ordinary least-squares), estimates the individual contribution of each mixture component or element to the respondent's rating of that mixture. Conjoint analysis was developed more than 50 years ago (Luce & Tukey, 1964), and boasts a large literature, both in academics and in practical application (Green & Krieger, 1991; Wittink & Cattin, 1989). More recently, it has been modified to be a self-authoring system, first on the Internet (Moskowitz, Gofman, Itty, Katz, Manchaia, & Ma,2001).

By testing mixtures rather than single components (see the AGRO-PELLETS ideas above), the researcher accomplishes at least five objectives:

1. Makes the study more natural. People don't deal with single ideas in their daily lives. They deal with mixtures of ideas, bundles, combinations. It's hard for a person to abstract out the response to a single element or aspect, such as a price or a brand name. It is the combination of these elements which have 'ecological reality,' which are the stuff of daily existence.
2. Identifies the individual contributions of the elements, the so-called 'part-worths' of the components of the mixture. To do this requires that the set of combinations, the so-called mixtures or vignettes, be arranged in a specific way, so that the same element appears against many backgrounds, and that each element is independent of every other element. That is, each element behaves as an independent 'actor.'
3. The respondents who participate cannot really discern the underlying 'recipes.' To these respondents, the combinations, these vignettes, seem to be a blooming, buzzing confusion. The respondents simply look at each vignette in turn, and assign a rating. When the rating question ranges from low (don't like it at all) to high (like it very much), the number assigned shows the degree of liking of the entire mixture of messages or ideas.
4. Statistics, regression analysis specifically, deconstructs the ratings to the contribution of each element. Even though the respondent or panelist swears

that he or show CANNOT tell which element is important, the deconstruction of the responses to these systematically varied combinations reveals what each element contributes.

5. When each person evaluates a set of vignettes designed to be its own experimental design, the regression analysis builds an equation for each person, and show the contribution of each element to the ratings of a specific individual.

All of the above can be, and should be done 'behind the scenes,' automatically, allowing the researcher to focus on discovery, not on mathematics. Today, for the most part, many researchers focus on the elegance of the method, on their technical virtuosity of the analysis, rather than on the clear opportunity to use conjoint analysis to inspire the mind.

The foregoing presented the mechanics. The idea is quite simple. Instead of asking a person 'what's important,' do a simple experiment. Mix and match the ideas into combinations by experimental design, and ask a person to rate the combinations, which is a more natural action than rating individual elements. Then use regression, either for the total data (all people combined into one group) or for the individual data (person by person) to show 'what wins, what loses. The bottom-line result of this experiment is to challenge the person to think creatively, but within a structured system (Moskowitz & Gofman, 2004). The system, embedded in the APP, ends up directing the person to think, test, and learn, on topics of interest to the person. Furthermore, almost anything of interest, studied in this way, may generate knowledge of deep value, partly due to the creativity of the person, partly due to the discipline which is forced upon the creative process, a discipline which inheres in the system but does not constrain thinking.

The Researcher and Respondent Experiences

At this point it is best to work with a concrete example, staying with the topic of the AGRO-PELLET, but this time embedding the topic into an APP designed to teach and to excite, as well as to obtain valuable data, an additional motivation for a researcher who discovers that his or her learning has additional value to others.

Step 1: We begin with the set-up for the study in Exhibit 6. The research is set up on a smartphone, putting the APP, the research, and indeed the entire experience in the research of anyone with a smartphone. Exhibit 6 shows the researcher first naming the study.

Figure 3. Setting up the study. The screen shows the first step in setting up the study on a smartphone.

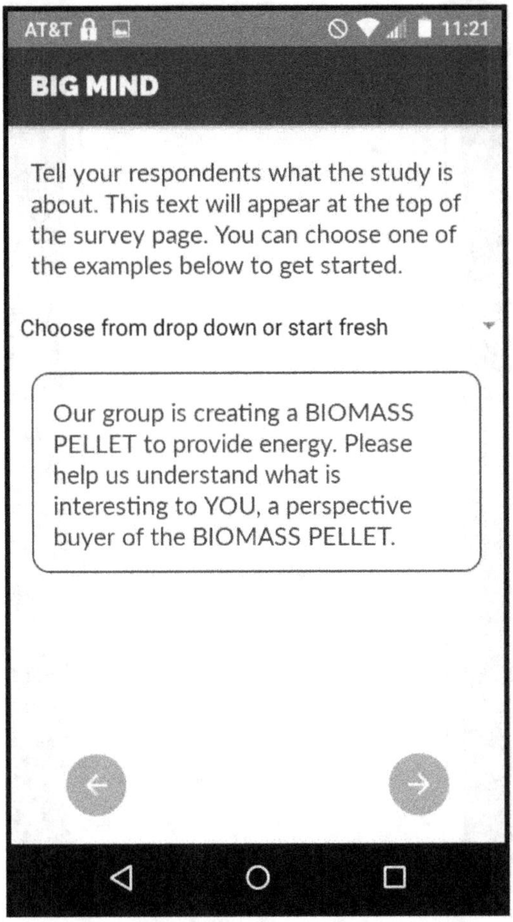

Step 2: S shown in Figure 4 Step 2 requires the researcher to write out what the study should cover. Again, the objective here is to push the researcher in to a disciplined study, providing the framework, encouraging the creativity, and then leaving the natural excitement of doing and learning to emerge. This information will later be incorporated into the report.

Step 3: The researcher identifies four aspects or silos of ideas. It is best for the novice researcher to think of these four aspects as four questions, asked in a meaningful order. The order of questions is important in order to tell a story, and follows in spirit the way a newspaper reporter would write a story, using 'what, who, where, why, when, and perhaps how.' Exhibit 8 shows the set of four aspects or silos, created as questions to be answered. Experience with making the aspects

Figure 4. The researcher writes down what the study is about.

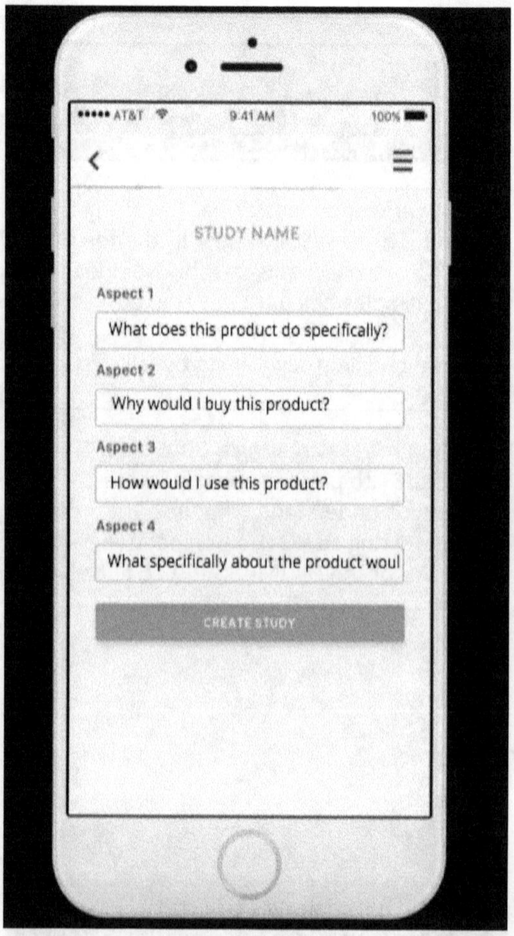

or silos into questions is that once the researcher grasps the notion of questions followed by a set of answers of each question, the experience is easier, not at all intimidating, and more fun. It is at this stage that the researcher begins to think critically about whether the questions tell a story, whether the questions are in the right order, and even whether the questions need to be rephrased or perhaps removed in favor of another question.

Step 4: The researcher provides four answers to each question, one question at a time. The easiest way to do Step 4 is to look at the question and answer the question. At first the answers may be short, curt phrases, but with practice the novice researcher will learn to put the answers into a more felicitous language. It's a matter of practice. From observations over three decades, it has become increasingly clear that 'practice does make perfect.' The researcher, beginning

Figure 5. The four aspects (silos), presented as questions.

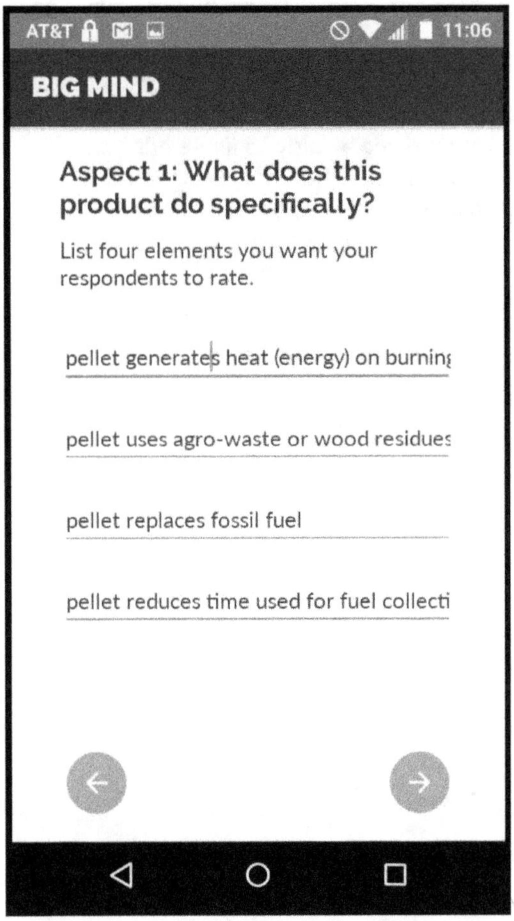

diffidently with short, curt, almost sterile answers, ends up writing simple but powerful sentences, answers which comprise word pictures in a declarative statement. The phrases in Exhibit 9 come from a first-time researcher, who is just learning how to provide both the set of questions, and the set of four answers to each question.

Step 5: The APP adds three additional classification questions, presented at the start of the interview, before the experimentally designed vignettes are presented. Two of the questions are fixed, age, and gender. The third is optional, in this case the question of what is most important. Exhibit 10 a screenshot of this question.

Figure 6. Four elements presented as answers to aspect 1, i.e., question 1

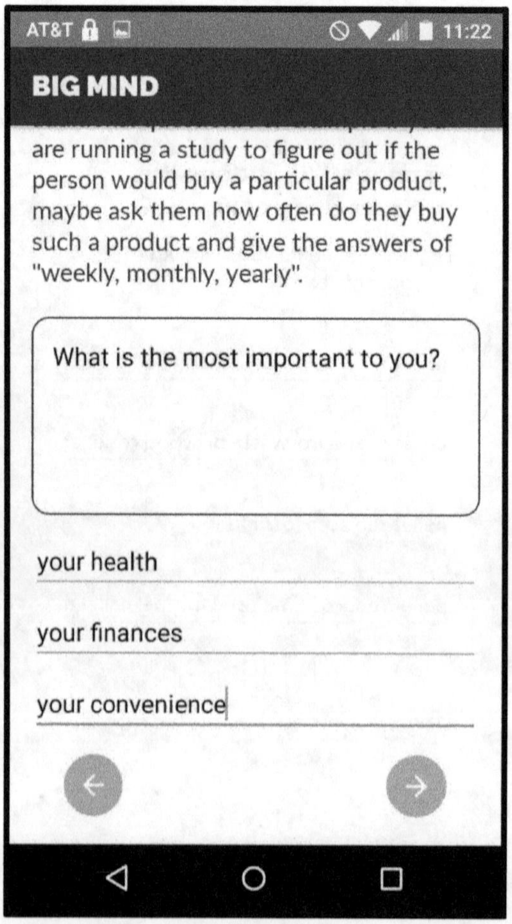

Step 6: The interview. The APP uses a pre-set collection of experimental designs. Each experimental design comprises 24 combinations, vignettes, created by the underlying experimental design. The experimental design specifies which particular elements will appear together. Each element appears exactly five times across the 24 vignettes. Some vignettes are incomplete, comprising only three elements, with one question missing and therefore no answer to that question appearing in the vignette. The respondent never sees the question, only the combination of 'answers.' Exhibit 11 shows one test vignette.

The foregoing strategy of presenting both complete and incomplete vignettes in a single set of 24 is deliberate, allowing the researcher to estimate in absolute terms the contribution of each of the 16 elements to the ratings. Each respondent evaluates a unique set of vignettes, allowing anyone, even without knowledge, to explore a topic. One need not know the 'right order of combinations' and the 'right combinations to test.'

Some Comments on the Steps

The experimental design just illustrated presents a systematized framework for setting up an experiment. The structure of the experiment is different from the topic of the experiment. One could master the structure very easily, but take a long time learning how to create meaningful questions and write answers pleasant to read, expressed in felicitous language. Or one might remain a novice, using simple phrases, almost 'boiled down,' without much other than the raw idea. This type of sterile stimulus is often used in business to understand the power of simple ideas.

The sterile stimulus is not appropriate to a novice researcher whom we are trying to excite, whom we are trying to teach to think, and who will enjoy the experience. We must use realistic phrases, of the type one typically reads, of the type which conveys meaning both by content and by the style of writing. By mixing together ideas and creating paragraphs we naturally migrate to elements which are phrases, rather than elements which are boiled down. By having elements which are cognitively rich, have meaning and expressed in a meaningful way, the research ends up showing how real people respond to real people respond to real stimuli. We see how the elements win and lose. The elements about AGRO-PELLETS are meaningful to us. We can see whether some ways of describing elements are better than others.

A parenthetical note: The skeptic looking at these two approaches, direct rating versus deconstructed contribution, might say that they should produce identical results when compared to each other. That is correct. The focus here is NOT on which of the two methods is better, but rather which of the methods, if either, can excite a young person to become a researcher. What is better – to have the young novice evaluate simple stimuli and compare them on ratings, or do an experiment, where the stimuli are expressed in more natural language, where the respondent reads a vignette, and all of a sudden it can be seen which idea pulls the mind's eye?

The Excitement of Discovery Begins

We call this section 'excitement of discovery,' although more seasoned researchers, writing for their peers and for history in reports and archival journals will label this section as 'Analyses and Results.' Since, however, we are using conjoint to teach people to think and to enjoy discovery, we will retain this notion of excitement, because in fact the act of looking at the data brings in the joy of discovery.

Figure 7. The third classification question, requiring the respondent to choose which aspect is most important

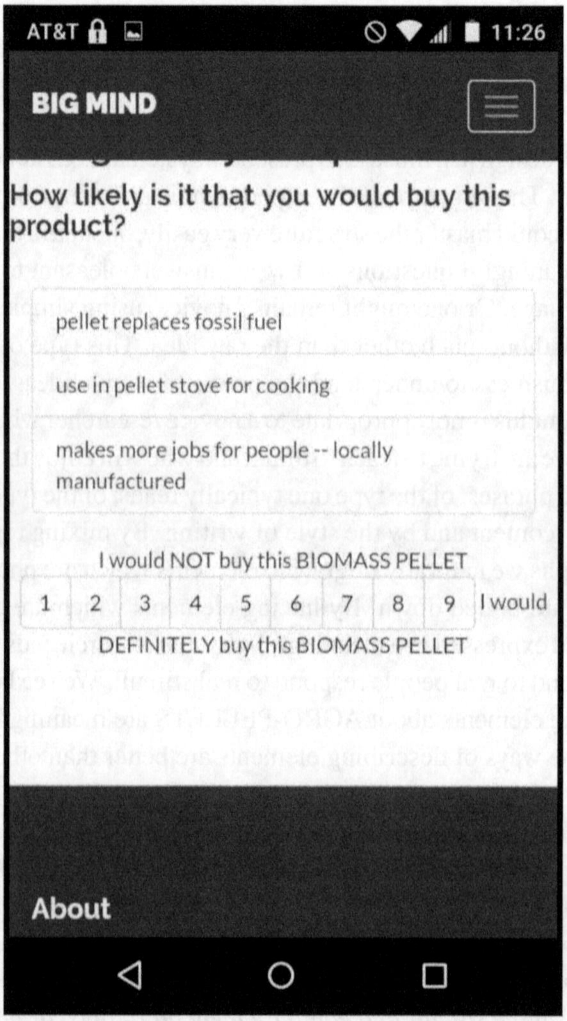

We begin with the analysis, an integral part of the process, but done behind-the-scenes, in the APP. Purists might argue that it is incumbent to teach the researcher about the methods of analysis, with those methods being the true focus of learning. The reality is that, in the metaphor of today (2017), we are learning how to read time, not how to create a watch. Exhibit 12 shows the stages of analysis, explicated in a non-technical manner.

The results appear in Exhibit 13. Our focus should be on the following:

Figure 8. Example of a single vignette. The vignette is created according to an underlying experimental design. The questions are never seen by the respondents. Only the answers are seen, in a simple advertisement-like paragraph, with one element atop the other in the order originally designated.

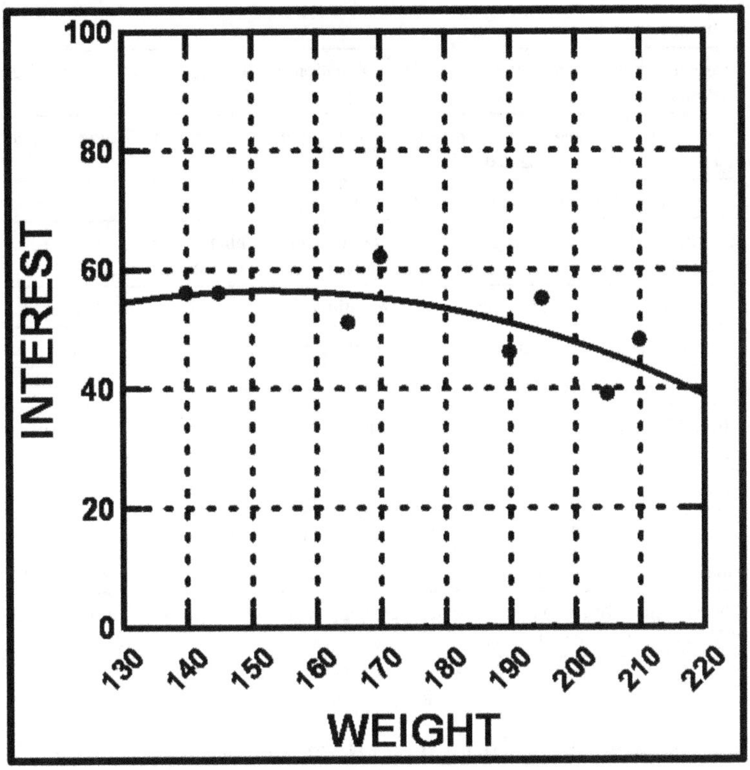

1. The additive constant, a measure of the basic interest in the proposition (business which sells the AGRO-PELLET).
2. The individual coefficients or impact values, which are the coefficients from the model. We have shaded the positive elements or answers, to show those which drive a strong positive response (I'm interested), and those which drive a strong negative response (I'm NOT interested)
3. It is important for the researcher that these strong performing elements be presented in a way which makes the patterns 'jump out.' Once the researcher sees 'what works,' it becomes exciting to think about 'why,' and about 'what this means.'

Table 4. The stages of analysis

1.	Each vignette comprises 32-4 elements (answers to a question), but not the question
2.	The question is a way to prompt the four different answers.
3.	Respondents looked at 24 vignettes (combinations)
4.	Each combination is different
5.	Every respondent evaluates a unique set of 24 combinations or vignettes ..covers a wide range of combinations
6.	Cannot be 'gamed'… respondents soon simply respond, giving their intuitive feeling .. which is important ... that's how they make decisions
7.	The respondent rates each combination on an anchored 9-point scale
8.	Replace rating of 1-6 with 0, rating of 7-9 with 100, making is a binary response (doesn't fit, not interested in the service or product; does fit, am interested in the service or product)
9.	Use OLS (ordinary least-squares, curve fitting) to estimate contribution of every element
10.	Each person has an additive constant (estimated rating if no elements…purely estimated ... a baseline)
11.	Each person generates 16 coefficients, impact values, one per element
12.	So we have 17 numbers; additive constant (baseline) and the pulling power (coefficient) of each element
13.	So we know each mind
14.	Now we simply average the data from people in appropriate groups
15.	A group could be how they say they feel about certain values (health, convenience, income)
16.	Could be the pattern of responses (mind-set segments) … people who see the world of the AGRO-PELLET business in different ways.

The first discovery comes from the performance of the total panel. When we look at the results, we should stop for a moment and ask 'what is the story about nature that our data tell us?' When we construct meaningful elements, statements which convey messages, we can almost sense the inside of the mind of the average, getting a feeling of what's important and what's not important. It's almost gratifying to realize that the respondents may not even be aware of their own attitudes. Exhibit 11 shows the data from the total panel, from three groups self-defined by what's important, and the two groups defined by the patterns of the 16 coefficients.

It's not necessary to go into the actual results themselves. The patterns emerge clearly. It is the job of the researcher to sit back and ask 'what is the story?' All that the researcher needs is contained within the elements. It's a matter of looking at the elements, and weaving together a coherent description of what ties together the positive elements in a group, and what ties together the negative elements. When we look at positive elements versus negative elements, the positive elements are generally more important as hints about what motivates the particular group...

1. **Total Panel:** Average the response of all 74 respondents
2. **Importance:** At the start of the study, before the respondents evaluate the 24 vignettes, ask the respondent three 'classification' questions. The first two are gender and age. The third, left to the discretion of the researcher, is, for this study 'Select which of these factors is most important to you: Health, Finances, Convenience.
3. The mind-set segments are created though the statistical method of clustering. The pattern of all 16 elements, defined by their coefficients, is used to divide respondents into two groups, mind-set segments, and later into three mind-set segment. Members in the same segment show similar patterns of coefficients.

Increasing the Excitement – Exploring Well-Defined and Newly-Discovered Subgroups

The experiment with AGRO-PELLETS reveals what messages work, and what messages don't work. Exhibit 11 presents the opportunity for the researcher to move beyond the data, look for a 'story,' asking 'what's going on here?' Of key importance is that the are expressed in ordinary language, and not in the telegraphed, so-called bulletized language of business.

We now move to increase the critical thinking, and the excitement. Recall we created an individual-level model or equation for each panelist, each study participant. We see results for the total panel and all the key subgroups in Exhibit 11. The important thing now is to look for a pattern, a story in the data, perhaps the story of the AGRO-PELLETS going on in the mind of the respondent, as the respondent evaluates different vignettes. Although we cannot go into the respondent's mind, nonetheless we get a sense of what is important. Keep in mind that the rating question is 'purchase intent.' Thus, the high positive numbers correspond to those elements driving interest in purchasing the AGRO-PELLETS, whereas the high negative numbers correspond to those elements driving away from purchase, towards rejection or at least indifference.

The structure of the study, in the form of subgroup (column) by element (row) tells a lot, and makes the task easy, fun and shareable for the researcher. Once a person understands how to read the table, it becomes quite straightforward to look at a column of data, search for the high positives, and create the story if a story is to be told. The elements are meaningful, in and of themselves.

It's important that the researcher stop for a moment, and look at the 'big picture.' Is there different story for respondents who say that they are interested in health, versus those who are interested in financial security, versus those who are interested in convenient. The data from our AGRO-PELLET study comprises the results from

Table 5. Data from the study. The data are presented separately for total panel, for three groups defined by how respondents classified themselves in terms of what's important, and two mind-set segments.

	Total	Important -- Health	Important - Finances	Important – Convenience	Mind-set Segment 1 Buy based on understanding the product	Mind-set Seg 2 I basically like the idea ..I am interested in making my
Base size	74	54	10	10	22	52
Additive Constant	70	67	76	80	36	84
What does this product do specifically?						
pellet uses agro-waste or wood residues	6	11	-3	-9	11	4
pellet reduces time used for fuel collection and transportation for domestic purposes	3	4	9	-7	18	-3
pellet replaces fossil fuel	2	3	4	-7	7	-1
pellet generates heat (energy) on burning	-1	1	-5	-8	11	-6
Why would I buy this product?						
cheaper than other forms of energy	3	5	1	-2	15	-1
greatly reduces harmful effects because it doesn't burn wood or coal	1	3	-8	-1	6	-1
environmentally friendly	1	3	-4	-11	9	-3
reduces cooking time for food	-5	-5	1	-12	-6	-5
How would I use this product?						
use in pellet heaters to heat a house	4	4	5	6	0	6
use in boilers in industry	2	1	-7	15	2	2
use in pellet burners to heat air in factories and businesses	1	-1	12	3	-4	3
use in pellet stove for cooking	0	-1	3	0	-2	1
What specifically about the product would I tell my friends and family?						
cheaper than fossil fuels like LPG, coal, kerosene, diesel	6	9	1	-4	22	0
carbon-neutral -- reduces carbon footprint	6	8	-8	10	18	1
reduce problem of waste disposal -- uses agro-waste	5	7	4	-5	12	2
makes more jobs for people -- locally manufactured	1	3	-11	3	18	-6

74 people, so we do have respondents from all three groups, as they define themselves in the classification question, done ahead of the actual evaluation of vignettes.

What important is not the story itself, but the journey to make the story. All we have are clues from the elements. It is our job, or really the job of anyone looking at the data, to abstract the pattern and suggest what's going on. One aspect of the

Figure 9.

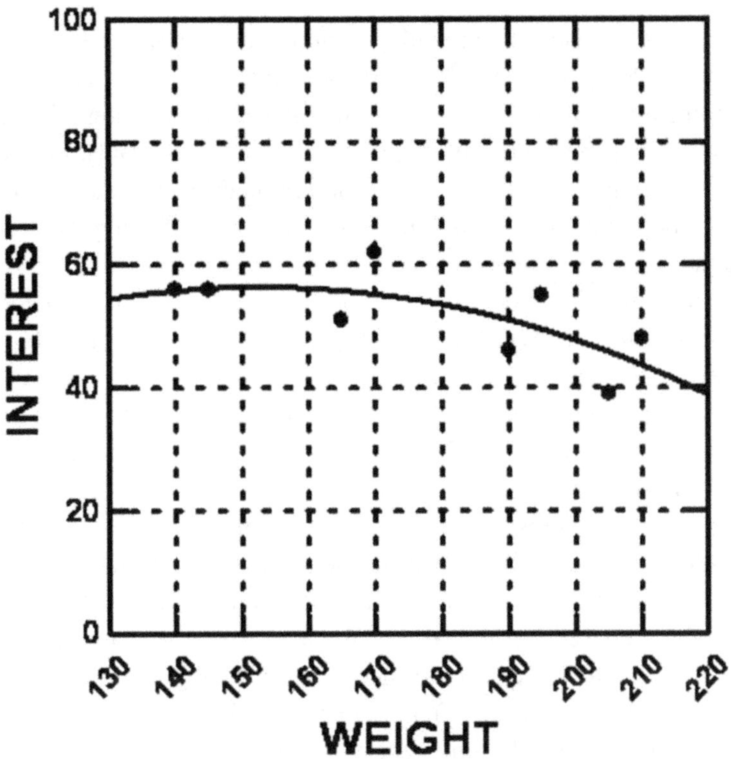

pattern is which numbers are high. Another aspect is the distribution of elements with negative numbers. Thus, for the group which choose 'convenience' as the most important factor, we see that talking about 'what the product DOES' is negative. The story? "Tell me how to use it, and tell me it reduces the carbon footprint." These people look at the product as something to be consumed, and safe for the environment.

Looking at subgroups also forces the new researcher to think about people to people differences, to wonder whether there is any relation between the topic being investigated and some meaningful division of people. At first the exercise might be a bit tedious, such as looking for differences between males and females. Since, however, the stimuli are meaningful, quite often gender differences observed in the reaction or coefficient or utility of an element leads to the important question 'why is this happening?' It is that question that we want to emerge from the study. The experimental design of ideas as described above leads naturally to this inquiry.

Encountering Mind-Sets, the True joy of Discovery

What if one were to discover something entirely new, perhaps new to the world, never realized before, or at least never demonstrated before by anyone publicly. It is this moment which often 'hooks' the researcher, transforming the researcher from a passive experimenter to a lifelong devotee of discovery and knowledge. That 'discovery of the entirely new' is what conjoint analysis can do, almost forcing the discovery onto the initially unsuspecting researcher, effecting its own magical transformation.

How then is this discovery made? More important, how can this discovery become part of virtually EVERY STUDY, in a structured, predictable fashion, without needing the benevolence of good fortune? The answer is by clustering or combining together people with similar patterns of coefficients or impact values, so that the groups of respondents become those similar in mind-sets, as shown by the pattern of positive responses to elements.

Recall that each of our respondents generates his or her own individual model for the AGRO-PELLETS product, showing the degree to which the individual elements 'drive' interest. When we blindly combine the different patterns into a single 'pot,' we end up with a consensus, an average. We miss the 'fine-grain' details, details which could be critical, but details washed away by averaging.

What happens when there are different 'mind-sets' in the population, people with different viewpoints about the same every-day experience? What if the research were able to discover them? What if our researcher could become an Isaac Newton, discovering forces, not of the physical world but rather forces of the mind? What a wonderful opportunity to learn about the world, even if the start of that voyage of learning is the set of 'mind-sets' about AGRO-PELLETS, rather than the laws of motion and gravity. Still, a major discovery.,

Exhibit 11, the final two columns on the right, show clearly different groups, mind-sets, based upon the pattern of responses to the different elements. The computer program uses a well-known set of computer programs called 'clustering programs.' These programs divide the 74 respondents in our study, or any set of respondents in any study, putting the respondents into smaller groups, clusters, based upon the pattern of their coefficients. Respondents within a cluster show similar patterns of coefficients, respondent in different clusters show different patterns. The clustering program is purely statistical, mind-less, and works on mathematical criteria. It is left to the wisdom of the researcher to choose the number of clusters, ideally as few as possible, but in turn clusters which tell a story. These criteria are parsimony (as few clusters as possible), and interpretability (the clusters tell different, seemingly meaningful stories, based upon the coefficients or impact values of the 16 elements).

To help cement that insight, we need only consider the strongest positive and the strongest negative elements for each segment, and compare those strongest performing elements against the performance of these same elements for the total panel. What emerges is a story, typically a very clear story, and in turn an excited researcher, who in a very simple fashion has made a discovery. Furthermore, the discovery may be obvious, e.g., when we work in the world of AGRO-PELLETS. But what about the same type of discovery, different mind-sets, when we work in a world of say ethics and other socially relevant issues?

Bringing the Excitement to the Masses

At the time of this writing many people in the world possess computers or tablets, and even more people possess smartphones, phones which have computer-like properties. To help spread the vision of 'learning through experiment,' the authors have created a free computer program, an APP, which allows anyone in the world to be a researcher. The only things required are a smartphone, access to respondents (people who can participate, either on their own smartphone or on a computer), and some imagination. The APP goes through the exercise described above in detail, in a way that is both fun and educational.

As in any other experience using an APP, there are a series of simple steps that one follows. The reader will see that the educational focus is on discovery, and not on mathematics. The objective here is to have the researcher discover something new about the world, at least the world of people, the world of thought. Thus, the APP, based upon the principles of experimental design and the emerging empirical science of Mind Genomics, represents, one might say, a student-version of this tool, geared to education, to critical thinking, and most important to the joy of discovery.

Tapping Into the User Motivation

Today's smart phone users are daily bombarded with APPs for their smart phones, their tablet, and so forth. As we venture into this world of enhanced, experiential learning, research and discovery, the question naturally occurs: 'Why this APP, instead of APPs which are games, fun, exciting?' This APP is for education, to teach a person how to think, how to experiment, discover, and grow. That's the fun, rather than diverting amusement of gallery type games of chance, or games of adventure and challenge, massively on-line competitive games. The question 'WHY' becomes very important in such a competitive environment.

The answer to the WHY comes from discussions with prospective users, and their responses. Here are the touch points for the APP, and the benefit at each touch point:

1. A way for people to make money. Perhaps the strongest motivation for the APP is that it is a way for people to do experiments, with the hope that their results excite buyers who purchase the data, thus giving them 'unexpected' money for each purchase, at least for current data less than a year old. Perhaps with the financial incentive, people will begin to think critically about just what topics interest people, and are likely to drive a purchase for the full data set.
2. A way for people to establish their credibility and demonstrate their achievements through the results of a study. The topic of the study, the elements, and the results of the study reflect mightily on the researcher. The researcher can point to the web-pages of several studies, these web pages showing the information block and the flash results (results for the total panel and perhaps two mind-sets). A prospective employer can look at the web pages of a job candidate to see the nature of the candidate's thinking. Organizations can scour the web pages, searching for studies, and thus people, who appear to be able to run interesting, and for some companies, relevant studies. Essentially the web page becomes a way to advertise one's own creativity in a structured manner, where everyone has the same chance as everyone else. Presented a counter showing the number of 'purchases' of a person's data provides a further metric of the researcher, at least in terms of that researcher identifying topics and elements leading to purchase.
3. Very young students (ages 7-9) learning to read. These young students are at the start of their reading career, or may be older students who have not received the proper education. The experimental design comprising four silos and four elements per silo can be made more concrete by make the exercise simpler, such as '*telling a story about what we did today*.' The story begins with four silos, the parts of the story, and proceeds with four elements for each silo. The child's task is, with teacher coding, to create the four silos for a specific scenario such as 'going to the park to play,' to put the four silos into the proper order, to provide the four elements for each silo, and then either participate in the study, and/or convince other people to participate. Afterwards, the children can look at the results, and discuss what they learn from the data, such as 'which is the most fun' from the set of 16, or '*what are these two or three mind-sets...does that mean that people think about fun differently*?
4. Young students, ages 9-14. These young students understand mathematics. They are members of a cohort called 'digital natives.' They understand how to work the cell phone. They know how to read and write, to compute, and most of all, how to think. They are cognitively well developed, and have no fear of the digital world. Their reaction, when the idea is presented is 'interest.' They don't see the practical application as yet. They look at the APP as something

'cool,' with which to have fun, learn, and perhaps do something in school. They do not yet have specific needs.

5. Students working alone. By the time a student is in the second year in high school, the family discussion may focus around what the student wants to do with his or her life. The students talk among themselves. With the economic uncertainties of the past decade have left many students with a startling sense of disequilibrium They see the change. As English Poet Laureate Alfred Lord Tennyson writes in the Morte d'Arthur,

The old order changeth yielding place to new
And G-d fulfills himself in many ways
Lest one good custom should corrupt the world.

The APP provides a tool by which the high school student can cope with change, developing a skill and a set of studies to be demonstrated as one's own ability and achievement in documented form. Imagine the intellectual growth of a student who completes a set of 8-10 related studies, on a topic such as judgments of the ethicality of actions in different situations. One study with 50 respondents will teach the student about the way to think, test elements, understand the response patterns, and finally discover new-to-the-world segments in the way people perceive the ethicality of actions. A set of eight studies dealing with the issue of ethics in business, personal life, education, and so forth produces a scholar, even in high school. The work product may transcend a set of tables, and instead be incorporated into a set of PowerPoint® presentations, or even a book. All this coming from the high school student.

6. Students working in teams. During the years 2011-2013, The Department of Mathematics of Queens College, City University of New York, featured Mathematics 110, introduced by Professor Martin Braun of the Mathematics Department, and supported by Professor and Chief Operating Office of Queens College, Professor Susan Henderson. The objective was to use a form of the APP to encourage teams of students to identify an interesting problem, and create the study. The topics ranged from filling a stadium to creating a new coffee to enhancing social media. The exercises allowed groups of 2-4 students, working as a team, to create the study, execute the study with real respondents from commercial on-line panels, and then analyze the data, and present the results in an evening conference attended by key college administration. The students received the same

type of education as do graduate students in business schools, and once again creating a tangible work-product to show for their efforts, as well as the experience of thinking creatively and critically.

7. Students looking for jobs. With the increasingly difficult economy, those seeking jobs may use the APP to research the messaging of the prospective employer, and the messaging of the employer's competitors. All of the information was and remains publicly available on the Internet. The outcome is a presentation to the prospective employer, a presentation which produces 'new news.' From direct reports of those using the approach just described, the prospective employers are presented with a great deal of new information, putting the candidate into a favored position of 'knowing' as much or perhaps even more than the interviewer. At this point, of course, it is important to behave in the proper manner because to some degree the interviewee 'knows more,' leading to a more comfortable feeling, but a feeling that must stop short of arrogant cockiness which might be masking discomfort.
8. Young researchers using the APP to acquire publishable data in an affordable way. We refer here to the topics where the opinion of people is the measure of all things. Clearly, we are not referring to issues such as biological science, but rather issues dealing with topics and the way the topics are perceived and judged. Mind Genomics, the underlying science, has been applied to the law, to economics, to psychological issues, health issues, and so forth. There is every reason to believe that the assiduous research can quickly assemble a publishable corpus of structured information. The APP is only an enabling tool, aiding the mind of the researcher.
9. Young people offering their services to investigate topics, either for socially relevant situations or as consultants to local companies. Young people need experience. Today's education promotes such real-world experience through internships. Often the internships consist of menial jobs, clerical work, which gives some experience but not the type needed for intellectual and professional development. Armed with the technology provided by the APP the student can volunteer in a social organization to investigate a topic, or offer consulting and research services to a local business trying to find out what to communicate to customers.
10. Companies and organizations, public and private, 'crowdsourcing' solutions to opportunities or to problems. We might imagine what would happen with, say, 100,000 or more researchers using the APP, and a central registry of such individuals, known through their email

addresses. The company might wish to determine what would be the best features of a drinkable yogurt appropriate for after sports. Or a local government might be interested in how to get people to read more. Or perhaps a national government might be interested in idea about stopping the epidemic of opioid abuse. All of these issues might be framed simply. The organization requesting the crowdsourcing would guarantee to fund the first 100 studies, each study dealing with the topic, comprising the design of four silos, 16 elements, run with easy-to-find people, and with a base size of 50 respondents. The funding might be a guarantee of $80 to the researcher, and the direct payment of the research fee to the on-line panel provider, and a special website, publicly available, which features the researcher's work, if so desired. The likely direct costs for such crowdsourcing is approximately $400/study. Thus 100 studies, the product of 100 diverse minds, with 'tested and vetted' data would cost $40,000. In turn, for national problems of great significance, 1,000 studies, ten times as may, would cost a mere $400,000, this for the results from 1,000 minds experimenting with the problem, each experiment conducted with 50 real people.

11. Society and government as a whole. Society and government would benefit by creating a '*wiki of the mind*,' with ideas provided by people, with structured data, and with responses of real people who take the task serious, namely the respondents from the on-line panel. In turn, such a database can be mined to understand trends, to understand differences across people, and fundamentally to create a resource to better understand the mind of man. Such a resource exists, of course, right now. It is called a library. The library, however, is not a living, breathing organism, growing, and evolving. The library comprises static knowledge, writing that has passed hurdles and been published. The 'wiki of the mind' is dynamic, created by contributions, both of the researcher and of the respondent.
12. Professionals in the conflict resolution business, who want to get a sense of which aspects of an argument drive the desired 'response.' As one example, consider law students faced with a problem to work through, or negotiators faced with the demands of two sides. By putting the legal case or conflict into the form of a four-silo, sixteen-element study, and submitting the study to a random or selected group of respondents, it become possible to understand which arguments are persuasive, at least to untrained minds but actual people nonetheless.
13. Discovering the components of a new invention, or the convincing messages about the new invention. Entrepreneurs who are just starting

out often have an idea but no money, yet the need to discover what in their offering 'resonates' with people. Investors want to know whether or not the entrepreneur has 'tested the idea' with people, and if so, then which part of the idea resonates. The APP allows that testing as a very low cost.

It bears repeating, however, that there is no 'free lunch.' The price for testing is low, really the cost of the respondents. The analysis is free. The data, specifically the information block and the flash results, however, are publicly available at no cost, and the deep results are available at a very modest price. The trade-off, is a reasonably powerful analytic engine, affordable because it is priced at low cost, but with the basic results freely available, and the deep results available at a nominal price, far lower, by one or two orders of magnitude from the price of a bespoke project.

End Words

As we present this new approach to critical thinking, it is important to note that we are not really inventing a technology as much as we are modifying what already exists, bringing the technology into the world of the student. Today's students do not think critically, at least most of them do not. The number of references is in the millions when we ask Google® to give us 'hits' to the question "Critical Thinking?

Technical Tutorial: How to Read the Data From a Conjoint Measurement Study

We will confine ourselves here to a specific example, a conjoint study which comprises four independent variables or silos, each independent with four elements, bringing us to 16 elements. We choose this specific design because it will be the design that we use in our world-wide efforts to teach creative thinking through the 'Big Mind APP.' By following the set of steps, the reader should quickly understand both the underlying mathematics and the interpretation. It's also important to realize that to teach 'thinking' is not to teach mathematics. Mathematics is simply an underlying tool, making the experiment possible, and in fact rather quite straightforward.

1. **The Raw Materials:** Conjoint analysis deals with the power of different ideas or messages to sway the person who is making a decision. We begin with a topic, such as 'What do we say to make a person want to buy the AGRO-PELLETS?' The topic is the experience of selling AGRO-PELLETS so that people will say 'Yes … I want to buy that."

2. The specific silos, framed as questions. The respondent never sees the questions. The researcher must put in the four questions and make sure that they are in the correct order. With practice, the researcher eventually can recognize when the order of questions produces the outline for an interesting story. It takes practice, however. Forcing the researcher to specify the questions and their order becomes part of the training for critical thinking.
   Here is one order, which may work, but could be strengthened. Intuitively, the order of questions simply does not seem correct
   a. How would I use this product?
   b. What specifically about the product would I tell my friends and family?
   c. Why would I buy this product?
   d. What does this product do specifically
   Here is an improved order
   a. What does this product do specifically?
   b. Why would I buy this product?
   c. How would I use this product?
   d. What specifically about the product would I tell my friends and family?
   We don't know how well the concepts will perform, as rated by the respondents. That depends upon the elements. We do know, however, that the revised order of the silos makes a bit more sense, at least subjectively to the writer, and probably to the researcher as well.
3. **Select the Elements:** It is the elements which must do most of the work to convince a person about these AGRO-PELLETS. Each element in a silo should answer the question posed by the silo, but as a phrase which stands alone. The phrase should make sense. From many studies the data continues to show that elements which present a word-picture are better than elements which are fluffy, without presenting a word-picture. The good and the poor elements can mean the same thing. The good answer draws a word picture, and is reader-friendly, presenting text that is of the same quality as one might read in a magazine or on a billboard. The poor answer is simpler, stark, of the type one might encounter in a business boardroom, where the ideas are 'telegraphed' in the interest of time, and where every already knows the agenda and what the issues happen to be.
   a. A 'good element' in terms of structure: use in pellet heaters to heat a house
   b. A 'poor element' in terms of structure: heats the house
4. Create the respondent instruction page. The respondent instruction is simple. It comprises a few lines, instructing the respondent what the study is about,

as well as the rating scale. The tendency of many respondents is to 'analyze' the concept, line by line. The orientation page instructs the respondents to treat the combination as a singular idea, one vignette, read the vignette, and answer quickly. Finally, the orientation page tells the respondents that all the vignettes are different. The same element will appear a number of times. A conscientious respondent may feel that the same vignette has appeared because the element is familiar. The statement that al the vignettes are unique helps allay that insecurity that 'I've seen this before…haven't I?' For the APP version, where text space is at a minimum, the respondent instructions may have to be shortened, and somewhat compromised, to make the interview easier, less onerous, less visually taxing.,

5. **The Rating Scale:** The rating scale is the vehicle by which the respondent can communicate with the researcher. We want to emphasize that there are no perfect scales. The scale has to make sense in terms of what it requires the respondent to judge. The specifics of the scale are often a matter of argument by practitioners, some of whom believe that the scale should have an even number of points, others who believe that the scale should have an odd number of points, and so on. For the APP we often use an anchored 1-9 scale, anchored only at 1 and at 9, with verbal anchors to make the scale clear, and unambiguous. We do so, for a really simple reason, ergonomics. With a 1-9 scale, respondent need only press a single key to assign a rating, with the computer programming 'grabbing' the rating, and proceeding automatically to the next question. The respondent is not subjected to the onerous task of reading the stimulus, assigning a rating of perhaps two or three digits, and pressing 'next.' That latter task, two strokes instead of one, may seem simple, but not when there are 24 vignettes to read. One stroke saved is a lot of respondent-energy spared.
6. **The Classification Questions:** The Big Mind APP was designed to encourage critical thinking, and in doing so acquire truly 'solid data' from real people, data that can be presented to the education, science, and business communities, just to name a few prospective audiences. In order to accomplish that objective, we need to discover 'who the person is.' The APP was originally designed as a simple system for students, for those who are learning to think and to experiment. The APP was not designed to replace higher-level methods, not meant for studies with more elements (beyond the 16), or more detailed understanding of the respondent by means of a long classification questionnaire. In the interests of maintaining a low-cost system for the researcher, and an easy, fast study for the respondent, we allow three classification questions. Two are fixed, age and gender, respectively. Third classification question is of the researcher's

choosing. A researcher interested in knowing more about the respondents can link in another study to find out more information.

7. **Launch the Project:** Once the study is 'designed,' i.e., with the appropriate silos, elements, rating question, and so forth, all the researcher has to do is 'launch the study,' preparing it for respondents. Launching is nothing more packing the study in a form to be sent to respondents, after which the study is sent to either a list of email addresses (personal addressees) or to a professional panel company which specializes in recruiting panelists for these types of studies. The study itself lasts about four minutes in the field.
8. Each respondent evaluates a unique set of combinations, allowing the study to 'span the space.' The panelist or respondent agrees to participate, receives the orientation page, reads it, and begins to evaluate 24 combinations of elements. The combinations vary from one person to another, but follow a straightforward experiment design. Each of the 50-150 respondents evaluate a unique set of 24 vignettes, created according to a recipe book, the experimental design. The fundamental design is the same, but is permuted to create isomorphic variants (Moskowitz & Gofman, 2004). The permutation strategy ensures that many of the possible combinations are covered across the different respondents, rather than forcing all respondents to evaluate the same set of combinations. Mathematically, we strive for 'spanning the space' with the different respondents, rather than using the respondents to help to reduce the uncertainty by replicating the experiment precisely, thus producing a better estimate of the mean rating for each of a limited set of 24 vignettes, tested by everyone.
9. **Transform the Data:** Our respondents use an anchored 9-point scale to rate their interest in this AGRO-PELLETS product. In the world of marketing and consumer research many practitioners feel comfortable with a binary scale, no or yes. It's easier to think in these defined categories than to think about degree. To accord with their practice we transform the 1-9 scale into two regions. Region 1, the 'lower 2/3' of the scale, ratings 1-6, we transform to 0. Region 2, the 'higher 1/3' of the scale, ratings 7-9, we transform to 100. The choice of WHERE to divide the scale is ours to make. Over the past 35 years, since the early 1980's, it has been most productive to divide the scale in the 2/3, 1/3 fashion as just described. We also do one other simple transformation, adding a very small number ($<10^{-5}$) to each value, 0 or 100, so that the numbers ever so slightly differ from each other. This transformation to make the numbers very slightly different will end up allowing the regression analysis to proceed.
10. Estimate the parameters of the 74 individual'equations or models.' Each of our 74 respondents evaluated a unique set of 24 vignettes, our test concepts. The vignettes are not random, despite the respondent's inability to discern a pattern. The vignettes are created according to an experimental design, so that

the elements appear independently of each other, in a statistical sense. The experimental design, and thus the statistical independence, allow for a very simple regression model using OLS, ordinary least squares. The regression equation is very simple, of the form:

$$\text{Binary Rating (0/100)} = k_0 + k_1(_{A1}) + k_2(_{A2}) + \ldots .k_{16}(_{D4})$$

11. We start to understand the data by averaging the results from the total panel, all 74 respondents who participated. Exhibit 13 above shows the data from the total panel, from the three groups who chose what was most important (health, income, convenience), and from the two mind-set segments. We repeat some of that data in Exhibit 14, this time sorted from high to low, based on the response from the total panel. We only show part of the data, specifically the best two performing elements for total panel, and the worst two performing elements for total panel. We look at how these four elements perform by all the key subgroups
    a. The additive constant, k_0, defined as the conditional probability of a concept being rated 7-9 on the 9-point scale in the absence of elements. Of course, none of the 24 concepts contained 0 elements. However, the additive constant gives us a sense of what would have happened, a sense of a baseline. When it comes time to interpret these results, often the magnitude of the baseline tells its own story. Is the baseline low? When the baseline is low, it is the elements which must do the work. Is the baseline high? When the baseline is high, the elements don't really matter. Our data suggest very high baselines for every group except Mind-set segment 1. Segment 1 wants to understand the product itself, meaning the base level of interest in the AGRO-PELLET is low 36, but the elements can compensate. The elements must do a lot of the work.
    b. The value of the coefficient, i.e., the 'impact' that the element has on driving the binary rating. From many thousands of studies over the past 35 years, we can say that elements with values around +6 to +8 or higher are meaningful, i.e., they correspond to real changes. Our respondents are telling us 'this is an important message to me for making me like or want to buys AGRO-PELLETS.' When we see elements that are around -6 to -8 or lower, they are also meaningful, but they detract from acceptance.
    c. When we read the results, looking at the total panel, we are looking at averages across the whole population of respondents. Sometimes the story is very clear, sometimes only one or two elements really make a difference.

d. When we look at subgroups defined by how the respondents describe themselves, we often see a somewhat clearer story than we would see from the total panel results

e. When we look at subgroups defined by clustering the response patterns, the so-called Mind-Sets, we often see far more striking, compelling, and interpretable differences. The reason for the differences emerging so strongly comes from the effect of clustering, which puts people with opposing, mutually counteracting patterns, into different groups. Once a group comprises people who 'think alike,' at least for these elements, the different underlying patterns emerge far more clearly. The story becomes more cogent. It then it an issue whether there are two, three, four or even more mind-sets. The decision as to the number of mind-sets there are is left to the researcher. As the number of mind-sets increases, the differences emerge more clearly, but at the expense of parsimony. It's best to work with as few mind-sets as possible.

Table 6. Reduced presentation of results from the 74 respondents, showing detailed results for four elements. These four elements are the two strongest performers among total panel, and the two weakest performers, i.e., the two elements driving towards purchase, and the two elements driving away from purchase, respectively.

	Total	Important -- Health	Important - Finances	Important – Convenience	Mind-set Segment 1 Buy based on understanding the product	Mind-set Seg 2 I basically like the idea ..I am interested in making my life better
Base size	74	54	10	10	22	52
Additive Constant	70	67	76	80	36	84
pellet uses agro-waste or wood residues	6	11	-3	-9	**11**	4
cheaper than fossil fuels like LPG, coal, kerosene, diesel	6	9	1	-4	**22**	0
pellet generates heat (energy) on burning	-1	1	-5	-8	**11**	-6
reduces cooking time for food	-5	-5	1	-12	-6	-5

REFERENCES

Box, G. E. P., Hunter, J., & Hunter, S. (1978). *Statistics For Experimenters*. New York, NY: John Wiley & Sons.

Green, P. E., & Krieger, A. M. (1991). Segmenting markets with conjoint analysis; IN. *Journal of Marketing*, *55*(4), 20–31. doi:10.2307/1251954

Luce, R. D., & Tukey, J. W. (1964). Conjoint analysis: A new form of fundamental measurement; IN. *Journal of Mathematical Psychology*, *1*, 1–36. doi:10.1016/0022-2496(64)90015-X

Moskowitz, H.R., & Gofman, A. (2004). *System and method for performing conjoint analysis*. Academic Press.

Moskowitz, H. R., Gofman, A., Itty, B., Katz, R., Machaiah, M., & Ma, Z. (2001). Rapid, inexpensive, actionable concept generation and optimization – the use and promise of self-authoring conjoint analysis for the foodservice industry. *Food Service Technology*, *1*(3-4), 149–16. doi:10.1046/j.1471-5740.2001.00021.x

Moskowitz, H. R., Porretta, S., & Silcher, M. (2005). *Concept Research in Food Product Design & Development*. Ames, IA: Blackwell Publishing Professional. doi:10.1002/9780470290132

Provisional patent application, 60/538,787, filed January 23, 2004.

Schuurman, N. (2013). Tweet me your talk: Geographical learning and knowledge production 2.0. *The Professional Geographer*, *65*(3), 369–377. doi:10.1080/00330124.2012.693873

Wittink, D. R., & Cattin, P. (1989). Commercial use of conjoint analysis: An update; IN. *Journal of Marketing*, *53*(3), 91–96. doi:10.2307/1251345

Chapter 4
Attrition Risk Management

Anugamini Priya Srivastava
Symbiosis International University, India

ABSTRACT

A company cannot be successful if it fails to retain talent in the organization. They have to manage effectively their resources, comprising financial, psychical, and human resources. This is important because higher attrition rate can have various consequences that an attrition incident can cause. It can affect profitability, customer loyalty, revenue, and market image. This chapter aims to identify the antecedents and precedents of attrition in different sectors and evaluates the data received to understand the actual scenarios and its implication on future. This aspect is very important as employee attrition and retention strategies influence the trajectory of the organization.

INTRODUCTION

With the advancement in the area of human resource management, importance of humans in organization has increased. The more diverse workforce is coming under one roof, the more crucial the role of human resource managers is becoming in an organization. Organizations invest huge sums of money to recruit select and place the right person at the right job. Organization invests in training and induction program, provide rewards and compensations to attract and retain talents in their organizations (Bhatnagar, 2007). However, with the change in the mindset of the upcoming population, the employee attrition or employee turnover is creating a big risk towards the sustainability of the organization.

Some of the reasons that are creating attrition risk issues are job hopping, employee low job satisfaction, low compensation, disputes with colleagues and

DOI: 10.4018/978-1-5225-4038-0.ch004

Copyright © 2018, IGI Global. Copying or distributing in print or electronic forms without written permission of IGI Global is prohibited.

supervisors etc. The word 'attrition' refers to gradual loss of employees over time. When employees from an organization tend to leave the job frequently, it creates risk for the company and when this culture of leaving the job increases in an organization, it generates huge lot of concerns for the organization in terms of money and time invested in recruiting those candidates. It influences the overall work process and the profitability status of the company.

- *The word 'attrition' refers to gradual loss of employees over time*

On the other hand, when a company fails to satisfy the psychological expectations of employees, attrition happen. Every organization is supposed to nurture talents in their organization to compete in the market. Their employees are their asset to let them stand and survive in the market. However, when organization does not focus on the quality, skills, knowledge and potential of their employees, then there are higher chances to lose them soon. Higher level of influences the market image of the organization and reduces the chances of bright students to apply in the company in future. It may also lead to customer attrition as the customers were connected to the organization through that particular employee.

Thus, employee attrition is a big risk to the organization and requires effective management. This chapter deals with the varied aspect of attrition risk management and aims to give more awareness regarding the theoretical as well as research aspect of the topic.

Understanding teacher attrition is particularly important in contexts where economically and socially the costs of attrition are unbearable, teachers are becoming increasingly professionally and geographically mobile, and new management regimes are changing the nature of teachers' work (Hatcher, 1994). Yet, the causes and effects of teacher attrition vary across cultures and socio-economic situations, teachers' ages and specialties, and according to the research methodology employed (Chapman, 1994; Gritz & Theobold, 1996).

MEANING OF ATTRITION

The term attrition refers to total number of employees who have left the organization due to some reason. It can be defined as "A reduction in the number of employees through retirement, resignation or death" and also we can say it as "The rate of shrinkage in size or number".

Attrition can be voluntary or involuntary attrition. Voluntary attrition means attrition due to the own will of the employee. This may happen due to personal or professional reasons because of which employee resigns from the organization. This type of attrition is very prevalent in IT/ITES/Retail/Hospitality industries (Bennett, Blum, Long,& Roman, 1993).

Involuntary attrition occurs when employee has to leave the job at the hands of their employer. It can either in the form of being 'fired' or 'laid off'.in most of the cases of being fired is considered as more of dishonorable way of leaving an organization (Guthrie, 2001).

FEATURES OF ATTRITION

Employee attrition has following crucial features

1. During attrition, employees leave the organisation.
2. Attrition can be due to organisational reasons or personal reasons
3. Employee attrition is a form of warning to management indicating the critical concerns with the physical composition of the organisation
4. It indicates the unhealthy situation of the organisation
5. It cost human values and money to the organisation.
6. It hinders the overall flow of work in the organisation.
7. It may also lead to customer attrition.
8. It causes loss to the organisation in terms of money invested on their training.

RETENTION

Theoretically, retention refers to "systematic effort by employers to create and foster an environment that encourages current employees to remain employed by having policies and practices in place that addresses their diverse needs" (Sandhya & Kumar 2011). Employee retention refers to the company's policies to avert talented employees from leaving the job. Now a day when people are more involved in hoping the jobs to get better career opportunities, pays and recognition, it has become very difficult for the company manager to retain talented employees and maintain their competitive edge. Along with the loss of competitive edge and core competency, company's inability to retain talents cause multiple negative outcomes that are discussed in this chapter.

Figure 1.

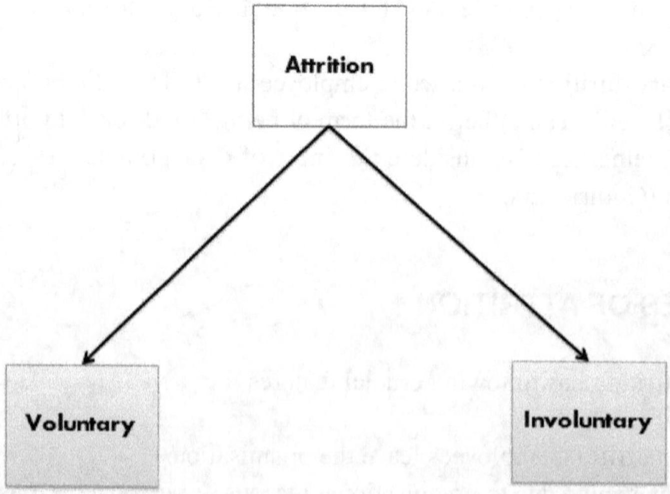

REASONS OF ATTRITION

Attritions can occur due to several personal as well as professional reasons. Some of the key reasons for higher level of attrition at work place are-

Everyday Indignities

Rude behavior displayed by the supervisors is considered as the key reason for attrition. Such everyday indignity based behavior not only influences the productivity of the individual but also affects the work environment negatively; thus, force them to quit the job. Such behavior includes rudeness, undue blames, back-biting, favoritism, and retaliations. Consistent indignities make employees to feel resentful and feel low about them.

Imbalance in Work-Life

Another reason for employee attrition is work life imbalance. In a job which has high demands from the employee, includes late hour workings and weekend work tend to put high pressures on a single employee. Due to this employee are forced to opt amid their professional life and personal life. This not only affects their overall performance and commitment in the organisation but also disturbs their family life (Carter, & Baghurst,2014).

Mismatch Between Expectations and Reality

Many a times there occurs a mismatch between what has been promised to candidate at the time of interview and what actually he/she receives. This mismatch cause mistrust among employees. They start doubting other things for which the company may go the other way. They begin to feel breached and lose their interest at the work place.

Misalignment of Employee

Every manager should attempt to hire employees who can sync with the culture and goals of the organization. When they fail to hire such an employee, both organization and the employee have to suffer. If the person misaligns with the qualification required to complete the job and finds it hard to meet the cultural grounds, it becomes a misfit for the whole organization. It makes it hard for the employee to survive and thus affects their intentions to perform well.

Sense of Being Undervalued

Every individual desire to attain recognition and rewards for the work they have executed. It is natural for a human being. Through recognition employee not only receive credit for their contribution but also attain positive reinforcement to do the same in the future. It is an effective way to communicate appraisals for optimistic efforts. However, when they do not receive such acknowledgment, their work commitment reduces gradually with time (Srivastava, &, Dhar, 2016).

Key Facts

As per the report provided by NASSCOM, the employee attrition in Indian ITES & BPO have risen dramatically causing 1.5 times of the annual salary. Some of the key reasons that are causing high attrition rate are-

- Improper work timings
- Family pressure
- Health issues due to work life misbalancing
- Pressure from peer
- Lack of opportunities for growth in the company
- Other better career options
- And compensation

Lack of Coaching and Feedback

Feedback and coaching by the managers play an important role in the improvement of an employee. A true and honest feedback can avail employees an opportunity to improve themselves, uplift their performance in the future and enable them grow and build successful teams and organizations. However, an ineffective manager lags in giving true feedback even though he/she understand that true feedback and simultaneous coaching can help employees to give their best. Such situation reduces employee faith in supervisor and thus force them to leave the organization.

Concern With Micro Managing

Many a times, managers while micro managing, feel in-secured about their employee ability to perform and complete the work on time. This insecurity binds employees from using their skills to accomplish the job and thus makes them feel low and unsatisfied. Organisations need to make their employees feel 'empowered' to raise their commitment with the organisation and their satisfaction with the job. They should be given freedom and authority to decide and give ownership to their jobs. In turn, employee will accept the responsibility and embrace that trust bestowed by the company with enthusiasm and pride of ownership.

Natural v/s Positional Managing Skills

Based on the performance, many employees are promoted to the position of a manager. Though it might be possible that they do not pursue actual leadership or management skills. Their ability to execute previous job might be very good though getting along people and motivating them to work better might not be his/her trait. This will affect not only his/her confidence to work but also may lead to raise their intentions to leave. Organizations should analyze the skills of people and those who are naturally skilled to get along people and motivate them to get the results, they should be awarded with higher positions.

Instability in the Organisation

Another reason of attrition is instability in the organization. To eliminate the monotony of doing a single job, management on regular basis tend to reorganize, shuffle and change the direction of the people. Such activities disconnect people from the common goal of the organization and place them in a confusing state regarding their job roles, priorities and managerial expectations. Further it leads to frustration and inefficiencies.

Rewarding pay

Studies have found that money and compensation isn't the only thing that motivates employees to stay committed to the organization. It is the career growth options and pay hike provided by the other companies that makes them to leave the existing job. Even though the companies are not able to pay better hikes due to economic crisis, they should at least pay a competitive as well as rewarding pay to retain the talents. It will make them feel valued and will retain their commitment towards the company (Bisht, & Singh, 2012).

Research Says: Gender and Attrition

Despite women's success entering the professions in the USA, the attrition of women from these fields is staggering. The attrition rate among female professionals is almost three times that of their male counterparts. In a 1993 national survey, 12.1% of women versus 4.0% of men in law were out of the labor force 10 years after graduation. The ratio remained roughly the same among MBAs (7.8 vs. 2.2%) and physicians (10.7 vs. 3.7%; Baker, 2002). Among 715 newspaper journalists surveyed, 30% of women 27 years and younger reported that they intended to leave the field (Reinardy, 2009). A leading professional services firm also reported losing half the women in each class within the five to seven years from recruitment to partnership (McCracken, 2000). The existing research in academia confirms that faculty women are also more likely to leave their jobs than are men (e.g., Bickel et al., 2002; Cropsey et al., 2008; Hensel, 1991; Xu, 2008). Deutsch, F. M., & Yao, B. (2014). Gender differences in faculty attrition in the USA. *Community, Work & Family, 17*(4), 392-408.

Workload v/s Returns

Whenever an employee works hard to accomplish the targets on time, he/she expects rewards in return. But when they do not receive such recognition or rewards they tend to feel breached. Employee's faith and confidence in the organization will tend to get shaken thus affecting their performance and their overall productivity. Therefore, every company should attempt to give raises to the compensation packages of their employees with the rise in organizational performance and profitability. The organization should treat employees as key assets rather than just consumables to get the work done, without sharing the fruits of their efforts. By giving such critical enablers of success, employee will have more confidence in their organizations

Opportunity for Growth

Organizations lose good talents when they fail to provide better growth opportunity to their employees. When employee feel trapped in dead end jobs or positions, there are forced to job hop from one company to another in order to grow in terms of status and pay. The most successful and employee oriented organizations help their employees to learn new skills and gain new knowledge to update themselves in their current positions and give them better prospects to grow in future. Employees are inclined to stay committed to an organization when they sense higher growth potential and comparable compensation in the company (Mitchell, Holtom, & Lee, 2001)

EFFECT OF ATTRITION ON CUSTOMERS

Employee attrition has major impact on the customer organisation relationship. The two kinds of effect that attrition has on the customers are-

Erosion of Service Brand Image

Brand image refers to as the general perceptions or beliefs regarding the brand (Keller 1993). It depends upon the service provided by the service employee and their interactions with their customers. The more effective and easier is it for the customers to solve their issues and handle the queries by different contact points in firms' communication structure, the more positive will be the brand image (Subramony, & Holtom,2012).

When unit level employees leave the organization, it results into wearing away of the firm's customer value. In other words, it affects the service brand image of the organisation. An optimistic brand image can support the service firms to distinguish themselves from their rivalries. However, loss of employees and thus the customer's perception can negatively affect the organisation overall performance (Holtbrügge, Friedmann, & Puck, 2010).

Reduction Customer Evaluation of Service Delivery

Customer usually relate brand with the trustworthiness, innovativeness and professionalism of the employees who provide value to them. Positive perception makes customers to remain loyal with the firm and make repurchase decision and provide word of mouth promotions and referrals. It further enhances the financial brand equity and support the firm to expand their brand abilities in the long run. On the other hand, employee high turnover from the organisation an also has negative effect on the customer evaluation of service delivery. The customer evaluation of service delivery indicates customer's perception of the unit's effectiveness in delivering core service offerings.

Effect on Unit's Customer Orientation

The sales, customer service and other customer facing staffs comprise a crucial relation between the firms and the customer. The more they stay loyal to the employee or say the firm's representative, the more they remain loyal to the firm. Frequent interactions with the customer helps the employee in maintaining a personal touch and deeper understanding of individual customer's needs and choices. Therefore, it gives employees discretion to solve the customer's problems in their own ways. However, downsizing of employees lead to loss of customers as it will negatively affect the unit's collective level of customer orientation (Ellett, Ellis, & Westbrook, 2007).

Effect of Attrition on the Organization

Employee turnover from the organisation has a key impact on the overall functioning of the company. The customer facing employees are the ones who actually get the customers connected with the organisation. Loss of such employee can have following consequences towards the organisation.

Disruption of the Services

When the customer facing employees leave the organisation, as mentioned above, it affects the relationship of customer with the company. Attrition of such employees, thus causes disruption in the delivery of the service.

Interruption in Normal Operations

Every work in an organisation is interdependent and interrelated to one other. When an employee leaves the job it affects the smoother functioning of the other related and dependent jobs, thus causing unwanted delays in normal operations.

Effect of Organisational Costings

Employees' voluntary attrition not only causes interruption in customer organisation network, delays in operations, it also forces organisation to recruit and select new people and train them for the task. This requires additional time and effort to re-orient the new staff and additional emotional energy to rebuild the relationship with the new partner (Holtom, Mitchell, Lee, & Eberly, 2008).

Low Level of Delivering High Quality Service

Attrition in the long run affects the overall ability of the organization to distribute high quality service. Due to loss of customer facing employee, they fail to understand the nature of individual customer problems and thus are not able to manage and solve it effectively.

Offset Business Outcomes

Serving customers effectively can be treated as the key strategic asset towards organization success. Though employee attrition, along with affecting the ability to provide good quality services, affects the profitability, productivity and customer satisfaction in the short run. Although such layoffs or downsizing might reduce the overall labour cost, it can also affect the related business outcomes in negative manner. It can also spread of fear among the existing employees due to job insecurity and this will worsen the situation further, if not managed properly.

Breach of Psychological Contract

A psychological contract refers to implied agreement among the employee and the employer. It indicates that each of the party in an employment contract has some or the other expectation from the another one. This is not provided in the written form, but still exist when someone joins a company or a firm. However, when any of the party sense non fulfilment of the expectation, they tend to lose their interest in job and thus intend to leave the company in the short run. This non fulfilment of the expectation is termed as breach of 'psychological contract'.

Win-Win Situation Against Competitors

Better understanding towards customer needs and satisfaction of those needs bring s the competence to the company to win against the competitors. However, employee attrition negates the competitive advantage situation and thus provides better opportunity for the competitors to capture the customers' loyalty and investment.

FACTORS AFFECTING EMPLOYEE TURNOVER/ATTRITION

Attrition has become a prominent issue for the present day organizations. It is hampering the functioning of the organization, due to which it is attracting the attention of numerous scholars (Rebeťák, & Farkašová, 2015). Number of studies have been conducted till date. A brief review of the same is given below.

Level of Relationship Transparency

Kumar and Yakhlef (2016), stated that loss of customer facing employee can have a negative implication on the company. By conducting a survey on Indian Knowledge intense service organization, they showed to avoid threat of employee attrition and to manage client relationships, organization should emphasize on 'relationship transparency model'. Through relationship transparency information and knowledge can retained and transferred effectively, even the employee leaves the organization. Further, through effective succession plans and timely management intervention can reduce or minimize the chances of negative customer perception and their fear for un certainty. Hence it will lead to fortification of the trust based relationship with the organization.

Manager's Support

In another study, Li, Kim and Zhao (2017) proposed a 'trickle down model' and showed in a sample of casino employees, that manager support at the workplace plays an important role in minimizing the chances of employee attrition and nurturing an optimistic and reliable settings. Such a setting allows employees to trust their managers and provide better performance at work. The author stated that when managers provide their support to frontline employees, in turn the employees reciprocate through citizenship behavior, i.e. their voluntary behavior to go beyond their role and benefit the organization. This further reduces their intentions to leave the organizations.

Working Conditions

Identifying the basis of employee attrition, Macdonald (1999) carried a literature review on teacher's attrition from educational institutions. He mentioned that frequent cases of teacher attrition have led to teacher shortage in educational industry, thus causing wastage of resources, expertise and knowledge. Since the teacher's profession tends to have a low status perception and have to work in poor working conditions, this forces teachers to leave the profession early. This study suggested for the maintenance of comprehensive databases on teaching personnel and solve the problems that are causing higher percentage of teacher's attrition.

Work Values and Organisational Values

De Cooman et al., (2009) analyzed the reasons which cause attrition among organization and grounded on the theory of 'attraction- selection- attrition model' evaluated the relationship between work values and organization values. In other words, this study examined the importance of work values towards organizational commitment and their fit in the organization and the key role of person organization misfit as a reason for employee attrition. Cooman and his colleagues showed that people socialize with each other at work place and try to understand and learn the organizational values. When they find a good fit with the organization, they retain their commitment and loyalty towards the organization. However, when they sense a misfit, they tend to leave the organizations.

Contextual Factors

Lapointe & Vandenberghe (2017) indicated few more reasons that cause attrition among employee. This study proposed the role of contextual factors - job scope and development opportunities as having critical influence on employee's intention to stay in the job or leave it. Grounded on the theory of 'Social exchange theory' the authors showed that when employees have strong feeling that their career will prosper in an organizational setting and they will get more opportunities to learn and develop, they tend to stay committed with the organization. Contrary to this, in the absence of such opportunities, even though the mentor supervision is effective, they tend to lose their interest in the job and thus leave the job, causing higher attrition rates.

Safety Provisions and Implementation

In line with, Huang et al., (2016) carried a study on truck drivers and stated issues with the safety provisions i.e. the safety climate, in the organization a reason for employee attrition. The study showed that the higher level of safety in the organization are important aspects that help in deriving injury reducing behavior and developing safer work surroundings. Supporting the 'social exchange theory', when employee perceive their organization as providing all safety provisions and facilities, they have less tendency to fear for any kind of injury and thus stay committed with the organization. However, contrary to this, when the safety facilities are not justified, it increases the chances of accidents and injury and thus causing low job satisfaction and higher attrition.

Perceived Benefits and Compensation

Hsieh & Su (2007) conducted a longitudinal survey on certified care assistants and identified personal factors, work related factors, the managerial structure, welfare system, style of leadership and the work environment to play important role towards employee intentions to leave the organization. This study argued that it is the personal interest of the employees that helps them to sustain in this care industry. Their feeling to care the elderly, perceived benefits received in terms of money and supportive leadership are some of the reasons that encourage them, to stay in the organization. However, factors like low wages and heavy workloads, long working hours and related level of stress, and poor financial benefits are the ones that contribute to the careers attrition from this industry.

Political Structure

In line with, Urwin et al., (2010) found the challenges that were leading to attrition of students from nursing courses. This study discussed the micro i.e. individual, meso i.e., political and macro i.e. professional level reasons which are forcing students to dropout from nursing courses. Further, they mentioned the issues like challenges in defining the meaning of attrition, changes in education system and changes in political structure as the reason due to which students are leaving the nursing courses.

Customer Incivility

A study carried on by Han, Bonn, & Cho (2016), in hospitality industry mentioned that customer incivility at work i.e. the conditions where employees has to face rude behavior of their customer which is in disrespectful or insulting manner, as one of the current issue which is causing employee attrition from the hospitality industry like hotels and restaurants. Customer incivility cause burnout i.e., the highest level of stress, among hotel employees and thus, forcing them to leave the organization.

Recruitment Efforts

In the research conducted on health employee in Pomerania, Haring et al., (2009) highlighted the role of extended recruitment efforts on attrition bias. The authors showed that late recruitment at the initial point, unemployment, low level of education, females and the smoking habit are the few aspects which predicted attrition at a higher percentage.

Satiani et al., (2013) evaluated the trend in retention of academic surgeons and reviewed faculty attrition rates, their tendency to leave the academic surgery. They suggested that proper retention planning is the key to reduce the attrition rates. This planning should include "enculturation, mentoring of professional satisfaction, formalized mentoring of younger surgeons, retaining academic couples and a part-time workforce, leadership and talent management, exit interviews, and competitive financial packages." (p. 944)

Theory of Reciprocity

Akgunduz & Sanli (2017) mentioned that employees tend to represent positive reciprocal behavior when they sense that their interests are protected and the organization is committed for their career growth. Based on the social exchange theory and norm of reciprocity theory, they investigated the extent to which employee advocacy i.e. "state of being a volunteer on acting in the name of the interests of the employees, and shows the transparency of the employee policy of the organization" (p.119) and perceived organizational support i.e. "general belief that the organization cares for the contributions and welfare of its employees" (p. 119) cause employee turnover or attrition through the statistical analysis on a sample of hotels.

Self-Efficacy

Bryer, Peterson-Graziose & Nikolaidou (2015) conducted a survey on nurses and analyzed the reasons for their attrition for the nursing profession. This study stated that the self-efficacy i.e. belief for own tendency to face adverse situations, of the nurses has a significant effect on their intention to leave the organization.

Gender and Work Life Balance

Deutsch & Yao (2014) evaluated gender differences as the basis for employee attrition. They found that females were the ones who were leaving the organization more in numbers apart from the high number of retirees. The major reason for the attrition of female faculty was sorted as work life conflict i.e. difficulty of coordinating two careers. Another reason was job dissatisfaction shown in this study that lead to attrition of female faculty. This study suggested modulation of spousal policies to support female faculty to coordinate both the work and personal life.

Performance Appraisals Bias

Similarly, Agarwal & Mehta (2014) analyzed performance appraisals and working environment as the reason for higher attrition rates in ITES of India. They stated that employee who sense higher biasness in performance appraisal and were not able to meet the expectations of working environment, tend to feel low about themselves. Consequently, they have less job satisfaction and thus this increases their intention to leave the organization.

Demographics

Latha, K. L. (2013) showed that demographics of an individual also play an important role in influencing once intention for attrition. Her study indicated that age, educational qualifications, and work experience not only influence the internal motivation level of individual but also affect their intention to leave the company.

HOW TO IDENTIFY AND REDUCE ATTRITION

Attrition rates can be calculated by adopting following equation

Attrition = (No. of employees who left in the year / average employees in the year) x 100

In this way, a manager can evaluate the attrition rates and accordingly take steps to manage the attrition rate across the organization. In order to reduce the intensity and frequency of employee attrition or turnover, employer need to understand the nature of the problem behind it. Following are the two ways prominent and the common in the organization through which the reasons behind attrition can be identified and thus can be sorted in future:

Exit Interviews

Exit interviews are conducted to identify the reasons from an employee who is leaving the organization. This is suggestively to be the best way to gather information regarding the problems lying inside the work environment, the perceptions of employees towards the organization, issues underlying between the supervisor and the subordinate or subordinate to subordinate and the feedback on manager's leadership capabilities. Usually this interview is conducted just before the employee leaves the company or sometimes when they have already left the organization. However, studies suggest to carry this interview shortly after the notice of resignation is given by the employee. Further, special caution has to be taken by the employer for who shall take this interview. It should not be taken by the manager who is supposed to write the reference for that particular employee in future. Preferably, the interviewer should be some external agent before whom the employee can give accurate reasons and opinions regarding his separation from the organization. Moreover, this is important to maintain the anonymity and confidentiality of employee's response. When such assurance is there, employees are in better position to express true feeling and opinions. This interview is normally carried out using a questionnaire or through one to one interactions.

Surveys

Another way to understand the reasons for employee attrition is conducting surveys. Many companies carry out confidential attitude surveys to understand the possible reasons of the employees who have left the company for more than six months. It involves questions on the reasons for intention to leave and is sent to former employees in a confidential manner. However, the response rates are very poor in this situation. The questions can be open ended or multi choice answers type, but has to be easy, understandable and fairly short.

COSTS OF ATTRITION

The recruitment and selection of an employee into an organization involves huge amount of time. Along with that company incurs huge sum on their overall selection induction and training processed, with an aim to prepare them as an asset of the company. However, when an employee leaves the organization, it costs to the company in economic terms. Following are the three major costs that are suffered by the company:

Recruitment Cost

This includes cost incurred on the recruitment process to hire a new person. This process involved sub costs for "background screening, time spent on sourcing replacement, time spent on recruitment and selection, travel expenses, re-location costs, if any in Training/ramp-up time and background/reference screening" (Ratna, & Chawla, 2012, p.36).

Administration Cost

Administration cost include cost like setting up communication systems, desktop, telephone, email ids, adding employees to HR system, setting id cards, access cards etc.

Training and Development Cost

Training and development cost involves expenditures incurred on developing new employees. It does include many direct and indirect costs, which can involve arrangements for training materials, technology for training, employee benefits and trainers' time schedule (Srivastava, & Dhar, 2017).

MANAGING RISK OF ATTRITION

Till now, it is clear that attrition is purely a risk to the company in multiple terms. Based on the reasons of attrition, following are the key steps that can be taken to reduce the attrition rates.

Knowledge Based Pay

Organization should try to give rewarding and competitive pay based on the KSAEs i.e. Knowledge, skills, attitude and experience. This will let the employees to sense the commitment of organization towards their employees and will encourage employees to stay in the organization in the long run.

Development Opportunities

The company should give their employees better prospects to develop their skills and knowledge and indicate better career in the future. They should focus on enhancing the learning experience and its effect on the earning abilities of the employees

Employee Engagement

The work given to an employee should be designed in such a manner that avoids boredom and monotony. It should be such that engages employee on continuous basis. If the job requires repetitive tasks, then periodical transfers or rotations of employee should be done to lessen the monotony of performing the same job day after day, and to increase the chances to have knowledge of all the related tasks. Such action would increase employee's motivation to work amd stay committed to the organization.

Adjust Recruitment and Selection Policies

Based on the frequency of people leaving the organization, the human resource managers should try to adjust their recruitment and selection policies. This is suggested to avoid organization-person fit errors and get the person who can adjust in the organization for long run and stay committed to the organization and while increasing its productivity and performance. The aim of the policies should be to get the 'right person at the right job', to avoid any future separations of the employees from the company causing attrition.

Inclusion of Technology

To avoid attrition and the risk related to its management, companies can leverage the relevance of technology and its usage to complete the tasks. This will improve the expertise of the company in technical terms without causing any risk of attrition.

Declaration of Career Growth

The recruiter should declare the terms and polices regarding one's career path and must define it clearly to avoid any kind of breach of psychological contract in future. If this aspect is taken care in the initial stage, this can reduce the chances of employee turnover or attrition in the future.

Encourage the Feeling of Being Valued

Employer should give non-financial rewards to acknowledge the good performers in the organization. Personal appraisals or a pat on the back in time or celebrating small achievement will employees will let them feel being valued and will increase their job satisfaction and commitment.

Periodical Address by the Senior Management

In organizations, where senior manager takes their time to interact with their employee and address them periodically, tend to have more committed employees. Such addresses let employees be considered as a part of the big family, thus motivating them to give their best to the company.

Reinforcement Through Company Mission

The employee should be re-informed about the mission of the company and the importance of their role towards it. This will make them motivated to learn more and do their part of job effectively. They should also involve sharing of learning and experience to all so that new comers can get influenced and work efficiently.

Creative and Flexible Attendance

The attendance should not be very rigid. It should be related with motivating people to be on time. Though it should consider the other aspects of an employee by developing flexible and creative attendance system and should consider the personal problems in identifying their commitment towards work in the form of attendance.

Awareness Among Employee

The employee of the organization should be, from time to time, made aware of their role importance towards the organization performance and success. This will motivate them to work in motivated manner.

SUMMARY

Human resource are the key elements or say the assets of every organization. The more talented the human resource remains; the more competitive edge the company gets. However, when the company fails to satisfy the employee needs or the employee lacks interest in the assigned tasks it causes attrition. Therefore, every company should consider the related facts and try to retain the talent in their organization.

REFERENCES

Agarwal, R. N., & Mehta, A. (2014). Impact of performance appraisal and working environment on the job satisfaction and attrition problem in the Indian IT industry. *Paradigm, 18*(1), 73–85.

Akgunduz, Y., & Sanli, S. C. (2017). The effect of employee advocacy and perceived organizational support on job embeddedness and turnover intention in hotels. *Journal of Hospitality and Tourism Management, 31*, 118–125. doi:10.1016/j.jhtm.2016.12.002

Bennett, N., Blum, T. C., Long, R. G., & Roman, P. M. (1993). A firm-level analysis of employee attrition. *Group & Organization Management, 18*(4), 482–499. doi:10.1177/1059601193184006

Bhatnagar, J. (2007). Talent management strategy of employee engagement in Indian ITES employees: Key to retention. *Employee Relations, 29*(6), 640–663. doi:10.1108/01425450710826122

Bisht, N. S., & Singh, L. K. (2012). Understanding antecedents to attrition for employees with varying levels of experience in Indian software industry professionals. *Global Business and Management Research, 4*(1), 99.

Bryer, J., Peterson-Graziose, V., & Nikolaidou, M. (2015). Self-esteem and self-efficacy as predictors of attrition in RN-BS completion students: A descriptive correlational study. *Teaching and Learning in Nursing, 10*(1), 30–34. doi:10.1016/j.teln.2014.08.004

Carter, D., & Baghurst, T. (2014). The influence of servant leadership on restaurant employee engagement. *Journal of Business Ethics, 124*(3), 453–464. doi:10.1007/s10551-013-1882-0

De Cooman, R., De Gieter, S., Pepermans, R., Hermans, S., Du Bois, C., Caers, R., & Jegers, M. (2009). Person–organization fit: Testing socialization and attraction–selection–attrition hypotheses. *Journal of Vocational Behavior, 74*(1), 102–107. doi:10.1016/j.jvb.2008.10.010

Deutsch, F. M., & Yao, B. (2014). Gender differences in faculty attrition in the USA. *Community Work & Family, 17*(4), 392–408. doi:10.1080/13668803.2014.885880

Ellett, A. J., Ellis, J. I., Westbrook, T. M., & Dews, D. (2007). A qualitative study of 369 child welfare professionals' perspectives about factors contributing to employee retention and turnover. *Children and Youth Services Review, 29*(2), 264–281. doi:10.1016/j.childyouth.2006.07.005

Employee attrition and retention. (n.d.). *Shodhganga*. Retrieved from http://shodhganga.inflibnet.ac.in/bitstream/10603/15957/10/10_chapter%202.pdf

Guthrie, J. P. (2001). High-involvement work practices, turnover, and productivity: Evidence from New Zealand. *Academy of Management Journal*, *44*(1), 180–190. doi:10.2307/3069345

Han, S. J., Bonn, M. A., & Cho, M. (2016). The relationship between customer incivility, restaurant frontline service employee burnout and turnover intention. *International Journal of Hospitality Management*, *52*, 97–106. doi:10.1016/j.ijhm.2015.10.002

Haring, R., Alte, D., Völzke, H., Sauer, S., Wallaschofski, H., John, U., & Schmidt, C. O. (2009). Extended recruitment efforts minimize attrition but not necessarily bias. *Journal of Clinical Epidemiology*, *62*(3), 252–260. doi:10.1016/j.jclinepi.2008.06.010 PMID:18834716

Holtbrügge, D., Friedmann, C. B., & Puck, J. F. (2010). Recruitment and retention in foreign firms in India: A resource-based view. *Human Resource Management*, *49*(3), 439–455. doi:10.1002/hrm.20353

Holtom, B. C., Mitchell, T. R., Lee, T. W., & Eberly, M. B. (2008). 5 Turnover and Retention Research: A Glance at the Past, a Closer Review of the Present, and a Venture into the Future. *The Academy of Management Annals*, *2*(1), 231–274. doi:10.1080/19416520802211552

Hsieh, P. C., & Su, H. F. (2007). Retention and attrition of certified care assistants in the long-term care industry from the Taipei area: An interview survey. *International Journal of Nursing Studies*, *44*(1), 93–104. doi:10.1016/j.ijnurstu.2005.11.024 PMID:16413554

Huang, Y. H., Lee, J., McFadden, A. C., Murphy, L. A., Robertson, M. M., Cheung, J. H., & Zohar, D. (2016). Beyond safety outcomes: An investigation of the impact of safety climate on job satisfaction, employee engagement and turnover using social exchange theory as the theoretical framework. *Applied Ergonomics*, *55*, 248–257. doi:10.1016/j.apergo.2015.10.007 PMID:26611987

Kumar, N., & Yakhlef, A. (2016). Managing business-to-business relationships under conditions of employee attrition: A transparency approach. *Industrial Marketing Management*, *56*, 143–155. doi:10.1016/j.indmarman.2016.01.002

Lapointe, É., & Vandenberghe, C. (2017). Supervisory mentoring and employee affective commitment and turnover: The critical role of contextual factors. *Journal of Vocational Behavior*, *98*, 98–107. doi:10.1016/j.jvb.2016.10.004

Latha, K. L. (2013). A study on employee attrition and retention in manufacturing industries. *BVIMSR's Journal of Management Research*, *5*(1), 1–23.

Li, J. J., Kim, W. G., & Zhao, X. R. (2017). Multilevel model of management support and casino employee turnover intention. *Tourism Management*, *59*, 193–204. doi:10.1016/j.tourman.2016.08.006

Macdonald, D. (1999). Teacher attrition: A review of literature. *Teaching and Teacher Education*, *15*(8), 835–848. doi:10.1016/S0742-051X(99)00031-1

Mitchell, T. R., Holtom, B. C., & Lee, T. W. (2001). How to keep your best employees: Developing an effective retention policy. *The Academy of Management Executive*, *15*(4), 96–108. doi:10.5465/AME.2001.5897929

Ratna, R., & Chawla, S. (2012). Key factors of retention and retention strategies in telecom sector. *Global Management Review*, *6*(3).

Rebeťák, M., & Farkašová, V. (2015). Managing High–Potential Employees. *Procedia Economics and Finance*, *23*, 867–871. doi:10.1016/S2212-5671(15)00437-2

Sandhya, K. K., & Kumar, D. (2011). Employee retention by motivation. *Indian Journal of Science and Technology*, *4*(12), 1778–1782.

Satiani, B., Williams, T. E., Brod, H., Way, D. P., & Ellison, E. C. (2013). A review of trends in attrition rates for surgical faculty: A case for a sustainable retention strategy to cope with demographic and economic realities. *Journal of the American College of Surgeons*, *216*(5), 944–953. doi:10.1016/j.jamcollsurg.2012.12.052 PMID:23522787

Srivastava, A. P., & Dhar, R. L. (2016). Authentic leadership for teacher's academic optimism: Moderating effect of training comprehensiveness. *European Journal of Training and Development*, *40*(5), 321–344.

Srivastava, A. P., & Dhar, R. L. (2017). Authentic Leadership and Extra Role Behavior: A School Based Integrated Model. *Current Psychology (New Brunswick, N.J.)*, •••, 1–14.

Subramony, M., & Holtom, B. C. (2012). The long-term influence of service employee attrition on customer outcomes and profits. *Journal of Service Research*, *15*(4), 460–473. doi:10.1177/1094670512452792

Urwin, S., Stanley, R., Jones, M., Gallagher, A., Wainwright, P., & Perkins, A. (2010). Understanding student nurse attrition: Learning from the literature. *Nurse Education Today*, *30*(2), 202–207. doi:10.1016/j.nedt.2009.07.014 PMID:19910083

Chapter 5
Service Innovation and Its Consequences:
The Growing Imperative of Knowledge Sharing and Donating on Quality of Service Innovation Techniques

Mrinal Tyagi
BML Munjal University, India

Hrishikesh Hulyalkar
BML Munjal University, India

Harshvardhan Kothari
BML Munjal University, India

Amrita Kapoor
BML Munjal University, India

Aishwarya Bhatia
BML Munjal University, India

Alisha Vij
BML Munjal University, India

ABSTRACT

The corporate world in the present times pays special heed to the skills, knowledge, and attitude of an employee as these characteristics plays a crucial part in the success of the organization where the employee works. In this chapter, the authors map the various aspects that are completely indispensable for the learning and development of the employee given by the leader ultimately transforming the employee into a

DOI: 10.4018/978-1-5225-4038-0.ch005

Copyright © 2018, IGI Global. Copying or distributing in print or electronic forms without written permission of IGI Global is prohibited.

more efficient and responsible professional. Pervading the relevant knowledge to the employee and the organization by a leader can cause tremendous change in the behavior and performance of the employee. This exchange of knowledge results in a more focused approach and instills a sense of belief within the employee, and this creates a camaraderie that leads to smooth working and creates a milieu of trust and confidence in turn benefiting the organization in the long run.

INTRODUCTION

Innovation make repetition to erode and make path for creative and more efficient way of solving a problem and yet innovation is not confined by any area where it can be used. When we talk about service innovation in organization it is present (and required) at all the levels of the hierarchy starting from the Operational level going all the way to the top Strategic Level where the decision-making takes place. And therefore, service innovation is not just needed to bring new ideas on the table but rather to make people think out of the box and enable them to come up with solution that were previously never thought about. But Service Innovation can be elusive most of the times due to inadequate nurturing of talent or as it often happens by turning a blind eye towards a new method or approach and taking a conservative stand by avoiding taking that calculative risk when required.

Innovation are derived within the organization by a Transformational Leader with the intention to cultivating excellent ways of going about a specific problem that the organization might be facing by giving the proper information or knowledge to the employees and curating them on periodic basis. Service Innovation acts as an asset to any organization implementing because the propensity of an employee to come up with unique ways of solving a problem or to even conceive a new method of doing something starts to build up. And in today's competitive corporate environment where the 'Age of Customer' rules the roost success is anything but repetitive. Hence, innovation is indispensable to organization these days.

Service Innovation depends on several external factors apart from the leadership transformation given by the leader in the organization as discussed earlier in the text. We would be taking these external factors such as Knowledge Sharing, Knowledge Donation and Innovation Climate.

When an employee and a leader (manager or boss) work together in the same premises communication takes place. This exchange of information gives the employees new insights on how the organization works, what are the expectation of the organization from the employee, how the organization previously has been

Figure 1. **Factors of Service Innovation**

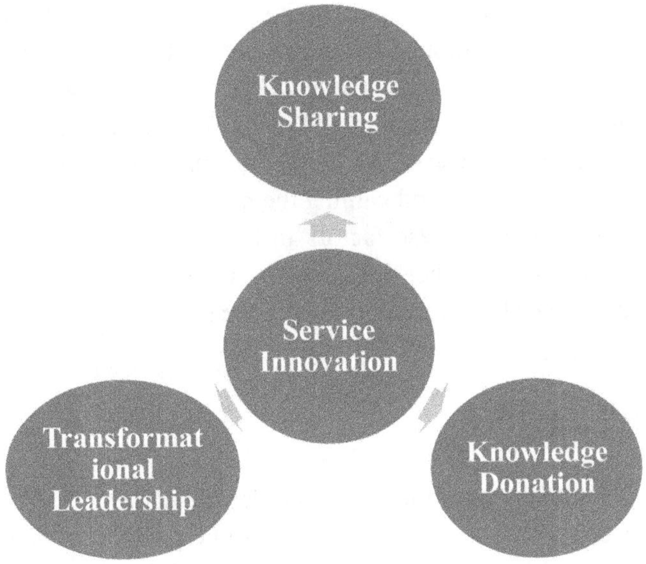

operating or how the employee can add value to the organization by his/her work. All of this happens if the communication is robust and healthy where both the leader (the employer) and the employee learn from each other and creates value for the organization bringing new and noble ideas on the table.

Often an organization succumbs to the chasm created by the lack of interaction between the leader and the employee due to attitudinal or cynical issue from either the leaders' or the employees side. Knowledge Sharing is one of the fundamental aspect in ordering a Service Innovation at workplace.

While the archives and repositories of information extracted, used and stored are created it is also important to let the doors of these archives open to all the employees and members of the organization open. The knowledge garnered by a leader can be useful to several people in the organization and it is imperative on the part of the leader to let the reach and access of this historical data(information) be available to all the interested people who want to use it. In this way, the information pervaded through the organization faster and to more and more number of people.

No amount of knowledge and communication is effective if it is not intended for the betterment of an individual and therefore the role of a leader is of such high importance in organization and anywhere else. A Transformational Leader takes charge of the approach that are needed to achieve the goals for the organizations and empowers the employees with confidence, enthusiasm, positive attitude and knowledge to enable them to contribute in the attainment of the result for themselves and for the organization at large. A Transformational Leader acts as a catalyst for creating a Service Innovation by imparting the needful knowledge and resources to the employees of the organization all of which helps in initiating a process of creating more leaders than mere followers to the leader himself! Also, a Transformational Leader tries to foster an environment of perfection and excellence by motivating the employees and team mates to strive for getting the maximum from the opportunity by following legitimate means and gaining the maximum.

We would be examining these factors in the following section by deducing Hypothesis and checking whether these factors stands the statistical tests and gets proven by the data recorded after interviewing the people.

LITERATURE REVIEW

With the changing dynamics of the industry today the understanding of innovation has also changed looking a problem from only one perspective and following a standard approach will not reap the desired result (Harrison et al. 1996). And therefore, Service Innovation is required so that new ideas and different filters can be utilized to analyze and dismantle the dilemma at hand so that plausible solution can be zeroed down. Service Innovation stands for restructuring the entire approach of going about a defined problem statement and finding optimal solution for it (Coelho & Henseler,2012).

The environment at a workplace can shape the behavior of an employee and impact his/her working. The establishment of a relationship and trust amongst the employee and the leader can be proportionate and improve the performance of the employee if proper guidance and motivation is extended. Also, the knowledge sharing starts to take place which in turn enhances the learning and application of the fundamental being directed to the employee. All of this helps the organization to achieve its goals (Cabrera et al. 2006).

The crafting of the new way of providing services to the customers by tackling the problems being faced requires the updating of the knowledge with the latest trends and developments. If this is properly practiced, then the approach with which the services are extended to the customers can be reprogrammed and improved all of which enhances the experience for the end users (Cheng, 2011).

The camaraderie between the employer and the employee can lead to better working experience eventually giving the best experience to the customer which ultimately results in the achievement of the organizational goals. The interpersonal behavior can lead to the efficient exchange of information pertinent to the holistic development of and employee with which innovative ideas can be derived and the entire premise can be improved (Oke et al. 2013).

By creating an environment of learning and interaction the organization can achieve better performances and positive attitude from the employees by establishing a due process where the delegation of the responsibilities is taken care of.

In an organization, there are some long-term goals and some short terms goals both having their own set of importance and the attainment of both goals makes an organization rise in terms of its reputation in the market. The role of a transformational leaders becomes vital here since the leaders makes sure that accomplishment of both goals is done with respect to the employees' capabilities. The role of a leader is also important as the continuum of values in an organization is kept intact and define the culture that becomes the beacon for the organization giving a statement to its employees (Eisenbeiss et al. 2008).

The more the organization becomes knowledge driven the better the bonding between its employees and the leaders or managers flourishes. The dissemination of the knowledge from the top of the hierarchy to the lower level creates a good relationship amongst the employees and at the same time the information exchange takes place at regular interval. By the virtue of these interaction and exchange of information the periodic targets of the organization keep on completing. The overall development of an employee in terms of the learning and behavior also enhances (Jaiswal et al. 2015).

In an organization, there can be different employees with different style of thinking and approaching a problem or defining these diverse people and their proclivity can be used in tailoring the new ways and techniques to solve a problem or state a way of accomplishing goals for the organization. The pre-conceived notion that are there in an employee prior joining the organization or even teams in which they work can be often detrimental for the completion of a project by fostering an Innovative Climate these impediments can be eradicated and the end results for the organization and the employee's personal development can be achieved efficiently (Hsu & Fan, 2010)

RESEARCH METHODOLOGY

Sample and Data Collection

For our study, we had a total of 256 respondents who participated in filling the surveys and providing their insights on the topics. These respondents came from diverse industry background each providing their unique experience to add value to the study. Out of all the respondents 64% were Male and 36% were Female. Also, 85% of the respondents came from the Private organization and the rest were from Public and Not for Profit Organizations. The mean of the sample was 25.7 years and mean time with organization was 5.1 years.

Results and Findings

The overall exploratory power of the model was 58.5% which is fair. The mean scores for Knowledge Sharing, Knowledge Donating and Service Innovation Behavior were 3.69, 3.14 and 3.762 respectively. Service Innovation was the most important aspect for the respondents followed by Knowledge Sharing with a mean score of 3.69

The Co-Relation for the different factors such as Service Innovation - Innovation Climate, Innovation Climate – Knowledge Sharing, Transformational Leadership and Knowledge Donating were found out. Out of which the strongest Co-Relation value was for Transformational Leadership and Innovation Climate with a Co- Relation score of 68.5% and the second most strong co relation score was for Transformational Leadership and Service Innovation Climate with 63.8%.

With Service innovation as the Dependent Variable and Knowledge Sharing, Knowledge Donating and Transformational Leadership as the Independent Variable. The data based on the responses received from the respondents we have deduced a regression equation for the model.

Service Innovation = 0.387 + 0.458 Knowledge Sharing + 0.015 Knowledge Donating + 0.226 Transformational Leadership + 0.240 Innovation Climate

Where 0.387 is the intercept for the regression equation. The equation also shows that with one unit increase in Service Innovation there will be 0.458 units increase in the knowledge sharing and 0.015 units increase in the Knowledge Donating. With a unit increase in the Service Innovation there will be an increase of 0.226 units

Table 1. Descriptive Statistics

	Mean	Std. Deviation	N
KnowledgeSharing	3.6977	.75956	256
KnowledgeDonating	3.1445	.82152	256
EmployeeServiceInnovativeBehavior	3.7624	.74350	256
TransformationalLeadership	3.6616	.68169	256
InnovationClimate	3.3647	.59446	256

in Transformational Leadership and an increase of 0.240 units in the Innovation Climate respectively.

Overall the model for the study is a good fit model with all the statistical value within the accepted range and the results are validated sans any fallacies.

CONCLUSION

Overall as per the analysis the importance of a conducive environment of knowledge sharing and effective communication between a leader and an employee is an absolute must to have in an organization. The more the organization interacts within itself more is the trust and mutual respects gets instilled causing the organization to become a learning organization which helps it to achieve its goals effectively and efficiently. The role of a leader in the organization is indispensable and a transformational leader acts as a catalyst in shaping the employees as per the organization needs and culture while in the process enhances the employees as professionals and individuals both.

REFERENCES

Cabrera, A., Collins, W. C., & Salgado, J. F. (2006). Determinants of individual engagement in knowledge sharing. *International Journal of Human Resource Management*, *17*(2), 245–264. doi:10.1080/09585190500404614

Cheng, J. H. (2011). Inter-organizational relationships and knowledge sharing in green supply chains—Moderating by relational benefits and guanxi. *Transportation Research Part E, Logistics and Transportation Review*, *47*(6), 837–849. doi:10.1016/j.tre.2010.12.008

Coelho, P. S., & Henseler, J. (2012). Creating customer loyalty through service customization. *European Journal of Marketing*, *46*(3/4), 331–356. doi:10.1108/03090561211202503

Eisenbeiss, S. A., van Knippenberg, D., & Boerner, S. (2008). Transformational leadership and team innovation: Integrating team climate principles. *The Journal of Applied Psychology*, *93*(6), 1438–1446. doi:10.1037/a0012716 PMID:19025260

Harrison, B., Kelley, M. R., & Gant, J. (1996). Innovative firm behavior and local milieu: Exploring the intersection of agglomeration, firm effects, and technological change. *Economic Geography*, *72*(3), 233–258. doi:10.2307/144400

Hsu, M. L., & Fan, H. L. (2010). Organizational innovation climate and creative outcomes: Exploring the moderating effect of time pressure. *Creativity Research Journal*, *22*(4), 378–386. doi:10.1080/10400419.2010.523400

Jaiswal, N. K., & Dhar, R. L. (2015). Transformational leadership, innovation climate, creative self-efficacy and employee creativity: A multilevel study. *International Journal of Hospitality Management*, *51*, 30–41. doi:10.1016/j.ijhm.2015.07.002

Oke, A., Prajogo, D. I., & Jayaram, J. (2013). Strengthening the innovation chain: The role of internal innovation climate and strategic relationships with supply chain partners. *The Journal of Supply Chain Management*, *49*(4), 43–58. doi:10.1111/jscm.12031

Chapter 6
Role of TQM in Sustained Business Performance in Indian Automotive Supply Chain

Sanjiv Narula
BML Munjal University, India

Satwinder Pal
Hero Moto Corp, India

Vinay Saini
Hero Moto Corp, India

Prabhat Saxena
Hero MotoCorp, India

Ajay Goyal
Hero Moto Corp, India

Mohit Yadav
BML Munjal University, India

ABSTRACT

This chapter creates a place in which TQM (total quality management) differs from business sustainability. Management can focus themselves more accurately when they understand the missing link between these two aspects. It also helps to reduce and eliminate certain wastes related to cost and efficiency and helps to produce better quality with minimum waste. In this study, a TQM framework is developed

DOI: 10.4018/978-1-5225-4038-0.ch006

Copyright © 2018, IGI Global. Copying or distributing in print or electronic forms without written permission of IGI Global is prohibited.

according to a comprehensive literature review: primary data collection through a structured questionnaire and interview of performers/nonperformers at various levels in different organizations. Analysis of data is used to establish the relationship between attributes of TQM and business sustainability. TQM enhances the cost effectiveness while helping suppliers to produce enhanced quality to their customers and with minimum efforts and lesser rejection. Analysis of data is used to establish the relationship between attributes of TQM and cost effectiveness in an organization.

INTRODUCTION

TQM and Business Sustainability TQM Helps Organizations in

- Sustained improvement at world class level at least for ten years.
- Will be market leader in products and services that it provides worldwide.
- Evidence that improved results were due to quality improvement initiatives.
- Critical business process will at World Class level – bench mark for other organization.
- Vision of the future state is the mind-set –midterm, long term plans.
- Develop more aggressive targets for the future.

Purpose of the Project

Our Primary Objective of the research is to

- Identify the TQM Factors associated with Business Sustainability.
- How Organizations Sustain leadership.

Background

Today's Global Business Environment current scenario poses Challenge of Maintaining growth and market share (Figure 1)

Literature Review

Quality is the ability of a product or service to consistently meet or exceed customer expectations

Figure 1. Challenges in the market

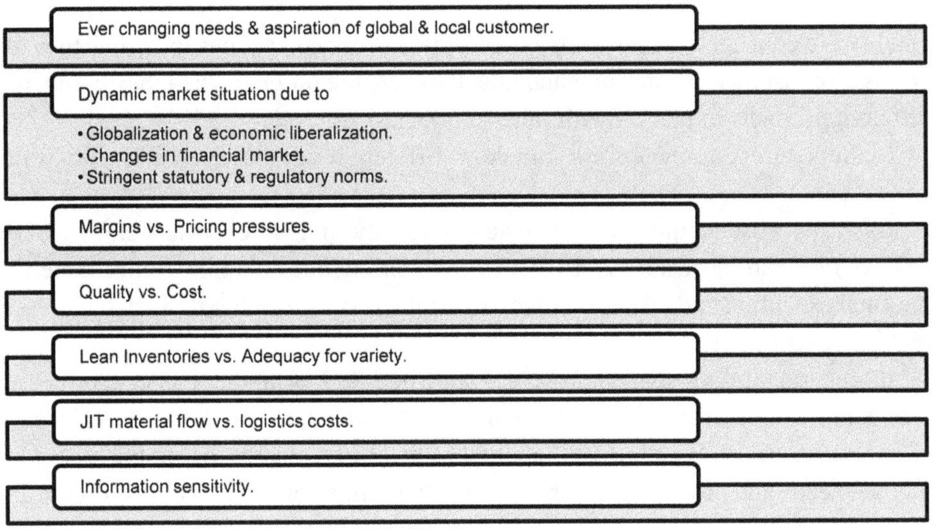

We can improve quality while adhering to the customers demand and we can also enhance appetite of our buyers towards our product, it will not just only leads to improve our production but also broaden our abilities while making more profit at the end. Now the main question arises that what are those parameters which are related to quality?

- Quality of a motor vehicle is to cost efficiently mobilize its customer.
- Quality of a clock is to show accurate time.
- Quality of a heater is to efficiently warm the environment with minimum cost and fuel efficiency.

We do not buy a product but we buy its function and value, its performance which based on the value of its usability and our need on how much extent it meets.

Quality is variable w.r.t. person to person and it is compared with attributes such as cost, efficiency, market and needs.

If you produce quality beyond customers need and want they will not appreciate you for that work they want their needs meet with certain level of economy, all they care about. But they will not tolerate anything below their need.

Quality means for front line operators too meets the SOP of the process operators first of all needs to understand what good quality production process is.

Transition of Quality Concept

Quality is a concept which has attributes related to consumers but somehow they all varies by consumer to consumer and how they rate the product when they compares different products in market with other products.

Manufacturer parameters are somehow different when they look at quality w.r.t. consumers.

Basically cost of quality is adjusted manually and by experience, The SOP follows the Plan-Do-Check-Act (PDCA), which includes planning work done till the final execution and after that checking of the results weather they matches with requirements or not.

Its general thinking that quality costs but when we look at the final economics of production sales and after warranty then we can easily understands that actually cost of quality saves much more cost than it takes, but there must be a fine line that how much it needs and how much it can be saved by putting certain processes (Figure 2).

Rule of 1:100 of Quality Cost

Quality and Cost

The total quality management (TQM) is the quality that allows relation between cost of conformance and cost of non- conformance, it also allows control production cost while super enhancing their productivity which can be seen in those companies those who has such quality measures

Like in Toyota (japan) and its worldwide subsidiaries they have total quality management and other manufacturers of other continents like in America FORD also has its own systems

Cost of quality = *Cost of conformance* + *Cost of non-conformance*

- "Cost of the conformance is that, which providing products or services as per required standards". Also it is the value of the amount to be sanctioned. It is called "Prevention & Appraisal costs".
- "Cost of the non-conf.ormance is the failure cost associated with process. This is also taken as failure cost which derived to fulfill failures that are generated due to low quality.

Figure 2. Stages of Rectification of Defects

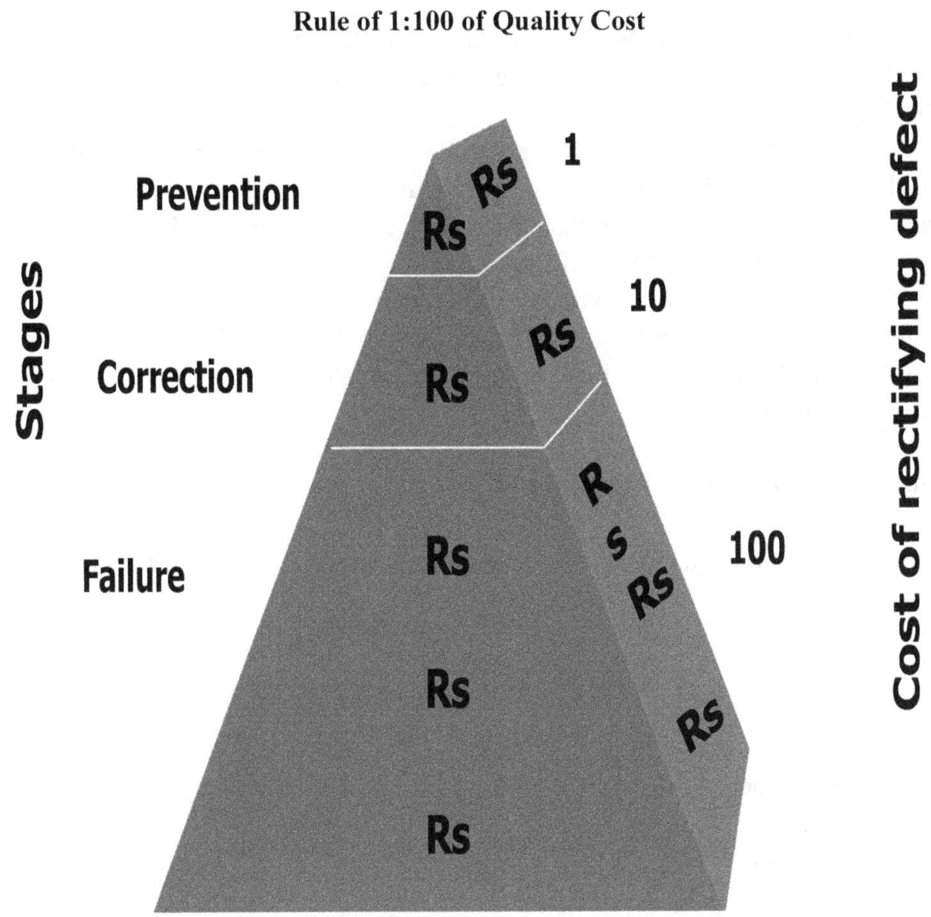

Quality and Profit Margin

With improved quality any company can charge improved profit margins that are also considered as payment from better quality aspects, good quality producers can charge much more premium amount which is derived from the value of their quality products.

Some companies like HONDA and TOYOTA have their policy to not charge quality gains in terms of high value gained from product selling price but they tends to make money from economies of scales and tend to conquer more and more market share of their respective markets.

Quality w.r.t. Inventory

When companies acquires 96% success and mere 4% remaining error but they still needs to analyze that what went wrong in order to stop or reduce that 4% error so that it may not rise in future.

In Toyota they see inventory as a curtain which hides 16 types of losses that can be rise when looking into management issues these losses are manageable only when tackled at right time and that can only be done if we have online production system not inventory FIFO or LIFO.

Again it is argued about inventory aspects that how much benefit it provides to company but the trade-off is that it may or may not be cost effective when traded with issues which compares loss due to lesser inventory and loss due to low cost of produced commodities.

Eight Dimensions of Quality

Eight dimensions of quality gives necessary framework that can be used for analysis of needs w.r.t. TQM

1. Performance
2. Features
3. Reliability
4. Conformance
5. Durability
6. Serviceability
7. Aesthetics
8. Perceived Quality

Performance

Performance is the basic objective that needs to quantify needs of user and producer. They are basically measurable products and can be attributed with necessary elements of needs and desires of user and producer.

It depends on industry to industry like in airlines and car manufacturing company performance are judged on different criteria.

Features

According to Garvin (1988, p-49) features are the bells and whistle of products, a second dimension of quality. He called this feature as secondary characteristics that supplement the products functioning. Example of this dimension can be the free drink offer in plane flight or automatic tuner in a color TV. He explained that some time it become very difficult to separate between the primary (Performance) and secondary characteristics.

Reliability

According to Clark (1996, p-43) reliability of a product is likelihood of malfunctioning or failing with in specific time period. According to Garvin (1988, p-49) it shows product failure in span of certain time. He further explains reliability as the mean time before failure or the failure rate per unit.

These are more often validated with durable goods

Conformance

According to Garvin (1988, p-49) "a related dimension of quality is conformance or degree to which a products design and operating characteristic meet pre-established standards". It is closely associated with process control and sampling techniques. Specification limits are matched against the inherent capabilities of a manufacturing process. They related to manufacturing approach of a company because it directly improves field quality gains.

Durability

According to Clark (1996, p-42) durability can be simply define as the life of a product which one might reasonably expect from it. Good example of that could be of Television, number of hours it would last. Now measuring the durability of the product include the ease of use, cost of maintenance and the cost of model. Similarly. Durability becomes the amount of use one gets from a product before it is replaced or broken down. It becomes more crucial when the product is not repairable or it contains heavy cost to regain its original position.

Serviceability

According to Garvin (1988, p-49) serviceability can be defined "as the speed of courtesy, competence and ease of repairs. Consumers are not only concerned about the breakdown of product but also about the elapsed time before service is restored".

Some time they complained about the repairing charges and some time they complain about frequently occurring problems. Companies increase their efforts on recognition of serviceability competitive potential and a desire to differentiate themselves through increased responsiveness Similarly Clark (1996, p-43) define serviceability very simply as speed and easy while we repair them

Aesthetics in Nature

According to Garvin (1988, p-49) Aesthetic and perceived quality are closely related to each other. Aesthetics could be defines as products look, feels, sounds, taste or smells. Aesthetics shows the outer combination of product attributes the best defines the consumer's needs & interests are the dimension of quality.

According to Garvin the brands most successful in establishing strong market position were the ones most clearly differentiated strong market position were the ones most clearly differentiated on these characteristics. Whereas, Clark define (1996, p-42) in very simple way as, the over appeal of the product that could be fit, feel, finish and smell.

Perceived Quality

According to Garvin (1988, p-49) Consumer always does not have complete information about the products and its features. They just come to know about the product that is shown by advertising.

Usually it tends to go far away when it is compared with the ground reality that what consumers are getting. Recently researches showed that the consumers often perceive country of manufacture as an indication of quality. Reputation is primary contribution to perceived quality.

It has two major segments

1. Quality that leads to drawing perfection
2. Conformance to that drawing's design

Quality that Leads to Drawing Perfection

According to Oakland (1995, p- 9)

quality of design is measure how well the product or service is designed to achieve the agreed requirement. The most important features of design with regard to achieving quality are the specification. Specifications must also exist at the internal supplier/ customer interfaces if one is pursue company-wide quality.

It is not just enough that marketing department of organization explain the wants and demand of customers, that marketing department of organization explain the wants and demand of customers.

Conformance to that Drawing's Design

According to Oakland (1995, p-10)

the quality of conformance defines the extent to which the service or product achieve the quality of design. He explains that what the customer will receive will be confirmed to design-to-design and operating cost is tied firmly to the level of conformance achieved. A high level of inspection or checking at the end is often indicative of attempts to inspect in quality.

An important part of setting the initial requirement for conformance, however is meeting all the design and operating characteristics that customer want and its performance as specified by them. This will decrease the spiraling cost and viability as well.

Correlates of Quality

Price

Price may have difference have more then one meaning. People think about price negatively. They often relate the price to that they must want. People perceived higher price as the symbol of quality and prestige. If manager believe that perception and consumer purchase decision are positively correlated with price.

Therefore, for a company it becomes a mean of differentiating a product. Therefore, it may be or may be not perceived or actual quality is being measured and whether or not managers are using price as a mean of product differentiation.

Cost

There are different approaches concerning the cost and quality of products. According to first approach, quality and costs are positively related.

The different arises when it tackle with the basic attributes of

- Expenses
- Labor hours

- Construction
- Derivatives related to material
- Policies of companies
- Policies of the land

Need for the Culture That Brings Quality

In order to get high quality products the companies may be reluctant to change culture but it is the most basic need of the organization to change the perception towards quality when they look at their company culture.

It flows from top to bottom: CEO to operator, although it takes biggest effort to achieve this target but also it yields biggest results

It comprises of-

- Change in mentality of management
- Work style of middle management
- More SOP oriented approach of line engineers
- Bound parameters (poka-yoke) for workers

Competitive Advantage

Through the process of strengthening core competence, competitive advantage would be yielded. Competitive advantage based on management ability to combine technology and corporate production, so that the corporation will be able to adapt quickly enough to serve rapid changing of opportunities.

In order not to lose core competencies, company must aware of several issues such as failing to learn within an alliance, dependence on outsourcing, forging opportunities to establish competencies that are evolving in existing businesses, not taking advantage of economies of scale and scope in core products, advertently divest core competences.

Organization develops these strategies to have a favorable competition strategy in the industry. The main aim of this strategy is to have competitive and profitable position within industry competition. Porter and Millar describes 1985, P.12) Competitive strategies of firms depend upon its comparative position within the competitive industry. Profitability of the firm defines the situation of the firm whether company is below or average industry. The average performance of the firm in long run depends upon company sustainable advantage. Though a firm can do have number of strength and weakness but Porter defines a firm can have two fundamental types of competitive advantage, either it could be low cost or product differentiation. He further explains that cost advantage depends upon the stem of the industry structure. Porter calls these two strategies as a generic strategy. Both of these strategies adopt different route to competitive benefit. The differentiation strategies and cost leadership strategies seek to have competitive benefit in broad range of different type of industry segment. While focus strategies aim always cost benefit or differentiation .All these activities are called the process of adding values, called value chain process. Porter explains that values chain activities like-strategy, approach to implementing its strategy and underlying economics activities. Values chains of industry and difference among competitor's values chains are key source of differentiation. A values chains process of a company is combination of company primary and supportive activities. A primary activity are composed of inbound logistic, industry operations, outbound logistic, marketing, sales and finally services whereas the support activities are composed of firm infrastructure such as H R management, technological development, and procurement

Cost of the Leadership

Cost leadership derives more efficient way of the aspects which are related to adoption of design and production after that distribution to the market .

Usually companies have more scope when it comes to provide scope to operate in the industry, many time it does operate in related to industry as well. He explains that the source of cost advantage depends upon the structure of the organization. Those companies who achieved cost leadership are actually leaders in their segments.

At low prices relatively to its competitors translates into higher rate of return. This strategy focuses on cost reduction by produce large amount of production with economies of scales. The main theme of strategy is to produce low cost and made available to very large customer.

Data Collection

Following are the Different Solved Questionnaire's Values Filled by Experts

Lets have a set of pairwise comparison matrices. Below is given the Blank Questionnaire given to each respondents/ Experts for giving their rankings

Analysis

Value of each element of table column is then divided by the sum mentioned of the corresponding column. We got the below matrix shown in Table 5. For cross checking/verification purpose sum of each column is checked. It should be 1.

Figure 3. Analyzing factor table

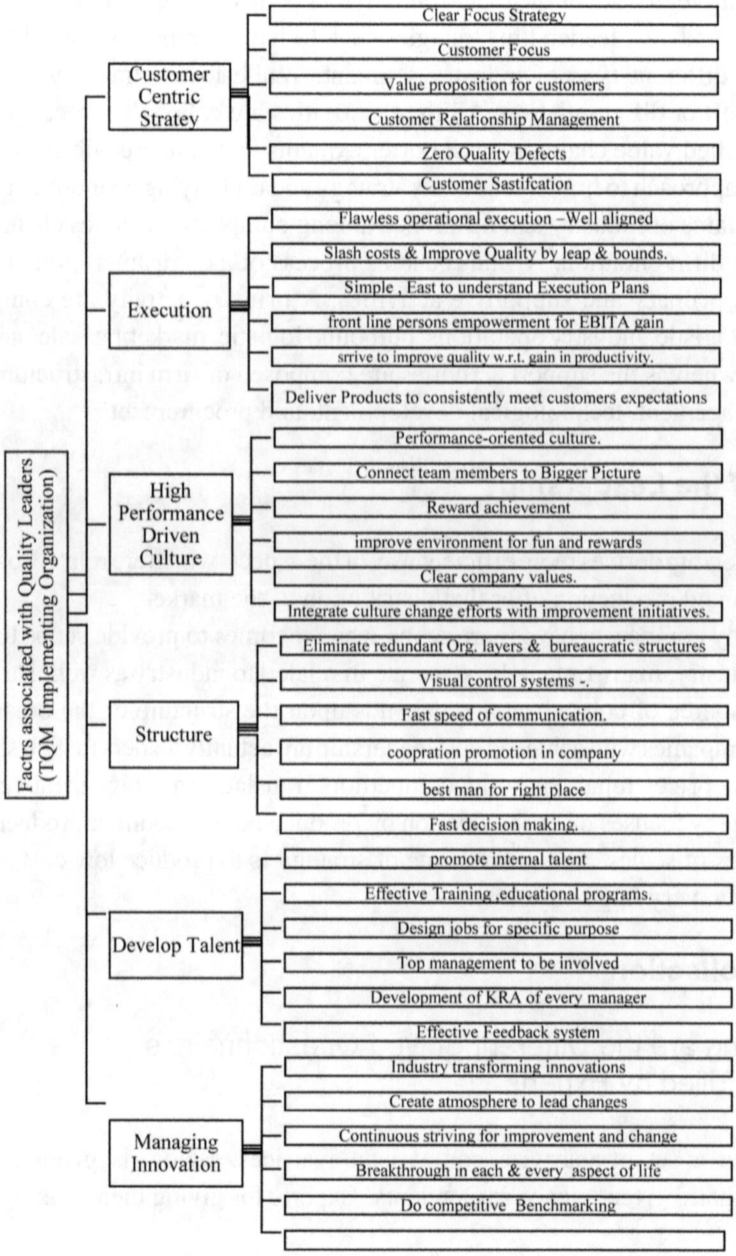

Table 1. Paired Comparison Matrix

	Main – Attributes	Extreme	Very Strong	Strong	Moderate	Equal	Moderate	Strong	Very Strong	Extreme	*Main- Attributes*
A1	Visionary Customer Driven Leadership Strategy	9	7	5	3	1	3	5	7	9	Execution
	Visionary Customer Driven Leadership Strategy										High Performance Driven Culture
	Visionary Customer Driven Leadership Strategy										Structure
	Visionary Customer Driven Leadership Strategy										Develop Talent
	Visionary Customer Driven Leadership Strategy										Managing Innovation
	Execution										High Performance Driven Culture
	Execution										Structure
	Execution										Develop Talent
	Execution										Managing Innovation
	High Performance Driven Culture										Structure
	High Performance Driven Culture										Develop Talent
	High Performance Driven Culture										Managing Innovation
	Structure										Develop Talent
	Structure										Managing Innovation
	Develop Talent										Managing Innovation

Table 2. Step 1-Geometric Mean

		Using Analytical Hierarchy Process:					
		Visionary Customer Driven Leadership Strategy	**Execution**	**High Performance Driven Culture**	**Structure**	**Develop Talent**	**Managing Innovation**
Geometric mean	Visionary Customer Driven Leadership Strategy	1.00	2.05	0.69	0.83	0.17	0.26
	Execution	0.49	1.00	2.24	3.56	0.27	0.37
	High Performance Driven Culture	1.44	0.45	1.00	2.17	1.62	0.60
	Structure	1.20	0.28	0.46	1.00	0.58	0.35
	Develop Talent	5.83	3.71	0.62	1.64	1.00	2.50
	Managing Innovation	3.87	2.69	1.66	2.84	0.55	1.00

CONCLUSION

As CI/RI is 0.1 which means the model is consistent

- Factor F5(Develop talent) is ranked no 1
- Factor F6(Managing Innovation) is ranked no 2

Data Analysis by De Metal Process

We have considered DEMATEL Process for finding those factors which are influencing other factors

Following are the different solved questionnaire's values filled by 12 experts

A DEMATEL "method is used to evaluate the causal relations among the criteria/factors. It has been widely accepted as one of the best tools to solve the cause and effect relationship among the evaluation criteria (Chiu et al., 2006, Tzeng et al., 2009, Wu and Lee, 2007, Lin and Tzeng, 2009). This method is applied to analyze and form the relationship of cause and effect among evaluation criteria or to derive interrelationship among factors (Lin and Tzeng, 2009). The procedure of DEMATEL method is presented below:

Table 3. Step 2 to 6- Normalization of Matrix & Weight Matrix

		Using Analytical Hierarchy Process:					
		Visionary Customer Driven Leadership Strategy	**Execution**	**High Performance Driven Culture**	**Structure**	**Develop Talent**	**Managing Innovation**
Step 2 Normalize Matrix	Visionary Customer Driven Leadership Strategy	0.07	0.20	0.10	0.07	0.04	0.05
	Execution	0.04	0.10	0.34	0.30	0.06	0.07
	High Performance Driven Culture	0.10	0.04	0.15	0.18	0.39	0.12
	Structure	0.09	0.03	0.07	0.08	0.14	0.07
	Develop Talent	0.42	0.36	0.09	0.14	0.24	0.49
	Managing Innovation	0.28	0.26	0.25	0.24	0.13	0.20
	For checking take sum	1	1	1	1	1	1
Step 3 Find out the Weight of Matrix	Visionary Customer Driven Leadership Strategy	0.09	Rank 5	8.98%			
	Execution	0.15	Rank 4	15.03%			
	High Performance Driven Culture	0.16	Rank 3	16.38%			
	Structure	0.08	Rank 6	7.89%			
	Develop Talent	0.29	Rank 1	29.10%			
	Managing Innovation	0.23	Rank 2	22.62%			
Step 4	Matrix multiplication of weight matrix with Main matrix is done. To find out ratio we divide corresponding elements of product matrix mentioned below with weightage mentioned in table	Product	Ratios				
		0.69	7.64				
		1.00	6.68				
		1.14	6.95				
		0.55	6.99				
		2.17	7.46				
		1.63	7.23				
Step 5	Consistency index (average of ratios - order of matrix)/ (order of matrix -1)		0.23				
Step 6	Random index(CI/ RI) CI/Random consistency for matrix size 8		0.10	RI is 1.24			CI/RI

Process Followed

Step 1: "Gather Experts' Opinion and Calculate the Average Matrix 'A':"

This is the same matrix which we made for AHP method. This matrix is made after gathering the expert's opinion & by averaging all the corresponding ranking of each pairwise comparison

Table 4. Expert Demographic property

Experts' Name	Code Name	Age	Qualification	Area of Expertise	Total Experience
Satwinder Pal Singh	A1	36	B.Tech(Mech)	Frame Plant	16 years
Sanjiv Narula	A2	36	B.Tech(Mech)	Supplier Quality	17 years
Suryakant	A3	39	B.Tech(Mech)	Engine Plant	20 years
Vinay Saini	A4	36	B.Tech(Mech)	Quality Assurance	17 years
Prabhat Saxena	A5	28	B.Tech(Mech)	Engine Assy	10 years
Ashwini Vohra	A6	39	M.Tech(Mech)	Project Engineering	18 years
Manmohan suri	A7	46	M.Tech(Mech)	Weld shop	25 years
Sachin Gupta	A8	38	M.Tech(Mech)	Quality Assurance	20 years
Vikas Sharma	A9	40	M.B.A	Business	21 years
Rajiv Gupta	A10	40	B.COM.	Business	24 years
Ajit Kapoor	A11	48	BA,LLB	Lawyer	25 years
Meenakshi	A12	35	MSC,I.T.	Teacher	14 years

Figure 4. The Process of the DEMATEL Method

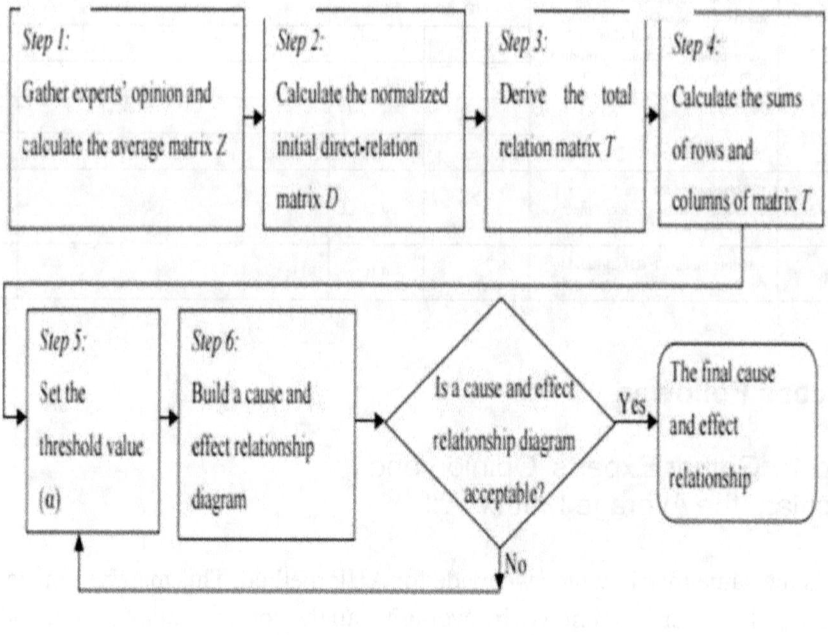

Table 5. Expert Opinion

Experts	**Influencing Score One Factor to Another**						
		F1	F2	F3	F4	F5	F6
A1	F1	0	1	0	1	0	1
	F2	4	0	1	3	0	1
	F3	4	4	0	3	0	1
	F4	3	1	4	0	1	1
	F5	4	4	4	4	0	4
	F6	4	3	3	4	1	0
A2	F1	0	1	4	1	0	1
	F2	1	0	1	4	0	4
	F3	3	4	0	3	3	1
	F4	2	1	4	0	1	4
	F5	1	4	1	4	0	4
	F6	1	1	1	4	1	0
A3	F1	0	1	0	1	0	4
	F2	4	0	1	2	4	1
	F3	4	4	0	3	4	1
	F4	3	1	4	0	1	1
	F5	4	4	4	4	0	4
	F6	4	3	3	4	1	0
A4	F1	0	1	2	1	0	4
	F2	4	0	1	1	3	1
	F3	4	4	0	1	0	4
	F4	3	1	4	0	1	1
	F5	4	4	4	4	0	4
	F6	4	3	3	4	1	0
A5	F1	0	1	2	1	0	1
	F2	4	0	1	4	4	1
	F3	4	3	0	1	0	1
	F4	3	1	4	0	1	1
	F5	4	4	4	4	0	4
	F6	4	3	3	4	1	0
A6	F1	0	1	4	4	0	2
	F2	4	0	1	4	3	1
	F3	4	4	0	2	3	1
	F4	1	4	0	0	1	1
	F5	2	2	4	4	0	4
	F6	4	2	2	4	1	0

continued on following page

Table 5. Continued

A7	F1	0	1	0	1	3	1
	F2	4	0	1	3	0	1
	F3	4	4	0	4	3	1
	F4	3	1	4	0	1	1
	F5	4	4	4	4	0	4
	F6	4	3	3	4	1	0
A8	F1	0	1	0	1	2	1
	F2	4	0	1	3	0	1
	F3	4	4	0	4	0	1
	F4	3	1	4	0	1	1
	F5	4	4	4	4	0	4
	F6	4	3	3	4	1	0
A9	F1	0	1	0	1	0	3
	F2	4	0	1	1	4	1
	F3	4	4	0	3	0	2
	F4	3	1	4	0	1	1
	F5	4	4	4	4	0	4
	F6	4	3	3	4	1	0
A10	F1	0	1	0	1	0	4
	F2	4	0	1	4	0	1
	F3	4	4	0	3	0	4
	F4	3	1	4	0	1	1
	F5	4	4	4	4	0	4
	F6	4	3	3	4	1	0
A11	F1	0	1	0	1	0	1
	F2	4	0	1	1	0	4
	F3	4	4	0	3	0	1
	F4	3	1	4	0	1	1
	F5	4	4	4	4	0	4
	F6	4	4	3	4	1	0
A12	F1	0	1	0	1	0	1
	F2	4	0	1	4	0	4
	F3	4	4	0	3	0	4
	F4	3	1	4	0	1	1
	F5	4	4	4	4	0	4
	F6	4	3	3	4	1	0

Table 6. Dematel Steps from 2 to 10

Steps	Factor	F1	F2	F3	F4	F5	F6	ROW TOTAL
Step 2	F1	0.000	1.000	1.000	1.250	0.417	2.000	**5.667**
	F2	3.750	0.000	1.000	2.833	1.500	1.750	**10.833**
	F3	3.917	3.917	0.000	2.750	1.083	1.833	**13.500**
	F4	2.750	1.250	3.667	0.000	1.000	1.250	**9.917**
	F5	3.583	3.833	3.750	4.000	0.000	4.000	**19.167**
	F6	3.750	2.833	2.750	4.000	1.000	0.000	**14.333**
STEP 3	COLOUMN TOTAL	17.750	12.833	12.167	14.833	5.000	10.833	
STEP 4	MAX COL	19.167	0.052					
STEP 5	MAX ROW	17.750	0.056					
STEP 6	MIN OF TWO		0.052					
STEP 7	F1	0.000	0.052	0.052	0.065	0.022	0.104	
MATRIX, D=M*A	F2	0.196	0.000	0.052	0.148	0.078	0.091	
	F3	0.204	0.204	0.000	0.143	0.057	0.096	
	F4	0.143	0.065	0.191	0.000	0.052	0.065	
	F5	0.187	0.200	0.196	0.209	0.000	0.209	
	F6	0.196	0.148	0.143	0.209	0.052	0.000	
STEP 8		F1	F2	F3	F4	F5	F6	
PREPARE I	F1	1.000	0.000	0.000	0.000	0.000	0.000	
	F2	0.000	1.000	0.000	0.000	0.000	0.000	
	F3	0.000	0.000	1.000	0.000	0.000	0.000	
	F4	0.000	0.000	0.000	1.000	0.000	0.000	
	F5	0.000	0.000	0.000	0.000	1.000	0.000	
	F6	0.000	0.000	0.000	0.000	0.000	1.000	
		F1	F2	F3	F4	F5	F6	
STEP 9	F1	1.000	-0.052	-0.052	-0.065	-0.022	-0.104	
IDENTITY MATRIX - D	F2	-0.196	1.000	-0.052	-0.148	-0.078	-0.091	
	F3	-0.204	-0.204	1.000	-0.143	-0.057	-0.096	
	F4	-0.143	-0.065	-0.191	1.000	-0.052	-0.065	

continued on following page

Table 6. Continued

	F5	-0.187	-0.200	-0.196	-0.209	1.000	-0.209	
	F6	-0.196	-0.148	-0.143	-0.209	-0.052	1.000	
Step 10: Prepare a Matrix by doing the Inverse of [matrix I – matrix D]								
		F1	F2	F3	F4	F5	F6	
	F1	1.118	0.131	0.130	0.157	0.059	0.164	
INVERSE OF I-D	F2	0.368	1.134	0.190	0.290	0.133	0.207	
select matrix, put equal sign, select ID matrix, then press ctrl shift enter	F3	0.420	0.340	1.160	0.320	0.130	0.234	
	F4	0.320	0.200	0.294	1.152	0.109	0.178	
	F5	0.520	0.424	0.414	0.471	1.113	0.396	
	F6	0.427	0.306	0.303	0.385	0.131	1.154	

Table 7. Dematel step 11

STEP 11		F1	F2	F3	F4	F5	F6
	F1	0.1178	0.1311	0.1302	0.1573	0.0587	0.1636
T=D*(INVERSE OF I-D)	F2	0.3676	0.1340	0.1895	0.2898	0.1334	0.2068
select matrix, put equal sign, mmult (d matrix & INVERSE OF I-D),then press ctrl shift enter	F3	0.4197	0.3404	0.1599	0.3201	0.1302	0.2339
	F4	0.3196	0.1999	0.2943	0.1524	0.1086	0.1776
	F5	0.5205	0.4235	0.4138	0.4708	0.1130	0.3955
	F6	0.4271	0.3060	0.3029	0.3846	0.1306	0.1538

- **Step 2:** "Calculate the sum of Columns CT of matrix A"
- **Step 3:** "Calculate sum of Rows RT of matrix A"
- **Step 4:** "Find out the inverse of maximum value of sum of Columns CT (Obtained in step 2)"
- **Step 5:** "Find out the inverse of maximum value of sum of Rows RT (Obtained in step 3) "
- **Step 6:**" Find out M- the minimum value obtained from Step 4 & 5"
- **Step 7**: "Prepare a Matrix D by multiplying each & every element by the value M = 0.2667"
- **Step 8**:" Prepare a Unit/Identity Matrix"
- **Step 9:** "Prepare a Matrix by subtraction of matrix I – matrix D"

Table 9. Scatter Diagram

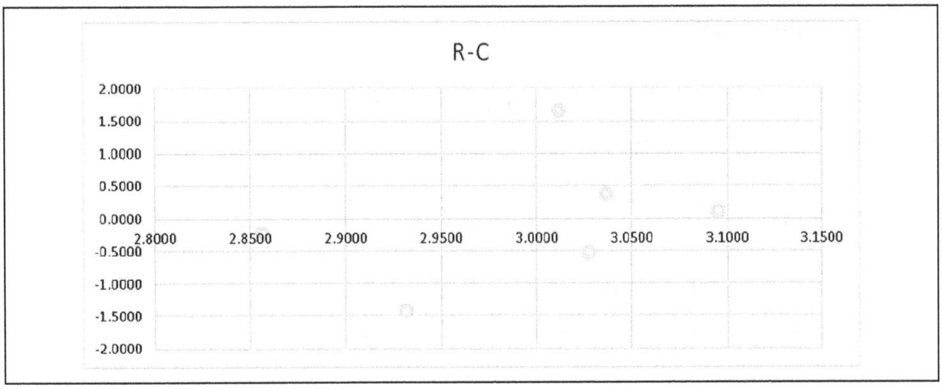

Table 8. Dematel step 12 to 17

	Step 13		Step 14	step 15	step 16	step 17	
step 12	sum of row	sum of col	R+C	R-C	Rank	Impact	
F1	0.7587	2.1723	2.9310	-1.413	6	effect	influenced by others
F2	1.3211	1.5350	2.8561	-0.213	4	effect	influenced by others
F3	1.6042	1.4907	3.0949	0.113	5	cause	influence to others
F4	1.2524	1.7750	3.0274	-0.522	3	effect	influenced by others
F5	2.3371	0.6745	3.0116	1.662	1	cause	influence to others
F6	1.7050	1.3312	3.0362	0.373	2	cause	influence to others

- **Step 10:**" Draw/find out Cause & Effect relationship based on RT-CT value. If RT-CT value is negative then the factor has Effect relationship other the factor is having Cause relationship."
- **Step 11:** Prepare a Matrix T by multiplying the Matrix D by the Inverse of [matrix I – matrix D]
- **Step 12,13,14,15:** Find out Sum of Rows RT, Sum of columns CT, RT +CT, RT-CT
- **Step 16 Step 16:** Rank/priorities the factors based on RT +CT value
- **Step 17:** Draw/find out Cause & Effect relationship based on RT-CT value. If RT-CT value is negative then the factor has Effect relationship other the factor is having Cause relationship.
- **Step 18:** Calculate Threshold value

Threshold value = Sum of the Sum of Columns CT/64= 0.2494

1. According to DEMATEL

Factor 3 (High Performance driven culture), 5 (Develop Talent), 6 (Managing Innovation) are influencing on other factors

2. According to AHP

Factor F5 (Develop talent) is ranked no 1
Factor F6 (Managing Innovation) is ranked no 2

- By Implementation of TQM research identifies 4 Primary elements and 2 secondary elements that correlates the corporation or firm's performance w.r.t. TQM.
- Winner in the field have mastered their attributes in all 4 primary and 2 secondary ones.
- Keep all the 4+2 elements alive, if one falls others will follow.
- The 4+2elemets are to be performed with their full efficiency to provide a winner.
- Consistence is most important to survive at the top.

Figure 5. Inter-relationships between various factors

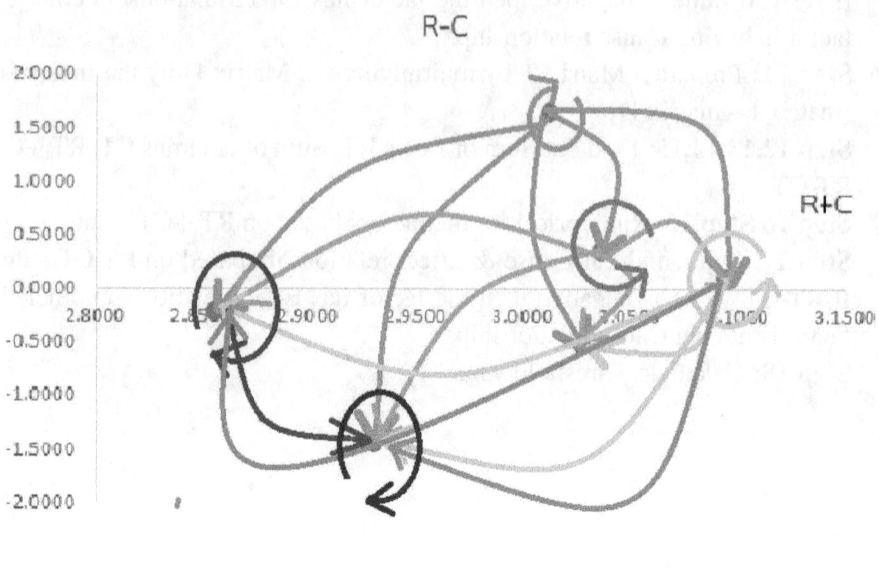

REFERENCES

Chiu, Y. J., Chen, H. C., Tzeng, G. H., & Shyu, J. Z. (2006). Marketing strategy based on customer behaviour for the LCD-TV. *International Journal of Management and Decision Making, 7*(2-3), 143-165.

Clark, E. R., & Dubovec, J. (1994). *U.S. Patent No. 5,296,805*. Washington, DC: U.S. Patent and Trademark Office.

Garvin, D. A. (1988). *Managing quality: The strategic and competitive edge*. Simon and Schuster.

Lin, C. L., & Tzeng, G. H. (2009). A value-created system of science (technology) park by using DEMATEL. *Expert Systems with Applications, 36*(6), 9683–9697. doi:10.1016/j.eswa.2008.11.040

Oakland, J. S. (1995). *Total quality management: Text with cases*. London, U.K.: Butterworth–Heinemann.

Porter, M. E., & Millar, V. E. (1985). *How information gives you competitive advantage*. Academic Press.

Tseng, M. L. (2009). A causal and effect decision making model of service quality expectation using grey-fuzzy DEMATEL approach. *Expert Systems with Applications, 36*(4), 7738–7748. doi:10.1016/j.eswa.2008.09.011

Wu, W. W., & Lee, Y. T. (2007). Developing global managers' competencies using the fuzzy DEMATEL method. *Expert Systems with Applications, 32*(2), 499–507. doi:10.1016/j.eswa.2005.12.005

Chapter 7
People Need People:
A Study of Instrument FIRO-B

Teena Bharti
Indian Institute of Technology Roorkee, India

ABSTRACT

Relationships are an unavoidable part of life, and yet can be a prospective source of pressure at workplace or organizations. In organisations, performance, delivery, and efficiency are required, often from mere acquaintances. To perform better, individuals need to work on trust and a strong establishment of noble working connections. The fundamental interpersonal relations orientation-behavior (FIRO-B) instrument focuses on these needs, distinguishing the drivers basic to the practices that shape connections for people inside an association. This chapter, therefore, deals with various aspects of the interpersonal relationship and why there is a need to emphasize on these particular areas.

INTRODUCTION

The FIRO-B instrument was developed in the late 1950's by W. Schutz, measures practices determined by relational needs in 3 dimensions—Need for Inclusion, Need for Control, and Need for Affection—and discourses how these practices can influence one's communications with other individuals (Hammer & Schnell, 2000). The tool depicts the communication of these 3 classes of relational needs along with two measurements: expressed and wanted. This instrument repairs broken connections/ relationships and takes good, useful and functional connections to a more elevated amount. The key opens the potential of work environment collaborations. Notwithstanding his own particular perceptions of gathering conduct, Schutz was impacted by the works of Fromm, Adorno, Freud, Jung and others.

DOI: 10.4018/978-1-5225-4038-0.ch007

Copyright © 2018, IGI Global. Copying or distributing in print or electronic forms without written permission of IGI Global is prohibited.

He formulated the Fundamental Interpersonal Relationship Orientation-Behaviour theory to help in the comprehension and anticipation of how selected military groups would cooperate. To build up the FIRO-B hypothesis, he started with the preface that "individuals require individuals." He utilized the phrase relational to show any collaboration, envisioned or genuine, happening between or among individuals. Also, he utilized the phrase need to depict a psychological situation that, if not fulfilled or satisfied, prompts a situation of nervousness or uneasiness.

BACKGROUND

In 1744, the word "relationship" first came into existence, but was not applied "specifically to romantic or sexual relationships" until 1944. On the other hand, *Interpersonal relationship* is a close and strong connection between individuals that may vary in duration from short to a persistent one. To be in an interpersonal relationship it is very important to share the common objective i.e. should have some commonality, trusting each other is of utmost importance otherwise it would feed the doubts and result in a conflict, being attached and transparency should be given due preference. This connection may be based on corollary, affection, cohesion, business relations, or some other type of collective commitment.

Levinger (1983) asserted that interpersonal relationships are dynamic in nature and keeps on changing continuously. He proposed a relationship model defining various stages of interpersonal relation. The different stages are depicted in figure 1 as shown below:

The various stages can be describes as under:

1. **Acquaintanceship:** It is the default stage of any relationship. Getting to be noticeably familiar relies upon past connections, physical nearness, early introductions, and an assortment of different variables. On the off chance that two individuals start to like each other, preceded with cooperations may prompt the following stage, yet colleague can proceed uncertainly. Another illustration is affiliation. In the context of workplace, this stage houses the people on the outskirts of an individual's social circle, the co-worker followed by pep- talks and inconsequential conversations.
2. **Buildup:** Amid the development stage, the two individuals included have an expanded level of trust and solace with each other. In an expert setting, this can appear as a counselor part, the beginnings of a mentorship, or as individuals from a group or council. The individual needs to put a lot of effort as it takes the relationship to next level.

3. **Continuation:** In this stage, there's an extending of trust and responsibility regarding the relationship, and a comparing increment in the measure of impact both individuals can result in.
   This is the perfect stage to have with your administrators, coordinate reports and tutors/mentees in the wake of working with them for a timeframe. This is the place you'll receive the rewards of better correspondence, enhanced efficiency and an expanded fulfillment with work. Expanded push to keep up the relationship at this level accompanies the expanded trust and impact. It doesn't need to be as consistent as in the development organize, yet it has to be important. Without that expansion in exertion, the relationship is probably going to begin decaying (arrange 4), prompting an arrival to the colleague or end stages.
4. **Deterioration:** Regardless of its negative essence, disintegration is regularly a characteristic and fundamental period of expert connections. Nobody works in a particular occupation everlastingly, and conditions every now and again prompt an adjustment in vicinity between individuals, or even an adjustment in the recurrence of contact. Without giving careful consideration to its upkeep, the relationship can return to a prior stage in the individual relationship continuum.
5. **Ending:** As with disintegration, there is no compelling reason to give the End stage's meanings a perception to impact your impression of this period of connections. It is greatly improbable that you will stay in contact with everybody you meet all through your whole expert vocation, thus end will be a characteristic stride in a number of your working environment connections.

Interpersonal relationships have their genesis in the milieu of cultural social and other inspirations. The framework could and might vary from family relations, friendship, marriage, relationships with colleagues or associates, workplaces, localities, and even at places of devotion. They might be regulated by custom, mutual agreement or law, and would be the basis of clusters or groups and humanity at large. Human is intrinsically social and is mainly shaped by his experiences with others. There are numerous outlooks to understand this inherent inspiration to relate with others.

In 1943, Maslow recommended that the need to belong was a key source of human motivation. He alleged that the need to belong was one of five human needs in the needs hierarchy, along with physiological needs, safety, self-esteem, and self-actualization. After physical or physiological and needs of safety are met an entity can then work to meet the need to belong and be adored or loved. According to his theory, if the first two needs are not satisfied, then an individual cannot completely adore or love other individual.

SOCIAL IDENTITY THEORY

In 1979, Tajfel anticipated that the groups which people were a part of or belonged to were an imperative source of self-esteem and pride irrespective of the type of group i.e. social class, family, clubs, football team etc. Groups give the members a sense of belonging to the social world: a sense of social identity.

THE NEED TO BELONG

Baumeister and Leary (1995) have reasoned that humans have a need to belong, which acts as the fundamental motivation. The *belongingness hypothesis* stated that human beings require to 'form and maintain strong, constant interpersonal relationships' and that this need 'is a powerful, vital, and extremely pervasive motivation'. According to the researchers, humans therefore have an innate need both to affiliate – that is, to seek the company of others – and to develop and maintain a number of positive, longlasting and substantial interpersonal relations. This need can only be satisfied by frequent interaction with familiar people united with persistent caring. Since this need can be almost as compelling as a need for food, human existence is shaped by the necessity to provide belongingness.

Table 1 depicts the belongingness hypothesis (Baumeister & Leary 1995) is consistent with the following characteristics of humans as shown below:

Table 1. Characteristics of Belongingness hypothesis (Baumeister & Leary, 1995)

Title	Characteristics
Belongingness Hypothesis	1. People in all cultures form into groups; social bonds form very easily within any society.
	2. Bowlby (1969) suggested throughout life, people form attachments willingly and eagerly and resist breaking them.
	3. A great deal of human cognitive processing is devoted to abilities such as language and empathy with facilitate interpersonal relationships.
	4. Sherif *et al.*1961; Tajfel 1970 supported that demonstrate that humans form into groups and show group allegiance even when there are no obvious benefits
	5. Many of the strongest emotions people experience are concerned with human relations. People greatly enjoy belonging and being desired or needed but have a fear and dislike of being rejected. People experience happiness, elation and contentment when relationships are going healthy, and anxiety, loneliness, jealousy, grief and depression when they are not.
	6. Critchley *et al.* 2000; Berkman *et al.* 2000 suggested that people who lack belongingness have high levels of mental and physical illness as a result of lack of attachment in terms of well-being, adjustment, health and others.

THE NEED TO ATTACH

The developmental psychologists suggest that, because of the need of humans to form relationships in order to survive, the first specific relationship that an infant makes is very important in their later stage development. Schaffer (1996) established that this relationship is denoted as an *attachment,* which could be defined as a long-lasting, eloquent tie at emotional level to a specific individual. Also, Bowlby (1969) who put forward the Theory of Attachment summarized tendency to bond to one main person as *monotropy*, since the first or main attachment serves as an core model of working, which is the basis of an individual's expectation and direction regarding relations in later life, the consequences of not forming this crucial bond are liable to be very damaging. Nevertheless, despite specific criticism, there seems little doubt that attachments are crucial in a young child's life and that the nature of these attachments have long-term consequences.

People intrinsically enjoy the company of others, so mixing with friends and, even sometimes strangers, offers a positive experience. Harris *et al.* (2007) supported that Brain imaging studies show that the same regions of the brain are activated by simply interacting with other people as by other social rewards, indicating that individuals like to associate with other individuals merely for its own sake. And naturally, the desire to associate is affected by the particular individual with whom we are interacting or the specific situation, i.e. the desire to associate increases if the people and/or situation are interesting and fun.

Depending upon the uncertain, confusing or ambiguous circumstances individuals tend to seek guidance from others in order to respond appropriately in a given situation. Owing to stressful conditions, individuals try to ease or lessen anxiety levels by turning to compassionate people who might offer information as to how to deal with the situation. Also, people who are in a troubling situation often receive support and consideration from others.

On the other hand, there are certain situations in which an individual tend to compare himself with other individuals and association provides the means of doing this, often called as Social Comparison. In 1991, Buunk & Yperen founded that people who are uncertain about their marriage; especially if they are unhappy with it, like to discuss this with people in a similar situation, i.e. to make social comparisons. In 1954, Festinger suggested that people want to compare their own feelings and reactions with those of others in the same situation especially a fearful situation, known as *Social comparison theory*, which was later expanded by Suls & Wheeler (2000). Further, researchers argued that struggle or competition for attention is one of the most important things in a person's life and there are occasions in which an individual seek of the company of other individuals in order to get attention, appreciation or approval.

It is a common parlence without doubt people like to be respected and valued by society and their affiliates which act as a satisfying tool in accomplishing their ambitions and desires. Human being carry non-identical differential trait with different motives to satisfy. For example, If someone is diagnosed of having lung cancer he would seek an advice from people with identical suffering or experts in their aforesaid field i.e. oncology to provide information, reduce anxiety and mental support. Last family and friends also act as an emotional parapet in difficult times. Empathy, sympathy and social information gathering is bound to happen during the phase.

Human brain and its acquaintances are very volatile and dynamic variable which reacts as per its own information gathering and reaction postulated. This could be seen in the study conducted by Argyle (1994) which demonstrated that people are particularly keen to be with others under pleasant conditions as well as the threatening ones. Further, Fox's survey indicated that human beings prefer to be unaccompanied under certain unpleasant circumstances, such as when they are nervous and tense before a critical interview or have just failed a test, and under circumstances that require concentration, such as when they need to revise for an important test.

Research on affiliation has tended to concentrate mainly on artificial situations, usually stressful ones, in which the desire or otherwise to be with another person can be easily measured.

HISTORY OF FIRO-B

The Fundamental Interpersonal Relations Orientation–Behaviour (FIRO-B) instrument was created in the late 1950s by William Schutz, PhD. Schutz developed the FIRO-B theory to aid in the understanding and predicting of how high-performance military teams would work together. The basic assumption of schutz model believes that people get together in agroup and it is conclusively contained by 3 variables namely affection/openness, control and inclusion

Schutz developed an instrument of measurement that contains six scales of nine-item questions, and which became the version B, where B stands for Behavior. This technique was created to analyse how group members feel when it comes to inclusion, control, and affection/openness or to be able to get feedback from people in a group. Before going into intricacies of the topic lets study the thread bear the concepts attached to it.

WHAT ARE THE INTERPERSONAL NEEDS?

As per the research conducted by Schutz, developed FIRO-B instrument to assess in *interpersonal needs* the theory is way beyond the existing Maslow's theory and added the concepts of Inclusion, Control, and Affection citing, these 3 factors play a dominant role in strongly motivating the stake holders.

Inclusion, synonymous to Involvement, is about the need to belong. It is a human tendency to be recognized, appreciated, included across different circles of society; it could be namely a literary group, coffee house membership, library membership etc. This leads to strongly motivating the hidden personality traits of an individual. At times, it has been found that expressed inclusion is a very dominant player in personality development.

Control interchangeably known as influence, is a need of interpersonal relationship which triggers the individual's behaviour. It deals with an individual being incharge of something. It talks about how driven an individual is to outperform others and taking the sole responsibility. Expressed Control is the need to lead, provide structure, influence, and make the decisions. Whereas wanted Control deals with how much an individual want others to provide structure, lead, set the goals, etc.For example in a team an individual who influences, initiates and takes the responsibility is ought to reflect expressed control whereas the members who follow that individual are bound to show wanted control. The immediate and strong desire for opportunity and autonomy from obligation may restrain their adequacy in a relation.

Affection synonymous to connection is about individual to individual interaction and emotional ties between individuals. Wanted need for affection deals with how much closeness and warmth one needs from other individuals. Considering how regularly an individual reveals the emotions to people and that how eagerly an individual tune in to theirs. How vital is it for an individual to be ideal by others? On the other hand, Expressed Affection is about how willing is an individual to develop a warm and intimate relationship with the other individuals. In view of contrasts in this relational need, a few people might be seen as unapproachable, while others might be baffled in a relationship in light of the fact that the other individual doesn't acknowledge the profundity and force that they need and need.

WHAT IS THE INTERPERSONAL ORIENTATION?

Interpersonal orientation (IO) is generally defined as individual dissimilarities in inclination for social relation or interaction. The influence of Interpersonal Orientation, however, likely depends on the nature of frequency or complementarity within the interpersonal context.

UNDERSTANDING FIRO

FIRO or Fundamental Interpersonal Relationship Orientation is a well-established theory of relational or interpersonal necessities that claims to reason for both why and what of an individual's activities toward other individual. According to Schutz, all human beings possess three needs namely needs for inclusion, control, and affection, to a greater or lesser degree. In developing this theory, the premises or foundation was that "People need people." Therefore, the keyterm interpersonal indicated any interaction, imagined or real, stirring between individuals. The theory demonstrates the term need to define a psychological situation that, if not fulfilled, can land an individual into a situation of anxiety or discomfort.

The theory postulated that interpersonal needs could be clustered into 3 categories: Need for Inclusion, Need for Control, and Need for Affection and the FIRO-B model defined the interaction of these 3 types of interpersonal needs along with 2 magnitudes of behaviour: expressed and wanted.

The FIRO-B evaluation or assessment has a wide usage including the following areas:

- Leadership development
- Individual interpersonal effectiveness
- Team building
- Retention

Table 2 gives an overview of the characteristics of an individual associated with the three types of interpersonal needs as desired by an individual for his existence.

In 2000, Hammer & Schnell highlighted that the instrument measures behaviors driven by interpersonal needs and discourses how these behaviours can impact one's relations with other individuals. The FIRO-B model is built on the philosophy

Table 2. Characteristics associated with the three Interpersonal Needs

Inclusion	Control	Affection
Recognition	Authority	Consensus-Orientated
Distinction	Power	Private
Attention	Responsible	Empathetic
Participation	Influence	Sensitive
Involved	Directive	Affirming
Association	Managerial	Open
acknowledgement	Decisive	Closeness
Connection	Leader	Supportive
Belonging	Regulated	Warmth
Acceptance	Consistent	Faithfulness

that fulfillment of the above mentioned interpersonal needs works as motivation in individual's day to day life. In 1993, they highlighted that the instrument also processes the degree to which each of the above mentioned needs is wanted or expressed by an individual. Expressed needs refers to the behaviour that individuals exhibit towards others, whereas wanted needs refers to the behaviour individuals choose to have unveiled towards them by other individuals (Schutz, 1958). It also gives an idea of the overall needs (say Total Control) along with the total behaviours (say Total Wanted), and provides the total Need Score for Interpersonal Relationship.

Briefly defined FIRO Theory recognizes 3 basic needs that all individuals share: the need to feel noteworthy, proficient and affable. It recommends that these wants express themselves across 3 levels of human association or interaction: feelings, behavior and self-concept. Within every level there are 3 distinct areas of human concern: inclusion, control and openness or affection. Schutz (1958) signified that in order to attain a satisfying self-concept every individual seeks to negotiate just the exact expanse of inclusion, control and openness that they yearn to feel significant or noteworthy, proficient and affable and inturn feel good about them. The better the individuals genuinely feel about themselves, the more they like and feel unstinting and appropriately springy toward other individuals. This facilitates them to work better with other individuals and to achieve higher levels of contentment in every area of our work and life.

FIRO Theory Postulates That

- Feelings are driven by Self-concept,
- Behavior is driven by Feelings, and
- Results are driven by Behaviour.

The concept provides the groundwork for accepting and getting to know how to develop sustainable, high-trust and collective relations. Behaviour is driven by self-concept, which advances at the very existence of our being. The self-concept signifies how an individual feels about himself, which inturn reflects how he feel about others and as a result self-feelings relate to the interpersonal feeling level with the need to feel important, likable and competent.

CONCEPT OF SELF

How an individual feels about himself dictates the behaviour and inturn influences each and everyone around them. To be dynamic, fruitful, innovative, creative and ethical all evolve around the very existence. What motivates individual's conduct is vital for unbridling potential and productivity of human. Also, people relate to each other from the superficial or exterior layer of behaviour .That behaviour, conversely, is stirred by the present state of non-threat or threat experienced by the self-concept. The outside world perceives only the behaviour of individual but not the susceptibility an individual might be facing at the primary level. If the external behavior is demonstrating a practice of defense mechanism, (blaming, ridiculing, attacking or criticizing), then it is likely that the self-concept is feeling susceptible and their might be various external threats to oneself. This sense of threat activates an emotion of fear, causing an individual to activate his guards and a fear-response is demonstrated in our behaviour. Figure 2 helps in giving a better understanding of the concept of self as depicted under:

EVOLUTION

The FIRO theory and other associated philosophies developed over a period of time that have been discussed in numerous publications (Schutz, 1955, 1958, 1977, 1967, 1988, 1984). In 1976, the theory was successful tested on over six thousand individuals from the public school community. Later, it was applied to include the body of human, as the base for describing why people are selective and opts for a particular thing (Schutz, 1984). In 1984, Doherty & Colangelo used the theory to establish the major theories of therapy for families. After that, it has been utilised as the foundation for categorizing styles to policy-making and to outline a new method of making decisions, came to be known as **Concordance** (Schutz, 1987).

NEW MEASURE ASSOCIATED WITH FIRO

In 1955, Schutz introduced three new instruments later came to be known as Elements and constituted the second generation.

- **Element B:** Behavior is a degree of the extent of interpersonal behavior: Need for Inclusion, Need for Control, and Need for Openness primarily built to help unite clusters whose affiliates work well collected, that is, are compatible. Element B is a revision and apprising of the FIRO-B. While FIRO-B analyses only 6 aspects, Element B takes into account additional 12 measures which is being utilized by Human resource Professionals, Trainers, Coaches and Consultants use this highly reliable and validated instrument to identify the behavioral patterns of individuals, help people better understand

and interpret their own as well as others' behavior and create action plans. Figure 3 gives an overview of what Behaviour comprises of:

Table 3 demonstrates the six cell model being developed to understand FIRO-B. It is a copyright of Key Talent Partners ltd and is widely used to gain an insight into individual's behaviour.

CHANGES FROM AFFECTION TO OPENNESS

As described above, the FIRO theory suggested three areas for understanding human interaction. After putting years of research, Schutz found that the term "affection" was problematic.

- Empirically it was hard to differentiate affection behavior from affection feelings in constructing the tool (Schutz, 1977). The notion of affection refers predominantly to feelings rather than to behaviour.
- Consequently, "affection" was transformed to the indispensable behavioral element of affection, "openness." And later on the 3 dimensions of behavior then converted to inclusion, control, and openness.
- **Element F:** Feelings is a measure of the dimensions of interpersonal feelings. With respect to feelings, Element F examines the following constructs i.e. Competence Significance and Likability. Element F is a revision of FIRO-F. Figure 4 gives an overview of what Behaviour comprises of:
- **Element S:** Similarly, Self is a measure of the dimensions of the self-concept which comprises of Aliveness, Self-determination, Self-awareness, Self-competence Self-significance and Self-liking. Figure 5 gives an overview of what Behaviour comprises of:

Table 3. Six Cell Model (copyright key talent partners ltd)

Variables	Inclusion	Control	Affection
EXPRESSED BEHAVIOUR	**EXPRESSED INCLUSION** (I initiate, try to join a group to be with people).	**EXPRESSED CONTROL** (I try to influence others and seeks pleasure in organising them)	**EXPRESSED AFFECTION** (I feel comfortable in expressing personal feelings and gets close to people).
WANTED BEHAVIOUR	**wanted INCLUSION** (I want others to belong to me and initiate first).	**WANTED CONTROL** (I am comfortable when someone else tries to influence me and wants other to take the responsibility)	**WANTED AFFECTION** (I want others to share their feelings and be close to me and act warmly towards me).

IMPORTANCE OF INTERPERSONAL RELATIONSHIP AT WORKPLACE

Outside the nuclear family it is employment that provides for most people [a] social context and demonstrates in daily experience that 'no [person] is an island entire of itself', and that the purposes of a collectivity transcend the purposes of an individual. (Jahoda, 1982)

Interpersonal relations in the oganisations are an inspectable reality all those working in the context of any workplace. As specified by Jahoda (1982), in the context of relationship that employees find a social purpose. Researchers lean towards to primarily on the implications of *negative* interpersonal relations in organisations, on employee and organisational outcome/ achievement of desired goal. If a researcher analysis from employee viewpoint the studies invariably find that higher level of job dissatisfaction, intent to turnover negative mental and physical health are certain outcome which have caused by interpersonal interaction as aggression, incivility and social exclusion (Williams, 2001).

On the other hand, researchers emphasised that as negative interpersonal relations are somewhat related to unwanted or negative outcomes, similarly positive interpersonal relations can be associated with improved performance in the organisation and better productivity (Heaphy & Dutton, 2008). Positive relations inculcate positive attitude which helps an individual in achieving greater things and fulfill the aimed objective which on a larger canvas help in fulfilling the need for belongingness.

Baumeister and Leary (1995) postulated that need to belong acts as a catalyst in guiding an individual's involuntary and voluntary thoughts, behaviors and emotions. Further, he added that primarily two criteria should be met i.e. the interactions or relations must be regular and non-aversive and secondly, they must ensure a long-lasting and stable relationship, in order to fulfill the need to belongingness. Therefore, the organisations or workplace nurtures the development of regular interactions and persistent relations.

The need to belong provides an integrative structure on positive interpersonal relations at workplace and therefore it is very important to develop a clear understanding of why relations are an indispensable part of any organisation. As illustrated by Heaphy and Dutton (2008), a connection involves the mindfulness of both the parties that must acknowledge that the interaction has already taken place and was of momentary nature. On the other hand, a relationship looks for stability and endurance. Therefore, both relationships and connections involve the sentience and involvement of the parties involved. Further, they added that appraisal of such an exposure is mandatory in order to experience a relation or establish a connection with the other individual.

OUTCOMES OF POSITIVE INTERPERSONAL RELATIONSHIP AT WORKPLACE

Cohen and Wills (1985) documented that being a part of any social system helps in reducing the stress levels in employees and further increase the productivity of an individual in an organisations. For example, in the TMX, if the leader is perceived to be a good listener then he is ought to harness employee social support, trust relationship and felling of belongingness (Alvesson & Sveningsson, 2003). Similarly, positive interpersonal relations with mentors have been linked with improved job-related outcomes, such as better salary, managerial raise (Allen et al., 2004) mobility of career (Scandura, 1992), rewards, recognition, and a chance to create a base of supremacy (Hunt & Michael, 1983).

Manniero (1989) advocated that informal relations at workplace also help in achieving positive job- related outcomes along with the personal outcomes. For example, when co-workers or team members are attracted towards each other it helps in developing a positive outlook and leads to better performance, commitment, team cohesion and decreases the intention to turnover (Berman et al., 2002; Feeley et al., 2008; Winstead et al., 1995; Riordan & Griffeth, 1995). Thus, workplace friendship helps in achieving better results at the organizational level. Further, Riach & Wilson, 2007 established that there has been a strong relation between workplace romances and the employee happiness, favourable work environment, psychological aids and improved health conditions of employees (Heaphy & Dutton, 2008).

Researchers believe that positive interpersonal relation also helps in employee identification (Dutton et al., 1994) which is associated with motivation, satisfaction, cohesion, inter- group conflict and compliance (Kramer, 1991). In addition, Liden et al., (2000) elucidated that positive interpersonal relations act as an antecedent to organizational commitment whereas Kostova and Roth (2003) supported that positive interpersonal relationship at workplace results in better team performance, as they encourage individual's behaviour that are intended to increase team efficiency and efficacy.

FOSTERING POSITIVE INTERPERSONAL RELATIONSHIPS AT WORK

As discussed earlier, positive interpersonal relations at workplace fulfills the individual's need to be in the right place (Baumeister & Leary, 1995). Thus, there arises a need to understand the organizational level effect of such relations.

ORGANIZATIONAL LEVEL EFFECTS

Baumeister and Leary (1995) propounded that the workplaces in which personalities are employed forms the prevailing background of their interactions in the workplace. For some, the working environment might be a particularly stable setting, in which they can hope to see recognizable faces in unsurprising spots at unsurprising circumstances; consequently, this area will concentrate on how associations can guarantee that these steady connections are non-aversive. At a large scale level, the association itself might be seen as strong.

Wallace et al., (2009) propagated that hierarchical sustenance or support i.e., representatives' observation that the association esteems their information and is worried for their prosperity (Eisenberger et al., 1986) directed the connection between test stressors (the unpleasant however possibly sensible requests put on workers) and representatives' part based execution (i.e., representatives' execution obligations). Notwithstanding the provision offered by the association, representatives' view of their "fit" with their association may likewise advance positive results. Kristof-Brown et al., (2005) meta-diagnostically inspected the impacts of individual association fit on individual results where individual association fit is characterized by the similarity between the individual and the association, with respect to esteem comparability (Kristof, 1996; Chatman, 1989; Verquer et al., 2003) or objective consistency (Witt & Nye, 1992). Along these lines, it has been clearly established that more unequivocally people see that they are "suitable" for their association, the better their job-related results appear to be.

Schneider & Reichers (1983) demonstrated that an association's atmosphere is its recognizable practices and methods. Further, researchers argued that the advancement of an atmosphere of equality and justice, or respectful and reasonable correspondence among representatives might encourage constructive relational connections or relations (George & Bettenhausen 1990; Heaphy & Dutton, 2008). Also, Baker & Dutton (2007) proposed that these practices, which might incorporate coordinating new workers with a coach or mentor, help representatives in understanding the suitable standards of collaboration, which can encourage positive associations. In the context of socialization process, Chao et al.(1992) found that representatives with guides will probably set up fruitful and fulfilling work connections than their non-coached associates. Bies and Moag (1986) identified 4 criteria for communication i.e. communications must be perceived as true, appropriate, respectful and justification should be provided if necessary. The study concluded that keeping in mind the requisites of communication in an organisation might help an employee in developing interpersonal relations and hence better performance.

Dutton and Heaphy (2003) contended that a pioneer's social mindfulness (i.e., his or her ability to see and respond to a representative's full of feeling state) will energize constructive associations on the grounds that such pioneers can help workers manage and repair relational associations. In fact, Postmes et al., (2001) contended that authoritative pioneers, as agents of administration, were all the more unequivocally identified with representatives' feeling of hierarchical having a place than were the workers' "casual and social-enthusiastic communications with associates and proximate partners".

Further, Heaphy and Dutton (2008) argued that front-runners who promote a mutual identity and interdependence among workers are better able to minimalize perceived dissimilarities between people, which should end in a stronger foundation for positive interactions at organisation. The minimalization of dissimilarities has important implications for diverse organizational work groups (i.e., work groups composed of individuals who vary in race, gender, age, ethnicity or other observable characteristics), which have become far more common in recent years. In general, there is evidence that individuals who perceive themselves to be not at all like their association and additionally partners have a tendency to be less disposed to relate to and focus on the association and more prone to pull back. Hence, the minimalization of perceived contrasts may help advance worker distinguishing proof and duty, and in this manner their feeling of having a place.

Cornelis et al., (2006) emphasized that the fairness followed by the leader's decision- making processes is related with the employee's relations along with their relations with others. On the other hand unfairness if followed would result in negative interpersonal relations in an organisation. Further, Tyler & Lind (1988; 1992) supported that when a pioneer treats an authoritative part reasonably, the pioneer is flagging his or her values to different individuals from the association and therefore, affects an essential part in empowering positive associations and sentiments of having a place (Tyler et al., 1996). Researchers argued that effective coordination in relations is encouraged by quality of communication as well as the relationship which also emphasizes on fostering mutual respect for an individual's skillset or competence that helps in creating a bond between the employees of organisation. Thus, when a leader focuses on procedural fairness, interactional justice, relational attentiveness, trust development, transformational leadership and quality of communication, a context is being created in which workers readily meet their need to belong.

DYADIC INTERPERSONAL RELATIONSHIPS

Dyadic relationship means the relationship between two individuals. George & Bettenhausen, 1990 established that organisations are made of individuals and the relations with each other and it is this relationship which determines the need to belong for every individual. Argyris (1996) proposed that working environment companionship gives an establishment whereupon beneficial hierarchical social frameworks can be created Levinger (1979) expressed that dyadic relationships have their genesis in Social exchange theory which propounds that individuals incur both rewards and cost from their interaction with other individuals. As indicated the theory, people might be roused to seek after a relationship when they see the prizes to exceed the expenses.

Kristof et al. (2005) analysed the supervisor- person fit and meta- analytically established that the relationship is being affected by the values (Krishnan, 2002), their objectives (Witt, 1998) and personality.

Kinships in the working environment may specifically fulfill a person's have to have a place, as these connections are relied upon to be non-aversive, because of the meaning of "fellowship", and also successive, stable, and persevering. As per Berman et al. (2002), working environment kinships are "nonexclusive work environment relationships that include common trust, responsibility, proportional loving and shared interests or qualities". They are deliberate connections in which individuals interface with each other as one of a kind people as opposed to as tradable part inhabitants (example director, associate) (Wright, 1984), and are characterized by a mix of the level of common concern and shared relationship past that was required by their hierarchical parts (Winstead et al., 1995).

Further, Randel & Ranft (2007) propagated that job facilitation motivation and relationship motivation help in establishing workplace relations which inturn might not satisfy th e individual's need to belong. Berman et al. (2002) in his study that a professional's view of both the expenses and rewards of work environment kinships and found that while administrators perceived expenses related with representative fellowships (e.g., an expanded potential for circumstances in which companion and business related interests struggle, political weakness, and stressed free judgment), they had a tendency to consider kinships to be critical and significant to their association (Rousseau, 1995).

Over a period of time the meaning of workplace had undergone change flat structures, cordial relations, greater load expectations which corresponds to increase in time investment (Turner et al., 2002). Also, Thau et al., (2007) operationalized having a place as the disparity between members' self-announced view of their real and their coveted social closeness with their associates being measured by Aron et al., (1992) to identify the perceived relationship analyzing the self and others. Further the instrument underwent change and Thau et al., focused on treating the other circle as their fellow workers. The difference between the two instruments helps in getting an index for belongingness.

Edwards and Peccei (2007) defined belongingness of workplace as the degree of an individual's relationship with his or her association or workplace. This operationalization is in accordance with Ashforth and Mael (1989), who termed one's feeling of belongingness with a specific classification of society or an association as "identification". Edwards and Peccei characterized authoritative recognizable proof as "a mental linkage between the individual and the association whereby the individual feels a profound, self-characterizing full of feeling and intellectual bond with the association as a social substance".

Thus, Relational connections at work favorably affect both individual and hierarchical factors. Several researchers contest that fellowships at work can improve singular representative demeanors, for example, work satisfaction, duty, engagement and perceived support from organisation (Cherniss, 1991; Morrision, 2009; Ellingwood, 2001; Riordan & Griffeth, 1995; Song & Olshfski, 2008; Robinson et al., 1998; Zagenczyk et al., 2010). Also, researchers (Anderson and Martin, 1995; Morrison, 2009; Fine et al., 1986; Song & Olshfski, 2008; Sias & Jablin, 1995;) added that a negative attitude if carried by an individual at workplace can hamper his growth and performance in an organisation. But if the employee starts discussing and sharing the reason for that particular attitude then the condition can be brought under control and the individual can continue to work in the similar manner.

In today's corporate world, there is a requirement for work to be done as speedy as could be allowed, and for this reason, working experts need better connection between each other. Proficient relations can be kept up by successful working environment correspondence and collaboration in an organisation. Relational connections steadily develop great group cooperation with different individuals. Then again, these connections may disintegrate when an individual leaves the gathering and quits being in touch (Seibert, 2010).

ISSUES RELATED TO INTERPERSONAL RELATIONSHIP

Though no one can deny the importance of interpersonal relationship in an individual's life, but there are various issues which proliferate as soon as a relation comes into existence be it the life at large or workplace. As researchers from psychological and organizational field have clearly indicated that due to the ease of data collection, cross- sectional survey, convenience sampling, self- report data and various other reasons the results might turn out to be something different if the above mentioned factors are not considered while conducting a study. Another major concern is that it is very difficult to obtain the field data as their lies a contrast in the top professionals and the external team of research.

Further while conducting a study in an organisations the researcher must align the items to be studied according to the temper of the organisation and make the authorities understand the significance of the study. Maintenance of cordial and harmonious relations is vital for the growth and survival of any organisation. Healthy relations result in augmented effectiveness and therefore, prosperity, decreased intent to turnover and other palpable benefits to the organization.

Also, the limitation of time restricts a researcher from obtaining more information than what is obtainable and hence the objective could not be accomplished. Perhaps, the main cause or source of poor organizational interpersonal relations leading to inefficiency and employee unrest is mental stress which might be proliferating because of the unhealthy and less number of interpersonal interactions from both management and employees.

Indeed, even in families there are contrasts of sentiment, misconception, contradictions, fight, conflicts imitate with others, who are all blood relations. Leaving family bond, the working environment is a business association where winning is the prime concern both for the business and workers. In each work setting, multifaceted connections exist with the association of entrepreneur, chief or prompt manager and representatives of that association. It is extremely basic that at whatever point contrasts of supposition emerge, one ordinarily adheres on to one's perspective dismissing or overlooking the other people's perspective. When it comes to the other person then individual's start expecting that he should stand out and thus the role of interpersonal relationship becomes important from an organizational point of view.

While working in an organisation an individual has to manage conflicts efficiently and should understand the causes of conflict in the organisation. With its huge collection of dynamic and interpersonal connections, the working environment is a productive ground for strife. Perceiving and managing the variables that may conceivably prompt conflicts can positively affect working environment agreement and profitability. Conflicts in the organisations are ignited by the clash of goals, needs, values and interests between two or more workers and particularly about the consequence or outcome. Its sources can include a variety of interpersonal, organizational or external factors. Interpersonal Conflict between employees is perhaps the most palpable one which takes place in every organisation and needs to be catered for its smooth functioning.

Workplaces are considered to be melting pots of ages, personality types, ethnicity and race to which an individual belongs, thus, leaving a room for interpersonal clashes and conflicts between incompatible personality types. This includes gender, sexual discrimination racial, or harassment under its umbrella. To manage such conflicts organisations adopt various methods or strategies like interviews, confidential surveys and discussion groups to mitigate the situation nd arrive a solution which could help the organisation to grow. For example the tension between a project lead and the members of team are heightened by the differences in the way they perceive their responsibilities. There arises a situation which is potential for interpersonal conflict in the allocation of the roles, responsibilities, workload not undermining the fact that all the above mentioned factors lead to burnout, resentment as well as unnecessary argument and competition. The organisations, therefore, have started adopting open way communication and nurturing an atmosphere of positive interpersonal relationship which could make an organisation a productive workplace relying on the accommodating relations of each of its members. If the organisations undermine the interest of their employees and discourages them to air their opinion, views and feelings then the interpersonal conflict would be shifted to the subconscious and would grow, leading to the development of feelings of misunderstanding, resentment and dissatisfaction.

Thus, it can be derived that conflicts are normally a part of our personal and professional lives leading to distort the interpersonal relationships and therefore affecting the work environment, reducing efficiency and productivity. However, they can be harnessed to reroute the negative outcome into positive ones which needs that the organisations must recognize, communicate and make the necessary changes such that the conflicts can strengthen the relations at workplace in order to create a healthy and supportive climate.

Further, FIRO-B is not a very comprehensive instrument reason being it analysis the behaviour and not the personality of an individual. It doesn't make an organisation to have perceptions that whether the individual is good or bad for the workplace. It does not measure the career interests, expectations, objectives and achievements of an individual owing to which their might occur a role conflict. The behaviour of an individual is determined by the interaction of personality and the needs and therefore, is very dynamic in nature.

FUTURE RESEARCH DIRECTIONS

Interpersonal relationships are very dynamic in nature and are the essence of our existence Productivity is the conventional road to growth which occurs mainly on account of harmonious interpersonal relations. Healthy interpersonal relations in a business endeavor are based on our exposure to the world and the attitude towards it which prompt advance and strength. In a nation like India, where the educational level of the general population is still at the base level, and to the center, at an alarming stage, is at a disturbing level for sure. By and large, education assumes an indispensable part in the getting down to association of the mental constructs and the personality of the general population such that any attempt with most extreme participation would bring about productive outcomes for the organisation.

The chapter highlighted the importance of positive relationships in an organisation such that they are not only beneficial or fruitful for the organisation but also help in overall development of individual employees. Several researchers (Bernstein, 2003; Dutton & Glynn, 2008;; Dutton et al., 2006) conducted a study on a research group at the University of Michhigan and established that the mission statement of an organisation not only energize and transform the organisation but also assures the importance of interpersonal relationship (Center for Positive Organizational Scholarship (POS)). While a greater emphasis has been laid on the interpersonal relations in an organisation, there is a dearth of literature available and various avenues are still unexplored so there arises a need of future study. For instance, the research available in the social categorization and demography literatures demonstrated that personnel compare their own demographical characteristics (e.g., sex, race) with those of the other members of the group they are a part of, for example in a team the members have to tendency to outperform each other (Chattopadhyay et al., 2004) which leads to self- categorization and have negative consequences such as sour relationships at workplace, reduced productivity and hampers the organizational citizenship behaviour (Chattopadhyay, 1999).

Further, Williams et al., (2007) supported that the study on personality and social- categorization highlighted the effects of diversity on positive relationship at workplace whereas it did not take into account the multi-linguality as well the work-life balance and the role of optimism in sustaining or developing long- enduring relationships in the organisation. In line, Chattopadhyay, et al., (2008) indicated that dissimilarities among the employees had greater effect on the efficiency and productivity in collocated groups as compared to the groups which are distributed but outlooked the location, environment and cultural perspective of organisation.

In addition to the previous researches related with the workplace interrelationship and the gender diversity, there is a lacuna in the context that research should also analyse how the individual's need to belong varies keeping in mid the cultural aspect in context of India. This might help the organisations in getting accustomed to the cultural specifications and the needs of the employees leading to harnessing human capital. Also, the methods in which organizations may effectively meet the need to belong of employees when the job description requires them to work in seclusion and/or when they have to be engaged with large member virtual teams (Fiol & O'Connor, 2005) is yet to be examined at length.

Another intricacy of the interpersonal relations in an organisation is that the need to belong and affection somewhat seems to be blurred in an organizational setting and thus needs to be clearly stated and mentioned keeping in mind the safety and security of female employees in the organisation. Another highlighted domain is that there are individuals those who prefer to be alone and hence do not have a need to belong (Masterson and Stamper, 2003) which again leads to conflict if working in a team. Therefore, an employee- job fit should be taken care of in an organisation for its sustainability and growth.

CONCLUSION

Human resources are made up of living human beings. They want freedom of thought, of speech, of movement, of expression, etc to reach their maximum and thus outperforming their capacity. When organisations treat them as objects, encroach on their expectations, conflicts burnouts, and tensions come into the picture which effects the work environment. The organisations are more interested in getting to know the predictors of negative interpersonal relationships as compared to the positive relations reason being the intimidation of such situation needs to have a plan to tackle and keeps going the regular business or activity of organisation. The above view has been supported by Atkinson (2000) emphasizing that we understand normality by getting to know the meaning of abnormality. In brief, the requirement for Inclusion indicates the amount to which people need social communications and relationship with others. The requirement for Control Inclusion indicates the extent to which people need to lead and impact others and in addition the degree to which they like to be affected and driven (Hammer and Schnell, 2000). The requirement for Affection alludes to the passionate associations amongst individuals and the degree to which people try to set up associations with others, especially one-on-one connections (Waterman and Rogers, 1996). Therefore, to determine an individual's behaviour an insight must be gained into what is needed by an individual and how it supports his preferences for life. Thus, the chapter concludes that human, being a social animal highly incorporates interpersonal relationship in their life and defines it the soul basis of existence.

REFERENCES

Allen, T. D., Eby, L. T., Poteet, M. L., Lentz, E., & Lima, L. (2004). *Career benefits associated with mentoring for protégés: A meta-analysis*. Academic Press.

Anderson, C. M., & Martin, M. M. (1995). Why employees speak to coworkers and bosses: Motives, gender, and organizational satisfaction. *The Journal of Business Communication, 32*(3), 249-265.

Aron, A., Aron, E. N., & Smollan, D. (1992). Inclusion of Other in the Self Scale and the structure of interpersonal closeness. *Journal of Personality and Social Psychology, 63*(4), 596–612. doi:10.1037/0022-3514.63.4.596

Ashforth, B. E., & Mael, F. (1989). Social identity theory and the organization. *Academy of Management Review, 14*(1), 20–39.

Baker, W., & Dutton, J. E. (2007). *Enabling Positive Social Capital in Organizations*. Academic Press.

Baumeister, R. F., & Leary, M. R. (1995). The need to belong: Desire for interpersonal attachments as a fundamental human motivation. *Psychological Bulletin, 117*(3), 497–529. doi:10.1037/0033-2909.117.3.497 PMID:7777651

Berman, E. M., West, J. P., & Richter, M. N. Jr. (2002). Workplace relations: Friendship patterns and consequences (according to managers). *Public Administration Review, 62*(2), 217–230. doi:10.1111/0033-3352.00172

Bernstein, B. (2003). *Class, codes and control: Applied studies towards a sociology of language* (Vol. 2). Psychology Press.

Bies, R. J., Moag, J. F., Lewicki, R. J., Sheppard, B. H., & Bazerman, M. H. (1986). *Research on negotiations in organizations*. Academic Press.

Bowlby, J. (1969). *Attachment and loss* (Vol. 3). Random House.

Furman, W., & Buhrmester, D. (2009). Methods and measures: The network of relationships inventory: Behavioral systems version. *International Journal of Behavioral Development, 33*, 470–478.

Buunk, B. P., & Van Yperen, N. W. (1991). Referential comparisons, relational comparisons, and exchange orientation: Their relation to marital satisfaction. *Personality and Social Psychology Bulletin, 17*(6), 709–717. doi:10.1177/0146167291176015

Chao, G. T., Walz, P., & Gardner, P. D. (1992). Formal and informal mentorships: A comparison on mentoring functions and contrast with nonmentored counterparts. *Personnel Psychology*, *45*(3), 619–636. doi:10.1111/j.1744-6570.1992.tb00863.x

Chatman, J. A. (1989, August). Matching people and organizations: Selection and socialization in public accounting firms. In Academy of Management proceedings (Vol. 1989, No. 1, pp. 199-203). Academy of Management.

Chattopadhyay, P., George, E., & Shulman, A. D. (2008). The asymmetrical influence of sex dissimilarity in distributive vs. colocated work groups. *Organization Science*, *19*(4), 581–593. doi:10.1287/orsc.1070.0324

Chattopadhyay, P., Tluchowska, M., & George, E. (2004). Identifying the ingroup: A closer look at the influence of demographic dissimilarity on employee social identity. *Academy of Management Review*, *29*(2), 180–202.

Cherniss, C. (1991). Career commitment in human service professionals: A biographical study. *Human Relations*, *44*(5), 419–437. doi:10.1177/001872679104400501

Cohen, S., & Wills, T. A. (1985). Stress, social support, and the buffering hypothesis. *Psychological Bulletin*, *98*(2), 310–357. doi:10.1037/0033-2909.98.2.310 PMID:3901065

Colbert, B. A. (2004). The complex resource-based view: Implications for theory and practice in strategic human resource management. *Academy of Management Review*, *29*(3), 341–358.

Cornelis, I., Van Hiel, A., & De Cremer, D. (2006). Effects of procedural fairness and leader support on interpersonal relationships among group members. *Group Dynamics*, *10*(4), 309–328. doi:10.1037/1089-2699.10.4.309

Dutton, J. E., & Glynn, M. A. (2008). The SAGE handbook of organizational behavior: Vol. 1. *Positive organizational scholarship*. SAGE.

Dutton, J. E., & Heaphy, E. D. (2003). The power of high-quality connections. *Positive Organizational Scholarship: Foundations of a New Discipline, 3*, 263-278.

Edwards, M. R., & Peccei, R. (2007). Organizational identification: Development and testing of a conceptually grounded measure. *European Journal of Work and Organizational Psychology*, *16*(1), 25–57. doi:10.1080/13594320601088195

Eisenberger, R., Armeli, S., Rexwinkel, B., Lynch, P. D., & Rhoades, L. (2001). Reciprocation of perceived organizational support. *The Journal of Applied Psychology*, *86*(1), 42–51. doi:10.1037/0021-9010.86.1.42 PMID:11302232

Ellingwood, S. (2002). *The collective advantage*. Academic Press.

Feeley, T. H., Hwang, J., & Barnett, G. A. (2008). Predicting employee turnover from friendship networks. *Journal of Applied Communication Research, 36*(1), 56–73. doi:10.1080/00909880701799790

Festinger, L. (1954). A theory of social comparison processes. *Human Relations, 7*(2), 117–140. doi:10.1177/001872675400700202

George, J. M., & Bettenhausen, K. (1990). Understanding prosocial behavior, sales performance, and turnover: A group-level analysis in a service context. *The Journal of Applied Psychology, 75*(6), 698–709. doi:10.1037/0021-9010.75.6.698

Hammer, A. L., & Schnell, E. R. (2000). *FIRO-B® Technical Guide*. Mountain View, CA: CPP, Inc.

Heaphy, E. D., & Dutton, J. E. (2008). Positive social interactions and the human body at work: Linking organizations and physiology. *Academy of Management Review, 33*(1), 137–162. doi:10.5465/AMR.2008.27749365

Hunt, D. M., & Michael, C. (1983). Mentorship: A career training and development tool. *Academy of Management Review, 8*(3), 475–485.

Jahoda, M. (1982). *Employment and unemployment: A social-psychological analysis* (Vol. 1). CUP Archive.

Kostova, T., & Roth, K. (2003). Social capital in multinational corporations and a micro-macro model of its formation. *Academy of Management Review, 28*(2), 297–317.

Kramer, R. M. (1991). Intergroup Relations and Organizational Dilemmas-The role of categorization processes. *Research in Organizational Behavior, 13*, 191–228.

Kristof-Brown, A. L., Zimmerman, R. D., & Johnson, E. C. (2005). Consequences of individuals' fit at work: A meta-analysis of person–job, person–organization, person–group, and person–supervisor fit. *Personnel Psychology, 58*(2), 281–342. doi:10.1111/j.1744-6570.2005.00672.x

Levinger, G. (1979). A social exchange view on the dissolution of pair relationships. *Social Exchange in Developing Relationships, 3*, 169-193.

Liden, R. C., Wayne, S. J., & Sparrowe, R. T. (2000). An examination of the mediating role of psychological empowerment on the relations between the job, interpersonal relationships, and work outcomes. *The Journal of Applied Psychology, 85*(3), 407–416. doi:10.1037/0021-9010.85.3.407 PMID:10900815

M.Sias, P., & Jablin, F. M. (1995, September). Differential Superior-Subordinate Relations, Perceptions of Fairness, and Coworker Communication. *Human Communication Research*, *22*(1), 5–38 doi:10.1111/j.1468-2958.1995.tb00360.x

Maslow, A. H. (1943). A theory of human motivation. *Psychological Review*, *50*(4), 370–396. doi:10.1037/h0054346

Morrison, R. L. (2009). Are women tending and befriending in the workplace? Gender differences in the relationship between workplace friendships and organizational outcomes. *Sex Roles*, *60*(1-2), 1–13. doi:10.1007/s11199-008-9513-4

Postmes, T., Tanis, M., & De Wit, B. (2001). Communication and commitment in organizations: A social identity approach. *Group Processes & Intergroup Relations*, *4*(3), 227–246. doi:10.1177/1368430201004003004

Randel, A. E., & Ranft, A. L. (2007). Motivations to maintain social ties with coworkers the moderating role of turnover intentions on information exchange. *Group & Organization Management*, *32*(2), 208–232. doi:10.1177/1059601106286778

Riach, K., & Wilson, F. (2007). Don't screw the crew: Exploring the rules of engagement in organizational romance. *British Journal of Management*, *18*(1), 79–92. doi:10.1111/j.1467-8551.2006.00503.x

Riordan, C. M., & Griffeth, R. W. (1995). The opportunity for friendship in the workplace: An underexplored construct. *Journal of Business and Psychology*, *10*(2), 141–154. doi:10.1007/BF02249575

Robinson, S. L., & Greenberg, J. (1998). Employees behaving badly: Dimensions, determinants and dilemmas in the study of workplace deviance. *Journal of Organizational Behavior (1986-1998)*, 1.

Rousseau, D. M. (1998). The'problem'of the psychological contract considered. *Journal of Organizational Behavior*, *19*(S1), 665–671. doi:10.1002/(SICI)1099-1379(1998)19:1+<665::AID-JOB972>3.0.CO;2-X

Scandura, T. A. (1992). Mentorship and career mobility: An empirical investigation. *Journal of Organizational Behavior*, *13*(2), 169–174. doi:10.1002/job.4030130206

Schaffer, H. R. (1996). *Social development*. Blackwell Publishing.

Schneider, B., & Reichers, A. E. (1983). On the etiology of climates. *Personnel Psychology*, *36*(1), 19–39. doi:10.1111/j.1744-6570.1983.tb00500.x

Schutz, W. (1977). *FIRO Awareness Scales*. Consulting Psychologists Press.

Schutz, W. (1992). Beyond FIRO-B—Three new theory-derived measures—Element B: Behavior, Element F: Feelings, Element S: Self. *Psychological Reports, 70*(3), 915–937. doi:10.2466/pr0.1992.70.3.915 PMID:1620783

Schutz, W. C. (1955). What makes groups productive? *Human Relations, 8*(4), 429–465. doi:10.1177/001872675500800404

Schutz, W. C. (1958). *FIRO: A three-dimensional theory of interpersonal behavior.* Academic Press.

Seibert, S. E., Wang, G., & Courtright, S. H. (2011). *Antecedents and consequences of psychological and team empowerment in organizations: a meta-analytic review.* Academic Press.

Sherif, M., Harvey, O. J., White, B. J., & Hood, W. R. (1961). *The robber's cave experiment: Intergroup conflict and cooperation.* Academic Press.

Song, S. H., & Olshfski, D. (2008). Friends at Work A Comparative Study of Work Attitudes in Seoul City Government and New Jersey State Government. *Administration & Society, 40*(2), 147–169. doi:10.1177/0095399707312827

Suls, J., & Wheeler, L. (2000). *Handbook of social comparison.* New York: Kluwer.

Szeliski, V., & Paradiso, L. J. (1936). Demand for Boots and Shoes as Affected by Price Levels and National Income. *Econometrica, 4*, 338–355.

Sveningsson, S., & Alvesson, M. (2003). Managing managerial identities: Organizational fragmentation, discourse and identity struggle. *Human Relations, 56*(10), 1163–1193. doi:10.1177/00187267035610001

Tajfel, H., & Turner, J. C. (1979). An integrative theory of intergroup conflict. *The Social Psychology of Intergroup Relations, 33*(47), 74.

Thau, S., Aquino, K., & Poortvliet, P. M. (2007). Self-defeating behaviors in organizations: The relationship between thwarted belonging and interpersonal work behaviors. *The Journal of Applied Psychology, 92*(3), 840–847. doi:10.1037/0021-9010.92.3.840 PMID:17484563

Turner, N., Barling, J., & Zacharatos, A. (2002). Positive psychology at work. Handbook of Positive Psychology, 52, 715-728.

Tyler, T. R., & Lind, E. A. (1992). A relational model of authority in groups. *Advances in Experimental Social Psychology, 25*, 115–191. doi:10.1016/S0065-2601(08)60283-X

Verquer, M. L., Beehr, T. A., & Wagner, S. H. (2003). A meta-analysis of relations between person–organization fit and work attitudes. *Journal of Vocational Behavior*, *63*(3), 473–489. doi:10.1016/S0001-8791(02)00036-2

Wallace, J. C., Edwards, B. D., Arnold, T., Frazier, M. L., & Finch, D. M. (2009). Work stressors, role-based performance, and the moderating influence of organizational support. *The Journal of Applied Psychology*, *94*(1), 254–262. doi:10.1037/a0013090 PMID:19186910

Williams, H. M., Parker, S. K., & Turner, N. (2007). Perceived dissimilarity and perspective taking within work teams. *Group & Organization Management*, *32*(5), 569–597. doi:10.1177/1059601106293769

Winstead, B. A., Derlega, V. J., Montgomery, M. J., & Pilkington, C. (1995). The quality of friendships at work and job satisfaction. *Journal of Social and Personal Relationships*, *12*(2), 199–215. doi:10.1177/0265407595122003

Witt, L. A., & Nye, L. G. (1992). Gender and the relationship between perceived fairness of pay or promotion and job satisfaction. *The Journal of Applied Psychology*, *77*(6), 910–917. doi:10.1037/0021-9010.77.6.910 PMID:1468995

Witt, U. (1998). Imagination and leadership–the neglected dimension of an evolutionary theory of the firm. *Journal of Economic Behavior & Organization*, *35*(2), 161–177. doi:10.1016/S0167-2681(98)00058-4

Wright, R. A., & Brehm, J. W. (1984). The impact of task difficulty upon perceptions of arousal and goal attractiveness in an avoidance paradigm. *Motivation and Emotion*, *8*(2), 171–181. doi:10.1007/BF00993072

Zagenczyk, T. J., Scott, K. D., Gibney, R., Murrell, A. J., & Thatcher, J. B. (2010). Social influence and perceived organizational support: A social networks analysis. *Organizational Behavior and Human Decision Processes*, *111*(2), 127–138. doi:10.1016/j.obhdp.2009.11.004

Chapter 8
Jio-Bharti Airtel Data War and Strategy

Anil Kumar
BML Munjal University, India

Mohan Balaji
BML Munjal University, India

Ujjwal Krishna
BML Munjal University, India

Mohit Yadav
BML Munjal University, India

ABSTRACT

The chapter examines various viewpoints in regards to Reliance Jio and Bharti Airtel. This includes the entry of Jio in the telecom space along with the difference in the market Jio bought right after its introduction of the services for public. The focus area for the research has been the secondary sources. A complete understanding of both these companies has been taken into account for this study to pick up the points that both Jio and Bharti have been lacking upon and areas in which one has surpassed the other by attracting a new set of consumers into their family. The chapter as recorded by the facts presented through the Telecom Regulatory Authority of India Analytics Portal witnessed that Jio proved to have an upper hand in terms of the quality of service, which included data speed and tariffs. The other side of the story shows Bharti Airtel's lack of dominance in 4G experience delivery after Jio's entrance.

DOI: 10.4018/978-1-5225-4038-0.ch008

Copyright © 2018, IGI Global. Copying or distributing in print or electronic forms without written permission of IGI Global is prohibited.

INTRODUCTION

It was in 2009 when the 4G Spectrum of the Indian Telecom Industry was at auction and an unlisted firm named Infotel Broadband Service limited got down into the race and bagged all the 22 telecom circles broadband spectrum. In 2010, Reliance Industries bought 96% stake in Infotel Broadband Service Limited which resulted in Reliance industries becoming the Parent Company and Infotel Broadband being their Telecom Subsidiary. In 2013, Infotel Broadband Service limited was renamed as Reliance Jio Infocomm Limited (RJIL) .The Company initially went of with beta testing by late 2015 with initial users being the Reliance Family Members i.e. their Employees. After successful results of the testing Phase, Jio launched its commercial service for the general public on 5th September 2016. Reliance Jio Infocomm Limited is owned by one of the most powerful personality in India - Mukesh Ambani whose is the Chairman of Reliance Industries Limited. Reliance Industries as a conglomerate has diversified verticals for business which includes Petrochemical, Retail, Textiles, Energy etc. It is one of the Prominent Business Groups of India which has been featured in Forbes 500 list for the highest market capitalization in Indian Industry.

On September 5, 2016 Jio launched its commercial operation for the public by providing services under a suite called the "Welcome offer" through which the user would be entitled to get unlimited data, sms & calls throughout the national circles with access over other operators as well. The initial entry of Jio created curiosity among consumers as True 4G Experience was guaranteed and that too without any charges. This led the Incumbents like Airtel, Vodafone and Idea to get a pressure of increase in the competition. Not much of the surprise within the initial months of the Welcome offer the majority of Incumbents Consumers went on to join the Jio offer. The reaction with which Bharti and other player responded didn't helped them as the Regulatory Violation which the players reported as against Jio to the Telecom Regulatory Authority of India(TRAI) which quoted violation of the Telecom Services through the freebies that were offered by Jio. In addition to the above move Bharti reportedly didn't supported Jio further and blocked the Point of Interconnection (PoI) which resulted in Call Failures by the Jio users. All these chain of activities had framed a competitive stage for both the players in the near future and with the mind-set Jio has been addressing its users it would not be wrong to categorise that the Consumer has been the Ultimate Winner who has been capitalizing on this opportunity to earn and experience a true digital world with an array of freebies.

What India seeks in the coming years is to be a digital economy and with that vision the Current Government has worked tremendously till date which has also been complimented very well by the Pioneer of Reliance, Mr. Mukesh Ambani through the Introduction of a True Digital Experience called "Jio". The Public Private Partnership model initiated by the government of India through this Jio experience seems to be a reality in real time. Also, with the aim of getting the economy digitally runned which required the adoption of Public to the Internet World and with Jio this task have also been seeked to be achieved in majority of the states in India with the Introduction of Low Budget True 4G Smartphones and Complementary Data to get hold of the Digital India. Moreover with a promise and commitment to a better and bright India Jio has been working towards the End to End Digital Solutions which clearly reflects its Social Responsibility towards Indian Population.

LITERATURE REVIEW

An article (Khanna & Pathak, 2016) which mentioned the beginning of the rivalry among Jio and Bharti states that when on September 5, 2016 Reliance Industries chairman announced the news of Jio entry into the Indian Telecom Sector while addressing the shareholders in the 42nd Annual General Meeting of the Company the announcement itself created a humungous impact on the Balance Sheets of the Incumbent firms. The Editor specifically mentioned that while Reliance Industries Chairman was addressing the shareholders and unveiled the Jio Brand with its offering for the public with the basic plans during that time one of the Major Incumbent Player Bharti recorded a dip of about 9% in its net worth and similarly a dip was recorded in other small players as well. The Article specifically talked about how at the initial level of Introduction of the Services to the general public Jio made an impact on the existing player in the market i.e. Bharti with its lucrative plans for the Public with as low as Rs. 51 per GB for Data and announcing No Charges for the Calling facility it sent out a message to rivals that new standards and norms were being created to which rival need to address.

One of the most prominent paper article (Sahay, 2017) quoted on the status of the Telecom Space aggressive customer dominated strategy which the existing players have been adopting since Jio has started capitalizing on the Market value of the Telecom Business in India which resulted into shrink revenues at the previous quarters ended. The customer centric philosophy of Jio and the marketing tactic they have employed so far has let the existing firms like Bharti to reconsider their entire model. The Editor has gone in further research of the attrition rivalry which Jio has somehow let the other players feel the heat off. None of the stone has been let unturned by Jio when it comes to its custom tailored consumer oriented product offering which has let them provide data under the regulatory framework of Telecom Regulatory Authority of India (TRAI) guidelines of Fair Usage Policy (FUP). All these mentions done by the editor gives an idea of the spark which Jio has been giving its Rivals at each stage of the business but also has excelled them so far very fairly. One of Very basic enrolment tactic Jio employed as stated in the article was providing free services through its initial "Welcome Offer" which later turned onto "Happy New Year" to continue the services without charges to build upon the customer base and as soon as the Company touched its targeted customer base i.e. 100 million users it introduced Prime Membership offering to keep users intact through a nominal payment. This Move of Jio let Bharti also step into the field of customer retention which they so far have been trying to keep the user intact by proving a similar offering though not identical to its existing users to have them connected with Brand Bharti.

Another Article (Taneja, 2017) states how Jio's entry in the telecom market impacted the Incumbents as well as the smaller player of the market. Soon after the proposed Merger of Vodafone-Idea, Airtel announced its intention to acquire Norwegian's Telecom Arm Telenor. It also mentioned the way this merger would benefit Bharti Airtel in the telecom market space as it could curb their losses reported in the previous quarters. This Consolidation being taken place in the Industry has been the due to the nightmares by Jio's entry. With Companies opting for Mergers and Acquisitions the Indian Telecom sector had seen a drastic change within the past few months. One of the Major reason reported for these activities was the huge Infrastructure costs players had to invest to exist in the market and with Jio entry it proved a very difficult task for these telecom players. International Data Corporation had valued the industry at $37 billion in 2016 which defines how crucial the Telecom Industry is in India.

Some points covered by (WebTeam, 2017) states that the Telecom Player Jio had been so far successful in creating nightmares for the Incumbents which include the Threat of achieving the Return on Investment (ROI) which has been noted by Bharti and other player as well because the initial spectrum costs incurred by these players have been huge and as Jio offered slashed Tariffs which led the others players like Bharti in order to deal with it also offered drops in the Tariffs. This move has led Bharti and Vodafone the major Incumbent player to re-work on the statistics as the earlier statistics have failed badly and the stated Average Revenue per user (APU) have not been achieved by both players in the recent months. Another aspect which add on to this is the Free Voice Calling that Jio had started with by this strategy Players like Bharti are on the verge of the same question figuring out ways to get return on Investment and being Calling segment free the only option which remains is Data that being too competitive because of tariff rates. Even though the Revenue consideration be kept aside by Players like Bharti but Consumer Retention would still haunt them as Portability provides a lucrative way to switch between Service Providers for the Consumers and it doesn't incur any switching cost for them as well which also prove to a threat. When considering the Business Strategic perspective of the Telecom Companies Mergers and Acquisitions to compete with Jio doesn't sound too great from that perspective as in order to compete with the other player in Industry it would compel the firms to consider such decisions but that might not end up in the true favour of the Stakeholders off the firm.

METHODOLOGY

The study involved research through secondary sources which included Websites and Articles. The Article considered for the research were from Live mint, Daily News Analysis (DNA), Vccircle, Indian Express and the Herald Goa.The Website considered for the study include the Telecom Regulatory Authority of India (TRAI) official analytics web page through which the Trends amongst the Telecom operators in India on various aspects such as Usage Frequency, Data Tariffs, Data Speed and Voice Connectivity were studied.

Research Findings

Bharti Airtel have been in the Indian Telecom Space since 1995 with a user base of over 400 million as of 2017 which categorises it to being the third largest operator in the world. To its contrary, Reliance Jio which was established in 2016 and within 170 days of its incorporation and revelation of services to the public its user base crossed 100 million. Although Airtel has been a dominant player for long in the Industry but with Jio emerging as a strong competitor has led Airtel Policies being completely revamped since then. These changes came into place seeking the impact on revenue that companies generate on a user.

One of the change that Bharti deployed early at the entry of Jio was in "Tariffs" which can be seen in the Below Table.

As showcased in Table 1 the Data Tariffs that were charged by Bharti Airtel from its users pre Jio Entry. These tariffs were more service provider friendly as these rates catered to the providers in earning good amount of revenue per user. This equation soon got changed and tariffs started to be more consumer friendly than service provider friendly which can be seen in Table2.

As the Competition explored in the Telecom space the first things which saw its impact was Tariff's cost and that too at a large extent that the service provider's value creation perspective has got a clear denial in this race. In a comparative framework of Table 1 and 2 one tends to clearly understand that the Service Provider Approach has been turned down to Consumer Centric Approach. No point of revenue generation has been touched since September, 2016 since Jio became commercially available for users and that to for free enrolments.

Table 1. Bharti Airtel Data Tariff Pre Jio Launch

MRP	Benefit	Validity	Charges after Free Usage
105	300 MB	30	3Ps/10KB
205	600 MB	30	3Ps/10KB
245	1 GB	30	0.5Ps/KB
345	1.5 GB	30	0.5Ps/KB
445	2 GB	30	0.5Ps/KB
595	3 GB	60	0.5Ps/KB
745	4 GB	30	0.5Ps/KB
845	3 GB	60	0.5Ps/KB

Source:http://trak.in/tags/business/2016/01/12/4g-internet-data-plans-comparison-2016-vodafone-airtel-idea/

Table 2. Bharti Airtel Data Tariff Compared with Jio Post its Entry

Operator	Reliance Jio Prime	Airtel
Price	Rs. 99 + Rs. 303	Rs. 345
Type	Prepaid	Prepaid
Bundled Data	28GB	28GB
Daily FUP	1GB	500MB Day + 500MB Night
Validity	28 Days	28 Days

Source: http://www.airtel.in/4g/index#!plans-and-devices/mobile/prepaid
https://www.jio.com/en-in/4g-plans

Another perspective of switching which goes simultaneously with Data Cost reduction is the Data speed. In a recent study conducted by "Ookla" on testing of the Speed that the Telecom Operators in India have been providing to its users was done and not to much too the surprise Jio being a True 4G service surpassed one another category against Airtel which had adversely impacted Bharti Consumption rate. The results of the test showed the following Speed Pattern as displayed in Figure1.

The above results published by Telecom Regulatory Authority of India showed the monthly trend of the download speed based upon the server in the region through which the test was conducted. Another published data which proves to be more alluring than the trends were the Average Speed observed by the consumers itself was revealed by Telecom Authorities and the results came to surprising even more on Bharti part as based upon the earlier discussion and certain facts it appeared to be a cut throat war amongst the two namely Jio and Bharti but to the surprise on part of the Average Speed of the 4G data as reported by the Telecom Authorities another player i.e. Idea in the Telecom Industry is giving a tough fight and with

Figure 1. Monthly Trend Download Speed
Source: http://www.myspeed.trai.gov.in/

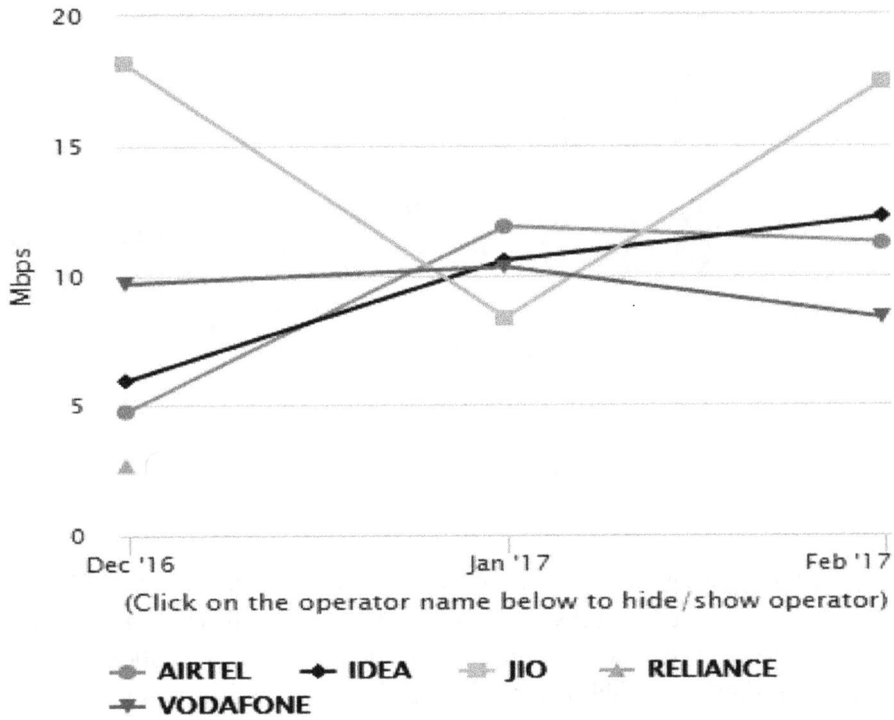

the recent stats it had surpassed Bharti in the Speed Experience by the Consumers. Though both Idea and Bharti an incumbent and present in the industry for a long time now understands the stiffness of the sector very well and being backed by two major corporate houses of India they won't be giving up any time soon even if Jio in its early days has been able to outplay both of them, there still exists possible fair play chances which both players would be looking to capitalise in the near future. The actual figures of the average download speed by all the major players in the industry has been showcased in figure 2 below.

CONCLUSION

Indian Telecom Sector has been the trending one right from the 2G Spectrum Service, the 3G activation service and more but the tremendous flow it observed from the consumer end was seen only when the government announced 4G spectrum sale. These auction itself provided a great acquisition deal in the Indian Telecom space.

Figure 2. Average User Download Speed
Source: http://www.myspeed.trai.gov.in/

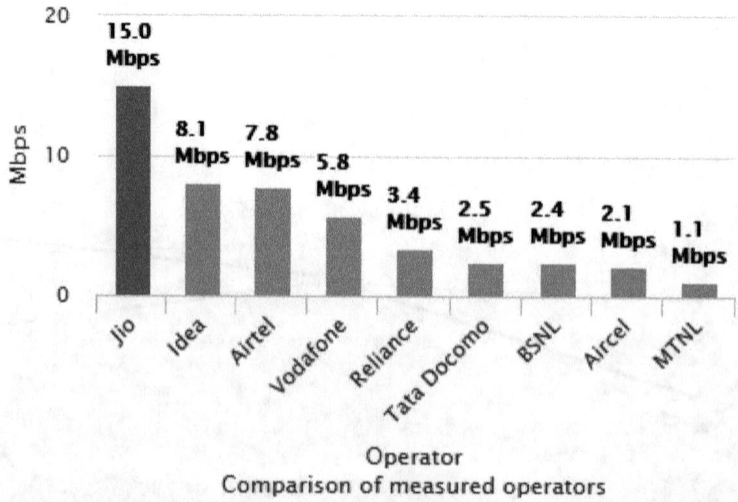

The spark of the great going ahead was felt by many when the news came of Reliance Industries entrance into the Telecom Space by striking a good deal from the Infotel Systems who won most of circle spectrum in auction. Most of the Analysts predicted that Reliance Entrance could be a beginning of a new Consumer Era in Telecom Space but no one amongst the public really wondered that it could actually change the face of the Communication over mobile. And as predicted by those analysts when Reliance started its operation and went publically available it created a real buzz amongst the consumer with initially starting off with "The Welcome Offer" on September 5, 2016. The offer implementation worked really well and within 170 days of its operation Jio enrolled more than 100 Million consumers. All these responses though had a favourable version for Jio but affected the incumbent player badly as within the first three months of Jio other companies like Bharti sought shrined customer base due to the switching between both operators which was opted by consumers. This soon emerged as a race between operators to seek win from consumers part and in the latest edition to this Jio still has been leading way far from players like Bharti in offering lucrative offers which are consumer benefit oriented keeping aside the revenue component to seek better consumer satisfaction for long term relationships. The latest from Jio to compete was the "Summer Surprise Offer" on March 31, 2017 that again offered 3 months free bundled usage leading to which Bharti has been again in talks to defend it. The major opportunity in terms of build on consumer base which Bharti has seeked through talks with Telenor by the way of merger to build strong base in order to successfully outperform the competitor.

Recommendations

Airtel was the first telecom to launch 4G airwaves in India it could have a gained them the first mover advantage but they weren't able to do so because of the lack of the availability of the technology of the smartphones & the offer given by Airtel was too high as it was priced same as 3G price and 4G takes more data compared to 3G. These things affected Airtel very much. Then Jio's entry caused a lot of disruption in the market which already was having price wars between incumbents. Since Airtel is an incumbent it has an advantage of increasing its penetration in rural segment & they can reduce the price to some extent which will help them to counter Jio. Airtel also has Pan India service except for Assam for which they can tie up with any other telecom. Technical wise Jio only works with the smartphone that has Volte whereas Airtel's 4G works in Normal LTE devices.

Jio should increase its presence in Rural India which would benefit it as it is one of the crucial segment in Telecom Industry as this will provide them a strong base to maintain its edge in the telecom industry. Rural Segment provides a considerable amount contribution of Revenue due to the lower reach of the Fixed Line segment. Since Jio is expanding its network to reach out to more, they are also emphasising to increase their Signal Towers where they lag most. This lagging is the only cause which may harm their survival in the telecom industry.

REFERENCES

Khanna, S., & Pathak, K. (2016, September). Reliance Jio sends a message to rivals: It's war. *Live Mint*. Retrieved March 2017, from http://www.livemint.com/Companies/D4leWGTopPio6OYUQg2CEP/Mukesh-Ambani-kicks-off-Reliance-Jio-services-at-company-AGM.html

Sahay, V. (2017, March). War of attrition in India's telecom space. *Herald Goa*. Retrieved March 2017, from http://www.heraldgoa.in/Business/In-Business/War-of-attrition-in-India%E2%80%99s-telecom-space/112623.html

Taneja, M. (2017, February). Bharti Airtel to acquire Telenor India as Jio threat grows. *VC Circle*. Retrieved March 2017, from http://www.vccircle.com/news/telecom/2017/02/23/bharti-airtel-acquire-telenor-india

WebTeam D. N. (2017, March). Beyond price and data war: There are other nightmares Reliance Jio could create for its competition. *Daily News and Analysis*. Retrieved March 2017, from http://www.dnaindia.com/money/report-beyond-price-and-data-war-there-are-other-nightmares-reliance-jio-could-create-for-its-competition-2345309

Chapter 9
How Does Empowering Leadership Contribute to Organizational Commitment of Millennials?
An Indian Perspective

Mohammad Faraz Naim
University of Petroleum & Energy Studies, India

ABSTRACT

This chapter explores the influence of empowering leadership on organizational commitment of Indian millennials. Also, the mediating effect of trust in the leader is examined. Primary data were collected from the sample of 440 IT employees working in Delhi/NCR. Structural equation modeling (SEM) was used to test the proposed relationships based on model fit and standard path coefficients. Findings indicate that empowering leadership has a significant positive effect on organizational commitment and trust in the leader, which also has a significant positive effect on organizational commitment, and trust in the leader has shown to have a partial mediating effect on the relationship between empowering leadership and organizational commitment of millennials. The chapter contributes to the limited empirical literature on the linkage between empowering leadership and organizational commitment in a generational context, specifically millennials in Indian context. The chapter provides a leadership-based approach to bolster organizational commitment of millennials.

DOI: 10.4018/978-1-5225-4038-0.ch009

Copyright © 2018, IGI Global. Copying or distributing in print or electronic forms without written permission of IGI Global is prohibited.

INTRODUCTION

In today's dynamic business environment characterized by competition, technological changes, and increasing quality demands; classic leadership theories have become insufficient and the emphasis in leadership has shifted from *command and control* to leadership *as a source of employee development and innovation* (Yukl, 2006). Also, such an environment calls for organizations to invest significantly to attract, select and retain employees with high levels of commitment (Schneide *et al.*, 2009). There is, therefore a need for research directed toward identifying the organizational factors that promote positive employee attitudes particularly, organizational commitment. In the same vein, organizations design strategies to empower their employees in a bid to foster commitment and retention rates, to stay competitive. This is drawn from the past research that supports hat empowered employees are associated with higher levels of job satisfaction, commitment, and performance. However, among the many enablers, one of the determinants of to infuse empowerment is leader-follower relationships (Kozlowski & Bell, 2003; Spreitzer, 2008).

The extant scholarship suggests that effective leadership plays a key role in influencing employee positive attitude and has, therefore, been the subject of extensive research. Yukl (2006) defines leadership as "the process of influencing others to understand and agree about what needs to be done and how to do it, and the process of facilitating individual and collective efforts to accomplish shared objectives" (p. 8). With the evolution of the leadership domain, other forms of leadership such as empowering leadership have attained academic attention. Empowering leadership encourages sharing of power, authority, and responsibility to the followers (Zhang & Zhou, 2014). Past evidences have shown a positive significant impact of empowering leadership on employee positive attitudes. However, most of this literature is related to team-environments and has not explored the IT work setting (Srivastava & Bertol, 2006). Research on empowering leadership, however, has not examined the mediating mechanism that determines the leader's influence on employee organizational outcomes at individual level.

In response to concerns about the lack of commitment and intention to stay among Indian Millennial employees, several studies have identified this challenge and called for strong leadership and trusting environment to create an engaged and committed workforce (Bhatnagar, 2007). Empowering leadership is viewed as behaviors that generate trust and organizational effectiveness (Avolio, Gardner, Walumbwa, Luthans, & May, 2004). This approach of leadership underscores the importance of fostering employee self-directedness achieved through sharing of power, and its positive implication on follower attitude and performance (Carson Tesluk, & Marrone, 2007; Srivastava & Bertol, 2006). The extant literature on leadership provides support for the mediating effects of trust in the leader and leadership influence on followers. Trust is considered the foundation of positive organizational cultures and, in essence, defines healthy workplaces (Khatri, Halbesleben, Petroski, & Meyer, 2007). Trustworthy leaders instill a willingness to put extra efforts and deep level of emotional attachment with the organization. The objective of this study was to examine the relationship between empowering leadership, trust in the leader, and organizational commitment using a Millennial employees' sample. The model incorporates trust in leadership to explain the mechanism by which empowering leadership, influences organizational commitment.

LITERATURE REVIEW AND HYPOTHESES DEVELOPMENT

Empowering Leadership and Organizational Commitment

Empowering leadership is defined as the extent to which supervisors express confidence in their employees' abilities, emphasize the significance of their employees' work, involve their employees in decision making, and reduce or remove bureaucratic constraints on their employees for better execution of tasks (Ahearne, Mathieu, & Rapp, 2005; Zhang & Zhou, 2014). http://www.emeraldinsight.com/doi/full/10.1108/13673271111119709 It is comprised of five dimensions: "leading by example, referring to a set of behaviors that show the leader's commitment to his or her own work as well as the work of his/her team members; coaching, referring to a set of behaviors that educate team members and help them to become self-reliant; participative decision making, referring to a leader's use of team members' information and input in making decisions; showing concern, referring to a collection of behaviors that demonstrate a general regard for team members' well-being; and informing, referring to the leader's dissemination of company wide information such as mission and philosophy as well as other importation information" (Arnold et al., 2000, in Xue, Bradley & Liang, (2011), p. 302). Empowering leadership can be viewed, therefore, as essentially an approach that offers prescriptions to leaders for arranging the distribution and exercise of power. Literature on empowering leadership is focused on two perspectives. The first is based on leader actions such as sharing power or decision-making discretion, and autonomy to employees, in order to motivate them (Kirkman & Rosen, 1999). The second perspective emphasizes on employees' response to empowerment, specifically employees' motivation to empowerment (Thomas & Velthouse, 1990).

Organizational commitment is defined as "the relative strength of an individual's identification with and involvement in a particular organization" (Mowday, Porter, & Steers, 2013, p. 27). Past evidences suggest that work experiences, personal and organizational factors are the enablers of organizational commitment (Eby, Freeman,

Rush, & Lance, 1999; Meyer et al., 2002). Leadership has been considered one such key organizational factor, which serves a strong predictor of organizational commitment is (Mowday et al., 2013). In the same vein, there is substantial evidence to support the association between leadership styles and organizational commitment in a variety of work context (Avolio et al., 2004; Bono & Judge, 2003; Lok and Crawford, 2004; Walumbwa & Lawler, 2003). The extant scholarship indicates that leaders that encourage responsibilities, provide opportunities for decision latitude, challenges, listen attentively and promote teamwork, are expected to evoke positive attitudinal response in followers manifested as higher levels of commitment to their organizations (Avolio et al., 2004; Kark & Shamir, 2002; Liden *et al.*, 2000; Seibert *et al.*, 2004; Wayne, Liden, & Sparrowe, 2000).

Therefore, we argue that through their empowering behaviors such as power sharing, decision making authority, autonomy, employee development; empowering leaders create a perception among followers, of being more capable and able to influence their job and organizations. If so, then they would also be expected to exhibit higher levels of commitment (Spreitzer, 1995). This is because employees who feel more empowered are more likely to reciprocate by being deeply committed to their organization (Eisenberger, Fasolo, & Davis-LaMastro, 1990; Kraimer, Seibert, & Liden, 1999). Further, past research indicates that empowered employees are focused; initiative-takers, and resilient, which in turn bolster their organizational commitment. In other words, employees' level of commitment is influenced to the extent to which they perceive their organization and the leader to acknowledge their contribution and care about their well-being. Importantly, leaders enhance employees' commitment by providing a supportive work environment characterized by concern for employees' well-being, adequate information sharing, and well-defined goals (Cheung, 2000). Further, this is consistent with the transformational leadership theory, which asserts a key role of role of empowerment to generate employee organizational commitment (Avolio, 1999; Yukl, 2006). Thus we hypothesize-

H1: Empowering leadership behaviors is positively related to employee organizational commitment.

Empowering Leadership and Trust in the Leader

Over the years the concept of trust has been the subject of wide academic attention in organizational behavior research (Dirks & Ferrin, 2002). Various scholars have suggested different definitions of trust. In broad terms, trust is defined as "a psychological state comprising the intention to accept vulnerability based upon positive expectations of the intentions or behavior of another" (Rousseau et al., 1998, p. 395). However, interpersonal trust, specifically, between a trustor (the subordinate) and the trustee (the superior/leader) has been the focal point in organizational behavior literature. Interpersonal trust is conceptualized as "a belief about a set of particular characteristics of another specific individual(s)" (Hassan & Ahmed, 2011, p. 164). While, leadership trust refers to leader-member relationship based on mutual respect, cooperation, commitment, reliability and equity (Dirks & Ferrin, 2002).

The extant literature indicates a strong effect of leadership on follower trust (Goodwin et al., 2011; Norman 2006). Empowering leaders generate follower trust through their empowering behaviors including encouraging participative decision making, removing bureaucratic barriers, exhibiting confidence and belief on them to resolve problems, leading by example, sharing information, coaching, demonstrating concern for them, treating them with respect, and recognizing their contributions (Ahearne, Mathieu & Rapp, 2005; Zhang a& Zhou, 2014). Though leaders are instrumental in developing the followers' trust, little research has examined the specific leadership styles which evoke trust. However, past scholarship acknowledges that transformational and authentic leadership are more effective in generating trust by demonstrating individualized concern and respect for followers (Jung & Avolio, 2000). Drawing from social exchange perspective, social relationships are formed, sustained or severed based on the perceived cost-benefit analysis. A sense of reciprocity develops when leaders exhibit concern for followers by providing them emotional and informational support, in turn, evoking positive psychological responses of trust (Cropanzano & Mitchell, 2005). In other words, in response to leader's empowering behaviors, employees feel more comfortable and willing to trust their supervisor. Thus we hypothesize-

H2a: Empowering leadership influences employees' trust in the leader.

Mediating Role of Trust

Despite being given considerable scholarly attention, trust has not been empirically tested for its mediating effects on leadership outcomes (Bartram & Casimir, 2007; Jung and Avolio, 2000). Like in any other social relationship, apart from certain behaviors there must be a mechanism that acts as s glue to keep the parties committed to cotniue the relationship. Therefore, followers must perceive trust in the leader in order to feel positively about the leader and the organization. This is based on the notion that trust plays a key role in productive interpersonal relationships including leader-member relationships. Leadership is considered trustworthy based on leadership's vision, strategy implementation, focus on followers' interests, and ability to communicate. Therefore, if followers develop a perception that the leader is not taking keen interest in their learning and welfare activities, it will dampen the level of trust in the leader and therefore it has deteriorating effect on their satisfaction, engagement, and commitment with the organization. In this regard, the leader's integrity, competence, and benevolence, is crucial as it has bearing on the decisions taken by leader, which directly influence followers future. If the leader scores highly on these trust-building factors, then it will signal a profitable future of followers in the organization, thus resulting in higher commitment (Dirks & Ferrin, 2002). Thus, we expect trust in leadership be associated with followers' positive attitudes, which in turn will be related to positive behaviors. Specifically, empowering leadership behaviors such as participative decision-making practices, supplying organizational support, and ensuring that expectations are met were related to greater trust in leadership.

Evidences from past behavioral research reveals that leadership trust is necessary for effective leadership (Barey, 2002; Morgan,and Zeffane, 2003). It has been empirically shown that leadership trust acts as mediator in influencing empowering leadership effect on organizational commitment and empowering behaviors are instrumental in generating trust (Laschinger, Finegan, Shamian, & Casier, 2000). Although, several scholars notes the association between trust in the leader and employee attitudinal outcomes such as satisfaction, commitment, leading to increased performance (Bartram & Casimir, 2007 Dirks & Ferrin, 2002; Korsgaard, Brodt, & Whitener, 2002). In particular, the past scholarship suggests a positive relationship of empowering leadership and organizational commitment in different work settings (Bono & Judge, 2003; Seibert *et al.*, 2004; Liden *et al.*, 2000; Walumbwa & Lawler, 2003). Further, Avolio, et al. (2004) corroborated that organizational commitment was higher for employees whose leaders display empowering behaviors such as participative decision-making, relationship building, teamwork, and avenues for followers' growth and development. Also, empowering behaviors have been shown to be linked with trust generation. Therefore, it is logical to argue here that empowering leadership will indirectly influence follower commitment through the development of trust in leader, which serves as the mechanism through which empowering leadership impacts employee organizational commitment. This is in agreement with the extant literature, which demonstrates a positive impact of empowering leadership on trust, which in turn, mediates its relationship with employee attitude (Bobbio, Bellan & Manganelli, 2012). Other studies reveal that in the presence of trust, empowering leadership leads to a positive attitude change. Thus the attitude of the employee towards an objective tends to change when the empowering leadership is exercised in the presence of trusting behaviors (Goodwin et al., 2011; Zhang & Zhou, 2014). In the similar vein, this study hypothesizes that trust mediates the effect of empowering leadership with attitude as an outcome. Thus we hypothesize-

H2b: Trust in the leader influences employees' organizational commitment

H3: The effects of empowering leadership on organizational commitment will be mediated by trust in the leader.

METHOD

Sample Description

The last decade or so has witnessed a spurt in IT industry in India. Consequently, the work setting for this study is a top-notch IT organization in Gurgaon, NCR. The organization operated 24 hours-a-day to provide IT solutions for clients from different countries. Although, management of IT organizations has traditionally been command and control type with stringent rules and deadlines, however, of late, there is a transformation in the management strategies highlighted by growing interest in employee empowerment (Gofton, 1999).

A cross-sectional survey design is used to gather primary data. The sample for this study is comprised of software programmers who belong to Millennial population i.e. born in between 1981-2000. The line managers were deemed fit for assuming leadership roles as they directly supervise their immediate subordinates. We made personal contact with HR Managers to persuade them to contribute in this study. We administered 650 questionnaires from October 2015 to December 2015. In all, 440 completely filled questionnaires were collected with a response rate of 67.69%. The average age of the executives was 23.2 years (S.D.=5.6), and they, on average, had worked in the organization for 3.5 years (S.D.=4.2). Out of this sample 54% are males and 46% are females, with an age group of 20-24 represented by 45% respondents, 25-29 by 32% and 29-34 by 23%, with an average working tenure with their immediate supervisors for 1.6 years (S.D.=1.7).

Figure 1. Theoretical Framework

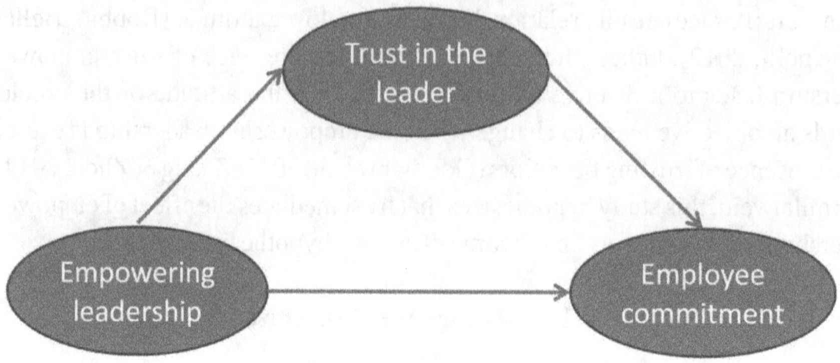

Instrumentation

Questionnaire items were adapted from pre-existing validated scales. The five-point Likert scale (1=strongly disagree, 5=strongly agree) was used as the measurement method.

Empowering leadership- We used the 12-item (α = .94) scale developed by Ahearne et al. (2005). A sample item is ''My supervisor expresses confidence in my ability to perform at a high level'.' Responses were measured on a 5-point Likert scale ranging from 1 ("strongly disagree") to 5 ("strongly agree").

Trust in Leadership: A 6-item (α = .83) scale by (Podsakoff et al. 1990) was used to measure trust. An example item is ''I have complete faith in the integrity of my manager/ supervisor''.

Organizational Commitment: It is measured by Mowday et al.'s (1979) 15-item (α = .86) organizational commitment questionnaire (CQ). An example is "I really feel as if this organization's problems are my own".

Controls

To avoid potentially misleading relationships between our study's variables and to enhance the validity of the study, the probable influence of age-group, gender, education, and experience were controlled. The coding schemata for the categorical control variables are shown in Table 1.

Table 1.

Construct	1	2	3	4	5	6	7	CR	AVE
1 .Age	-								
2. Gender	0.07	-							
3. Experience	0.10	0.06	-						
4. Tenure	0.05	0.10	0.05	-					
5 .Empowering Leadership	0.12	0.13	0.12	0.10	(0.94)			0.98	0.71
6.Trust in leader	0.10	0.11	0.10	0.15	0.36	(0.83)		0.93	0.82
7.Employee commitment	0.08	0.09	0.08	0.09	0.28	0.44	(0.86)	0.89	0.74

Figures in parenthesis denote Cronbach alpha; CR= Composite reliability; AVE=Average variance extracted (N=195)

Notes: * p< 0:05, ** p<0:01, Reliability estimates (Cronbach's alphas) are in parentheses.
Age-group (in years): 1= 20-24 (45%), 2= 25-29 (32%) and 3= 29-34 (23%).
Gender: 1 = Male (54%), 2 = Female (46%).
Education: 1 = Diploma (24%), 2 = Graduate (54%), 3 = Post Graduate (22%),
Experience (in years): 1= 0-2 (42%), 2 = 2-4 (30%), 3 = 4-6 (18%), 4= > 6 (10%)
Tenure with supervisor (in years) 1= 0-2 (62%), 2 = 2-4 (20%), 3 = 4-6 (18%)

Results

Preliminary Analysis

Data analysis for the present study was done using SPSS 21.0 and AMOS 7.0 softwares. Hypotheses testing were carried out through correlational analysis and regression technique. Reliability estimates, correlations, and descriptive statistics including standard deviations for all the variables under study are depicted in Table 1. Before proceeding for hypotheses testing, firstly the measurement model was examined for dimensionality, convergent, and discriminant validity through Confirmatory factor analysis.

In agreement with the extant research, CFA reveals that the five dimensions were significantly loaded on the empowering leadership construct (b= 0.86 to 0.95; a= 95 percent). The fit indices indicates the acceptable fit measures (χ^2/df= 3.284, p= 0.000, GFI= 95, CFI= 0.98, TLI= 0.97, NFI= 0.98, RMSEA= 0.073). For trust in the leader, scale fit indices show an adequately acceptable fit (χ^2/df= 3.112, GFI= 0.93, CFI= 0.97, TLI= 0.96, NFI= 0.96, RMSEA= 0.041). CFA reveals that the six itmes were significantly loaded on the trust in the leader construct (b= 0.84-0.91; a= 95 percent). While, the fifteen items assigned for measuring organizational commitment were averaged to one score of organizational commitment. Conducting CFA reveals that the scale fitted the data adequately (χ^2/df= 2.224, GFI= 0.95, AGFI= 0.92, CFI= 0.98, TLI= 0.96, NFI= 0.97, RMSEA= 0.070). Furthermore, results show that the fifteen items significantly loaded onto the organizational commitment construct with(b= 0.86-0.94; a= 95 percent).

Structural Model

As depicted in Table 3, the proposed model of empowering leadership, trust in the leader, and organizational commitment is found to exhibit acceptable fit indices (Hair et al. 2010). Findings of CFA reveal that the hypothesized model acceptable fit (χ^2/df = 2.01, GFI = 0.95, AGFI = 0.92, RMSEA = 0.078, CFI= 0.97; TLI= 0.97; NFI= 0.95). The value of coefficient paths were statistically significant ($p < 0.01$). Overall, the model explains 29 percent of the variance in organizational commitment.

Test of Hypotheses

Findings reveal that the standardized coefficient between empowering leadership and organizational commitment was significant (β =.70, $p < 0.01$) thus providing support for H1. Also, the relationship between empowering leadership and trust in

Table 2. Construct reliability, AVE, and correlations

Construct	Item	Mean	SD	Loading
Lead by Example	1	3.90	0.96	0.88*
	2	4.09	0.91	0.94*
	3	4.03	0.96	0.91*
	4	4.07	0.91	0.94*
Participative DM	1	4.03	0.89	0.93*
	2	4.10	0.87	0.95*
	3	4.14	0.83	0.95*
Coaching	1	3.89	0.93	0.92*
	2	3.97	0.87	0.93*
	3	3.93	0.92	0.92*
Informing	1	3.94	0.92	0.92*
	2	3.90	0.93	0.95*
	3	3.80	0.95	0.91*
	4	3.94	0.90	0.90*
Sharing Concern	1	3.73	0.95	0.86*
	2	3.89	0.88	0.92*
	3	4.11	0.86	0.86*
	4	3.91	0.88	0.90*
Trust in the Leader	1	3.80	0.79	0.89*
	2	3.79	1.01	0.87*
	3	3.80	1.11	0.85*
	4	3.81	1.05	0.88*
	5	3.80	0.88	0.84*
	6	3.82	1.09	0.91*
Affective	1	3.61	0.88	0.91*
	2	3.61	0.71	0.90*
	3	3.60	0.69	0.86*
	4	3.62	0.65	0.92*
	5	3.61	0.81	0.84*
Countenance	1	3.75	0.93	0.90*
	2	3.74	0.84	0.90*
	3	.3.75	0.82	0.94*
	4	3.73	0.75	0.89*
	5	3.73	0.69	0.88*
Normative	1	3.62	0.68	0.88*
	2	3.61	0.81	0.87*
	3	3.60	0.92	0.88
	4	3.62	0.82	0.84
	5	3.61	0.95	0.86

Table 3. Factor Loadings

Variables	χ^2/df	GFI	TLI	CFI	RMSEA
Empowering Leadership	3.284	.954	.073	.972	.983
Trust in the leader	3.112	.935	.960	.970	.041
Employee commitment	2.224	.958	.963	.986	.070

the leader was found to be positive with the standardized coefficient was significant (β =0.59, p<.01) that strongly supported H2a. Also, trust in the leader was positively related to organizational commitment. The standard path coefficient was significant (β = 0.63 . p<.01) supporting H2b. Finally, the direct standard path coefficient between leadership empowering and organizational commitment was significantly reduced to (β =0.36, p<.01) in the mediated model. Therefore, the result suggested partial mediation effect of trust in the leader between empowering leadership style and employee organizational commitment and thus partially supporting H3. Furthermore, the result reveals a 38% explained variance, which was well within the prescribed limit of 50%, the minimum threshold in accordance with Harman's single factor test (Podsakoff et al., 2012), thereby indicating that common method variance has been death with effectively.

DISCUSSION AND IMPLICATIONS

This paper aimed at examining the impact of empowering leadership on organizational commitment through the mediating role of trust in the leader. As proposed, the direct relationship between empowering leadership and organizational commitment was established, thus supporting H1. In other words, the findings demonstrate that Millennial executives supervised by empowering managers are more likely to be committed. The findings are consistent with previous research (Albrecht & Andreetta, 2011; Laschinger, Finegan & Shamian, 2001). Second, this study identified that empowering leadership positively influences perception of trust in the leader among Millennial followers, thereby supporting H2a; and that trust in the leader is shown to predict organizational commitment, thereby supporting H2b. Finally, the results of H3 lend support to a partial mediation of trust in the leader between empowering leadership and organizational commitment of Millennial employees. These results are in agreement with the empirical support driven from past literature that interpersonal trust has a positive significant impact of on organizational commitment (Dirks & Ferrin 2002; Nyham, 1999; Song, Kim & Kolb, 2009; Yang, 2005). Therefore, this study further confirms the findings of earlier studies and explains the impact of empowering leadership on organizational commitment.

The present study is significant for both managerial as well as theoretical perspective. From theoretical vantage point, the study contributes to limited empirical literature on the relationship between empowering leadership, trust in the leader, and organizational commitment. Although, substantial evidence is available for the influence of transformational and authentic leadership on trust and organizational commitment, still there is lack of studies on empowering leadership's impact on these outcomes. To the best of our knowledge, no study has examined the impact of empowering leadership on followers' trust in the leader Indian IT industry. Importantly, this study addresses the call for research to explore the mechanism underlying the impact of empowering leadership on organizational commitment (Dewettinck & Ameijde, 2011).Further there is an exigent need to enhance the IT Millennial employees' organizational commitment levels, given the present higher attrition rates in Indian IT industry especially among young generation employees i.e. Millennials (Naim & Lenka, 2017b). Recent estimates suggest Indian IT industry has experienced roughly 30 percent executive-level attrition rates in the last fiscal year (The Times of India, 2014).

From managerial vantage point, this study presents a strategy for HR managers to bolster employee organizational commitment rates. In this view, organizations should offer training and workshops to line managers or supervisors to improve their empowering behaviors to achieve reciprocal positive response from the executives. This argument is based on the notion that it is possible to impart empowering leadership behaviors through training interventions (Nielsena & Munir, 2009). These interventions would enable line managers or supervisors realize the significance of aligning Millennial executives' targets in alignment with their personal objectives. In addition, leveraging empowering behaviors fuel committed workforce, which is a sustainable source of competitive advantage in contemporary business landscape. Also, committed employees have higher likelihood of staying forth with the organization (Naim ^ Lenka, 2016). This is highly important in context of Indian IT industry, which registers high attrition rates in the Indian economy (Naim & Lenka, 2017a).

Limitations and Future Scope

This paper has some limitations, which could lead to directions for future research. Firstly, the relatively small sample size and cross-sectional nature limits its generalizability and causality. Secondly, as it was carried out in an IT organziation, empirical findings of the study could be more applicable in Asian countries as compared to Western ones Future studies should explore industries like IT, retail, or pharmaceutical. As quantitative research design has its obvious limitations so future studies should employ qualitative methods like focus interviews to further examine the results of this study.

REFERENCES

Ahearne, M., Mathieu, J., & Rapp, A. (2005). To empower or not to empower your sales force? An empirical examination of the influence of leadership empowerment behavior on customer satisfaction and performance. *The Journal of Applied Psychology*, *90*(5), 945–955. doi:10.1037/0021-9010.90.5.945 PMID:16162066

Albrecht, S. L., & Andreetta, M. (2011). The influence of empowering leadership, empowerment and engagement on affective commitment and turnover intentions in community health service workers: Test of a model. *Leadership in Health Services*, *24*(3), 228–237. doi:10.1108/17511871111151126

Arnold, J. A., Arad, S., Rhoades, J. A., & Drasgow, F. (2000). The empowering leadership questionnaire: The construction and validation of a new scale for measuring leader behaviors. *Journal of Organizational Behavior*, *21*(3), 249–269. doi:10.1002/(SICI)1099-1379(200005)21:3<249::AID-JOB10>3.0.CO;2-#

Avolio, B., Zhu, W., Koh, W., & Bhatia, P. (2004). Empowering leadership and organizational commitment: Mediating role of psychological empowerment and moderating role of structural distance. *Journal of Organizational Behavior*, *25*(8), 951–968. doi:10.1002/job.283

Avolio, B. J. (1999). *Full leadership development: Building the vital forces in organizations*. Thousand Oaks, CA: Sage.

Bartram, T., & Casimir, G. (2007). The relationship between leadership and follower in-role performance and satisfaction with the leader: The mediating effects of empowerment and trust in the leader. *Leadership and Organization Development Journal*, *28*(1), 4–19. doi:10.1108/01437730710718218

Bhatnagar, J. (2007). Talent management strategy of employee engagement in Indian ITES employees: Key to retention. *Employee Relations*, *29*(6), 640–663. doi:10.1108/01425450710826122

Bobbio, A., Bellan, M., & Manganelli, A. M. (2012). Empowering leadership, perceived organizational support, trust, and job burnout for nurses: A study in an Italian general hospital. *Health Care Management Review*, *37*(1), 77–87. doi:10.1097/HMR.0b013e31822242b2 PMID:21743337

Bono, J. E., & Judge, T. A. (2003). Self-concordance at work: Toward understanding the motivational effects of transformational leaders. *Academy of Management Journal, 46*(5), 554–571. doi:10.2307/30040649

Carson, J. B., Tesluk, P. E., & Marrone, J. A. (2007). Shared leadership in teams: An investigation of antecedent conditions and performance. *Academy of Management Journal, 50*(5), 1217–1234. doi:10.2307/20159921

Cheung, C. (2000). Commitment to the organization in exchange for support from the organization. *Social Behavior and Personality, 28*(2), 125–140. doi:10.2224/sbp.2000.28.2.125

Cropanzano, R., & Mitchell, M. S. (2005). Social exchange theory: An interdisciplinary review. *Journal of Management, 31*(6), 874–900. doi:10.1177/0149206305279602

Dewettinck, K., & Van Ameijde, M. (2011). Linking leadership empowerment behavior to employee attitudes and behavioral intentions: Testing the mediating role of psychological empowerment. *Personnel Review, 40*(3), 284–305. doi:10.1108/00483481111118621

Dirks, K., & Ferrin, D. (2002). Trust in leadership: Metaanalytic findings and implications for research and practice. *The Journal of Applied Psychology, 87*(4), 611–628. doi:10.1037/0021-9010.87.4.611 PMID:12184567

Dirks, K. T., & Ferrin, D. L. (2001). The role of trust in organizational settings. *Organization Science, 12*(4), 450–467. doi:10.1287/orsc.12.4.450.10640

Eby, L. T., Freeman, D. M., Rush, M. C., & Lance, C. E. (1999). Motivational bases of affective commitment: A partial test of an integrative theoretical model. *Journal of Occupational and Organizational Psychology, 72*(4), 463–483. doi:10.1348/096317999166798

Eisenberger, R., Fasolo, P., & Davis-LaMastro, V. (1990). Perceived organizational support and employee diligence, commitment, and innovation. *The Journal of Applied Psychology, 75*(1), 51–59. doi:10.1037/0021-9010.75.1.51

Gofton, K. (1999). Call-centers widen their field of vision. *Marketing, 22*, 20–32.

Goodwin, V. L., Whittington, J. L., Murray, B., & Nichols, T. (2011). Moderator or mediator? examining the role of trust in the transformational leadership paradigm. *Journal of Managerial Issues*, 409–425.

Hair, J. F., Black, W. C., Babin, B. J., & Anderson, R. E. (2010). *Multivariate Data Analysis: A Global Perspective*. Pearson Education International.

Hassan, A., & Ahmed, F. (2011). Authentic leadership, trust and work engagement. *International Journal of Humanities and Social Science*, *6*(3), 164–170.

Jung, D., & Avolio, B. (2000). Opening the black box: An experimental investigation of the mediating effects of trust and value congruence on empowering and transactional leadership. *Journal of Organizational Behavior*, *21*(8), 949–964. doi:10.1002/1099-1379(200012)21:8<949::AID-JOB64>3.0.CO;2-F

Kark, R., & Shamir, B. (2002). The dual effect of transformational leadership: priming relational and collective selves and further effects on followers. In B. J. Avolio & F. J. Yammarino (Eds.), *Transformational and charismatic leadership: The road ahead* (Vol. 2, pp. 67–91). Oxford, U.K.: Elsevier Science.

Khatri, N., Halbesleben, J. R., Petroski, G. F., & Meyer, W. (2007). Relationship between management philosophy and clinical outcomes. *Health Care Management Review*, *32*(2), 128–139. doi:10.1097/01.HMR.0000267789.17309.18 PMID:17438396

Kraimer, M. L., Seibert, S. E., & Liden, R. C. (1999). Psychological empowerment as a multi-dimensional construct: A construct validity test. *Educational and Psychological Measurement*, *59*(1), 127–142. doi:10.1177/0013164499591009

Krosgaard, M. A., Brodt, S. E., & Whitener, E. M. (2002). Trust in the face of conflict: The role of managerial trustworthy behavior and organizational context. *The Journal of Applied Psychology*, *87*(2), 312–324. doi:10.1037/0021-9010.87.2.312 PMID:12002959

Laschinger, H., Finegan, J., & Shamian, J. (2001). The impact of workplace empowerment and organizational trust on staff nurses' work satisfaction and organizational commitment. *Health Care Management Review*, *26*(3), 7–23. doi:10.1097/00004010-200107000-00002 PMID:11482178

Laschinger, H. K. S., Finegan, J., Shamian, J., & Casier, S. (2000). Organizational trust and empowerment in restructured healthcare settings: Effects on staff nurse commitment. *The Journal of Nursing Administration*, *30*(9), 413–425. doi:10.1097/00005110-200009000-00008 PMID:11006783

Liden, R. C., Wayne, S. J., & Sparrowe, R. T. (2000). An examination of the mediating role of psychological empowerment on the relations between the job, interpersonal relationships and work outcomes. *The Journal of Applied Psychology*, *85*(3), 407–416. doi:10.1037/0021-9010.85.3.407 PMID:10900815

Lok, P., & Crawford, J. (2004). The effect of organizational culture and leadership style on job satisfaction and organizational commitment: A cross-national comparison. *Journal of Management Development*, *23*(4), 321–338. doi:10.1108/02621710410529785

Meyer, J. P., Stanley, D. J., Herscovitch, L., & Topolnytsky, L. (2002). Affective, continuance, and normative commitment to the organization: A meta-analysis of antecedents, correlates, and consequences. *Journal of Vocational Behavior*, *61*(1), 20–52. doi:10.1006/jvbe.2001.1842

Morgan, D. E., & Zeffane, R. (2003). Employee involvement, organizational change and trust in management. *International Journal of Human Resource Management*, *14*(1), 55–75. doi:10.1080/09585190210158510

Mowday, R. T., Steers, R. M., & Porter, L. W. (1979). The measurement of organizational commitmen. *Journal of Vocational Behavior*, *14*(2), 224–247. doi:10.1016/0001-8791(79)90072-1

Naim, M. F., & Lenka, U. (2016). Knowledge sharing as an intervention for Gen Y employees' intention to stay. *Industrial and Commercial Training*, *48*(3), 142–148. doi:10.1108/ICT-01-2015-0011

Naim, M. F., & Lenka, U. (2017a). Talent management: A burgeoning strategic focus in Indian IT industry. *Industrial and Commercial Training*, *49*(3), 183–188. doi:10.1108/ICT-12-2016-0084

Naim, M. F., & Lenka, U. (2017b). Investigating the impact of social media on Gen Y employees' engagement: An empirical investigation. *International Journal of Human Capital and Information Technology Professionals*, *8*(3), 29–48. doi:10.4018/IJHCITP.2017070103

Nielsen, K., & Munir, F. (2009). How do transformational leaders influence followers' affective well-being? Exploring the mediating role of self-efficacy. *Work and Stress*, *23*(4), 313–329. doi:10.1080/02678370903385106

Norman, S. M. (2006). *The role of trust: Implications for psychological capital and authentic leadership* (Unpublished doctoral dissertation). University of Nebraska.

Nyhan, R. C. (1999). Increasing Affective Organizational Commitment in Public Organizations The Key Role of Interpersonal Trust. *Review of Public Personnel Administration*, *19*(3), 58–70. doi:10.1177/0734371X9901900305

Pearce, C. L., Sims, H. P. Jr, Cox, J. F., Ball, G., Schnell, K. A., Smith, K. A., & Trevino, L. (2003). Transactors, transformers and beyond: A multi-method development of a theoretical typology of leadership. *Journal of Management Development*, *22*(4), 273–307. doi:10.1108/02621710310467587

Podsakoff, P. M., Mackenzie, S. B., Moorman, R. H., & Fetter, R. (1990). Empowering leader behaviors and their effects on followers' trust in leader, satisfaction, and organizational citizenship behaviors. *The Leadership Quarterly*, *1*(2), 107–142. doi:10.1016/1048-9843(90)90009-7

Podsakoff, P. M., MacKenzie, S. B., & Podsakoff, N. P. (2012). Sources of method bias in social science research and recommendations on how to control it. *Annual Review of Psychology*, *63*(1), 539–569. doi:10.1146/annurev-psych-120710-100452 PMID:21838546

Rousseau, D., Sitkin, S., Burt, R., & Camerer, C. (1998). Not so different after all: A cross-discipline view of trust. *Academy of Management Review*, *23*(3), 393–404. doi:10.5465/AMR.1998.926617

Schneider, B., Macey, W. H., Barbera, K. M., & Martin, N. (2009). Driving customer satisfaction and financial success through employee engagement. *People and Strategy*, *32*(2), 22–34.

Song, J. H., Kim, H. M., & Kolb, J. A. (2009). The effect of learning organization culture on the relationship between interpersonal trust and organizational commitment. *Human Resource Development Quarterly*, *20*(2), 147–167. doi:10.1002/hrdq.20013

Spreitzer, G. M. (1995). Psychological empowerment in the workplace: Dimensions, measurement, and validation. *Academy of Management Journal*, *38*(5), 1442–1465. doi:10.2307/256865

Spreitzer, G. M. (2008). Taking stock: A review of more than twenty years of research on empowerment at work. Handbook of Organizational Behavior, 54-72.

Srivastava, A., Bartol, K. M., & Locke, E. A. (2006). Empowering leadership in management teams: Effects on knowledge sharing, efficacy, and performance. *Academy of Management Journal*, *49*(6), 1239–1251. doi:10.5465/AMJ.2006.23478718

The Times of India. (2014). *India's ITeS sector sees double-digit attrition rate*. Accessed 1 February, 2016 http://timesofindia.indiatimes.com/tech/jobs/Indias-ITeS-sector-sees-double-digit-attrition-rate/articleshow/37067873.cms

Thomas, K. W., & Velthouse, B. A. (1990). Cognitive elements of empowerment: An 'interpretive' model of intrinsic task motivation. *Academy of Management Review, 15*(4), 666–681.

Walumbwa, F. O., & Lawler, J. J. (2003). Building effective organizations: Transformational leadership, collectivist orientation, work-related attitudes, and withdrawal behaviors in three emerging economies. *International Journal of Human Resource Management, 14*(7), 1083–1101. doi:10.1080/0958519032000114219

Wayne, S., Liden, R., & Sparrowe, R. (2000). An Examination of the Mediating Role of Psychological Empowerment on the Relations Between the Job, Interpersonal Relationships, Work Outcomes. *The Journal of Applied Psychology, 85*(3), 407–416. doi:10.1037/0021-9010.85.3.407 PMID:10900815

Xue, Y., Bradley, J., & Liang, H. (2011). Team climate, empowering leadership, and knowledge sharing. *Journal of Knowledge Management, 15*(2), 299–312. doi:10.1108/13673271111119709

Yang, J. (2005). *The Role of Trust in Organizations: Do Foci and Bases Matter?* (Doctoral dissertation). Nanjing University, China.

Yukl, G. (2006). *Leadership in organizations* (6th ed.). Upper Saddle River, NJ: Pearson-Prentice Hall.

Chapter 10
Training for Ecommerce Adoption:
Macro Assessment of Determinants

Rohit Yadav
IIT Roorkee, India

Tripti Mahara
IIT Roorkee, India

ABSTRACT

This chapter empirically investigates the decision of small and medium-sized enterprises of wooden handicraft located in Saharanpur, India to adopt ecommerce. The study is motivated by the fact that even though the handicraft sector plays a vital role in the Indian economy in terms of exports and employment, it has not adopted ecommerce as one of the prominent sales channels for their products. Most of the studies in the literature focus on consumers, but here the focus is on the executives and the managers of SMEs. The study was done by surveying 163 sampled SMEs and the findings reveal that initial e-commerce adoption is mainly determined by organizational awareness and technological readiness. This chapter suggests training providers should focus on recipient and situation specific training to SMEs while designing programmes. Philosophy of one-size-fits-all is not suitable for handicraft training. Post-understanding determinants of initial and institutionalized ecommerce adoption require customized context-specific programmes with special focus are needed to be implemented.

INTRODUCTION

Small and Medium-sized Enterprises (SME) are mostly formulated by a single owner or a group and are generally family owned (Ritchie, 1993). SMEs organizational structure is usually flat. Nonetheless, it makes them more flexible (Scott et al., 1989). In their daily operations focused routine SMEs neglect people management issues.

DOI: 10.4018/978-1-5225-4038-0.ch010

Copyright © 2018, IGI Global. Copying or distributing in print or electronic forms without written permission of IGI Global is prohibited.

Technological progresses have brought in important transformations to the current production and operation methods. Even as SMEs imbibe these progressions in their daily processes, they neglect importance of skilled and trained workforce for their success. In particular, SMEs have to endure amendments during global competition. This puts considerable pressure and acts as a challenge for SMEs to manage both cost and quality while abiding diverse legal requirements, especially those SMEs functioning with labor intensive technologies in developing countries (e.g., Stewart and Beaver, 2003). Lots of SMEs constantly use questionable practices like child labor and violation of labor standards like minimum wage denial, poor work conditions. These SMEs have zero usage of professional management tools.

Porter (1990) said that countries with low natural gifts tend to invest in creation of superior factors, like education, upgrading communication systems and workforce training. Infrastructure linked to workforce quality and education is directly proportional to wholistic development of nation. Quality workforce is the most crucial factors that leads to competitive advantage (O'Malley and O'Gorman, 2001).

The majority SMEs does not possess any method of training that leads to vastly adopted practice of on-job training by master craftsmen. SMEs are complacent only on regular profit generation of workers. Consequently no formal appraisals and training systems are implemented by firms. To face survival and globalization, firms need to focus on training of employees to professionalize work atmosphere.

SMEs and Indian Scenario

India is a country with cultural diversity and has enormous range of handicraft items from different states. This sector is one of the biggest employers in rural India providing employment to more than 7.3 million people. Many artisans labors full time and numerous on part-time basis in this sector. This being an unorganized sector faces many hurdles and challenges like lack of raw material and funds, low productivity, unavailability of skilled artisans, lack of conducive environment, information asymmetry and dissemination (Chamikutty, 2013; Kumar and Rajeev, 2014).

With internet penetration of 34.8% and approximate 462 million internet users in July 2016, ecommerce industry is showing signs of phenomenal growth (Financial express, 2016). Initiatives like handicraft cluster and Flipkart alliance (PIB, 2014) brings skills upliftment and trained workforce into operations. A study by Giyar (2011), have done qualitative study to explore the ecommerce related practices in SMEs in wooden handicraft sector in Jodhpur, Rajasthan. Taking reference from Givar (2011) objective of this study is to identify macro touch points for design of future training and development of Saharanpur wooden handicraft cluster towards ecommerce adoption.

The annual value of the wooden handicraft industry of Saharanpur is worth around Rs 400 crore and it also supports the source of revenue for 150,000 artisans approximately (Yadav and Mahara, 2016) making it one of the important handicraft segment for study. Today, it is the principle center for wood carving. Wooden carvings result in decorated furnitures, furnishings for home, and gifts for all ages and toys for children's.

Assessment Framework of Ecommerce Adoption

The research is based on the Technology, Organization and Environment (TOE) (Tornatzky and Fleischer 1990) framework that has been used by numerous authors to understand different IT adoption especially ecommerce adoption in SMEs (Awa et al., 2016; Gangwar et al., 2015; Oliveira et al., 2014; Alshamaila et al., 2013), but to check the feasibility of this model in Indian SMEs context, preliminary qualitative research was undertaken. After studying the secondary data (literature), interviews were conducted with Managers/Owners of SMEs to understand ecommerce environment in cluster. TOE factors are consistent with previous researches, but along with them an additional factor called Strategy was discovered. Strategy refers to the planning that is done for ecommerce adoption. Level of ecommerce adoption may be different for one SME to another. To capture this variation, four stages of ecommerce adoption process in an organisation are defined (Molla and Licker, 2005a; Al-Somali, 2015). All the constructs of the proposed TOES (Technology, Organization, Environment, and Strategy) model are explained in table 1 and research model is depicted in figure 1. Here the term "Institutionalization" refers to the extent of ecommerce adoption and can be interactive, transactive or integrated (Molla and Licker, 2005a).

Figure 1. Ecommerce Adoption

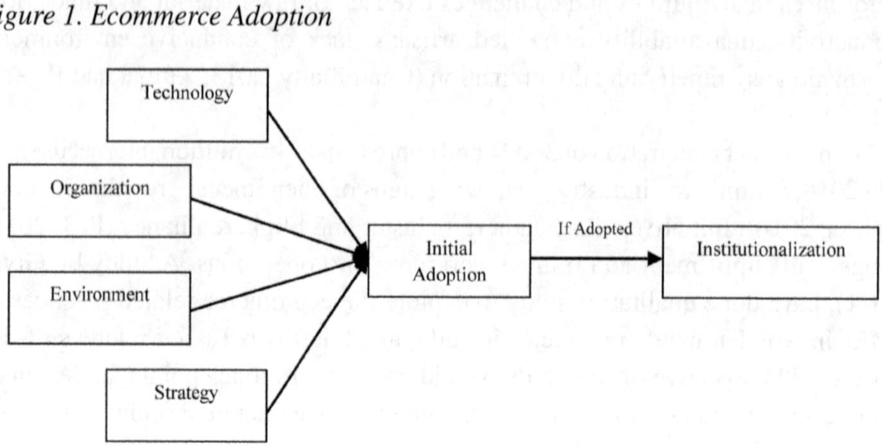

Table 1. Constructs of the Proposed Model

Factors/Construct	Description	Items	References
Organization			
Awareness of CEO/ Manager/Owner	It is defined as SMEs perception about benefits and risks of ecommerce adoption.		Molla and Licker, 2005a
Human Resources	It refers to the access and availability of staff or employees who have abundant experience and exposure to ICT. This is needed for ecommerce projects and initiatives.		Soliman and Janz, 2004; Molla and Licker, 2005a
Technology			
Tech Integration	It is defined as the integration of various components along the value chain. This will enhance SMEs capacity to conduct business electronically.		Oliveira and Martins, 2010a
Tech Readiness	It refers to a combination of factors that facilitate and enable the technological capacity of an organization to adopt ecommerce.		Iacovou et al., 1995; Lin, 2006; Oliveira and Martins, 2010a
Strategy			
Strategy	This factor depicts the importance of planning required for effective deployment of ecommerce. Planning is guided by strategic vision for ecommerce.		Somali et al., 2015; Molla and Licker, 2005a
Environment			
Market Forces e-Readiness	It evaluates the readiness of business partners of an organization such as suppliers and customers to conduct business online.		Molla and Licker, 2005a Li, 2008; Gibbs and Kraemer, 2004
Government Regulatory and Policy Support	It assesses the support provided by the government and various institutions to encourage, support, sustain and regulate activities related to ecommerce and its other requirements.		
Ecommerce Adoption			
Non-Interactive Ecommerce	It depicts access of firm in sense of static-web existence or e-mail access. Does it exist or not.		Al-Somali et al., 2015; Molla and Licker, 2005a and b
Interactive Ecommerce	Interactive ecommerce is achieved by a firm if it holds interactive web presence. This is achieved by usage of two-way communications with the consumers. It can involve online order, feedback forms, and different methods of interactions like queries acceptance from users.		Al-Somali et al., 2015; Molla and Licker, 2005a and b
Transactive Ecommerce	It shows that an organization has started buying and selling of products online.		Al-Somali et al., 2015; Molla and Licker, 2005a and b
Integrated Ecommerce	It shows that an organization has integrated various stakeholders like suppliers; customers back office to conduct business electronically.		Molla and Licker, 2005a and b

RESEARCH METHODOLOGY

Data Collection

A questionnaire based survey method was adopted for the study. In all, 500 SMEs were targeted using random sampling method. Till the closing stages of the pre set deadline, 163 responses were completely filled by respondents with a response rate is 32.6%.

Data Analysis

Principal Component Analysis (PCA) was conducted on 23 items are depicted in table 2. As a result of the analysis, 7 factors were extracted with the Eigen value greater than 1.

Table 3 presents the results of Pearson Correlation Matrix to check multicollinearity and results were found acceptable (Hair et al., 1998). None items with correlation value lower than 0.35 were observed and therefore results were acceptable (Churchill, 1979). The correlations were significant at $p < 0.05$.

Table 3 also depicts the validity results using Cronbach alpha as per Nunnally (1978) guidelines and results shows all constructs have alpha value above 0.7.

Model Test

The model was tested using discriminant function analysis (DFA) on data collected. It measures correlation between predictor variables and extracted discriminant function. Independent variables that had loading greater than or equal to ±0.40 were identified as significant contributors to the discriminant power of the function at $p < 0.01$ (Hair et al., 1995). Discriminant analysis requires testing the significance of the Discriminant model using F test (Wilks' lambda) that results in varied significance variables.

To analyze the data, two discriminant models are formed. The first model: *Initial Adoption of ecommerce* determines the readiness factors that are important to discriminate adopters from non-adopters of ecommerce. The samples include SMEs that have not achieved interactive ecommerce (n = 106) and those that have achieved interactive status (n = 57). The second model: *Institutionalization of ecommerce* tests hypotheses related to levels of ecommerce adoption. Assessment of integrated ecommerce adoption was not conducted as no SME was found to adopt integrated ecommerce level in Saharanpur wooden handicraft rural cluster. Thus, the samples include SMEs that have implemented interactive ecommerce (n = 32) and others that have started to adopt transactional ecommerce (n = 25).

Table 2. Results of Factor Analysis

Factors	Loadings						
	1	2	3	4	5	6	7
Awareness	.777						
	.784						
	.795						
	.779						
	.565						
	.802						
Human Resources		.794					
		.737					
		.634					
Technology Integration			.792				
			.889				
			.552				
Technology Readiness				.673			
				.796			
Market Forces E-readiness					.414		
					.888		
					.914		
Government Regulatory and Policy Support						.538	
						.448	
Strategy							.828
							.774
							.440
							.590

Table 3. Pearson Correlation Matrix and Cronbach Alpha

Constructs	1	2	3	4	5	6	7	Cronbach Alpha
1. Awareness	1							0.968
2. Human Resources	.889	1						0.807
3. Strategy	.812	.727	1					0.895
4. Market Forces e-readiness	.671	.597	.592	1				0.768
5. Government Regulatory and Policy Support	.540	.467	.360	.681	1			0.755
6. Technology Readiness	.887	.866	.815	.702	.499	1		0.847
7. Technology Integration	.770	.723	.788	.630	.353	.880	1	0.962

Initial Adoption of Ecommerce

Here, ecommerce adoption is operationalized as a dichotomy of whether or not an organization has attained an interactive ecommerce status. The results of the discriminant analysis together with the descriptive statistics are presented in Table 4. The model is statistically significant (Wilk's Lambda (λ) = 0.459; x^2 = 124.192; d.f. = 3; F =155.367; Canonical Correlation= 0.736; $p < 0.01$). The function correctly classifies 85.3% of the organisations in the sample (80.2% of the non-interactive adopters and 94.7% of the interactive adopters).

Institutionalization

Table 4 presents the results of discriminant analysis. The discriminant function analysis produces a statistically significant function (Wilk's Lambda (λ) = 0.311; x^2 = 62.402; d.f. = 3; F = 84.310; Canonical Correlation = .830; $p < 0.01$). This indicates that the model is satisfactorily significant in discriminating interactive and transactive ecommerce adopters. The function correctly classifies 89.5% of the organizations in the sample (96.9% of interactive ecommerce adoption and 96.0% of the transactive ecommerce adoption).

Table 4. Discriminant Analysis for Ecommerce Adoption

Constructs	Initial				Institutionalization			
	Discriminant Loadings	**Wilk's Lambda**	**F**	**Sig.**	**Discriminant Loadings**	**Wilk's Lambda**	**F**	**Sig.**
Awareness	**.861**	.507	155.353	.000	**.833**	.395	84.310	.000
Human Resources	**.645**	.647	87.259	.000	.105	.998	.102	.751
Strategy	**.681**	.622	97.300	.000	**.483**	.850	9.713	.003
Market Forces e-readiness	.305	.891	19.532	.000	-.118	.997	.145	.705
Government Regulatory and Policy Support	.343	.867	24.600	.000	**-.407**	.962	2.150	.048
Technology Readiness	**.674**	.627	95.110	.000	-.126	.966	1.917	.172
Technology Integration	**.558**	.710	65.319	.000	-.089	.998	.085	.771

DISCUSSIONS

The results of this study demonstrate Organization, Technology and Strategy factors are vital in initial adoption of ecommerce. Among all the constructs, awareness (Organization factor) is found most significant. The results are consistent with the previous findings of ecommerce adoption in developing countries. Without awareness of managers/owners/CEO of a SME, they are least likely to adopt new innovations and technologies (Ramdani and Kawalek, 2007). As noted in various studies that it is owner/manager/CEO whose awareness helps motivate, guide and encourage staff to adopt innovations in organization. It is the risk taking ability of the owner that helps in adoption of any new technology in organization. Without technology readiness and integration, it will not be feasible to integrate ecommerce into the SMEs business. The study also suggests that strategy positively influences initial and institutionalization stages of ecommerce adoption. Strategy reveals the importance of clear vision, legal policies information, communications, systematic changes required, long term goals and measures to taken by the SME for ecommerce adoption. At institutionalization level government regulatory and policy support is also crucial towards adoption of ecommerce. It is necessary to install trust in organizations to convert new innovations into opportunities for them. Without monetary and policy level support from government, adoption of ecommerce in rural areas of India will not be a huge success.

The study hoists significant propositions for both field experts and policy formulators. First, existing education curriculum cannot cater to the requirements of handicraft SMEs. Educational curriculum that addresses sector's numerous requirements for both management and artisanal skills is required. Secondly, firms are required to consider learning and training from a relevant perspective. Conversely, balanced formal and informal training emerges as the best method for SMEs to gain new learning's. Third, generally SMEs function under scarcity of resources, they must identify and selectively choose their capabilities and resources where investments are required that brings client satisfaction and cost advantage. All these points become crucial during global competition with mass production and low-end markets.

As evident in the study, adoption of ecommerce is hampered due to lack of awareness of its potential benefits. Hence it becomes crucial that various other stakeholders of this sector like vendors, export council, government etc. make the firms aware about benefits of ecommerce. Present study shows that not much of government support is available right now, but it is a critical factor to foster ecommerce adoption in the long run. To move SMEs from initial stage of adoption towards institutionalization specialized training courses and programs related to awareness, strategy and government policies with regulatory support is to be customized and provided. Well strategized training programme with the help of promotional seminars, workshops, on-site visits and presentations should be organized with stress on importance of ecommerce for competitiveness and productivity.

CONCLUSION

Adoption of ecommerce by SME cluster is affected by various factors and they all contribute significantly. Most of the factors are in need of special attention through training and development programmes. This study suggests training providers should focus on recipient and situation specific training to SMEs while designing programmes. Philosophy of one-size-fits-all is not suitable for handicraft training. Determinants of initial and institutionalized ecommerce adoption with training needs are of special focus to design context specific programmes for SMEs. As a fact, this field calls for lot of creativity and innovativeness on parts of designers of training programmes for SMEs.

Limitations and Future Research

The results only reflect Saharanpur wooden handicraft cluster perspectives on ecommerce adoption. The results may vary in different cultural and environmental settings. Hence, this study can be extended to various other handicraft SMEs located in other parts of the country. This will lead to a generalized framework that will aid the SMEs in handicraft sector to know determinants required for ecommerce adoption.

REFERENCES

Al-Somali, S. A., Gholami, R., & Clegg, B. (2015). A stage-oriented model (SOM) for Ecommerce adoption: A study of Saudi Arabian organisations. *Journal of Manufacturing Technology Management*, *26*(1), 2–35. doi:10.1108/JMTM-03-2013-0019

Alshamaila, Y., Papagiannidis, S., & Li, F. (2013). Cloud computing adoption by SMEs in the north east of England: A multi-perspective framework. *Journal of Enterprise Information Management*, *26*(3), 250–275. doi:10.1108/17410391311325225

Awa, H. O., Ukoha, O., & Emecheta, B. C. (2016). Using TOE theoretical framework to study the adoption of ERP solution. *Cogent Business and Management*, *3*(1), 1196571. doi:10.1080/23311975.2016.1196571

Chamikutty, P. (2013). *Problems facing the Indian artifacts sector*. Retrieved February 2, 2017. From https://social.yourstory.com/2013/06/crafting-a-livelihood-a-snapshot-of-the-indian-artifacts-sector-2/

Financial Express. (2016). Retrieved February 2, 2017. From http://www.financialexpress.com/industry/companies/Ecommerce-in-india-why-ishippo-com-is-eyeing-space-shunned-by-amazon-flipkart-snapdeal/290251/

Gangwar, H., Date, H., & Ramaswamy, R. (2015). Understanding determinants of cloud computing adoption using an integrated TAM-TOE model. *Journal of Enterprise Information Management*, *28*(1), 107–130. doi:10.1108/JEIM-08-2013-0065

Gibbs, J. L., & Kraemer, K. L. (2004). A cross-country investigation of the determinants of scope of e-commerce use: An institutional approach. *Electronic Markets*, *14*(2), 124–137. doi:10.1080/10196780410001675077

Giyar, M. R. (2011). A-*Study of Ecommerce Related Practices in Selected Small Scale Wooden Handicraft Enterprises*. Available at SSRN 1948146.

Hair, J. F., Anderson, R. E., Babin, B. J., & Black, W. C. (2010). *Multivariate data analysis: A global perspective* (Vol. 7). Upper Saddle River, NJ: Pearson.

Iacovou, C. L., Benbasat, I., & Dexter, A. S. (1995). Electronic data interchange and small organizations: Adoption and impact of technology. *Management Information Systems Quarterly*, *19*(4), 465–485. doi:10.2307/249629

Kumar, D., & Rajeev, P. V. (2014). Marketing challenges of handicraft retailers in changing environment. *ZENITH International Journal of Business Economics and Management Research*, *4*(10), 22–33.

Li, Y. H. (2008). An empirical investigation on the determinants of e-procurement adoption in Chinese manufacturing enterprises. In *2008 International Conference on Management Science and Engineering 15th Annual Conference Proceedings* (pp. 32-37). IEEE. doi:10.1109/ICMSE.2008.4668890

Lin, H. F. (2006). Interorganizational and organizational determinants of planning effectiveness for Internet-based interorganizational systems. *Information & Management*, *43*(4), 423–433. doi:10.1016/j.im.2005.10.004

Molla, A., & Licker, P. S. (2005a). Ecommerce adoption in developing countries: A model and instrument. *Information & Management*, *42*(6), 877–899. doi:10.1016/j.im.2004.09.002

Molla, A., & Licker, P. S. (2005b). Perceived e-readiness factors in ecommerce adoption: An empirical investigation in a developing country. *International Journal of Electronic Commerce*, *10*(1), 83–110.

Nunnally, J. C. (1978). *Psychometric theory* (2nd ed.). New York: McGraw-Hill.

O'malley, E., & O'gorman, C. (2001). Competitive advantage in the Irish indigenous software industry and the role of inward foreign direct investment. *European Planning Studies*, *9*(3), 303–321. doi:10.1080/713666484

Oliveira, T., & Martins, M. F. (2010a). Firms patterns of e-business adoption: Evidence for the European Union-27. *The Electronic Journal Information Systems Evaluation*, *13*(1), 47–56.

Oliveira, T., Thomas, M., & Espadanal, M. (2014). Assessing the determinants of cloud computing adoption: An analysis of the manufacturing and services sectors. *Information & Management*, *51*(5), 497–510. doi:10.1016/j.im.2014.03.006

PIB, Press Information Bureau. (2014). *Initiatives of the New Government in the Textile Sector, Govt of India, Ministry of Textiles*. Retrieved February 2, 2017. From http://pib.nic.in/newsite/PrintRelease.aspx?relid=110128

Porter, M. E. (1990). The competitive advantage of nations. *Harvard Business Review*, *68*(2), 73–93.

Ramdani, B., & Kawalek, P. (2007), SME adoption of enterprise systems in the Northwest of England. In *IFIP International Working Conference on Organizational Dynamics of Technology-Based Innovation* (pp. 409-429). Springer US. doi:10.1007/978-0-387-72804-9_27

Ritchie, J. (1993). Strategies for human resource management: Challenges in smaller and entrepreneurial organisations. *Human Resource Management*, 111–135.

Scott, M., Roberts, I., Holroyd, G., & Sawbridge, D. (1989). *Management and Industrial Relations in Small Firms*. Department of Employment Research Paper No. 70.

Soliman, K. S., & Janz, B. D. (2004). An exploratory study to identify the critical factors affecting the decision to establish Internet-based interorganizational information systems. *Information & Management*, *41*(6), 697–706. doi:10.1016/j.im.2003.06.001

Tornatzky, L. G., Fleischer, M., & Chakrabarti, A. K. (1990). *Processes of technological innovation*. Lexington Books.

Yadav, R., & Mahara, T. (2016). An exploratory study to investigate value chain of Saharanpur wooden carving handicraft cluster. *International Journal of System Assurance Engineering and Management*, 1-8.

Chapter 11
Factors Affecting High Employee Turnover in Indian Manufacturing Sector

Nishant Singh
Indian Institute of Technology Roorkee, India

ABSTRACT

This chapter is an attempt to explore the factors affecting high employee turnover (ET) in the Indian manufacturing sector. The study shows the association between meaningful work (MWF), organizational information and communication (OIC), and organizational trust (OT). The authors have chosen convenience sampling method and 211 respondents' data was collected from the five Indian manufacturing organizations located in Uttarakhand state. Reliability and validity (convergent and divergent) were also checked and found high. They used conditional process modeling to check the mediation effect of OIC. Findings suggest that MWF positively impacts OT and OIC positively impacts OT. Partial mediation effect of OIC was also captured on the relationship of MWF and OT. The managerial implications, limitations, and future scope were also discussed in detail. These implications provide the good insights to all the employers who are constantly seeking the solution to resolve the issues of attrition and high ET in their respective organizations.

INTRODUCTION

Nowadays organizations are facing various problems globally related to the high employee turnover issue and striving hard to keep their employees retained and let them feel valued. Specially, Indian employers are trying hard to retain their

DOI: 10.4018/978-1-5225-4038-0.ch011

Copyright © 2018, IGI Global. Copying or distributing in print or electronic forms without written permission of IGI Global is prohibited.

talented workforce for a longtime (Shashtri, 2008). ET has been a vital issue for the organizations and widely accepted as a major threat by the HR practitioners (Porter & Steers, 1973; Cotton & Tuttle, 1986; Griffeth et al., 2000). Although recruiting the potential candidates for the job is itself a big task and then to convert them in effective and efficient workforce is very tough. Employee turnover does not only imply the loss of human capital but also the loss of investment credited on the training process and knowledge provided by the organization. It means leaving the right employee is equal to the loss of intangible knowledge infused by the concern organization through the time (Balfour & Neff, 1993). Here the intention of the employee plays a big role to incite his thinking process towards leaving the organization. This turnover intention can be explained as ''the subjective estimation of an individual regarding the probability of leaving an organization in the near future'' (Mowday et al., 1982). Hence, predicting the employees' intention is necessary for the HR practitioners to deal with this problem precisely. Some studies examined these behavioral intentions as intention to leave, searching new prospects outside and quitting the organization. There are various empirical studies supporting the view of these intentions which can predict turnover rate better than any other variable in an organization (Steel & Ovalle 1984; Carmeli & Weisberg 2006). According to Dalton et al., (1982) from the organization perspective, there are two types of voluntary turnover 'functional and dysfunctional'. Functional turnover occurs when any employee leaves the organization voluntarily but it does not affect his organization much. In this case, organization does not get affected while losing such employees, may be because of their non-performance and lack of the unique skills. Moreover, dysfunctional turnover occurs when an employee leaves his organization voluntarily but organization gets very much affected. It might be because of losing the great talent who had unique skill, knowledge or talent which is perceived hard to get back. The aim of this study is to explore the factors which affect employee turnover most and study their relationship together in the Indian manufacturing industry. Thus, based on the above discussion two research questions arises here

Research Question 1: What are the factors influencing employee turnover across the globe?

Research Question 2: Which factors are essential and worthwhile to study in the Indian manufacturing industry?

To address the first question, we took the help of literature review and found that plenty of researches has already been done on ET, entails that meaningful work (Cortese, et al., 2013), organizational trust, commitment, learning capabilities (Tirelli & Goh, 2015), ethical climate (De Coninck, 2011), fair HR practices (Ertürk, 2014), psychological contracts fulfillment (Van den Heuvel et al., 2017), job satisfaction

(Schwepker, 2001) and communication (Kim & Lee, 2009; Madi, 2013; Xu et al., 2017) affects ET negatively across the globe in different sectors. Parts from these, there are some more reasons occurring for high turnover issue including low salary, lack of understanding with supervisor, communication barriers, and excess workload (Choi et al., 2015). After identifying the major factors and to address the second research question, we asked 100 employees working in different Indian manufacturing units in Uttarakhand state to name those factors which affect their leaving intention most. Their feedback revealed that meaningful work, organizational trust and organizational communication were the most influencing factors having the major impact on their intention to quit the organization. Also, we found that no research has been conducted so far to study these variables together in the Indian manufacturing sector. Hence our research will be focusing on MWF, OIC and OT.

LITERATURE REVIEW

People who have keen interest in their work and they succeed in life in the long run. Their performance is directly related to the passion towards their work. Famous novelist John Irving said that i never thought that I am doing any work, i don't consider my writing as work because i love it and i do it passionately which brought me happiness and success in life (Amabile, 1989, p. 56). Lips-Wiersma & Wright (2012) discussed the four dimensions of meaningful work such as service to others, developing the inner self, expressing full potential and unity with others were discussed in details and developed a new dynamic process to measure MFW. 'Inspiration' and 'reality' along with their dynamic relationship were identified to be an aspect searching for meaning in work and life. MFW concept is derived from humanities not from any management specific theory. Meaningful work has always captured the attention to be understood and studied thoroughly. The basic dilemma of management revolves around the concept of meaningfulness in the work. As per Pratt & Ashforth (2003) when work is considered meaningful, it helps every employee to understand 'why I am working here?'. Arnold et al. (2007) studied meaningful work as a mediator between transformational leadership and psychological well-being which helps leaders to transform their followers' belief to improve their well-being.

Organizational trust is defined as the promptness of a party to be careful about the behavior and actions of the other party (Mayer et al., 1995, p. 712). Trust is considered as a vital element to make the human relationship stronger and positive which helps building in supportive conducive environment and gives the feeling of attachment, belongingness and security (Mishra & Morrissey, 1990). Trust acts as a facilitator to link employees' relationship with their organization and supervisor. Organizational trust being an essential factor of organization, works as remedy to mitigate the turnover intention amongst the workers (Maertz et al., 2007). Various studies say that trust is positively associated with the job satisfaction, organizational commitment, performance, low absenteeism, positive attitude, low turnover rate and organizational citizenship behavior (Mayer et al., 1995; Butler et al, 1999; Dyer & Chu, 2003; Mayer & Gavin, 2005). After taking all these positive outcomes into account, OT appears to be a powerful tool leading to managerial effectiveness. Organizational trust or trust in organization is distinct from the employee trust towards his or her supervisor. It was explained that employee trust towards supervisor and organization constitute a new construct organizational trust as a whole (Nyhan & Marlowe, 1997). Brown et al., (2011) defined OT as one of the major determinants of workers' commitment and loyalty (CLI) and empirically tested 'how OT contributes to enhance the workers' performance'.

Organizational Information and Communication (OIC) is a process by which organization makes sure that their employees are aware about the goals and their involvement is recognized as a significant contribution to achieve the desired goals and foster job commitments (Anderson & Martin, 1995; Haskins, 1996). Organizational communication is a part of HR practices, which empowers employees and raises commitments amongst them (Stuart, 1999). Yamaguchi (2006) discussed about the four types of communication tactics 'rational, soft, promise exchange and hard tactics'. Rational communication tactics involve logical arguments and factual evidences, presented by the supervisor to let their subordinate come to a consensus. Soft communication tactics are comprised of creating favorable attitude, appealing feeling of loyalty and friendship towards the subordinates. Hard tactics are vice versa of the soft tactics; moreover, promise exchange tactics insures subordinates to fulfill all the promises made by their supervisor. Yamaguchi (2009) conducted a cross culture study between American and Japanese workers and found that communication tactics influence workers' trust in a significant way.

CONCEPTUAL FRAMEWORK

Meaningful Work (MWF) and Organizational Trust (OT)

(Herzberg et al., 1959) gave two factor theory of motivation and coined two terms 'intrinsic' and 'extrinsic' factors for motivation. According to the theory, work comes under the intrinsic factors which motivates the employees to work hard and positively affects their job satisfaction. Plausibly, it implies that work should be more focused and meaningful in nature. Scroggins (2008) also supported that meaningful work is negatively related to the intention of quitting and positively related to the job satisfaction and organization commitment. Plenty of studies (Rich,1997; Gilstrap &

Collins, 2012; Braun et al., 2013) suggest that job satisfaction is positively associated with organizational trust. So based on the above discussion we can hypnotize that

H1: Meaningful Work is positively related to Organizational Trust.

Organizational Information and Communication (OIC) and Organizational Trust (OT)

Thomas et al., (2009) proposed a model describing the relationship between communication and organizational trust. This model shows the association of 'quality of information' and 'quantity of information' to the organizational trust. Trust is said to be solely focused on belief which is generated through information, provided quality of information including accuracy, usefulness and timeliness is operationalized. Studies suggest that quality of information leads to higher trust within the organization (Benton et al., 1969; Folger & Konovsky, 1989; Konovsky & Cropanzano, 1991; Whitener et al., 1998; Simons, 2002). With the help of the above discussion, we can say that communication as in form of information acts as a facilitator to develop the organizational trust. Hence we hypnotize our second hypothesis here

H2: OIC is positively related to Organizational Trust.

OIC as a Mediator

Communication is said to be a central part of the management practices where managers indulge themself in some form of work of communication by spending their 75% average time (Klemmer & Snyder, 1972). The importance of communication as a strategic mediator has been studied deeply and explained that communication process mediates the relation between two parties involved (Ivanov, 2010). As our study is focused on the factors involved in employee turnover, we assume that OIC may mediate the relationship between meaningful work and organizational trust. So we conceptualize third hypothesis

H3: OIC significantly mediates the relationship between Meaningful Work and Organizational Trust.

Here is the proposed model for our study which is divided into two parts. The first part shows the total direct effect and second exhibits partial mediation effect.

Figure 1.

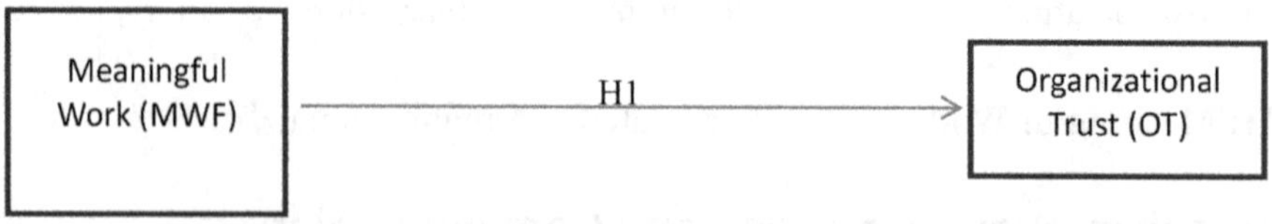

Hypothesized Model (I) – Total effect model

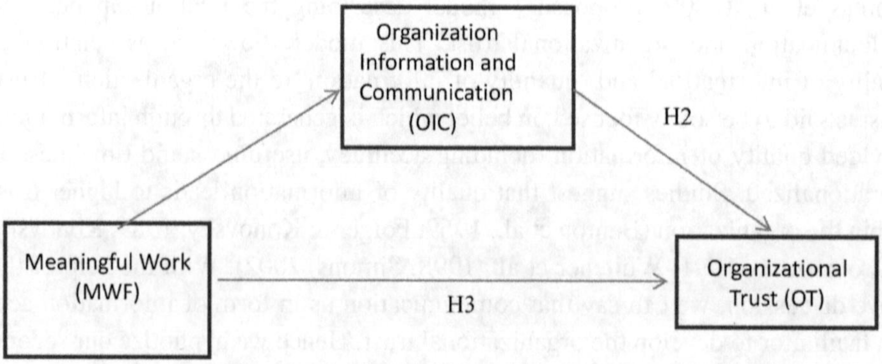

Hypothesized Model (II) – Total indirect effect model (Mediation effect)

RESEARCH APPROACH

Sample and Data Collection

This study is focused on the employees working in the Indian manufacturing industry, Uttarakhand. We have used convenience sampling method to collect data form the junior, middle and senior hierarchical levels. Researcher personally collected the data while assisting his supervisor in different training programs in these units. This study is emphasized on the Indian managers of the Indian manufacturing organizations, chosen from the different units of the Uttarakhand region. Total 225 respondents were targated between March 2016 to Sep 2016 in seven different phases. Fourteen respondents' data was eliminated due to the missing values and low standard deviation found. Data was containing 93% males and 6.63% females. Among all 56.40% graduates and 43.60% postgraduates were there and avearge income was recored 8 lakhs. The contribution of junior level employees was higher as 41.23%, followed by 22.75% middle and 11.85% senior level employees. The ratio of unmarried and married employees was 1: 3.5 and 58% employees were below 35 years of age. All the responses were captured on the Likert 5-point scale (1=strongly disagree, 2= disagree, 3= neutral, 4= agree & 5=strongly agree). We used conditional process modeling (Model 4) to analyze the mediation effect of compassion on the relation between meaningful work and organizational trust.

Measures

We have used the following scales and all the responses were captured through Likert five-point type scale (5= strongly disagree to 1= strongly agree).

Meaningful Work (MWF)

Seven items were taken to measure meaningful work. These were developed by Ashmos & Duchon. (2000).

Organizational Information and Communication (OIC)

There are four items in this scale taken from the empirical study done by Brown et al., (2011) with the help of WERS 2004.

Organizational Trust (OT)

There are four items in this scale taken from the empirical study done by Brown et al., (2011) with the help of WERS 2004.

RESULTS

Reliability and Validity

Reliability for all the three variables was checked through SPSS 23 version and found significant at 0.787 (MWF), 0.775 (OIC), 0.865 (OT) respectively. These values confirm the internal consistency within the acceptable limits (> 0.7) (Nunnally, 1978). Face validity was checked with the help of experts available in the field and 50 respondents were targeted initially to confirm the proper understanding of all the items included in the scales. Further, confirmatory factor analysis (CFA) was used to test the dimensions of all three variables which confirm that all the constructs were distinguished to each other. Model fitness was also checked through the latest version of SPSS 23 and AMOS. All the fit indices were taken into the account and found within the acceptable limit given by Anderson & Gerbing (1988). The theoretical model shows the overall model fit indices

X^2 /df <5), p = 0.000 AGFI >0.8), GFI >0.9), RMR <0.1, CFI >0.9, RMSEA <0.1

Model = 4,

X (Independent variable) = Meaningful Work (MWF), Y (Dependent variable) = Organizational Trust (OT), M (Mediator) = Organizational Information and Communication (OIC)

Table - I contains the results for all three hypotheses. MWF was significantly positively related to OT, as we hypothesized in hypothesis I (β =.4904, t = 5.3996, at p < 0.005). The relationship between MWF and OIC was found to be significantly positive (β =.3123, t = 3.6731, at p < 0.05). Third hypothesis was also found significant which says OIC is positively related to OT (β =.4008, t = 5.6949, at p < 0.01). MWF indirectly influenced OT through the effects of OIC. Hence, OIC partially mediated the relationship of MWF and OT. As we hypothesized in hypothesis

Table 1. Regression results for simple mediation

Variables	**β**	**SE**	**t**	**P**
Direct effect Model (Total effect of X on Y)				
MWF on OT	0.4904	0.0908	5.3996	0.000
Indirect effect Model (Compassion as mediator)				
MWF on OIC	0.3123	.0850	3.6731	.0003
OIC on OT	0.4008	.0704	5.6949	.0000
MWF on OT	0.3653	.0872	4.1880	.0000
Variable	**Value**	**SE**	**z**	**P**
Indirect effect and significance using normal distribution				
SOBEL	.1252	.0410	3.0537	.0023
Variable CI	**M**	**SE**	**LL 95% CI**	**UL 95%**
Bootstraps results for indirect effect				
Effect	.1252	.0407	.0590	.2198

Note: N=201, MWF= Meaningful Work, OIC= Organizational Information and Communication, OT = Organizational Trust, Bootstrap sample size = 5000, CI = Confidence Interval, LL = Lower Limit, UL = Upper Limit,

III, this indirect effect was found positive (.1252). The two tail significant test demonstrated the significant indirect effect (Sobel $z = 3.0537$, $p < 0.01$). We used bootstrap analysis which supported the SOBEL test results with lower limit 0.590 (95% CI) and upper limit .2198 (95% CI). This showed that both the limits were positive and did not contain zero. Therefore hypotheses I,II, and III were supported. The hypotheses results were summarized below.

Hypotheses results

- **H1**: MWF is positively related to OT . Supported
- **H2:** OIC work is positively related to OT Supported
- **H3:** OIC significantly mediates the relationship between
- MWF and OT Supported

DISCUSSION

This research provides several implications from the theoretical and managerial perspective. Results show the importance of MWF in building the OT. It is empirically tested that MWF positively impacts OT and OIC partially mediates the latter's relationship. The zest of the study suggests that organizations need to be more focused on the nature of the work which they are providing to their employees and supported by (Singh & Rangnekar, 2016). With the help of the measures of the meaningful work, they can investigate 'what their employees think about their current work?'. Studies suggest that job design (Wrzesniewski & Dutton, 2001) and job crafting are the alternative methods by which work can be made interesting and meaningful. Job crafting is thinking about job design in a new way which makes the employee efficient and able to cultivate the meaningfulness in the work. Researchers have nominated OT as a vital instrument which affects attitude and behavior of the employees. Studies demonstrate that trust is associated with positive employee behavior, exceeds contractual obligation demands, cooperation with supervisors and organizational citizenship behavior (Dirks & Ferrin, 2001; Cho & Ringquist, 2011). Employees, who have more trust in their organization, enjoy their work more and stay for a long time to seek more opportunities in their organization (Shahnawaz & Goswami, 2011; Balkan et al., 2014). Our results suggest that trust is directly proportion to the level of information and communication shared within the organization, so organization communication should be smooth and more focused in the organization. Notwithstanding, organization should also assess the quality and quantity of the information which is to be shared. This ensures the authenticity and mitigates the barriers between two parties involved in the communication. Moreover, to discuss the role of meaningful work in avoiding the high employee turnover, we can refer self-concept based theory. Shamir (1991) proposed the self-concept based theory and explained that employers need to more concentrate on matching the employee's self-concept with the job tasks so that employee can perceive his/her work meaningful. As our study is based on the Indian manufacturing units, we need to understand the nature of the industry first. Manufacturing industry demands rigorous planning, proper execution and more output. Delivering quality production within a specific time has been the prime focus. To achieve the desired targets, industry demands huge workforce, which could be divided into skilled, semi-skilled and unskilled. Managers hire the unskilled workforce and convert them into skilled by investing lot of time and money in form of training. Junior level employees play a big role to pave the way between workers and the middle and senior level employees. They impart information from the up to down and build a relationship between both the parties. This communication system provides a transparency in the organization so that workers will understand the top management' decisions and workers' union does not hinder the production process. Barriers make the communication process complicated and information get distorted. This type of problem increases the grievances amongst the workers and junior employees towards their seniors, that's how conflicts start in the organization. These conflicts lead to lack of OT and incite the leaving intentions of the employees. Organizations facing the high turnover rate, get difficulty in achieving the desired production goals and their growth gets diminished. Another interpretation of high employee turnover talks about the positive side of this process which says that high turnover removes the unsatisfied employees from the organization and leaves a less dissatisfied pool of employees. However, all the stayed employees may not be more satisfied than the left ones (Elger & Smith, 1999) but organization can retain them for a long period of time by providing good working environment, transformational leadership (Ariyabuddhiphongs & Kahn, 2017), meaningful work (Cortese et al., 2013) and psychological safety (Tiwari & Lenka, 2016). Psychological safety helps employees to work freely without the fear of retribution and facilitates in making a trustworthy relationship among employees which leads to high employee engagement and reduce the high ET. Employers should focus on building the talent hub by providing top management support, challenging tasks and continuous learning to their employees. Tiwari & Lenka (2015) suggested a conceptual model for developing the talent management model which also asserts that 'top management support, challenging tasks and continuous learning' create a positive environment where employees gain professional, social and personal competencies. Professional competencies comprise of communication skill, conflict resolution, technical expertise, execution excellence and goal-setting skills. Social competencies are building and managing a good relationship at the workplace through positive behavior, and social, emotional and cognitive skills. Moreover, personal competencies refer to the employees' personal traits and attributes such as self-awareness, self-confidence, and drive to develop own skills and capabilities. These above efforts act as facilitators to let their employees feel being valued in the organization by which they can perceive their work as meaningful which increases their trust and mitigate the intention to leave about their organization.

LIMITATIONS

Every research has its own limitations so we have here. The current research is done solely on the Indian manufacturing units in Uttarakhand. Manufacturing units are believed largely to be focusing on the production part rather than taking their employees' interest into the account so carefully. This sector has a different culture and practices to follow. As we collected our data from the junior, middle and senior level employees, our results may not be showing accurate mindset of a particular hierarchy level. It might be a cumulative thinking of all three different hierarchical levels rather than focusing on a particular level of employees. Moreover one more obvious limitation is the lack of the female employees in selected manufacturing units and study is limited to the Uttarakhand state only, where demographic factors may be prevalent. A related limitation is that the employee turnover is not empirically tested here with MWF, OIC and OT simultaneously. A theoretically connection was made and showed that these variables influence ET. To overcome these limitations a separate study need to be taken care of in the future where different industries may take place with large participation of female employees and ET as a variable can be empirically tested with its antecedents.

CONCLUSION

This research explores those factors which play a significant role in high employee turnover in the Indian manufacturing sector as well as talks about the HR practices which could be useful to mitigate this problem. We empirically tested that OIC partially mediates the relationship between MWF and OT. 'How these all three variables alienate the turnover intentions?' it was discussed in details. This research provides good inputs to the HR practitioners who are facing the high ET problem in their respective organizations. Results suggest that MWF is a concept which increases the positive intentions amongst all the employees and build a trust towards their organizations. If organization passes all the necessary information to their employees through all verticals and the right communication tactics are adopted, where employees are made sure to have known about each activity of their organization, improves better understanding and enhances OT.

REFERENCES

Amabile, T. M. (1989). *Growing up creative: Nurturing a lifetime of creativity*. Crown House Publishing Limited.

Anderson, C. M., & Martin, M. M. (1995). Why employees speak to coworkers and bosses: Motives, gender, and organizational satisfaction. *The Journal of Business Communication, 32*(3), 249-265.

Anderson, J. C., & Gerbing, D. W. (1988). Structural equation modeling in practice: A review and recommended two-step approach. *Psychological Bulletin, 103*(3), 411–423. doi:10.1037/0033-2909.103.3.411

Ariyabuddhiphongs, V., & Kahn, S. I. (2017). Transformational leadership and turnover intention: The mediating effects of trust and job performance on café employees in Thailand. *Journal of Human Resources in Hospitality & Tourism, 16*(2), 215–233. doi:10.1080/15332845.2016.1202730

Arnold, K. A., Turner, N., Barling, J., Kelloway, E. K., & McKee, M. C. (2007). Transformational leadership and psychological well-being: The mediating role of meaningful work. *Journal of Occupational Health Psychology, 12*(3), 193–203. doi:10.1037/1076-8998.12.3.193 PMID:17638487

Ashmos, D. P., & Duchon, D. (2000). Spirituality at work: A conceptualization and measure. *Journal of Management Inquiry, 9*(2), 134–145. doi:10.1177/105649260092008

Balfour, D. L., & Neff, D. M. (1993). Predicting and managing turnover in human service agencies: A case study of an organization in crisis. *The Personnel Administrator, 22*(3), 473–486. doi:10.1177/009102609302200310

Balkan, M. O., Serin, A. E., & Soran, S. (2014). The relationship between trust, turnover intentions and emotions: An application. *European Scientific Journal, 10*(2).

Benton, A., Gelber, E., Kelley, H., & Liebling, B. (1969). Reactions to various degrees of deceit in a mixed-motive relationship. *Journal of Personality and Social Psychology, 12*(2), 170–180. doi:10.1037/h0027570 PMID:5778349

Braun, S., Peus, C., Weisweiler, S., & Frey, D. (2013). Transformational leadership, job satisfaction, and team performance: A multilevel mediation model of trust. *The Leadership Quarterly, 24*(1), 270–283. doi:10.1016/j.leaqua.2012.11.006

Brown, S., McHardy, J., McNabb, R., & Taylor, K. (2011). Workplace performance, worker commitment, and loyalty. *Journal of Economics & Management Strategy, 20*(3), 925–955. doi:10.1111/j.1530-9134.2011.00306.x

Butler, J. K. Jr, Cantrell, R. S., & Flick, R. J. (1999). Transformation leadership behaviors, upward trust, and satisfaction in self-managed work teams. *Organization Development Journal*, *17*, 13–28.

Carmeli, A., & Weisberg, J. (2006). Exploring turnover intentions among three professional groups of employees. *Human Resource Development International*, *9*(2), 191–206. doi:10.1080/13678860600616305

Cho, Y. J., & Ringquist, E. J. (2011). Managerial trustworthiness and organizational outcomes. *Journal of Public Administration: Research and Theory*, *21*(1), 53–86. doi:10.1093/jopart/muq015

Choi, I. S., Son, Y. E., & Shin, K. A. (2015). *Statistical Yearbook of Social Worker*. Seoul: Korea Association of Social Worker.

Cortese, C. G., Gatti, P., & Ghislieri, C. (2013). Job demands, meaningful work, and turnover intention among nurses. *La Medicina del Lavoro*, *105*(1), 37–47. PMID:24552093

Cotton, J. L., & Tuttle, J. M. (1986). Employee turnover: A meta-analysis and review with implications for research. *Academy of Management Review*, *11*(1), 55–70.

Dalton, D. R., Todor, W. D., & Krackhardt, D. M. (1982). Turnover overstated: The functional taxonomy. *Academy of Management Review*, *7*(1), 117–123.

DeConinck, J. B. (2011). The effects of ethical climate on organizational identification, supervisory trust, and turnover among salespeople. *Journal of Business Research*, *64*(6), 617–624. doi:10.1016/j.jbusres.2010.06.014

Dirks, K. T., & Ferrin, D. L. (2001). The role of trust in organizational settings. *Organization Science*, *12*(4), 450–467. doi:10.1287/orsc.12.4.450.10640

Dyer, J. H., & Chu, W. (2003). The role of trustworthiness in reducing transaction costs and improving performance: Empirical evidence from the United States, Japan, and Korea. *Organization Science*, *14*(1), 57–68. doi:10.1287/orsc.14.1.57.12806

Elger, C., & Smith, T. (1999). Good enough production' and the shaping of worker cooperation, compliance and non-compliance in Japanese transplants. In *International Labour Process Conference*. Royal Holloway University of London.

Ertürk, A. (2014). Influences of HR practices, social exchange, and trust on turnover intentions of public IT professionals. *Public Personnel Management*, *43*(1), 140–175. doi:10.1177/0091026013517875

Folger, R., & Konovsky, M. A. (1989). Effects of procedural and distributive justice on reactions to pay raise decisions. *Academy of Management Journal*, *32*(1), 115–130. doi:10.2307/256422

Gilstrap, J. B., & Collins, B. J. (2012). The importance of being trustworthy: Trust as a mediator of the relationship between leader behaviors and employee job satisfaction. *Journal of Leadership & Organizational Studies*, *19*(2), 152–163. doi:10.1177/1548051811431827

Griffeth, R. W., Hom, P. W., & Gaertner, S. (2000). A meta-analysis of antecedents and correlates of employee turnover: Update, moderator tests, and research implications for the next millennium. *Journal of Management*, *26*(3), 463–488. doi:10.1177/014920630002600305

Haskins, W. A. (1996). Freedom of speech: construct for creating a culture which empowers organizational members. *The Journal of Business Communication, 33*(1), 85-97.

Hayes, A. F. (2013). *Introduction to mediation, moderation, and conditional process analysis: A regression-based approach*. Guilford Press.

Herzberg, F., Mausner, B., & Snyderman, B. B. (1959). *The Motivation to Work* (2nd ed.). New York, NY: Wiley.

Ivanov, M. (2010). Communication via a strategic mediator. *Journal of Economic Theory*, *145*(2), 869–884. doi:10.1016/j.jet.2009.08.001

Kashyap, V., & Rangnekar, S. (2016). The mediating role of trust: Investigating the relationships among employer brand perception and turnover intentions. *Global Business Review*, *17*(3), 64–75. doi:10.1177/0972150916631083

Kim, H., & Lee, S. Y. (2009). Supervisory communication, burnout, and turnover intention among social workers in health care settings. *Social Work in Health Care*, *48*(4), 364–385. doi:10.1080/00981380802598499 PMID:19396707

Klemmer, E. T., & Snyder, F. W. (1972). Measurement of time spent communicating. *Journal of Communication*, *22*(2), 142–158. doi:10.1111/j.1460-2466.1972.tb00141.x

Konovsky, M. A., & Cropanzano, R. (1991). Perceived fairness of employee drug testing as a predictor of employee attitudes and job performance. *The Journal of Applied Psychology*, *76*(5), 698–707. doi:10.1037/0021-9010.76.5.698 PMID:1960142

Lips-Wiersma, M., & Wright, S. (2012). Measuring the meaning of meaningful work: Development and validation of the Comprehensive Meaningful Work Scale (CMWS). *Group & Organization Management, 37*(5), 655–685. doi:10.1177/1059601112461578

Madi, M. Y. A. (2013). *Communication, Job Satisfaction and Employees Turnover in Multinational Engineering Organizations in the United Arab Emirates* (Doctoral dissertation). The British University in Dubai.

Maertz, C. P., Griffeth, R. W., Campbell, N. S., & Allen, D. G. (2007). The effects of perceived organizational support and perceived supervisor support on employee turnover. *Journal of Organizational Behavior, 28*(8), 1059–1075. doi:10.1002/job.472

Mayer, R. C., Davis, J. H., & Schoorman, F. D. (1995). An integrative model of organizational trust. *Academy of Management Review, 20*(3), 709–734.

Mayer, R. C., & Gavin, M. B. (2005). Trust in management and performance: Who minds the shop while the employees watch the boss? *Academy of Management Journal, 48*(5), 874–888. doi:10.5465/AMJ.2005.18803928

Mishra, J., & Morrissey, M. A. (1990). Trust in employee/employer relationships: A survey of West Michigan managers. *Public Personnel Management, 19*(4), 443–486. doi:10.1177/009102609001900408

Mowday, R. T., Porter, L. W., & Steers, R. M. (1982). *Employee-organization linkage. The psychology of commitment absenteeism, and turn over*. London: Academic Press Inc.

Nunnally, J. C. (1978). *Psychometric theory*. New York: McGraw-Hill.

Nyhan, R. C., & Marlowe, H. A. Jr. (1997). Development and psychometric properties of the organizational trust inventory. *Evaluation Review, 21*(5), 614–635. doi:10.1177/0193841X9702100505

Porter, L. W., & Steers, R. M. (1973). Organizational, work, and personal factors in employee turnover and absenteeism. *Psychological Bulletin, 80*(2), 151–176. doi:10.1037/h0034829

Pratt, M. G., & Ashforth, B. E. (2003). Fostering meaningfulness in working and at work. *Positive Organizational Scholarship: Foundations of a new discipline*, 309-327.

Rich, G. A. (1997). The sales manager as a role model: Effects on trust, job satisfaction, and performance of salespeople. *Journal of the Academy of Marketing Science, 25*(4), 319–328. doi:10.1177/0092070397254004

Schwepker, C. H. Jr. (2001). Ethical climate's relationship to job satisfaction, organizational commitment, and turnover intention in the salesforce. *Journal of Business Research*, *54*(1), 39–52. doi:10.1016/S0148-2963(00)00125-9

Scroggins, W. A. (2008). Antecedents and outcomes of experienced meaningful work: A person-job fit perspective. *Journal of Business Inquiry*, *7*(1), 68–78.

Shahnawaz, M. G., & Goswami, K. (2011). Effect of psychological contract violation on organizational commitment, trust and turnover intention in private and public sector Indian organizations. *Vision: The Journal of Business Perspective*, *15*(3), 209–217. doi:10.1177/097226291101500301

Shamir, B. (1991). Meaning, self and motivation in organizations. *Organization Studies*, *12*(3), 405–424. doi:10.1177/017084069101200304

Shastri, R. K. (2008). A strategic action plan for managing non government with special reference of India definition of NGOs. *International NGO Journal*, *3*(3), 74–76.

Simons, T. (2002). The high cost of lost trust. *Harvard Business Review*, *80*(9), 18–19. PMID:12389455

Singh, N., & Rangnekar, S. (2016). Relationship between meaningful work and organizational trust: A study of techno-managers in the Indian power sector. *Proceedings of GLOGIFT*, *16*, 247–255.

Steel, R. P., & Ovalle, N. K. (1984). A review and meta-analysis of research on the relationship between behavioral intentions and employee turnover. *The Journal of Applied Psychology*, *69*(4), 673–686. doi:10.1037/0021-9010.69.4.673

Stuart, H. (1999). Towards a definitive model of the corporate identity management process. *Corporate Communications*, *4*(4), 200–207. doi:10.1108/13563289910299328

Thomas, G. F., Zolin, R., & Hartman, J. L. (2009). The central role of communication in developing trust and its effects on employee involvement. *Journal of Business Communication*, *46*(3), 287–310. doi:10.1177/0021943609333522

Tirelli, A., & Goh, S. C. (2015). The relationship between trust, learning capability, affective organisational commitment and turnover intentions. *International Journal of Human Resources Development and Management*, *15*(1), 54–68. doi:10.1504/IJHRDM.2015.069971

Tiwari, B., & Lenka, U. (2015). Building and branding talent hub: An outlook. *Industrial and Commercial Training*, *47*(4), 208–213. doi:10.1108/ICT-11-2014-0077

Tiwari, B., & Lenka, U. (2016). Building psychological safety for employee engagement in post-recession. *Development and Learning in Organizations: An International Journal*, *30*(1), 19–22.

Van den Heuvel, S., van den Heuvel, S., Freese, C., Freese, C., Schalk, R., Schalk, R., & van Assen, M. (2017). How change information influences attitudes toward change and turnover intention: The role of engagement, psychological contract fulfillment, and trust. *Leadership and Organization Development Journal*, *38*(3), 398–418. doi:10.1108/LODJ-03-2015-0052

Whitener, E. M., Brodt, S. E., Korsgaard, M. A., & Werner, J. M. (1998). Managers as initiators of trust: An exchange relationship framework for understanding managerial trustworthy behavior. *Academy of Management Review*, *23*(3), 513–530.

Wrzesniewski, A., & Dutton, J. E. (2001). Crafting a job: Revisioning employees as active crafters of their work. *Academy of Management Review*, *26*(2), 179–201.

Xu, S., Martinez, L. R., & Lv, Q. (2017). Explaining the link between emotional labor and turnover intentions: The role of in-depth communication. *International Journal of Hospitality & Tourism Administration*, 1–19. doi:10.1080/15256480.2017.1324339

Yamaguchi, I. (2006). Multiple group factor analysis of organizational communications for sending the outcome of decision making in Japan–US companies. *Human Communication Studies*, *34*, 35–51.

Yamaguchi, I. (2009). Influences of organizational communication tactics on trust with procedural justice effects: A cross-cultural study between Japanese and American workers. *International Journal of Intercultural Relations*, *33*(1), 21–31. doi:10.1016/j.ijintrel.2009.01.002

Chapter 12
Applicability of Six Sigma in Human Resource Management

Nagaraj Shenoy
Dayananda Sagar Junior Business School, India

ABSTRACT

The role of HR has become like that of a firefighter, remembered only in emergencies. Their presence is felt only in their absence. HR is seen as a reactive staff function and a cost centre. The message is clear. Despite its best effort to keep organization together with uniform policy, norms, and values, HR is compelled to prove its financial worth to the organization. HR is under constant pressure for showing their results in quantifiable and financially measurable terms. Introducing Six Sigma in processes of HRM functions seems to be a solution to this problem. However, in some of "Total Six Sigma Organizations," the human resources department has been practically untouched by Six Sigma. The main reason being the difficulty in quantifying and measuring the financial returns of HR processes. But, some others feel that this is as easy as identifying the gaps and using the right formula. The real problem therefore lies in the perception of an individual HR professional. It takes an HR manager to think statistically and analyze how a process can be quantified.

PREAMBLE

Excellence is doing common things uncommonly well - Orison Swett Marden (1850-1924) American spiritual author in the 'New Thought Movement' and founder of 'Success Magazine'

DOI: 10.4018/978-1-5225-4038-0.ch012

Copyright © 2018, IGI Global. Copying or distributing in print or electronic forms without written permission of IGI Global is prohibited.

Perfection is an endless dream. Man's quest for flawless performance in all his work is leading him to the pursuit of constant improvement. Defects are dangerous as they have consequences much worse than earlier times. Modern times have compelled businesses to explore ways to improve their processes and work to ensure defect-free as their products and services to the extent possible. This exploration has led them to the discovery of many methods to improve the quality of their work.

Six Sigma is one such revolutionary concept that has transformed manufacturing industry in quality and excellence aspects. Six Sigma, which started as a process improvement tool to enhance quality perception of customers towards products and services, has transformed into a management philosophy for many organizations. It has changed the paradigm of excellence in every process and activity performed by industries. Most importantly, it has converted the qualitative aspect of 'Quality' into a 'measurable' variable.

BACKGROUND OF THE STUDY

Personnel Management - the earlier Avatar of Human Resource Management – used to be considered – perhaps rightly - only as a staff function. However, HRM is playing a multiplicity of roles, responsibilities, and more significantly, taking part in the strategic management process of a business. Nevertheless, HRM has not been given its rightful place in strategic management literature. Tacitly, in many organizations, it is still considered only a staff function. HR function itself is considered as a cost centre rather than a strategic unit.

The role of HR has become like that of firefighter, remembered only in emergencies; presence is felt only in their absence. In one of their case study of process improvement initiatives in an organization, Wyper & Harrison (2000, p. S720) observe that

prior to introduction of Six Sigma, the HR function did not enjoy a desirable reputation in the company. HR was seen as reactive, uncoordinated, over-manned and unprofessional, delivering poor, slow and non cost-effective services.

The message is clear. Despite its best effort to keep organization together with uniform policy, norms, and values, HR is compelled to prove its economic worth to the organization. The case of HR is similar to the controversy over the outcome of Government of India's 2001 Census where Indian housewives were considered as 'economically non-productive' as they are not generating any revenue. That is, HR is under constant pressure for showing their results in quantifiable and 'financially measurable' terms. Introducing Six Sigma in processes of HRM functions seems to be solution to this problem.

The participation of HR is indispensable for the successful implementation of any Six Sigma project in the organization. "Six sigma increases HR participation in employee, company, and customer development by integrating its function into management decisions, company strategy, as well as employee development" (DeFeo, 2000, pp. 1-6). But when it comes to applying Six Sigma to HR functions per se, the answer is not encouraging.

Some larger corporations have integrated Six Sigma so well into the corporate culture that it can be considered the DNA of the company. However, even in such companies, the human resources department, has been practically untouched by Six Sigma. (Gupta, 2005, pp. 1-2).

Some questions that arose in this regard were: 'How can HR be measured?'; 'How can you apply 3.4 defects per million opportunity rule to HR when no organization would have a million employees?' etc.

But this perception that Six Sigma cannot be applied to HR processes, for reasons whatsoever, is not shared by all.

Applying Six Sigma to HR is really no different than applying it anywhere else in the organization," says Jackie Nelson, Six Sigma Master Black Belt in HR at GE Consumer Finance. "The key is, 'What are the gaps?' Once you understand what the problem is, it is like a mathematical problem - you just apply the right formula to solve. (Heuring, 2004, pp. 76-80).

However, measuring HR processes is not an easy task either. It takes an organization to think statistically, analyze how a process can be quantified. An article by Griffiths (2005, p. 10) presents information on an international survey of over 200 companies to monitor the challenges facing HR. Results reveal that "Change management, leadership development and **Measuring HR Effectiveness** are the most challenging areas for HR practitioners across the globe, despite national and regional differences".

This situation demands HR to be more mathematics or statistics savvy. They need to find innovative ways to quantify their output, and its economic worth. A survey conducted by *Development Dimensions International* (1999, p. 9) showed that "there is still a lack of board level commitment to some fundamental HR practices despite recognition of the increasing importance of the human resources function". The survey also reveals that "only 31 percent of respondents (HR people) can calculate the cost of staff turnover". This indicates the state of condition of HR or the distance between the 'measurement' and HR professionals.

The real problem therefore, lies in the perception of an individual HR professional. Whether HR wants to remain in its supporting role in Six Sigma projects of other functions of the organization or enhance its role to take up some projects for its own domain, it is for the HR professionals to take the call.

HR PROFESSION: IN SEARCH OF RECOGNITION AND REWARD

Human Resource Management (HRM or simply HR) was conceptualized to address the shortcomings of its earlier version of employee management, Personnel Management, in organizations. Personnel Management was confined to limited to routine activity of managing the records of employee records and some disciplinary issues. Aswathappa (1999, p. 7) observed, "Personnel Management department itself was not treated with respect. It was filled with not very productive employees whose service could be used with minimal damage to the organization's ongoing operations".

HRM Basic Concepts

Coming out of the shadow of Personnel Management, HRM came with different concepts and definitions. Human Resource Management (HRM) has been defined as "managing (planning, organizing, directing, and controlling) the functions of employing, developing and compensating human resources resulting in the creation and development of human relations with a view to contribute proportionately (due to them) to the organizational individual and social goals" (Rao, 2004, p. 2). According to Ivancevich & Glueck (1989, p. 3) "HRM is concerned with the most effective use of people to achieve organizational and individual goals". Wikipedia (2017) defines "Human Resource Management (HRM or HR) as the management of human resources of an organization to maximize employee performance in service of an employer's strategic objectives". The HR function is concerned about attraction of best talent, selection, placement, training, compensation, and appraisal of an organization's workforce. It also monitors the functions such as statutory compliance, organizational culture, employee morale, etc. Dave Ulrich lists the functions of HR as, aligning HR and business strategy, re-engineering organization processes, listening and responding to employees, and managing transformation and change (Ulrich, 1997, pp. 53-188). In an organizational context, Bohlander & Snell (2005, pp. 33-34) feel "a Human Resources Manager has following responsibilities.

1. Advice and counsel
2. Service
3. Policy formulation and implementation
4. Employee advocacy"

Evolution of HRM Practices in India

While examining the evolution of 'people management' as a skill or profession, one would come across three distinct phases. In the beginning, before independence, the role had the form of 'Welfare Officer', that is, the person in the role had to be concerned with the welfare of the workers. Labour unions were trying to establish their identity and longing for some concern from the management apart from paying them a just wages. In such situation, the 'Welfare Officer' fitted the bill effectively.

The next phase arrived after the independence in 1947. As the nation's new leadership was genuinely concerned with the plight of labour class, they brought in a flood of legislations. All these legislations intended to safeguard the interests of the labour class. This led to the reversal of situation in the industrial environment. Braking out from the clutches of exploitation, workers through their unions started dictating terms and went to the level of posing unreasonable demands. The law and the government machinery however, were firmly with trade unions. The businessmen found the situation extremely suffocating. The role of people manager was mainly confined to deal with the legal aspects of relations with workers. The law degree considered essential for the role called 'Personnel Manager'. They started viewing all people management issues through legal glass. They spent more time in the corridors of courts than in the corporate premises.

Then came the LPG (Liberalization, Privatization, and Globalization) era. After 1991, the whole government machinery withdrew its legal along with its moral support to the trade unions. By this time, the very nature of workforce was gradually changing from physical workers to knowledge workers. The IT revolution led to the creation of knowledge economy. This created a level playing field for both businessmen and workers. 'Profit' ceased to be a 'bad word'. The third phase in the evolution of 'people management' called 'Human Resource Management' stressed the inevitability of the other party to both employer and employee. Now, in this phase, the focus was on the mutual helping and respecting relationship between employer and employee. 'Partnership' and 'Participation' became the buzzwords in the industrial relations scenario. The mantra for success became 'Cooperation' between' manager' and the 'managed'.

In such environment, HRM could not be confined to only routine functions of recruitment and retention. The HRM had to include in its function, the strategic concerns of the organization. "The transition to the next orbit hinges on the capability-building prowess of a company. Training and development of employees is, now a mandatory responsibility of the top management. In the highly competitive world of today, the Indian corporate requires a radical reorientation of its mindset even to stay abreast, let alone surging ahead". (Devarajan, 2011)

The Challenge of Human Resource Management

"The most significant resource of any organization is often said to be its people. Such claims appear in organization's annual reports and mission statements. Many people work in organization to gain, apart from money, recognition, achieve status, test and stretch their capabilities. The challenge of Human Resource Management is to minimize the obstacles and problems employees encounter while achieving this". (Rao, V S P, 2002, pp. 57-76)

Gomez-Mejia et al (2005, pp. 43-60) summarizes "the major HR challenges facing modern managers as below.

Information Source: Gomez-Mejia, Luis R.; Balkin, David B.; Cardy, Robert L.; Managing Human Resources, Pearson Education, Inc. 2005, Delhi."

Every organization strives to achieve excellence and HR has a significant role to play in it. Pattanayak (2005, p. 18) lists the following "important HR issues in achieving corporate excellence.

1. Aligning business strategy with HR strategy
2. Knowledge management and creating learning organization

Table 1. Key HR Challenges of Today's Managers

Environmental Challenges	Organizational Challenges	Individual Challenges
• Rapid Change • Dealing with Stress • The Internet Revolution • Greater Written Communication Skills • Job Redefinition • Breaking Down Labor Market Barriers • Keep Workers from Leaving • On-Line Learning • Enabling General Managerial Focus to HR • Workforce Diversity • Globalization • Legislation • Evolving Work and Family Roles • Skill Shortages and the Rise of the Service Sector	• Competitive Position: Cost, Quality or Distinctive Capabilities • Decentralization • Downsizing • Organizational Restructuring • Self-Managed Work Teams • The Growth of Small Businesses • Organizational Culture • Technology • Outsourcing	• Matching People and Organizations • Ethics and Social Responsibility • Productivity and Brain Drain • Empowerment • Brain Drain • Job Insecurity

3. Competence mapping and skill development through assessment centers
4. Developing moral excellence through ethics audit; and creating a value-based culture
5. Reorganization of work though job enlargement and enrichment
6. Development of mutual trust and synergy among work teams
7. Managing change through people
8. Restructuring and bringing about transformation in the organization to add value to the business
9. Bringing about rationalization of workforce through internal transfers and resorting to employee reduction, though not as first choice.
10. Holding opinion surveys to get a feel of the perception of employees and applying mid-course correction, if necessary."

Roles of a Modern HR Professional

The Responsibilities, Challenges and issues discussed above reveal the multiplicity of roles modern HR professional needs to play. Mutsuddi (2011, p. 14) lists "various such roles as below:

- HR Expert
- Management Theory Expert
- Mentor and Counselor
- Platform Speaker
- Influential Leader
- Objective and Ethical Leader
- Technologically Savvy Leader
- OD Expert
- Strategic Planning Expert
- Strategic Thinker
- Business Partner
- Moral Compass"

In spite of all these, HR in many organizations is striving hard to earn its place in management. It is irony that a department that has been assigned the work of determining the rewards and recognitions for its employees, seeking the same reward and recognition for its function.

Criticality of HRM Function for Software Industry

Human Resource is very critical for every industry. However, due to modern advancements in technology, especially automation technology has brought in radical changes in the perspective of manufacturing sector. The sound of a siren in big factories will not witness flood of workers coming out and getting in anymore. The technology has reduced their work force drastically, and so is organizations' dependency on them.

Nevertheless, the same is not the case with the most celebrated modern economy industry. Software Industry is still very much of depended on its human resource. In fact, newer avenues are explored in every passing day in Software Industry, more growth and development is taking place, resulting in enhanced need of talented human resource. Many a times, success and failure of a software firm depends on the quality of its human resource.

THE WORLD OF SIX SIGMA

All truth passes through three stages. First, it is ridiculed. Second, it is violently opposed. Third, it is accepted as being self-evident. - Arthur Schopenhauer (1788 –1860) German philosopher

Achieving perfection in whatever one does is a craze very few people possess. They strive hard to achieve the best quality in everything they do. This is true in case of organizations as well. Very few organizations long for doing it with the best possible way. Only such companies will rule the market. They alone satisfy the needs of customer. They are the organizations who register constant growth in sales, savings and profits. They have all the competitive advantages.

Naturally, every organization needs to achieve quality, though, for the benefits it offers to all its stakeholders. However, the big question is how. Many solutions have appeared in the horizon of industrial world, each offering its own benefits and inherent shortcomings. However, one improvement concept, that has stood the test of time, is Six Sigma. It has enjoyed the popularity as quality improvement philosophy for more than quarter century. It is still growing strong with finding newer application areas. It has passed through all the stages mentioned by Arthur Schopenhauer stated above.

Six Sigma was originally formulated at Motorola by Bill Smith around 1986. It was conceived as a set of practices developed to improve manufacturing processes for eliminating defects. In the later stage, its application was extended to other functions and other types of business processes as well. Six Sigma, in its evolution is highly influenced by preceding six decades of quality improvement methodologies such as Quality Control, Total Quality Management (TQM), Zero Defects, etc, developed by Shewhart, Deming, Juran, Ishikawa, Taguchi and others.

Six Sigma is a statistical concept and is driven by data. It measures quality of any product or service in terms of defects. It also refers to the process that leads to the creation of these products or services. The concept of 'defect' is also unique in Six Sigma terminology. In Six Sigma, a defect is defined as anything that could lead to customer dissatisfaction. "Six Sigma Quality" level is assumed to produce defects below 3.4 per million opportunities for any products, services or Processes. Six Sigma is conceptualized at Motorola and hence it is a trademark of Motorola, Inc.

Six Sigma is a statistical concept and involves the knowledge of many fundamental concepts and learning of the subject statistics to some extent. Hence, it is believed initially, that Six Sigma is only for engineers and statistics experts. To clarify on this myth, many write ups are found in the literature. Matchette (2006, pp. 19-21) finds that "the knowledge of the management is the only thing that is needed for adopting Six Sigma. If one can manage a process or function, then they can profitably use Six Sigma".

Statistical Concepts of Six Sigma

Sigma (σ) is statistical notation used to denote Standard Deviation. It is a measure of dispersion in statistics. It measures the 'Scatteredness' of the data in a given population. It is also explained as 'the root mean squared deviation' of the data from its mean. In other words, Standard Deviation measures the degree to which the individual data elements are dispersed from the mean of the group. That is, higher the value of standard deviation, the more dispersion in the data. In a normal distribution curve, if the data falls beyond a specified limit of sigma or standard deviation it can be called defect. The following table gives the number of defects – expressed in terms of Defects Per Million Opportunities (DPMO) and defectives percentages – for different sigma levels.

It may seem that 3 or 4 sigma level is good enough to ensure the satisfactory level of performance. The following table illustrates some of real world situations and its performance levels for different sigma levels.

The Approach of Six Sigma

Six Sigma intends to improve Operational Efficiency and Effectiveness (OEE). "Six Sigma is a business strategy that seeks to identify and eliminate causes of errors or defects or failures in business processes by focusing on outputs that are critical to customers". (Snee R. D., 1999, pp. 100-103). Thus it provides a competitive

Table 2. Probability of defects for different sigma levels

Sigma Level	Defects Per Million Opportunities (DPMO)	Percent Defective	Yield (%)
1	691,462	69%	30.85375
2	308,538	31%	69.14625
3	66,807	6.7%	93.31928
4	6,210	0.62%	99.37903
5	233	0.023%	99.97674
6	**3.4**	**0.00034%**	**99.99966**

Table 3. Real world examples of performance for different sigma levels

Situation/Example	In One Sigma World	In Three Sigma World	In Six Sigma World
Pieces of your mail lost per year (1,600 opportunities per year)	1,106	107	0.005
Number of telephone disconnections (7,000 talk minutes)	4,839	467	0.02
Erroneous business orders (250,000 opportunities per year)	172,924	16,694	0.85

edge to an organization. But its role is not limited to improved OEE and providing a competitive edge. It adds a whole new range of skills and competencies to an organization such as

scientific and disciplined problem solving and decision-making behaviour, and effective distribution of information over the organization. These skills help tackling the general problem of economic planning under constraints to knowledge. These competencies can be used to leverage a company's competitive strategy. (Mast, 2006, pp. 455-464)

Six Sigma allows an organization to achieve the constancy of purpose that is the secret to success, by focusing organization's efforts on understanding the variations in its processes and the defects that occur. This leads to achieve the following desired results: i) Money ii) Customer satisfaction iii) Quality iv) Impact on employees v) Growth vi) Competitive advantages. (Brue, 2005, p. 21)

Every organization in the business wants to achieve these results and Six Sigma helps them to achieve the same.

To achieve these objectives, in its methodology, Six Sigma begins with the Cost-Of-Poor-Quality (COPQ) that can trigger the movement of quality in an organization. Cost-Of-Poor-Quality (COPQ) is the cost of material, labour and overhead costs associated with the production of production of goods and services that does not meet customer expectation.

Six Sigma focuses on customer satisfaction as its topmost priority. It identifies Critical-To-Quality (CTQ) elements in a business process or product that is what matters most for the customers. Critical-To-Quality (CTQ) of a process are those elements, which significantly affect the output of that process. Identifying these elements is very important to figure out the ways to improvements, which can drastically reduce the cost and improve the quality. It leads to an effort to enhance quality from customer's perspective.

Setting benchmarks is another characteristics feature of Six Sigma methodology. Benchmarking is a method of setting standards for comparing a process. Benchmarks are set using standard or best practices of that process in the industry as basis. Then, ways to improve the chosen process to the level of benchmark process are explored. Benchmark helps Six Sigma to compare the progress made in the process.

Six Sigma Methodology

The Six Sigma follows two key methodologies. In line with Deming's methodology of PDCA (Plan-Do-Check-Act), the Six Sigma has DMAIC and DMADV methodologies. In this, acronym DMAIC stands for Define – Measure – Analyze – Improve – Control and DMADV stands for Define – Measure – Analyze – Design – Verify. DMAIC is generally employed for improving an existing manufacturing or business process while DMADV methodology is used to create new product or a new process design.

Six Sigma Roles and Responsibilities

The success of Six Sigma project depends on the people who are actively involved in implementing it. Six Sigma has a culture of assigning tasks to some personnel with specific roles and unique nomenclatures. American Society for Quality (ASQ) defines these roles as below:

Champions: Translate the company's vision, mission, goals and metrics to create an organizational deployment plan and identify individual projects. Identify resources and remove roadblocks.

Executives: Provide overall alignment by establishing the strategic focus of the Six Sigma program within the context of the organization's culture and vision.

Master Black Belt: Trains and coaches Black Belts and Green Belts. Functions more at the Six Sigma program level by developing key metrics and the strategic direction. Acts as an organization's Six Sigma technologist and internal consultant.

Black Belt: Leads problem-solving projects. Trains and coaches project teams.

Green Belt: Assists with data collection and analysis for Black Belt projects. Leads Green Belt projects or teams.

Yellow Belt: Participates as a project team member. Reviews process improvements that support the project.

White Belt: Can work on local problem-solving teams that support overall projects, but may not be part of a Six Sigma project team. Understands basic Six Sigma concepts from an awareness perspective. (ASQ, 2017, p. 1)

Financial Benefits of Six Sigma

Any improvement program, unless it shows the impact of an organization's bottom line, it will not have any takers. The financial benefits of the implementation of Six Sigma have been measured in many organizations and they are highly impressive. The global corporate giants like Motorola, Texas Instruments, IBM, Allied Signal, and most importantly General Electric, have implemented Six Sigma and saved literally billions of dollars. Later other companies like Ford, Dupont, Dow Chemical, Microsoft, and American Express followed the suit and reported similar benefits.

GE went from 3000 Six Sigma projects in 1996 to 6000 in 1997 when GE achieved $320 million in productivity gains and profits, more than double of their original goal of $150 million. The benefits were showing up in their financial results. By 1998, GE had generated $750 million in Six Sigma savings over and above their investment and would get $1.5 billion in savings the next year. In one GE business, admittedly extreme, found that by using Six Sigma, it could increase the capacity of their factories, eliminating the need for any capacity investment for a decade! (Welch & Byrne, 2001, pp. 325-340)

But Six Sigma is not only about money. It is more of a management philosophy, method of thinking, way of working, and above all commitment of an organization. In many top organizations like Dow Chemical, that are committed to Six Sigma, key managerial slots including HR managers, require Six Sigma certification. Jack Welch, considered as one among the greatest CEOs, initiated Six Sigma practices in General Electric, quoted as saying, "Six Sigma is the most important initiative General Electric has ever taken. It is part of the genetic code of our future leadership".

In the work of Fleming, Coffman, & Harter, (2005, pp. 106-114), they found out "fully engaged customers deliver a 23% premium over the average customer in terms of share of wallet, profitability, revenue, and relationship growth". They conclude that "high-level averages of corporate performance may provide good marketing copy, but they obscure the considerable variation within a company". They also find that "local performance variation is the scourge of organizations that aspire to high performance".

Comparisons with other Process/Quality Improvement Methodologies

Whenever a new Process/Quality Improvement concept is proposed, it is imperative to compare the methodology with its predecessors. Six Sigma is no exception. It had challenge of proving that it is 'different' from its earlier methodologies, especially Total Quality Management (TQM). Many Six Sigma practitioners have taken this task.

Anbari (2002, pp. 1-8) pointed out that

Six Sigma is more comprehensive than prior quality initiatives such as Total Quality Management (TQM) and Continuous Quality Improvement (CQI). The six sigma method includes measured and reported financial results, uses additional, more advanced data analysis tools, focuses on customer concerns, and uses project management tools and methodology. He summarized the six sigma management method as follows:

Six Sigma = TQM (or CQI) + Stronger Customer Focus + Additional Data Analysis Tools + Financial Results + Project Management

In their book "The Six Sigma Way," its authors Pande, Neuman, & Cavanage (2004, pp. 42-48) discuss the differences between TQM and Six Sigma. "The following table is summarized comparisons between TQM and Six Sigma.

Information Source: Pande, Peter S. et al, (2004), The Six Sigma Way, Tata McGraw Hill Publishing Company Limited, New Delhi", Page 42-48

Six Sigma concepts are also discussed with other two improvement concepts of Lean thinking and Theory of constraints. In an article Nave (2002, pp. 73-78), discussed "the basics of the three improvement methodologies and presented a model to understand their concepts and effects and similarities and differences as described in the following table with the essence of each methodology.

Table 4. Six Sigma versus TQM

Sl. No.	TQM Pitfall	Six Sigma Solution
1	Lack of Integration	Links to the Business and Personal "Bottom Line"
2	Leadership Apathy	Leadership at the Vanguard
3	A Fuzzy Concept	A Consistently Repeated Simple Message
4	An Unclear Goal	Setting a No-Nonsense, Ambitious Goal
5	Purist Attitude And Technical Zealotry	Adapting Tools and Degree of Rigor to the Circumstances
6	Failure To Breakdown Internal Barriers	Priority on Cross Functional Process Management
7	Incremental vs. Exponential Change	Incremental Exponential Change
8	Ineffective Training	Blackbelts, Greenbelts, Master Blackbelts
9	Focus on Product Quality	Attention to All Business Processes

Six Sigma and Organizational Leadership

Amernic, Craig, & Tourish (2007, pp. 1839-1872) made a detailed analysis of corpus of CEO letters of legendary Jack Welch to stockholders, during his tenure as CEO of GE, 1981–2000. They have attempted to understand the transformational leadership qualities of Jack Welch. They figure out and discuss "the five root metaphors that heightened Welch's persuasive and rhetorical impact on his audience as pedagogue, physician, architect, commander and saint". They find Six Sigma plays a key role in his endeavor throughout.

Larry Greiner conducts an interview with Steve Kerr, who was Vice President of Leadership Development and Chief Learning Officer for General Electric (GE). He had the responsibility for GE's renowned Leadership Education Center at Crotonville. Above all, he was acting as Welch's skillful consultant for 11 years. In this context, Larry Greiner interviews Steve Kerr on his years with Jack Welch at GE and comes out with some reflections.

"Larry Greiner's reflections were as below:

1. Corporate management education can be much more than a "packaged" training program.
2. Corporate transformation is created through dialogue among leaders, not through formal plans and strategies.
3. Knowledge management depends on social interaction, not computerized information systems". (Greiner, 2002, pp. 343-350)

Table 5. Comparison of Improvement Programs

Program	Six Sigma	Lean Thinking	Theory of Constraints
Theory	**Reduce variation**	**Remove waste**	**Manage constraints**
Application Guidelines	1. Define. 2. Measure 3. Analyze 4. Improve 5. Control	1. Identify value 2. Identify value stream 3. Flow 4. Pull 5. Perfection	1. Identify constraint 2. Exploit constraint. 3. Subordinate processes 4. Elevate constraint 5. Repeat cycle
Focus	Problem focused	Flow focused	Systems constraints
Assumptions	• A problem exists. • Figures and numbers are valued. • System output improves if variation in all processes is reduced.	• Waste removal will improve business performance. • Many small improvements are better than systems analysis.	• Emphasis on speed and volume • Uses existing systems • Process interdependence
Primary Effect	Uniform process output	Reduced flow time	Fast throughput
Secondary Effects	• Less waste • Fast throughput. • Less inventory • Fluctuation-performance measures for managers. • Improved quality.	• Less variation. • Uniform output. • Less inventory. • New accounting system. • Flow-performance measure for managers • Improved quality.	• Less inventory/waste. • Throughput cost accounting. • Throughput-performance measurement system. • Improved quality.
Criticisms	• System interaction not considered. • Processes improved independently.	• Statistical or system analysis not valued.	• Minimal worker input. • Data analysis not valued.

Source: Nave, D. (2002, March). How to Compare Six Sigma, Lean and the Theory of Constraints. *QUALITY PROGRESS*, pp. 73-78"

Six Sigma: The Way Ahead

Now, Six Sigma has come out of the myths, it was surrounded by, in the initial stages. Industry has realized that it is not difficult to understand what is Six Sigma. Business world has found out that Six Sigma is not only for engineers or statisticians; it is for anyone with a little analytical bent of mind, best and brightest from any field.

Industry has also realized that Six Sigma is not limited to any one segment. Any function, any process can be improved by Six Sigma techniques. In fact, today no field in the industry remains unreached by Six Sigma.

Therefore, the obvious question is about the road ahead for Six Sigma. The torchbearer of Six Sigma GE chooses to set higher benchmarks, change the metric concepts. Welch quotes, "Today we take it a step further. We measure span from our requested delivery date to (instead of exact delivery date) our customers' first revenue" (Welch & Byrne, 2001, p. 338). That is, 'after reaching the benchmark, raise it to next higher level or change the definition of benchmark itself' is the new excellence mantra for corporate. Six Sigma shows the way in this direction.

The Promise of Six Sigma for HRM

Non-quantifiability and non-measurability of HR functions and processes – though for some, is due to the inherent nature of HRM – depends much on organizational environment. In their work, Wyper & Harrison (2000, p. S720) observe that

HR employees were working hard to keep broken and ill-defined processes in place, with a level of application that bore no resemblance to the required results. The outputs of the key HR processes were not clearly defined. This image had a demoralizing effect on HR employees as they were aware that their considerable efforts were not appreciated in the business.

Six Sigma gives a hope in this situation. It is creating new wave in the organizations of all hues giving them a powerful tool, which provides for measuring any process and improving it systematically, and demonstrating results whose financial benefits are measurable.

The question raised in this context is why the HR professional should care so much for Six Sigma or about its applicability to HR functions. Albeanu, Hunter, & Radford in their book, quoting

"the experience of Orion Partners, list following ten key reasons why HR professionals should be interested in Six Sigma:

1. To create excellence in process delivery.
2. To reduce defects.
3. To increase efficiency.
4. To create a quality focused mindset.
5. To benefit from best practice.
6. To bring clarity to the processes of HR.
7. To use a structured scientific approach.
8. To speak the same language and improve communication.
9. To gain control over your processes.
10. To strengthen your business case". (Albeanu, Hunter, & Radford, 2012, pp. 1-3)

Yet, all said and done, the onus is still on HR professionals only. They only will have to device methodology to quantify the processes of their domain. They need to explore the ways to find the economic worth of their activities. Only then, they can claim their rightful share in the management.

REFERENCES

Albeanu, M., Hunter, I., & Radford, J. (2012). *Six Sigma in HR Transformation*. Surrey, UK: Gower Publishing.

Amernic, J., Craig, R., & Tourish, D. (2007). The transformational leader as pedagogue, physician, architect, commander, and saint: Five root metaphors in Jack Welch's letters to stockholders of General Electric. *Human Relations*, *60*(12), 1839–1872. doi:10.1177/0018726707084916

Anbari, F. T. (2002). Six Sigma Method and Its Applications in Project Management. In *Proceedings of the Project Management Institute Annual Seminars and Symposium*. San Antonio, TX: Project Management Institute.

ASQ. (2017, April 12). *Six Sigma Belts, Executives and Champions – What does it all mean?* Retrieved September 28, 2017, from American Society for Quality: http://asq.org/learn-about-quality/six-sigma/overview/belts-executives-champions.html

Aswathappa, K. (1999). *Human Resource and Personnel Management* (2nd ed.). New Delhi: Tata McGraw-Hill Publishing Company Limited.

Bohlander, G., & Snell, S. (2005). *Managing Human Resources* (13th ed.). Mason, OH: Thomson South-Western Publishing.

Brue, G. (2005). *Six Sigma for Managers*. New Delhi: Tata McGraw Hill Publishing Company Ltd.

DeFeo, J. A. (2000, Summer). Six Sigma: New Opportunities for HR, New Career Growth for Employees. *Employment Relations Today*, *27*(Summer), 1–6. doi:10.1002/ert.3910270202

Devarajan, R. (2011, April 12). *Emerging trends in HR management, Chennai*. Retrieved 12 12, 2012, from The Hindu: http://www.thehindu.com/books/emerging-trends-in-hr-management/article1691138.ece

Development Dimensions International. (1999, August). Good HR practice going unrecognised at the top. *Works Management*, *52*(8), 9.

Fleming, J. H., Coffman, C., & Harter, J. K. (2005, July - August). Manage your Human Sigma. *Harvard Business Review*, 106–114. PMID:16028821

Gomez-Mejia, L. R., Balkin, D. B., & Cardy, R. L. (2005). *Managing Human Resources*. Delhi: Pearson Education, Inc.

Greiner, L. (2002). Steve Kerr and His Years with Jack Welch at GE. *Journal of Management Inquiry*, *11*(4), 343–350. doi:10.1177/1056492602238840

Griffiths, J. (2005). Global consensus on top HR issues. *People Management*, *11*(16), 10.

Gupta, P. (2005). *Six Sigma in Human Resources*. Quality Digest.

Heuring, L. (2004, March). Six Sigma in Sight. *HR Magazine*, 76-80.

Ivancevich, J. M., & Glueck, W. G. (1989). *Foundations of Personnel/Human Resource Management*. Business Publications.

Mast, J. D. (2006). Six Sigma and Competitive Advantage. *Total Quality Management*, *17*(4), 455–464. doi:10.1080/14783360500528221

Matchette, D. R. (2006, July-August). Six Sigma for the DoD. *Defense AT, L*, 19–21.

Mutsuddi, I. (2011). *Essentials of Human Resource Management*. New Delhi: New Age International Publishers.

Nave, D. (2002, March). How to Compare Six Sigma, Lean and the Theory of Constraints. *Quality Progress*, 73-78.

Pande, P. S., Neuman, R. P., & Cavanage, R. R. (2004). *The Six Sigma Way*. New Delhi: Tata McGraw Hill Company Limited.

Pattanayak, B. (2005). *Human Resource Management* (3rd ed.). New Delhi: Printice Hall of India.

Rao, P. S. (2004). *Personal and Human Resource Management – Text and Cases*. Mumbai: Himalaya Publishing House.

Rao, V. S. P. (2002). *Human Resource Management – Text and Cases*. New Delhi: Excel Books.

Snee, R. D. (1999, September). Why should statisticians pay attention to Six Sigma? Quality Progress, 100-103.

Ulrich, D. (1997). *Human Resource Champions - The next agenda for adding value and delivering results*. Boston: Harvard Business School Press.

Welch, J., & Byrne, J. A. (2001). *JACK: Straight from the Gut*. New York: Warner Books Inc.

Welch, J., & Byrne, J. A. (2001). *JACK: Straight from the Gut*. New York: Warner Books Inc.

Wikipedia. (2017, September 30). *Human resource management*. Retrieved October 2, 2017, from Wikipedia: https://en.wikipedia.org/wiki/Human_resource_management

Wyper, B., & Harrison, A. (2000). Deployment of Six Sigma methodology in Human Resource function: A case study. *Total Quality Management*, *11*(4 & 5), S720. doi:10.1080/09544120050008129

Wyper, B., & Harrison, A. (2000). Deployment of Six Sigma methodology in Human Resource function: A case study. *Total Quality Management*, *11*(4 & 5), S720. doi:10.1080/09544120050008129

Chapter 13
Does Locus of Control Mediate the Relationship Between Personality Integration and Self-Disclosure?

Nagendra Singh Nehra
Indian Institute of Technology Roorkee, India

ABSTRACT

The topic of self-disclosure has been explored significantly and considered to greatly impact employees' relationships. Thus, this chapter explores the association between personality integration and self-disclosure considering how locus of control acts as a mediator. The sample was collected from public and private sector organizations in Uttarakhand. The data was collected through a cross-sectional survey-based research design, and a convenience sampling method was used. Thus, a total of 192 questionnaires were distributed during office hours. In the final analysis, only 189 responses were considered; the rest were discarded due to missing data. The authors use correlation and four-step hierarchical multiple regression analyses. Results show that internal locus of control partially mediates said association. Further, it was found that personality integration is positively associated with self-disclosure through internal locus of control. Additionally, external locus of control has a positive effect on self-disclosure. Implications and scope for future research is highlighted.

DOI: 10.4018/978-1-5225-4038-0.ch013

Copyright © 2018, IGI Global. Copying or distributing in print or electronic forms without written permission of IGI Global is prohibited.

PERSONALITY INTEGRATION AND SELF-DISCLOSURE: THE MEDIATING ROLE OF LOC

Introduction

Over the years, personality traits has been received significant attention in relation to job performance (Judge & Zapata, 2015), job satisfaction (Judge & Bono, 2001), and talent management (Sharma, 2014). Literature provides substantial evidence that locus of control (LoC) widely examined personality trait with respect to workplace related outcomes such as subjective well being, self-monitoring, stress, materialism in childhood, adolescence and adulthood (Benassi et al., 1988; Christopher et al., 2009). Besides this, many early studies reported on personality integration in relation to clinical and socio-psychology outcomes such as family communication, individual psychotherapy, self-concept in children, adults, and preadolescent males (Bowles & Wright, 1970; Cooley & Seeman, 1979), but still, there is dearth of research to elicit the association between personality integration and LoC at the workplace.

Moreover, self-disclosure is also an important attribute of individual personal effectiveness at workplace (Pareek & Purohit, 2011). Early studies found that self-disclosure play a pivotal role in developing and maintaining positive interpersonal relationship at workplace (Collins & Miller, 1994). Besides this, self-disclosure is widely examined personality trait with others traits self-concept, social acceptance, stress levels and internal energy (Posey et al., 2010; Şahin et al., 2010); but interestingly we have not found a singly study to explore the shared association between personality integration, LoC and self-disclosure at the workplace particularly in Indian context. Although, personality integration, LoC and self-disclosure are play an pivotal role in one personality and behavior at the workplace (Arpan & Roskos- Ewoldsen, 2005; Seeman, 1963; Spector, 1982). These personality traits found to effect the efficiency and productivity of individuals (Nicholls et al., 2015). Furthermore, the proposed association has highlight the uniqueness and orginiality of this study as; first, the said relationship has not been explored before and explore the relation would help to better understand how they effect each other at workplace; second, said relationhip would shed light on the relevance of proposed association in Indian unique management style at the workplace (Varma et al., 2005); third, India scores high on power distance and collectivism in relative comparison to wertern societies (Hofstede, 1984); fourth, research reported that unique socio-cultural attributes puts substantial impact on personality traits which eventually arises the necessity to study shared association in Indian management systems and practices at the workplace (Arora & Rangnekar, 2015; Nehra & Rangnekar, 2016; Nehra & Rangnekar, 2017; Nehra & Rangnekar, 2018). Of-course, on the basis of aforesaid peculiar characterstics, the present study seeks to fill this gap in literature by establishing the relationship between personality intergation and self-dislcosure while LoC (internal and external) as mediator therein, particularly in Indian context. Studying this association would explore what relationship exists among the study variables, and how, emphasizing these attributes, employees can be developed and hired so that they maintain and create a healthy work environment at the workplace. Thus, the objectives of this study are to determine: (a) whether personality integration has a significant positive relation with employees' LoC? (b) Does LoC (internal or external) have a significant positive relation with self-disclosure? (c) Does personality integration has a significant positive relation with self-disclosure (d) Does LoC (external & internal) mediate the relationship between personality integration and self-disclosure?. The proposed model is represented in figure 1.

LITERATURE REVIEW

Research explored the preeminent role of individual personality in multidimensional context which highlights its signicifant role in workplace psychology. Although in context to pscyhology, personality intergration is widely examined personality trait specific to clinical psychology and sociology psychology, but more importantly a dearth of studies to workplace psychology (Anchor, 1974; Doyne, 1969; Duncan, 1966; Hearn, 1967; Thomas & Seeman., 1969). Considering this, the relevance of existing study seeks to fill this gap through investigate the role of personality integration at the workplace in Indian context.

Personality Integration

Over the years, the concept personality integration has been received widespread attention between the practitioners and academicians particularly in clinical and socio-psychology (Bowles, & Wright, 1970; Cooley, & Seeman, 1979; Odom et al., 1971; Rubinstein, 1954). Since 1959 concept of personality integration was came in existence and stated as an approach for better understanding of optimal adjustment

Figure 1. Proposed Mediated Model

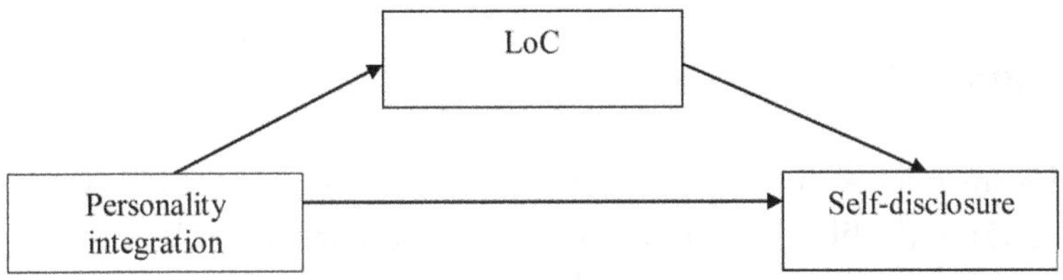

and effective behavior (Seeman, 1959). Besides this, many conceptualizations have been studied to explore the phenomena of personality integration. For instances, Cooley & Seeman, (1979) stated whether the individuals has vary levels of personality integration with their personal space boundaries in relationship with peers and parents. Results reveal that personality integration is significantly related to individual interpersonal relationships. Another pioneering research by Odom et al (1971) reported that children who are high on personality integration elicits higher degree of direct person-to-person interpersonal interaction; are more task oriented and has less tendency of psychological distance with parents. Further, Anchor (1974) reported that personality integration is a variable which likely to consider in proper matching between therapists and clients to build optimum circumstances for success in individual psychotherapy. Finally, personality integration considers as a quantitative aspect of individual personality dynamics (Rubinstein, 1954).

LoC

LoC refers as a common belief in the controllability of an event (Rotter, 1966). Research established two types of LoC – internal LoC (ILoC) and external LoC (ELoC). Internal LoC refers individual perception that they have control over events; whereas external LoC implies to the perception of individual that they have no control over events (Christopher et al, 2009). Prior researchreported that LoC consider as key variable to extract human behaviour at the workplace (Spector, 1982). LoC has been shown to have a positive relationship with emotional stability, self-esteem, job performance, generalized self-efficacy, and job satisfaction (Judge & Bono, 2001). Several studies have examined LoC as a personality trait with other traits like social adjustment, self-esteem, physical illness, depression, neuroticism, family dynamics, personal emotional adjustment, subjective well-being (Estrada et al., 2006; Morrison, 1997). Studies show that individual with neuroticism (low emotional stability) and high external LoC were more prone to stressors which led to illness (Horner, 1996, p.201). Research has also established that internal LoC associated negatively with depression and neuroticism, and external LoC related to depression (Clarke, 2004). Research also suggests that individuals high on internal LoC exhibit greater degrees of intimacy, while external LoC individuals exhibit lower degrees of intimacy (Mikulincer & Segal, 1991).

Self-Disclosure

Self-disclosure implies to sharing information about oneself with others (Falk & Wagner, 1985), and is likely to act as a base for developing close relationships (Forgas, 2011).The information shared can be descriptive or evaluative and can encompass of dreams, thoughts, goals aspirations, successes, failure, fear and as well as one's likes, dislikes (Ignatius & Kokkonen, 2007). An early study by Charmaz (1991) has reported two types of disclosure – spontaneous and protective. Spontaneous disclosure implies to freely expressing oneself without an attempt to control the extent of information when sharing. Protective disclosure entails emotional calculations and more caution when sharing information. In such disclosure, information is shared by excluding the vulnerable emotion which attenuated the risk of threat.

Research suggested that self-disclosure plays a pivotal role in framing social relationships (Ignatius & Kokkonen, 2007) and is an preeminent factor in disliking and liking an individual, which often leads to organizational friendships and social support (Macintosh, 2009a). Harris et al. (1999) reported that self-disclosure is a dynamic and complex process which is affected by various factors like emotional states, trust, flexibility, risk, confidentiality, self-presentation, cultural aspects, motivational aspects, and individual differences. Many studies have observed self-disclosure in relation with diverse traits, for example: LoC, self-concept, interpersonal conflict resolution (Şahin et al., 2009); self-monitoring, social encounters in New Zealand students (Hamid, 1994); self-disclosure, neuroticism, emotional stability (e.g., Burchill & Stiles, 1988; Yoo et al., 2010). Moreover, research suggested that self-disclosure represented by personal information sharing might seems to facilitate human social behavior at the workplace (e.g., Jourard, 1971). Research establishes that self-disclosure is commonly a positive experience that leads to build internal energy, support social acceptance, attenuated stress levels, and formation of intimate associations (Posey et al., 2010). Wheeless and Grotz (1977) suggested self-disclosure as entailing the following norms - depth, amount, intent, honesty and valence. The amount of self-disclosure shows degree and duration of disclosure; depth refers to an extent of intimacy; honesty implies to the correctness and accuracy with which individuals communicates; intent refers individual control and awareness over his or her self-disclosure; and valence is the degree to which positive nature of information being disclosed. Research has also suggested self-disclosure act as an important attribute of personal effectiveness (Pareek & Purohit, 2011). However, studies have found that in cases of extremely high and low degree of self-disclosure by individual, self-disclosure by the other party remains less (Cozby, 1972). Thus, self-disclosure elicits optimum responses from others when it is done in appropriate degrees and follow-up the self-disclosure norms (Wheeless & Grotz, 1977).

Personality Integration and LoC (Internal and External LoC)

An early study by (Anchor, 1974) is the best known research that indicates the attributes of individual who has higher degree of personality integration. More particularly in clinical psychology, research found that individual having higher degree of personality integration will have positive self-concept and is moderately well organized; thereby results in stable mood. Such individual would also exhibit the tendency of internal LoC and has capacity of congruence and acceptance between the others. Consistent to previous study, individuals high on personality integration have perceives themselves for his/her actions and accountable for them (Duncan, 1966). Besides this, individuals high on personality integration have high environmental contact and positive self concept, are moderately well organized, and relate to others affectively (Seeman, 1959; Seeman et al., 1963). They were also shows the feelings of safety and warmth with respect to the surrounding individual and environment (Thomas & Seeman, 1969). Such personality attributes are inherently embodied within those individual who are high on internal LoC and a reverse pattern observed in individuals having high on external LoC (Perlow & Latham, 1993). According to (Erikson, 1959), characteristics of personality integration are more likely to be displayed by those individuals having internal LoC. More importantly, individual having internal LoC are less likely to exhibit the aggressive behavior and have better level of psychological adjustment (DeNeve & Cooper, 1998). Whereas, individual having external LoC are more likely to display anxiety and depression and have believe that they cannot influence the outcome through appropriate actions (Morrison, 1997, p. 258). On the basis of above discussion, we can hypothesize that:

H1a: Personality integration has a positive relation with internal LoC.
H1b: Personality integration has a negative relation with external LoC.

LoC and Self-Disclosure

A primitive study by Ryckman et al. (1973) establishes the relationship between LoC and self-disclosure. The study reveals that individuals with an external LoC disclose less information (48%) as compared to individual with internal LoC (56%). Further, Ryckman et al. (1973) emphasized that women disclose moderately more personal information than men and the said relationship were tested in university setting whose potential respondents were students only. On other hand, research reported that external LoC demonstrated an association with anxiety and depression (Yağışan et al., 2007). Stiles (1987) found that individuals tend to self-disclose more in anxiety, anger, depression, and fear. These attributes reported in psychologically disturbed population. Moreover, identical findings were also reported in (e.g., Burchill & Stiles, 1988). Hamid (1994) found that Chinese students exhibited higher self-monitoring scores, external LoC, made less daily contact with other individuals, demonstrated higher levels of self-disclosure and were tasks oriented in relative comparison to New Zealand students. Therefore, we can hypothesize that:

H2a: Internal LoC has a positive relation with self-disclosure.
H2b: External LoC has a positive relation with self-disclosure.

Personality Integration and Self-Disclosure

Singh and Bhargava (1990) laid down five dimensions of emotional maturity: emotional stability, social adjustment, emotional progression, personality integration, and independence. Research reported that personality integration is one of dimension extracted from emotional maturity which is symbolic of an individual who has dynamic tendency for harmonious de-escalation and co-action of the inner conflict (Singh & Bhargava, 1990). Early research has also established that individuals high on personality integration have high environmental contact and positive self concept (Seeman, 1959; Seeman et al., 1963). Moreover, individuals high on personality integration showed feelings of safety and warmth with respect to the surrounding people and environment (Thomas & Seeman, 1971). Şahin et al. (2009) conducted research to examine the relation between self-concept, LoC, interpersonal conflict resolution approaches and self-disclosure more particularly in university students. Research found that self-concept is related to self-disclosure (Şahin et al., 2009). It can thus be argued that individual high on personality integration are positively associated to self-disclosure (via self-concept which is positively associated with both personality integration and self-disclosure). Thus, we can hypothesize that:

H3a: Personality integration has a positive relation with self-disclosure.

Mediating Effect of LoC

A plethora of studies have examined the mediating effect of LoC in relation to various others traits like stress and depression among childhood, adolescence, and adulthood, materialism and well-being, expectancy and self-esteem, (Benassi et al., 1988; Johnson et al., 2009; Sarrasin, 2014), interestingly no prior study has been conduced to examine the mediating effect of LoC in the relationship between personality integration and self-disclosure at workplace, particularly in Indian context.

The existing study seeks to fill this gap in literature by establishing the mediating effect of (internal and external) LoC in the association between personality integration and self-disclosure. Although, personality integration has been described as a positive personality trait encompass of capacity to freely express his/her feeling and is free to express them, and perceive the individuals and environment around them as safe and positive rather than threatening and hostile (Doyne, 1969; Hearn, 1968).

Further, individuals with high on personality integration exhibit higher perceptions about positive self-concept; stability in moods and higher degree of environment contact; thereby results in developing acceptance to others and congruence among the individuals (Odom et al., 1971). These suggest a relationship between the personality integration and self-disclosure. In addition, individuals high on internal LoC have strong perception about the controllability of events, and has faith in their capabilities and skills, thereby results in higher autonomy in their own behavior and demonstrated self-management style consistent with socially skilled attributes (Mikulincer & Segal, 1991). Therefore, it is anticipated that internal LoC will mediate the relationship between personality integration and self-disclosure. In contrast, individuals who perceive that they have no control over events (external LoC) might adopt emotion-focused coping strategies, resulting in possible apathy and isolation (Mikulincer & Segal, 1991, p. 807); thereby results in states of anxiety and depression. In addition, external LoC is more likely to associate with anxiety and depression, but interestingly individual tends to disclose more in depression and anxiety (Stiles, 1987; Stiles et al., 1992). Thus, we can also anticipate that external LoC will mediate the relationship between personality integration and self-disclosure. Therefore, we can hypothesize that:

H4a: Internal LoC will mediate the relation between personality integration and self-disclosure.

H4b: External LoC will mediate the relation between personality integration and self-disclosure.

METHODS

Sample and Procedure

The researchers telephonically contacted HR managers working in organizations in Uttarakhand. They were also explained how the findings of the study would benefit them. Before starting the survey, prior consent was obtained from managers for the survey. Thus, total 192 questionnaires were distributed during office hours (administered with a paper and pencil survey). Anonymity of responses and identities of respondents was assured. The questionnaires were collected immediately after the respondents filled them. Thus, total 192 questionnaires were distributed. However, in the final analysis, only 189 responses were considered; the rest were discarded due to missing data. About 11% of all participants were between 21 and 25 years of age, 32% were between 26 and 30 years, 23% were between 31 and 35 years, 16% were between 36 and 40 years, 8% were between 41 and 45 years, 4% were between 46 and 50 years, and 6% were above 50 years of age.

Personality Integration

Personality integration was measured through 10 items taken from Singh and Bhargava (1990) emotional maturity scale. Sample items included: "Having known that you are at fault, instead of accepting it, do you try to establish that you are right"; "Do you indulge freely without bothering about moral codes of conduct?". The participants are instructed to evaluate themselves on a response scale with responses varying from 5 = "strongly agree" to 1 = "strongly disagree". The present study found α = .92 (Nunnally, 1978).

LoC

We adopted (16-items) Work LoC Scale (Spector,1988). The scale offers split measurement among internal LoC and external LoC (p.336). The response scale varying from 6 = "strongly agree" to 1 = "strongly disagree". Agreement with statements such as "A job is what you make of it," and "On most jobs, people can pretty much accomplish whatever they set out to accomplish" indicate an internal LoC. Agreement with statements such as "Getting the job you want is mostly a matter of luck," and "Making money is primarily a matter of good fortune" indicate an external LoC. We formed specific subscales for internal LoC (α = .72), external LoC (α = .76) (Nunnally, 1978).

Self-Disclosure

Self-disclosure was measured through 5 items taken from Pareek & Purohit (2011) personal effectiveness scale. Respondents indicated the extent of agreement with statements on a response scale with responses varying from 5 = "strongly agree" to 1 = "strongly disagree". Agreements with statements such as "I enjoy talking with others about my personal concerns and matters," and "I express my opinion in a group or to a person without hesitations" indicate self-disclosure. The scale's was reported (α = 0.81) (Nunnally, 1978).

Control Variables

To control the adverse effect of age and gender on endogenous variables (Cho, 2007); we coded gender variables as (1) for males, (2) for females, and similarly age (years): (1) specify 21-25, (2) specify 26-30, (3) specify 31-35, (4) specify 36-40, (5) specify 41-45, (6) specify 46-50, (7) specify 51-55, (8) specify 56-60, (9) specify 61-65, (10) specify 66-70, and (11) specify 71-75 years.

Analyses

The normality of data checked through kurtosis and skewness indices. The maximum threshold values were 3.89 for kurtosis (less than 7) and 1.09 for skewness (less than 2) (West et al., 1995). We employed self-reported measures. Therefore, we utilize Harman's single factor test to overcome the common method bias (Podsakoff & Organ, 1986). Results demonstrated that single factor explained 22% variance that indicates no use of common method bias. Table 1 exhibits the standard deviations, correlations, and means among constructs. The correlation was performed among the study variables, and then carried out hierarchical multiple regression analyses to determine the type (mediating, indirect and direct) of association between them. We adopted guidelines laid down by Baron and Kenny was followed in the way suggested by Karatepe (2011).

RESULTS

Table 1 demonstrated the inter-correlations between study variables. It shows that internal LoC has a positive correlation with personality integration ($r = .146$, $p < .01$) as well as self-disclosure ($r = .328$, $p < .01$). As the correlation is not too high, it can be said that the problem of multicollinearity does not exist in this study. External LoC showed a negative significant correlation with personality integration ($r = -.150$, $p < .05$) but show a significant positive correlation with self-disclosure ($r = .260$, $p < .01$).Multiple hierarchical regression analysis was conducted to determine the type of association among personality integration, LoC (internal and external) and self disclosure. Findings are demonstrated in Table 2. As expected, personality integration was found a significant predictor of self-disclosure ($\beta = .372$, $p < .01$). Moreover, a direct impact of personality integration on internal LoC was measured.

Table 1. Standard Deviations, Means, and Intercorrelations of the variables

Variable	*M*	*SD*	1	2	3	4	5	6
1. Gender	1.213	.41	-					
2. Age	1.757	.64	.101	-				
3. ILoC	4.20	.63	.111**	.035*	[.72]			
4. ELoC	2.86	.75	-.055**	.023*	-.008**	[.76]		
5. Personality integration	3.08	1.39	.118	.221	.146**	-.150*	[.92]	
6. Self-disclosure	2.97	1.05	.240**	.251**	.328**	.260**	.486**	[.81]

Note. N=189. Cronbach's alpha is shown in parentheses along the diagonal.
**p< .05, **p< .01.*

Table 2. Hierarchical Multiple Regression Analysis: Direct Effect Among Personality Integration and Self-disclosure; Personality Integration and Internal LoC, External LoC

	Self-disclosure					Internal LoC					External LoC				
Predictor variables	**β (Step 1)**	**β (Step 2)**	R^2	ΔR^2	ΔF	**β (Step 1)**	**β (Step 2)**	R^2	ΔR^2	ΔF	**β (Step 1)**	**β (Step 2)**	R^2	ΔR^2	ΔF
Step 1 (Control Variables)			.110	–	11.40			.012	–	1.16			.020	–	1.86
Gender	.217	.237				-.110	-.090				-.141	-.151			
Age	.230	.372				-.010	-.012				-.018	-.016			
Step 2			.023	.036**	13.06**			.032	.016*	3.74*			.053	.011	6.45
Personality integration		.372**					.142*					.018			

Note. N=189.
*p< .05, **p< .01.

Table 2 demonstrates that personality integration (β = .142, p < .01) was related to internal LoC but not with external LoC (β = .018, p = .22). Thus, H1a & H3a are supported, but H1b is not supported. Likewise, internal LoC (β = .312, p < .05) was related to self-disclosure as well as to external LoC (β = .006, p < .05). Hence, H2a & H2b is supported. Thus, only internal LoC meets the guidelines of the MHRA (multiple hierarchical regression model) (Baron & Kenny, 1986) (see Table 3). We performed two additional step wise hierarchical multiple regressions with control variables (age and gender) in Step 1, personality integration in Step 2, and internal LoC in Step 3 against self-disclosure. As Table 4 exhibits, when internal LoC was controlled, personality integration contributed 1.8% (versus 3.6% with internal LoC uncontrolled) of variability in self-disclosure. Finally, a Sobel Test demonstrated that internal LoC significantly attenuated the relationship between personality integration and self-disclosure, z = 5.62, p < .001. Thus, the relationship between personality integration and self-disclosure was significantly reduced when internal LoC was controlled. Thus, H4a is supported.

Table 3. Hierarchical Multiple Regression Analysis: The Direct Effect of Internal LoC and External LoC on Self-disclosure

	Self-disclosure				
Predictor variables	**β (Step 1)**	**β (Step 2)**	R^2	ΔR^2	ΔF
Step 1 (Control Variables)			.110	–	11.408
Gender	.217	.221			
Age	.206	.085			
Step 2			.111	.020*	.316*
ILOC		.312*			
			.110	.011	.009
ELOC		.006			

Note. N=189.
*p< .05, **p< .01.

Table 4. Hierarchical Multiple Regression Analysis: Mediating Effects

	Self-disclosure					
Predictor variables	**β (Step 1)**	**β (Step 2)**	**β (Step 3)**	R^2	ΔR^2	ΔF
Step 1 (Control Variables)				.156	–	6.33
Gender	.060	-.044	-.033			
Age	.206	.087	.083			
Step 2				.235	.036**	13.06**
Personality integration		.372**	.325**			
Step 3				.254	.018*	5.07*
Internal LoC			.094**			

Note. N=189.
*p< .05, **p< .01.

It is noteworthy that personality integration did not show an association with external LoC and external LoC show an relationship with self-disclosure. Baron and Kenny (1986) stated that the mediating effect of a variable should be tested if: 1) independent variable is related to dependent variable; 2) independent variable is related mediator; 3) mediator variable is related to dependent variable; 4) association between dependent and independent variables should considerably be reduced when the mediator variable is present. As external LoC did not meet second of the aforementioned guidelines, its mediating effect was not tested. Thus, H4b is not supported.

DISCUSSION AND IMPLICATIONS

The existing study explores the association between personality integration and self-disclosure while examining the mediating effect of internal and external LoC on the relationship. We reported that no prior study has examined this association which highlights the unique contribution that this piece of work makes to existing body of literature. In addition, the present study tries to fill gap in the literature regarding inconsistency about the significance of internal LoC at workplace (Brockway & Njus, 1999). This association is important as its strong application in organizations would lead to develop individuals with self-monitoring and accountability characteristics of one personality; along with productive and healthy work environments.

Results exhibit that personality integration has a direct association with internal LoC, and is a significant predictor of self-disclosure. This finding carries an important implication for recruiters. It is recommended that personality tests assessing the level of a individual personality integration be made part of the selection process. In addition, measures for assessing whether an individual has external or internal

LoC should be included in the test. Individual who elicits scores indicating higher levels of personality integration and internal LoC must be considered for preeminent and accountable positions as such individual would be better equipped to handle pressure situations and assume responsibility for their actions. As findings suggest, personality integration is a predictor of self disclosure which means that an individual having personality integration would more likely to share appropriate degree and extent of information, maintain a positive view of others; forge good interpersonal relations at the workplace; creating a healthy and conducive working environment. Such instances would moderately be performed by those individuals who have higher degree of personality integration (Anchor, 1974; Hearn, 1968; Seeman et al., 1963). The another major finding that internal LoC has a significant relationship with self-disclosure underscores the above stated and emphasizes the relevance of giving priority to individuals exhibiting higher internal LoC when hiring. This is also highlighted by the fact that in our analysis, external LoC was found to be significantly and negatively associated with personality integration; which implies that individual with external LoC are less likely to be higher degree of personality integration (implying once again the significance of consider individual with internal LoC). More interestingly, the most obvious ways in which individuals exhibit disclosure is through both internal and external LoC. However, individuals having external LoC display inappropriate disclosure and not follow-up the norms of self-disclosure (such as depth, amount, intent, honesty and valence) (Burchill & Stiles, 1988; Stiles, 1987; Wheeless & Grotz, 1977; Yağışan et al., 2007). Furthermore, such self-disclosure more likely to exhibited in state of anger, anxiety, depression and fear which are found to be associated with external LoC. In contrast, a reverse pattern observed in individual having internal LoC. For instances, individuals having internal LoC found to be negatively associated with anxiety, depression, and display the ability of self-monitoring, emotional stability, and accountable for their actions (Morrison, 1997). Thus, we can suggest that individuals having internal LoC moderately display appropriate self-disclosure and follow-up self-disclosure norms.

The researchers recommended for training programmed at the workplace to train employees to develop stronger internal LoC. Internal LoC encompasses self-esteem and if their performance goes below standards, they themselves take initiatives to maintain the performance standards. Thereafter, no further need for more control and supervision. Thus, the study emphasized to develop a workforce that has a strong internal LoC. These suggestions are in line with those given by (Eden & Aviram, 1993; Nehra, N. S., & Rangnekar, S; Weiss & Sherman, 1973)

The study also has major implications for academics. A key finding of this study is that personality integration has association with self-disclosure via internal LoC. Our finding indicates that individual high on personality integration support the positive work environment and interpersonal relationships, which thereby results in increasing the chances of self-disclosure and sharing and follow-up the appropriate and correct information via internal LoC; in other words, appropriateness and follow-up the self-disclosure norms are inherently associated with internal LoC. Future research may further investigate the direct association between personality integration and self-disclosure may vary with respect to geographical context and subculture aspects (Hofstede, G., 1984; Ignatius & kokkonen, 2007, p. 377). Also, the present paper gives insights into the association shared by personality integration, LoC and self-disclosure. As this association has not been examined in the past, findings of this study would act as guidelines for researchers and academics for conducting further study.

Future Research Direction

The study has some limitations are as follows: first, the data only collected from organization specific to Uttarakhand, Northern India. Therefore, future research should be performed in various geographical regions having different culture. Second, the study suggests carrying longitudinal studies in future. Third, to overcome high R-R we suggest adopting mixed-mode methods (Shih & Fan, 2007).

REFERENCES

Anchor, K. N. (1974). *Personality integration and successful outcome in individual psychotherapy*. Academic Press.

Arbuckle, J. L. (2011). *AMOS 20*. Meadville, PA: SPSS.

Arora, R., & Rangnekar, S. (2015). The joint effects of personality and supervisory career mentoring in predicting occupational commitment. *Career Development International*, *20*(1), 63–80. doi:10.1108/CDI-12-2014-0156

Arpan, L. M., & Roskos-Ewoldsen, D. R. (2005). Stealing thunder: Analysis of the effects of proactive disclosure of crisis information. *Public Relations Review*, *31*(3), 425–433. doi:10.1016/j.pubrev.2005.05.003

Baron, R. M., & Kenny, D. A. (1986). The moderator–mediator variable distinction in social psychological research: Conceptual, strategic, and statistical considerations. *Journal of Personality and Social Psychology*, *51*(6), 1173–1182. doi:10.1037/0022-3514.51.6.1173 PMID:3806354

Benassi, V. A., Sweeney, P. D., & Dufour, C. L. (1988). Is there a relation between LoC orientation and depression? *Journal of Abnormal Psychology*, *97*(3), 357–367. doi:10.1037/0021-843X.97.3.357 PMID:3057032

Bowles, S., & Wright, L. (1970). Personality integration in preadolescent males. *Developmental Psychology*, *2*(1), 151. doi:10.1037/h0028612

Brockway, J., & Njus, D. (1999). Perceptions of competence and LoC for positive and negative outcomes. *Personality and Individual Differences*, *26*, 531–548. doi:10.1016/S0191-8869(98)00169-X

Burchill, S. L., & Stiles, W. B. (1988). Interactions of depressed college students with their roommates: Not necessarily negative. *Journal of Personality and Social Psychology*, *55*(3), 410–419. doi:10.1037/0022-3514.55.3.410 PMID:3171913

Charmaz, K. (1991). *Good days, bad days: The self in chronic illness and time*. Rutgers University Press.

Cho, J. (2007). *Psychological processes underlying the relationship between transformational leadership and multi-foci organizational citizenship behaviors: a multi-level approach* (PhD dissertation). The State University of New York, Buffalo, NY.

Christopher, A. N., Saliba, L., & Deadmarsh, E. J. (2009). Materialism and well-being: The mediating effect of LoC. *Personality and Individual Differences*, *46*(7), 682–686. doi:10.1016/j.paid.2009.01.003

Clarke, D. (2004). Neuroticism: Moderator or mediator in the relation between LoC and depression? *Personality and Individual Differences*, *37*(2), 245–258. doi:10.1016/j.paid.2003.08.015

Collins, N. L., & Miller, L. C. (1994). Self-disclosure and liking: A meta-analytic review. *Psychological Bulletin*, *116*(3), 457–475. doi:10.1037/0033-2909.116.3.457 PMID:7809308

Cooley, R. S., & Seeman, J. (1979). Personality integration and social schemata. *Journal of Personality*, *47*(2), 288–304. doi:10.1111/j.1467-6494.1979.tb00203.x

Cozby, P. C. (1972). Self-disclosure, reciprocity and liking. *Sociometry*, *35*(1), 151–160. doi:10.2307/2786555 PMID:5011335

DeNeve, K. M., & Cooper, H. (1998). The happy personality: A meta-analysis of 137 personality traits and subjective well-being. *Psychological Bulletin*, *124*(2), 197–229. doi:10.1037/0033-2909.124.2.197 PMID:9747186

Doyne, S. E. (1969). *Effects of a sensitivity training laboratory experience on self-disclosure, self-esteem, and social desirability* (Doctoral dissertation). George Peabody College for Teachers.

Duncan, C. B. (1966). A reputation test of personality integrations. *Journal of Personality and Social Psychology, 3*(5), 516–524. doi:10.1037/h0023297 PMID:5939600

Eden, D., & Aviram, A. (1993). Self-efficacy training to speed reemployment: Helping people to help themselves. *The Journal of Applied Psychology, 78*(3), 352–360. doi:10.1037/0021-9010.78.3.352

Erikson, E. H. (1959). Identity and the life cycle: Selected papers. *Psychological Issues*.

Estrada, L., Dupoux, E., & Wolman, C. (2006). The relationship between LoC and personal-emotional adjustment and social adjustment to college life in students with and without learning disabilities. *College Student Journal, 40*(1), 43–54.

Falk, D. R., & Wagner, P. N. (1985). Intimacy of self-disclosure and response processes as factors affecting the development of interpersonal relationships. *The Journal of Social Psychology, 125*(5), 557–570. doi:10.1080/00224545.1985.9712029

Forgas, J. P. (2011). Affective influences on self-disclosure: Mood effects on the intimacy and reciprocity of disclosing personal information. *Journal of Personality and Social Psychology, 100*(3), 449–461. doi:10.1037/a0021129 PMID:21171788

Hamid, P. N. (1994). Self-monitoring, LoC, and social encounters of Chinese and New Zealand students. *Journal of Cross-Cultural Psychology, 25*(3), 353–368. doi:10.1177/0022022194253004

Harris, S. M., Dersch, C. A., & Mittal, M. (1999). Look who's talking: Measuring self-disclosure in MFT. *Contemporary Family Therapy, 21*(3), 405–415. doi:10.1023/A:1021968517320

Hearn, C. B., Jr. (1968). *Personality integration and person perception in college males* (Doctoral dissertation). ProQuest Information & Learning.

Hofstede, G. (1984). Cultural dimensions in management and planning. *Asia Pacific Journal of Management, 1*(2), 81–99. doi:10.1007/BF01733682

Horner, K. L. (1996). LoC, neuroticism, and stressors: Combined influences on reported physical illness. *Personality and Individual Differences, 21*(2), 195–204. doi:10.1016/0191-8869(96)00067-0

Ignatius, E., & Kokkonen, M. (2007). Factors contributing to verbal self-disclosure. *Nordic Psychology*, *59*(4), 362–391. doi:10.1027/1901-2276.59.4.362

Johnson, S. J., Batey, M., & Holdsworth, L. (2009). Personality and health: The mediating role of trait emotional intelligence and work LoC. *Personality and Individual Differences*, *47*(5), 470–475. doi:10.1016/j.paid.2009.04.025

Jourard, S. M. (1971). *Self-disclosure: An experimental analysis of the transparent self*. Academic Press.

Judge, T. A., & Bono, J. E. (2001). Relationship of core self-evaluations traits—self-esteem, generalized self-efficacy, LoC, and emotional stability—with job satisfaction and job performance: A meta-analysis. *The Journal of Applied Psychology*, *86*(1), 80–92. doi:10.1037/0021-9010.86.1.80 PMID:11302235

Judge, T. A., & Zapata, C. P. (2015). The person-situation debate revisited: Effect of situation strength and trait activation on the validity of the Big Five personality traits in predicting job performance. *Academy of Management Journal*, *58*(4), 1149–1179. doi:10.5465/amj.2010.0837

Karatepe, O. M. (2011). Procedural justice, work engagement, and job outcomes: Evidence from Nigeria. *Journal of Hospitality Marketing & Management*, *20*(8), 855–878. doi:10.1080/19368623.2011.577688

Macintosh, G. (2009). Examining the antecedents of trust and rapport in services: Discovering new interrelationships. *Journal of Retailing and Consumer Services*, *16*(4), 298–305. doi:10.1016/j.jretconser.2009.02.001

Mikulincer, M., & Segal, J. (1991). Loneliness and the desire for intimacy: The intervening role of LoC. *Personality and Individual Differences*, *12*(8), 801–809. doi:10.1016/0191-8869(91)90146-3

Morrison, K. A. (1997). Personality correlates of the Five-Factor Model for a sample of business owners/managers: Associations with scores on self-monitoring, Type A behavior, LoC, and subjective well-being. *Psychological Reports*, *80*(1), 255–272. doi:10.2466/pr0.1997.80.1.255 PMID:9122336

Nehra, N. S., & Rangnekar, S. (2016). Relationship understanding between social adjustment and self-disclosure-results from the Indian power sector. *16th Global Conference on Flexible Systems and Flexibility*, 256-266.

Nehra, N. S., & Rangnekar, S. (2017). Relationship understanding between emotional stability, self-disclosure, and social adjustment. *Journal of Intercultural Communication Research*, *46*(6), 558–578. doi:10.1080/17475759.2017.1387165

Nehra, N. S., & Rangnekar, S. (2018). Linking the emotional maturity factors and self-disclosure: A study of Indian organizations. *International Journal of Organizational Analysis, 26*(2).

Nehra, N. S., & Rangnekar, S. (in press). Does emotional stability mediates the relationship between self-disclosure, personality integration, social adjustment. *International Journal of Business Excellence.*

Nicholls, A. R., Levy, A. R., & Perry, J. L. (2015). Emotional maturity, dispositional coping, and coping effectiveness among adolescent athletes. *Psychology of Sport and Exercise*, *17*, 32–39. doi:10.1016/j.psychsport.2014.11.004

Nunnally, J. C. (1978). *Psychometric theory* (2nd ed.). New York, NY: McGraw-Hill.

Odom, M. L., Seeman, J., & Newbrough, J. R. (1971). A study of family communication patterns and personality integration in children. *Child Psychiatry and Human Development*, *1*(4), 275–285. doi:10.1007/BF01441090 PMID:5163304

Pareek, U., & Purohit, S. (2011). *Training Instruments in HRD and OD*. McGraw Hill.

Perlow, R., & Latham, L. L. (1993). Relationship of client abuse with LoC and gender: A longitudinal study in mental retardation facilities. *The Journal of Applied Psychology*, *78*(5), 831–834. doi:10.1037/0021-9010.78.5.831 PMID:8253634

Podsakoff, P. M., & Organ, D. W. (1986). Self-reports in organizational research: Problems and prospects. *Journal of Management*, *12*(4), 531–544. doi:10.1177/014920638601200408

Posey, C., Lowry, P. B., Roberts, T. L., & Ellis, T. S. (2010). Proposing the online community self-disclosure model: The case of working professionals in France and the UK who use online communities. *European Journal of Information Systems*, *19*(2), 181–195. doi:10.1057/ejis.2010.15

Rotter, J. B. (1966). Generalized expectancies for internal versus external control of reinforcement. *Psychological Monographs*, *80*(1), 1–28. doi:10.1037/h0092976 PMID:5340840

Rubinstein, E. A. (1954). Personality integration and the perceptual process. *Journal of Clinical Psychology*, *10*(1), 23–29. doi:10.1002/1097-4679(195401)10:1<23::AID-JCLP2270100105>3.0.CO;2-X PMID:13117975

Ryckman, R. M., Sherman, M. F., & Burgess, G. D. (1973). LoC and self-disclosure of public and private information by college men and women: A brief note. *The Journal of Psychology*, *84*(2), 317–318. doi:10.1080/00223980.1973.9923845 PMID:4717162

Şahin, N. H., Basım, H. N., & Çetin, F. (2009). LoC and self-concept in interpersonal conflict resolution approaches. *Türk Psikiyatri Dergisi*, *20*, 153–163. PMID:19504366

Sarrasin, O., Mayor, E., & Faniko, K. (2014). Gender traits and cognitive appraisal in young adults: The mediating role of LoC. *Sex Roles*, *70*(3-4), 122–133. doi:10.1007/s11199-013-0336-6

Seeman, J. (1959). Toward a concept of personality integration. *The American Psychologist*, *14*(10), 633–637. doi:10.1037/h0042986

Seeman, J. (1963). Teacher judgments of high and low adjustment. *The Journal of Educational Research*, *57*(4), 213–216. doi:10.1080/00220671.1963.10883064

Seeman, J., Barry, E., & Ellinwood, C. (1963). Personality integration as a criterion of therapy outcome. *Psychotherapy (Chicago, Ill.)*, *1*(1), 14–16. doi:10.1037/h0088566

Sharma, N. (2014). Managing Talent for Sustainable Competitive Differentiation. *Parikalpana: KIIT Journal of Management*, *10*(1), 9–22.

Shih, T. H., & Fan, X. (2007). Response rates and mode preferences in web-mail mixed-mode surveys: A meta-analysis. *International Journal of Internet Science*, *2*(1), 59–82.

Singh, Y., & Bhargava, M. (1990). Manual for Emotional Maturity Scale. National Psychological Corporation.

Spector, P. E. (1982). Behavior in organizations as a function of employee's LoC. *Psychological Bulletin*, *91*(3), 482–497. doi:10.1037/0033-2909.91.3.482

Stiles, W. B. (1987). I have to talk to somebody. In Self-disclosure (pp. 257-282). Springer US.

Stiles, W. B., Shuster, P. L., & Harrigan, J. A. (1992). Disclosure and anxiety: A test of the fever model. *Journal of Personality and Social Psychology*, *63*(6), 980–988. doi:10.1037/0022-3514.63.6.980 PMID:1460564

Thomas, M., & Seeman, J. (1971). Criterion measures for therapy outcome: A study in personality integration. *Psychotherapy (Chicago, Ill.)*, *8*(1), 26–30. doi:10.1037/h0086619

Varma, A., Srinivas, E. S., & Stroh, L. K. (2005). A comparative study of the impact of leader-member exchange in US and Indian samples. *Cross Cultural Management*, *12*(1), 84–95. doi:10.1108/13527600510797971

Weiss, H., & Sherman, J. (1973). Internal-external control as a predictor of task effort and satisfaction subsequent to failure. *The Journal of Applied Psychology, 57*(2), 132–136. doi:10.1037/h0037054 PMID:4784756

West, S. G., Finch, J. F., & Curran, P. J. (1995). *Structural equation models with nonnormal variables: Problems and remedies.* Academic Press.

Wheeless, L. R., & Grotz, J. (1977). The measurement of trust and its relationship to self-disclosure. *Human Communication Research, 3*(3), 250–257. doi:10.1111/j.1468-2958.1977.tb00523.x

Yağışan, N., Sünbül, A. M., & Yücalan, Ö. B. (2007). Müzik bölümü öğrencilerinin benlik imgeleri ve denetim odaklarının incelenmesi. *Erciyes Üniversitesi Sosyal Bilimler Enstitüsü Dergisi, 1*(22), 243–262.

Yoo, G. J., Aviv, C., Levine, E. G., Ewing, C., & Au, A. (2010). Emotion work: Disclosing cancer. *Supportive Care in Cancer, 18*(2), 205–215. doi:10.1007/s00520-009-0646-y PMID:19434430

Chapter 14
Employee Retention:
Important Factors to Be Considered by Human Resource Professionals While Creating Retention

Karteek Ramalinga Ponnuru
BML Munjal University, India

Rashik Gupta
BML Munjal University, India

ABSTRACT

Attrition is a major problem in many Indian IT firms. On an average, attrition stands at around 14.5% in many major IT firms, making it a major problem. Attrition is not only a result of poor HR policies; it is also because of the many aspirations and need for career development for many young professionals. This gap between fulfilling the aspirations of the new entrants and the scope of development at any organization is the result of attrition. From the study, it has also been concluded that recognition, valuing one's individual opinion, and also the aspect of broadening and the scope of an organization to provide enough career development prospects in terms of training, executive education, and salary, etc. are also factors because of which many young professionals leave their respective organizations. Therefore, there is a need to amend the existing employee practices in order to meet the ever-changing momentum across the organizations and reduce the cost that happens due to attrition.

DOI: 10.4018/978-1-5225-4038-0.ch014

Copyright © 2018, IGI Global. Copying or distributing in print or electronic forms without written permission of IGI Global is prohibited.

INTRODUCTION

India has seen a precipitous shift from a manufacturing economy to a service based economy and internationally this has been the same scenario. With the growth of Indian service industry the growth of human capital has also grown exponentially because of the need of many technical and non-technical skills on which the industry generally relies on. One of the most critical factors for the growth of this industry is because of the strong HR practices these service organizations have enforced. Two key areas of the HR policies adopted by these companies are recruiting and retaining the workforce. The major chunk of these recruitments happen on university campuses across India. Companies generally take in fresh graduates, train them according to the requirements and set them up on different projects. But, this system is now being threatened by high rates of attrition and job hopping. For the year 2014-15 the service's sector has contributed to 57.9% of the total GDP in India (Planning Commission, 2015). It is estimated that the service sector would now contribute more to the Indian GDP in the coming years.

The Indian services industry is not only the big in terms of contribution to the GDP of the nation but also really huge when it comes to employing skilled workforce about 28% of the total workforce was employed by the services sector in the year 2012 (Singh, 2015) the success of this sector goes to the proper recruitment, capacity development, skill development and opportunities this sector has been providing for the employees of the sector. But, with the sprouting of many service sector companies especially IT companies, many of these companies have been facing a shortage of talent. India has one of the biggest youth populations, yet this gap between what the industry needs and the availability has become a looming problem for these companies and the opportunities for the experts in this sector has been increasing in an ever growing proportion. The biggest challenge now is to attract the right talent, train them and motivate them to stay with the organization for a longer time in an organization to reduce the cost of recruitment and training (Jessica Sze-Yin Ho, 2010)

On a general context, attrition can be attributed to push and pull factors (Jessica Sze-Yin Ho, 2010). Push factors are factors because of which employees would like to leave the organization. These factors are from the employee's side. Some of them involve switching jobs due to situational constraints or high levels of dissatisfaction. These factors can be identified through proper appraisal systems and analytics. These push factors can be addressed by talking to the employees and getting their feedback on various policies existing in the organization. Pull factors are factors which drive the individual to look for jobs outside the current organization. These factors are generally the *behind the scene* factors and are generally the driving factors that make the employee choose an alternative job. Addressing these factors is a big challenge because, these are the grey areas in the head of an employee and generally are not easily identifiable. Employees generally tend to be mouth shut on these factors. These factors might be a result of many undressed issues or biases held by the employees for a long time. Unless and until these factors are addressed the push factors cannot be zeroed down.

These factors can be further difficulty to be identified amongst the young talent workforce the IT organizations tend to hire for entry level positions because of the fact that the biggest proportion of the workforce is fresh out of college with little or absolutely no work experience and getting them onboard the companies work culture is a big challenge and involves a lot of induction sessions and programs which has to be borne by these companies. The purpose of this research paper is to understand what these push and pull factors are all about? What an average Indian professional who is fresh out of college looks for while deciding to stay up on a job or leave it for the better. Since, providing mitigation strategies to counter these push and pull factors are within the limits of the organizations, suggestions to reduce the attrition rate has also been provided. The remaining section of the paper has been structured in the following way:

Problem Statement

Until and unless we have a clear problem, we cannot find any optimal solution. And since none of the systems is perfect, there must always a problem associated with it. The challenge with the organizations today are facing is with the high attrition level among the new entrants. This task of retaining the employees for a longer tenure has become the utmost need for all the organizations. There could be a number of reasons which result in high attrition among the entry level executives, some of which are the salary's or the trust which the organizations are unable to create among these new entrants. But the challenge is even bigger. Today's markets lack in the number of candidates which are really employable especially in the Indian market where there are many institutions mushrooming everywhere across the country. We can say that there is a significant relationship between empowering the employees and intent to stay on a particular job. So talent retention is all about empowering employees so that they don't leave.

The research outcome of this study will reflect the degree of impact of many variables related to what many aspects what an entry level executives think before leaving a job so that the Human Resource department can work in this aspect so as to keep the entry level executives with the firm for a long time.

Figure 1. Research Methodology

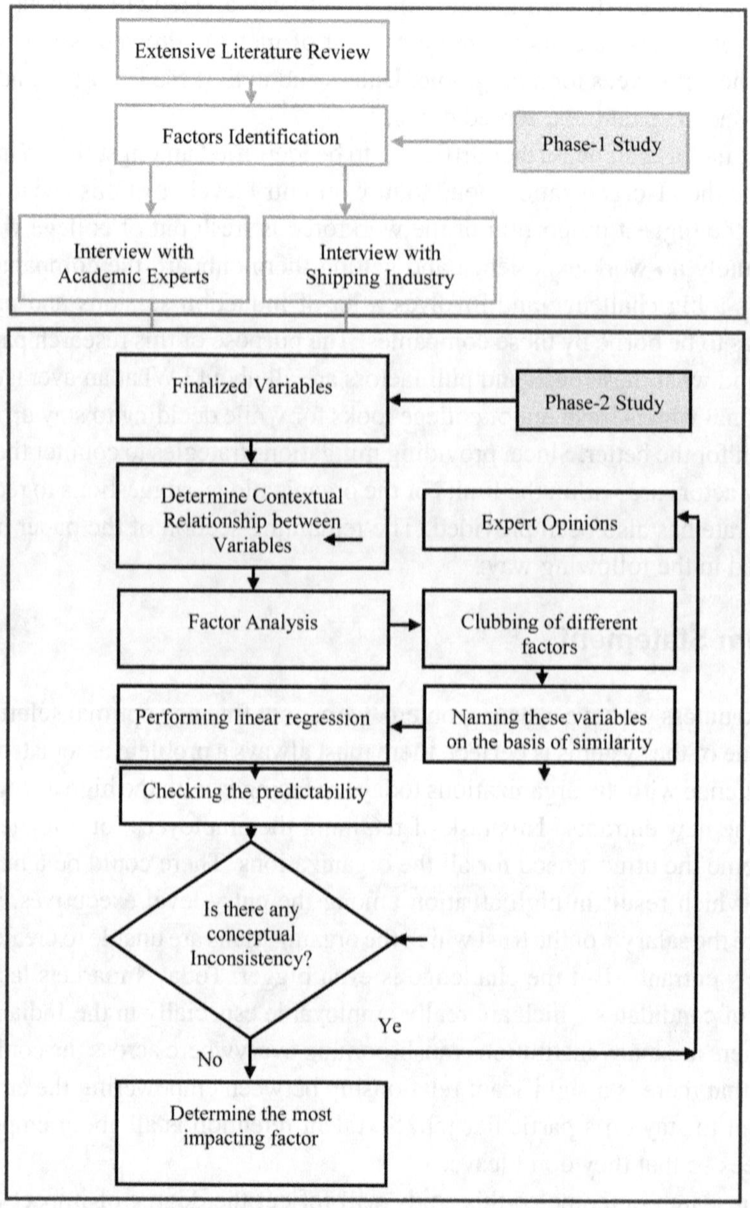

Literature Review

Today the biggest challenge which any Human Resource Professional is facing is retention of the potential employees. In past few years, most of the organizations have been following the practices of hiring campus recruits or third party employees at lesser salaries and replacing them with the higher salaried employees, making them do equivalent work. This behavior has reduced the loyalty of employees to their organizations, hence many new entrants start to leave the organization after gaining some experience. Human Resource department has been designing various programs and benefits for the entrants so that they feel more confident about their organizations and can rely for long term employment with them. Career Development is one of the programs which the organizations are deploying for the new entrants. In fact in a research by (Hall, 1998), career development opportunities is one of the most important variables as employees are more conscious about their career so they prefer a job where they can get more opportunities to develop their skills. A company that wants to strengthen its bond with its employees must invest in the development of their employees. (Hsu, 2003) also explains the importance of career development in his research paper. His research shows an indirect relationship between the number of Incentives which the organization has to offer to its candidate and the Intention to leave or a direct relationship with the Intention to work for longer tenure. In a research by (De Vos, 2008), there is some conflict or negative relation between the values the employees have the work which the Human Resource team does towards bridging that gap.

Some other researches focus on the relationship between the Supervisor and the sub-ordinate, or simply between the employee and the manager. In the research by Eisenberger and Associates, the perception of the employee and the view towards the organization is highly influenced with the relationship with the supervisor. Hence better the relationship, more fruitful will the outputs leading to positive results and hence retaining more employees. Open organizations or the Flat structure organizations like Google are the best example for this. They believe in empowering there employees by giving decision making to some degree in there hands. Also the work space design itself is such that It always creates a positive energy among its employees. In-fact a research by (Brill, 2001) workspace designs have a profound impact on workers and tend to live with job as long as satisfied).

Apart from this extrinsic factors some of the Intrinsic factors which play a role are the Physical or Psychological needs. As per the Maslow's hierarchal model, these come at the bottom of the pyramid and hence needs to be fulfilled much before any other need. These include basic which are necessary for living like food, space, money. Hence the important basic need which the organizations fill is the salary or the monetary benefits. According to (Shoaib, 2009), attractive remuneration packages are one of the very important factors of retention because it fulfills the financial and material desires as well as provide the means of being social by employee"s status and position of power in the organization. Many researchers demonstrate that there is a great deal of inter-individual difference in understanding the significance of financial rewards for employee retention. (Elliott, 2001) too mentions the various factors which play an important role in determining the satisfaction among the students towards recruitment and retention, among which salary plays an important part. Much of the other researches have focused on finding out other variables which influence the behavior. Some of these as cited include the family-work life balance through the flexible schedules, additional benefits through the child care assistance, maternity leave for the females as mandated by the government, childcare assistance, parental leave, childcare information and parental leave on organization commitment. Researchers showed that there is greater organizational commitment if employees had access to work life policies and also these employees articulated considerably with lower intent to renounce their profession (Grover and Crooker, 1995). In this research the objective is to use the attributes identified in the previous researches and validate and build a model on them.

Research Objectives and Framework

All the organizations are trying to capture the satisfaction of the employees through various feedback forms and try to build a Satisfaction Index on the basis of them. These are done by capturing the sentiments on the Likert scale, or by directly asking the feedback towards the services. The aim of this research is to build a quantifiable model by formulating techniques for the Human Resource executives while dealing with entry level executives, providing impacts of different variables related to how an entry level executive feels about their jobs and their future goals. By working on these aspects any firm would be able to retain their entry level executives.

Much of the study has already been done in this field and have tried to identify the important variables which influence the employees to leave the organization. This study aims at Identification of all the responsible factors by conducting a primary research. This is done by floating a questionnaire among hundreds of employees gathering their opinion on these key factors. We try to build a relationship between the identified items with the retention of the employees. Important part of this research is that the model building has been done keeping in mind Employee Retention as the dependent variable. Since the number of variables on which the opinions is collected is huge, hence a simple technique of dimensionality reduction has been applied. Exploratory Factor Analysis is a very good Dimensionality reduction technique which aims to club the number of identified variables into a particular number of factors depending on the correlation between them. Another advantage is that since the correlation part is already handled in this analysis, the model becomes near to perfect without any problem of multi collinearity. Later in the research Multi variate Regression has been deployed to build the model. The model is nothing but the linear relationship between the various factors identified and the dependent variable Employee Retention.

From the Figure 1, we can see that the research has been conducted into four steps, first one is the variables identification using Primary Research, where the next step is the Exploratory Factor Analysis, then by applying the Multi variate Regression Analysis a linear model has been built between the independent factors and the dependent variable.

Figure 3. Proposed Research Framework

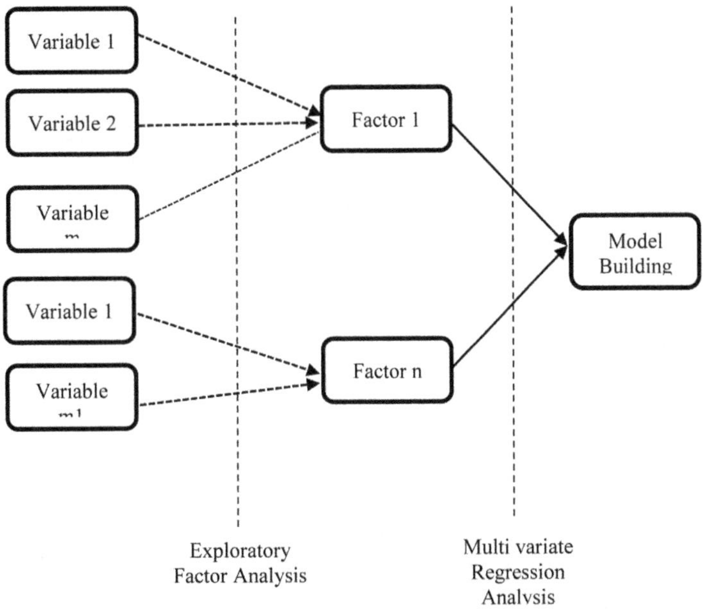

Figure 2. Research Framework by the steps followed in completing the research

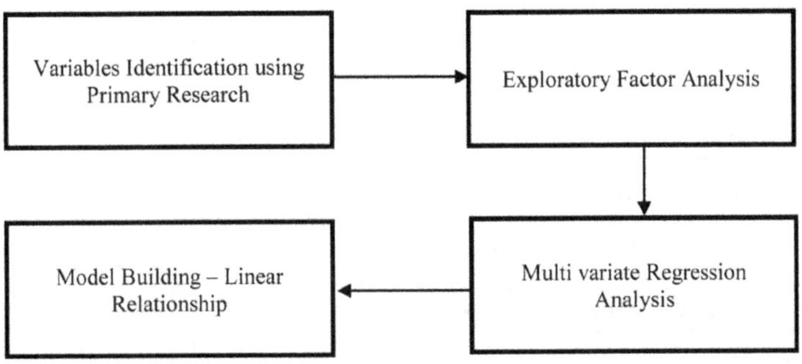

Table 1. Variables Identification and related citations

Type	Question	Citation
General Questions	Gender	(Bennett, 1993), (Subramony, 2012)
	Have you done your masters or not?	
	Did you get a job right after graduation	
	Do you plan to study more?	
Specific Questions	How do you feel about the career development program offered at your firm? How well does your direct supervisor/manager support you?	(Subramony, 2012), (Adhikari, 2009), (Ho, 2010) (Steel, 1984), (Benton, 1984), (Anthony, 1994)
	How well does your direct supervisor/manager value your opinion while decision making?	(James, 2013), (Bhatnagar, 2007), (Subraminy, 2012)
	Are you satisfied with the hygiene factors of your firm?	(Gupta, 2011)
	Are you satisfied with motivation your firm gives you?	(Banerjee, 2010)
	Are you satisfied with the reward system offered at your company?	(Nappinnai, 2013), (Banerjee, 2010), (Bennett, 1993)
	Are you satisfied with the work life policies your company adheres to?	(Nappinnai, 2013)
	Are you satisfied with the chances of promotion?	(Palan, 2007), (Jain, 2013), (Ingersoll, 2013)
	Are you satisfied with help being provided to you by other colleagues in your organization	(Nappinnai, 2013), (Banerjee, 2010), (Subramony, 2012)
	Are you satisfied with the allocation of rewards regarding work? Do you agree with the statement 'Too much work burdens you'?	(Singh, 2012), (Samson, 2013), (Nappinnai, 2013) (Singh, 2012)
	Do you feel your organization is doing good in terms of providing good work life balance	(Palan, 2007), (Singh, 2012)
	Is your organization doing good in terms of recognizing your skill	(Nappinnai, 2013)
	Do you feel it is important to learn while you work?	(Ingersoll, 2013)
	How important is job flexibility while learning?	(Ingersoll, 2013)
	Is your firm providing sufficient training in regards with your job?	(Samson, 2013)
	Are you satisfied with the compensation programs offered at your company?	(Gregory, 2005), (Samson, 2013), (Ingersoll, 2013)
	Do you perceive that your company is committed to you?	(Mehdi, 2012), (Davenport, 2010)
	Would you appreciate your company's efforts if they offer you distance education through major universities?	(Morgan, 1999)
	How likely are you going to leave your organization for better prospects elsewhere?	(Gregory, 2005), (Singh, 2012), (Palan, 2007), (Nappinnai, 2013)
	Would you leave your job for further education?	(Morgan, 1999)
	Do you think that your peers working in the other organizations are getting more pay than you?	(Gregory, 2005), (Singh, 2012), (Palan, 2007), (Nappinnai, 2013)
	Do you feel that giving international assignments would help in talent retention?	(Singh, 2012)
	Would you stay back in a company just to do an international assignment	(Singh, 2012), (Gregory, 2005), (Palan, 2007)
	Are you satisfied with the non-monetary compensation being provided to you in your company?	(Palan, 2007)
	Would you leave your company for an offer abroad?	(Singh, 2012), (Gregory, 2005)
	How likely are you to leave you current work place in the coming 2 years?	(Gregory, 2005), (Morgon, 2005), (Singh, 2012)

Table 2. Demographic Profile of the Respondents

		Number of Respondents	Percentage (%)
Gender	Male	162	64.8
	Female	88	35.2
Age	16-20	42	16.8
	21-25	147	58.8
	26-30	59	24.4
Education	Graduate	207	82.8
	Post-Graduate	43	17.2
Marital Status	Married	12	4.8
	Single	238	95.2

Research Methodology

This current study aims to identify the gap between the current systems deployed by the HR Departments towards the satisfaction of the employees and the expectations which the employees have for the same. This has been done in order to

- Identify the most influencing attributes among the new Entrants
- Build a relationship between these attributes and the Employee Retention among the new Executives

Data Collection

To fulfill the above objective, a primary research had been conducted to determine the factors based structure for Employee's Retention in the organization. From the past researches all the relevant variables had been collected, and some of the variables had been collected through direct feedback from the employees of PSUs and from self-experience. On the basis of above research, a questionnaire had been prepared which focuses primarily on 31 variables and try to prove the significant relationship

Table 2(b): Working Experience of the Respondents

		Number of Respondents	Percentage (%)
How long have you been working with organization	0 years	139	55.6
	1-5 years	98	39.2
	More than 5 years	13	5.2

between these variables and the Employee Retention. The whole research paper apart from the Demographics questions, the data had been collected on the Likert Scale on the rating 1-5. Likert Scale is very useful in Behavioral measurement, as it gives proper insights into the behavior of the consumer. All the variables Identified are mentioned in the Table 2, along with the Citations or references as to where these are gathered from.

Once the questionnaire had been prepared using Online Forms, the questionnaire had been floated among the employees of few MNCs and some of the PSUs to collect diverse data from different profiles. All the data has been collected in the age group 21-31, as this is the most relevant age of entering into the organization. From all the 31 identified variables, 27 had been put on the Likert Scale on the rating 1-5. Then by using Dimensionality reduction, the structural model is built which will act as an instrument for future reference of the HR executives.

Since the data has been collected among the newly entering employees, a total sample size of 250 had been collected for analysis. This sample size is enough for normality and removing any biases in the data. The data collected was interpreted using SPSS on which the data was fed into and two types of analysis namely factor analysis and multiple regression were run. Firstly, factor analysis segregated the data into seven different factors, the factors were named and then multiple regression was run and results were interpreted. Our dependent variable is' How likely are you to leave you current work place in the coming 2 years?' while the rest of the variables are called independent variables. We would like to see if an entry level executive would leave his/ her current work place and id yes why? And develop strategic HRM practices in order to retain them by focusing on the most important variables.

The table above shows the Demographic profile of all the respondents which would help us classify which segment of Employees are more likely to leave and the Table 2(b) shows the summary of Working Experience of all the respondents. This helps us getting insights in the data.

Data Analysis

The data collected had been analyzed through a number of analytical techniques. For these the Exploratory Factor Analysis and the Multivariate Regression has been used to reduce the number of variables into limited factors and then build a structural model which would be used as an instrument for measuring the factor of Employee Retention.

Table 3. Exploratory Factor Analysis output

Question	Variable	Factor Loading Value
Managerial Support		
How well does your direct supervisor/manager support you?	Supervisor Support	.558
Are you satisfied with the hygiene factors of your firm?	Hygiene Factors	.629
Are you satisfied with the reward system offered at your company?	Reward System	
Decision Making		
Are you satisfied with motivation your firm gives you?	Value of Opinion	.568
How well does your direct supervisor/manager value your opinion while decision making?	Motivational Factors	.771
How important is job flexibility while learning?	Job Flexibility	
Skill/Career Development		
Do you plan to study more?	Further Study plans	.817
Would you leave your job for further education?	Leaving job for studies	.894
How do you feel about the career development program offered at your firm?	Career Development Program	
Do you feel it is important to learn while you working?	Learning and Unlearning	
Current Education Level		
Have you done your masters or not?	Masters Education	.860
Did you get a job right after graduation	Job after graduating	.730
Organizational Commitment		
Do you perceive that your company is committed to you?	Commitment of Organization	.963
Would you appreciate your company's efforts if they offer you distance education through major universities?	Exec. – Distance Education	.963
Do you think that your peers working in the other organizations are getting more pay than you?	Peer Comparison	.962
Do you feel that giving international assignments would help in talent retention?	International Onsite projects	.962
Work life balance		
Are you satisfied with the work life policies your company adheres to?	Work Life scale	.503
Are you satisfied with the chances of promotion?	Promotions	.787
Are you satisfied with help being provided to you by other colleagues in your organization	Peer Help	.601
Are you satisfied with the allocation of rewards regarding work?	Reward System	.642
Do you agree with the statement 'Too much work burdens you'?	Need for work-life balance	.598
Do you feel your organization is doing good in terms of providing good work life balance	Providing work-life balance	.625
Recognition		
Is your organization doing good in terms of recognizing your skill	Skill Recognition	.728
Is your firm providing sufficient training in regards with your job?	Value for contribution	.681
Are you satisfied with the compensation programs offered at your company?	Feeling Equity	.682
How likely are you going to leave your organization for better prospects elsewhere?	Offsite Recognition	.885
Would you stay back in a company just to do an international assignment	Career Enhancement	.894
Are you satisfied with the non-monetary compensation being provided to you in your company?	Non-Monetary Compensation	.894
Would you leave your company for an offer abroad?	Abroad Aspirations	.894

Exploratory Factor Analysis

Exploratory Factor Analysis, as the name suggests acts as a powerful technique to reduce the dimensionality in the data set. Not only that the problem of Multi-collinearity is easily handled using EFA. The whole data has been in the SPSS version 21. After running the data on SPSS and using factor analysis we get the following rotated component matix. Through this matrix we can get to know which variables falls under which factor. The key criteria on which the EFA is finalized include:

1. **Correlation Matrix and the Anti Image Matrix:** This acts as an adequate tool to filter out the variables which are not appropriate for EFA analysis. Generally this shows correlation between variables and any poor value for correlation is dropped. In our case, if any value is lower than 0.5 then the variable is dropped.
2. **KMO (Kieser-Meyer-Olkin) Value:** To check if the sample is adequate enough the KMO value and Bartelett's value is referred. Generally KMO value more than 0.8 is preferred and in the research the KMO value has come out to be 0.86 and the Bartlett's significance value has been 0.000, which shows the sample is adequate enough.
3. **Factor Loading:** Defines how much correlation is there between the variables and between the variable and the factor. Generally it tends to vary between -1 to +1 and any value lower than 0.6 is considered low in correlation. In our case, almost all the values are near to or more than 0.6
4. Eigen value explains how much of the variance from the total is being explained by that particular factor. In the research we have considered 7 factors with Eigen value greater than 1

From the table 3 above, it can be seen that depending on the values of the Factor Loading, 7 factors are identified under which all the variables can be clubbed together.

Recognition (Factor 1): This defines the extent to which the organization is successful in recognizing the efforts of the employees. These recognition is not only in the form of the Monetary benefits, but also non-monetary benefits like awarding or prasing the hard work put by the employee infront of the whole team. Many organizations consider annual appraisals best recognition medium, but fewer organizations have started to feel that this is not enough. Like HCL one of the reputed firms of our Nation recognizes the high achievers every year by giving them the O2 award. Not only that the spot awards are also given to keep the employees motivated

Organizational Commitment (Factor 2): This factor defines the amount of perceived commitment the respondent feels the organization is giving him. Organizational commitment is one of the factors which motivate the employee to work with them, it tells them how important or special they feel while working for a particular organization. Many organizations take employees for granted and expect only their commitment towards the organization, but organizational commitment in turn is a commitment provided by the organization towards their employees

Work Life Balance (Factor 3): Work Life balance concept is not entirely new. Slogging at work is a long gone trend and many employers across the world accept this fact. Work Life balance is a strike between the amounts of work an employee does to complete his/ her KRA's and meet your KPI's while spending a private quality time with one's family. This balance is required for employees for their mental health and personal motivation

Skill/Career Development (Factor 4): Employers no longer hold the assumption that an employee would stick to the present job forever. It is a good notation and many organizations are now coming up with this concept of telling its employees the benefits of joining their organization. This career development track is one of the main aspects employees generally tend to look at. Employees generally look to improvise their skill set which would help them in their future endeavors. Skill/ Career Development looks at how well an employer helps its employees to gain new skills and fasten their career growth

Career Education Level (Factor 5): The Current Education level factor talks about the current level of education an employee has. If he/ she is an undergraduate, a post graduate or a doctorate in any field. This is important to know as this factor might have a high correlation with the future educational aspirations of an employee

Decision Making (Factor 6): This factor talks about the ability of an employee to take decisions or voice his feelings to facilitate the process of decision making. If an employee is given the ability to decide on any particular aspect he/ she would be feeling motivated and empowered. This is a very important factor to be considered as it talks about empowerment

Managerial Support (Factor 7): Grievances or problems are a part of any organization but the key lies in how an organization takes up its employee's grievances or problems and how it handles them. Managerial support is thus a very important aspect to be considered as it helps the employee to stay committed with the organization, gives a sense that the organization is listening to them and provides a sense of belongingness with the organization

Multi Variate Regression Analysis

The output from the Exploratory Factor Analysis is fed into the Regression Analysis to build a model between the dependent variable of Employee Retention and the Independent variable which are the Identified factors from EFA in our case. The general format of the equation from the multivariate Regression Analysis is

$$y = \beta_0 + \beta_1 x_1 + \beta_2 x_2 + \ldots\ldots + \beta_n x_n$$

Where β is the coefficient in the linear equation, y is the dependent variable, which is Employee Retention in our case, and x is the Independent variables, which is the list of all the Identified variables as explained in the Research Methodology section. The key criteria on which the Multi variate Regression Analysis is finalized include:

1. The Correlation Coefficient which is also called the R value is used measure the degree of relation between the variables. The direction of relation is determined by the sign in R value and the strength is determined by the value of R. Generally the value varies between -1 to +1, and any value which is more than 0.8 is considered to be good. In our model, the R value has come out to be 0.812 which shows that the model is having a good explanatory power.
2. The Coefficient of Determination or the R Squared value tells us about the goodness fit of the model. The value generally determines the amount of variance which the Independent variables (which are 7 factors output from EFA in our case) explains in the Dependent variable. The R Square value has come out to be 0.659 which shows that the model is optimal enough for consideration.
3. In case the number of Independent variables is more than 1, then Adjusted R Square value is referred. This value also tells about the goodness fit of the model. Generally a difference of no more than 0.05 should be there between R Squared value and Adjusted R square value. If the difference is more, then probably model lacks in number of variables. In our research the difference is less than 0.05.
4. Any problem of multi-collinearity is detected using the Variance Inflation Factor value. The VIF should be more than 3 for no multi-collinearity to be present.
5. P value or the Significance level tells us at what percentage the variable is coming out to be significant enough. Any variable with 95% significance, or p value less than 0.05 is considered
6. T-test for the good fit of the model, the value should be greater than 1.96

7. Test for auto-collinearity can be explained through the value of Durbin Watson. If the value is less than 2, then there is positive auto-correlation present in the data, and if the value is more than 2, then negative correlation is present. If the value is equal to 2, then the data is free from auto correlation. In the research we got Durbin Watson value as 1.96 which shows a minimal amount of auto-correlation present in the data.

As can be seen from the Table 4, the variables along with the coefficient value and the level significance is present. Some of the variables are positively impacting, whereas some of the variables are negatively impacting. The significance value or the p value from the t-test tells whether the variable should be considered or not. As per the table, two of the variables, i.e. the Organizational Commitment and the Managerial Support do not meet the requirement of 95% Significance level. Hence these are rejected from the model.

From the values in Table 4, the linear structural equation which can be built is as stated below:

$$\textit{Employee}\ \text{Retention} = 1.214 + 0.139\ \text{Recognition} + 0.137\ \text{Work Life Balance}$$
$$+\ 0.245\ \text{Skill Career Development - } 0.056\ \text{Career Educatoin} + 0.094\ \text{Decision Making}$$

From the model being developed above, it can be seen that of all the Independent variables, four of the variables are positively impacting, whereas one of the Independent variable, i.e. the Career Education is negatively impacting. Hence more you Investing into Recognition of Employees, Skills Development, and more you are empowering

Table 4. Multivariate Regression Output

Variable	Beta Value	Significance Level
Constant	1.214	.000
Recognition	.139	.000
Organizational Commitment	.023	.187
Work Life balance	.137	.000
Skill Career Development	.245	.000
Career Education level	-.056	.001
Decision making	.094	.000
Managerial Support	-.023	.193
R value:.812, R Squared Value:.659, Adjusted R Squared Value: .647		

the employee in decision making, better are the chances to retain him/her. Whereas more you are Investing your resources towards further education of employees, more options are opened for him and hence more chances to leave the organization.

Managerial Implications

May organizations are now looking at effectively utilizing their human resources to the best possible extent and many non-core activities are typically being outsourced to other organizations so as to bring down the cost of operation. Outsourcing has its own benefits and also has its disadvantages, many in the west seem to view it as mere cost cutting measure while it means business for Indian companies. With Employee attrition is now being viewed as a serious issue, with global attrition levels in many IT firms increasing and with the trend of entrepreneurship coming up where one is their own boss, many employees are leaving their organizations and entry level executives are no exception. Attrition has a cost associated with it and repeated cost of training and recruitment is a huge loss for the company. The authors have grouped their findings into two broad factors namely, critical and non-critical factors. Critical factors are factors which are important to be addressed while non critical factors can be perceived as not so important but they might drive the intensity of an employee to cling on to their decision to leave an organization.

Critical Factors

Critical factors are the push factors. Some of the critical factors the authors have identified are Recognition, Skill/ Career Development and Decision Making. The three variables mentioned have higher β values and hence grouped under the same head.

Non Critical Factors

The non-critical factors don't have a direct implication on the respondents view to leave the organization but in turn might be some of their driving forces. These are like the pull forces. The non-critical factors are organizational commitment and work life balance.

While the policy makers of the organizations make their HR retention policies especially for the entry level executives it is thus very important for them to look not only at the critical factors but also at the non-critical factors. Employees should be recognized for their contribution and one of the best way to capture this kind of recognition is to bring in a strong appraisal system in place. A 360 degree appraisal system might help in capturing not only the contribution of the employee but also his/ her level of expertise and also would be in a position to give some valid feedback.

The employer should not forget the fact that an employee would not last in a single job forever, thus it is the duty of the employer to make the employees stay in the organization for a longer time by helping them improve their skill set by providing them with career development trainings. Enhancement of the employees skills would not only make the employee feel that he/ she is being empowered it also forms a psychological contract with the employer and this really helps in retention.

Empowering the employee by giving them a chance to take decisions is a great way to show the employee that the organization listens to him/ her and values their individual opinion while decision making. To facilitate the same the organization should change their hierarchy model and go towards a flat organizational structure which really facilitates the art of decision making.

Organizational commitment is a great way to showcase the employee that the organization listens to them. This might not be a direct factor which triggers attrition but it surely acts as a pull factor. Employees prefer to stay with organizations which listens to their concerns and help them solve the problems. The second variable is work life balance, work life balance is no doubt very important but in this study it is having a lesser impact. This is because the respondents are mostly entry level executives who are just fresh out of college. For most of them career development is on the top of their priority. This doesn't mean that they don't seek work life balance. It is very important to note that a bad composition of work life balance may trigger the employee to leave the company and it is thus very important to have a proper work life balance structure.

Therefore the HR policies which should be made in accordance with the to deal with the attrition of the entry level executives should deal with factors such as recognition, career/ skill development and empowering the employees with decision making abilities while also looking at work life balance and organizational commitment.

Model Building

Once all the analysis is completed, the last phase is to build the model and validate it. Now from the structural equation developed above, a model is built to show which variables under which factor are impacting and in what direction. From all the data collected above, and from the analysis performed, the following model has been built, as shown in figure 4.

Figure 4. Model Building from the Research

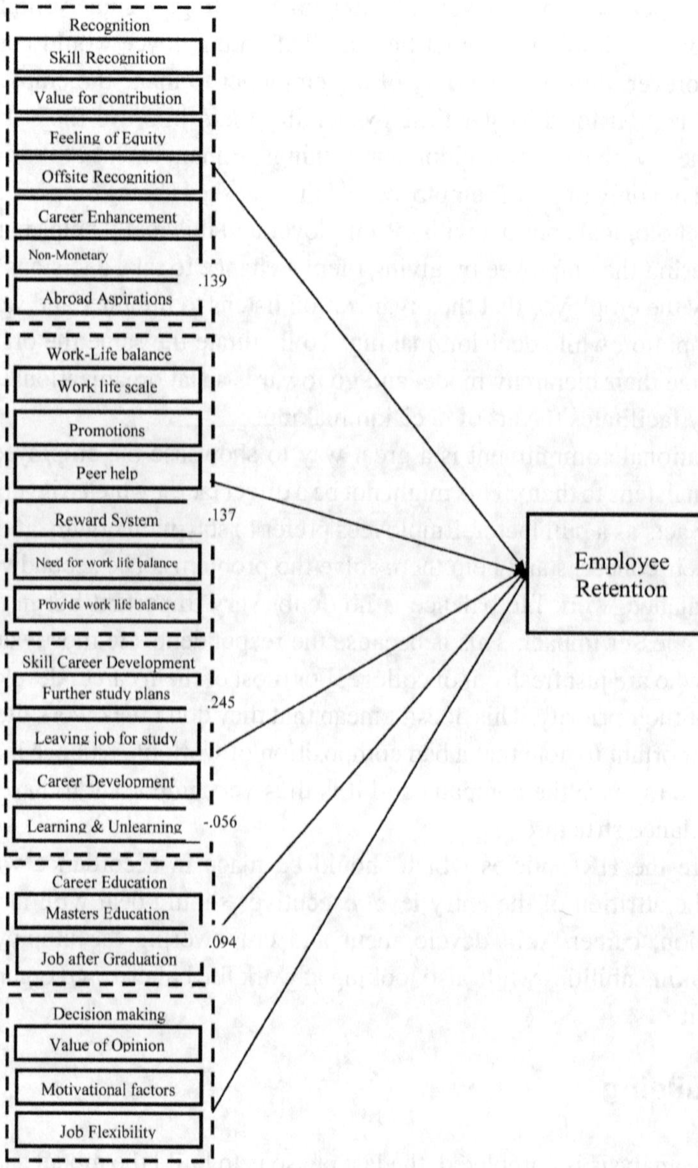

CONCLUSION

Employee management and better engagement is the key to stop attrition from any IT firm and the necessary HR interventions is a must. Attrition as explained is an unwanted cost and should be check on. The key to address attrition is to identify a workforce which is not only committed but also is keen to self-improvise themselves by continuous learning and unlearning. The key lies in a continuous positive relationship between the employee and the employer. Hire the right amount of people you can sustain and keep them continuously engaged. The second key is not only to have a transactional based contract but to have a psychological contract between the employee and employer. There might be many aspects which cannot reach the ears of the HR and this can be addressed through having a strong appraisal system and also a good mentor system where a senior can act as a mentor to the employee and report the same to the HR for further processing. Creating peer partnerships to nurture relationships amongst the employees is also important for peer and emotional support. The key *mantra* lies in changing the way an organization should look at their employees. Viewing them as co-creators of wealth and business partners and helping them achieve business acumen by continuous skill development would help them form a psychological contract with the employer and typically would last long with the same employer.

REFERENCES

Adhikari, A. (2009). Factors affecting employee attrition: A multiple regression approach. *IUP Journal of Management Research*, *8*(5), 38.

Anthony, L. V. L. (1994). *The relationship between transformational and transactional leadership and organizational culture, employee performance, and employee attrition* (Doctoral dissertation). University of Miami.

Banerjee, S., & Guha, S. (2010, January). Employee Attrition in Engineering Firms: Case Study of DCIPS Pvt. Ltd, India. *Proceedings of the 2010 International Conference on Industrial Engineering and Operations Management,* 9-10.

Barnett, R. C., & Hall, D. T. (2001). How to use Reduced Hours to win the War for Talent. *Organizational Dynamics*, *29*(3), 192–210. doi:10.1016/S0090-2616(01)00024-9

Bennett, N., Blum, T. C., Long, R. G., & Roman, P. M. (1993). A firm-level analysis of employee attrition. *Group & Organization Management*, *18*(4), 482–499. doi:10.1177/1059601193184006

Benton, F. W., Rosen, E. D., & Peters, J. L. (1982). *National survey of correctional institution employee attrition*. National Center for Public Productivity, John Jay College of Criminal Justice, CUNY.

Bhatnagar, J. (2007). Talent management strategy of employee engagement in Indian ITES employees: Key to retention. *Employee Relations*, *29*(6), 640–663. doi:10.1108/01425450710826122

210. Borstorff, P. C., & Marker, M. B. (2007). Turnover Drivers and Retention Factors Affecting Hourly Workers: What is Important? *Management Review: An International Journal*, *2*(1), 14–27.

Brill, M., Weidemann, S., Olsen, J., & Keable, B. O. S. T. I. (2001). *The Buffalo Organization for Social & Technological Innovation*. Associates.

Brill, M. S. (2001). *The Buffalo Organization for Social & Technological Innovation*. Associates.

Chew, J. (2004). *The impact of HRM practices on retention of core employees of Australian Organizations: An Empirical Study*. Greenhaus.

De Vos, A., & Meganck, A. (2008). What HR managers do versus what employees value: Exploring both parties' views on retention management from a psychological contract perspective. *Personnel Review*, *38*(1), 45–60. doi:10.1108/00483480910920705

De Vos, A., & Meganck, A. (2008). What HR managers do versus what employees value: Exploring both parties' views on retention management from a psychological contract perspective. *Personnel Review*, *38*(1), 45–60. doi:10.1108/00483480910920705

Elliott, K. M. (2001). Key factors influencing student satisfaction related to recruitment and retention. *Journal of Marketing for Higher Education*, 10.

Elliott, K. M., & Healy, M. A. (2001). Key factors influencing student satisfaction related to recruitment and retention. *Journal of Marketing for Higher Education*, *10*(4), 1–11. doi:10.1300/J050v10n04_01

Grover, S. L., & Crooker, K. J. (1995). Who appreciates family-responsive human resource policies: The impact of family-friendly policies on the organizational attachment of parents and non-parents. *Personnel Psychology*, *48*(2), 271–288. doi:10.1111/j.1744-6570.1995.tb01757.x

Gupta, S. S. (2011). *Employee Attrition and Retention: Exploring the Dimensions in the urban centric BPO Industry* (Doctoral dissertation). Jaypee Institute of Information Technology, Noida, India.

Hall, D. T., & Moss, J. E. (1998). The new protean career contract: Helping organizations and employees adapt. *Organizational Dynamics*, *26*(3), 22–37. doi:10.1016/S0090-2616(98)90012-2

Hall, D. T., & Moss, J. E. (1998). The new protean career contract: Helping organizations and employees adap. *Organizaotions Dynamics*, *26*(3), 22–37. doi:10.1016/S0090-2616(98)90012-2

Ho, J. S. Y., Downe, A. G., & Loke, S. P. (2010). Employee attrition in the Malaysian service industry: Push and pull factors. *The IUP Journal of Organizational Behavior*, *9*(1), 16–31.

Hsu, M. K., Jiang, J. J., Klein, G., & Tang, Z. (2003). Perceived career incentives and intent to leave. *Information & Management*, *40*(5), 361–369. doi:10.1016/S0378-7206(02)00018-6

Hsu, M. K., Jiang, J. J., Klein, G., & Tang, Z. (2003). Perceived career incentives and intent to leave. *Information & Management*, *40*(5), 361–369. doi:10.1016/S0378-7206(02)00018-6

Ingersoll, R. M. (2002). The teacher shortage: A case of wrong diagnosis and wrong prescription. *NASSP Bulletin*, *86*(631), 16–31. doi:10.1177/019263650208663103

Jain, M. (2013). Employee attrition-causes and remedies. *Journal of Social Welfare and Management*, *5*(2), 69–74.

James, M. J., & Faisal, U. (2013). *Empirical study on addressing high employee attrition in BPO industry focusing on employee salary and other factors in Karnataka and Kerala states of India*. Research Journal of Management Sciences.

Jessica Sze-Yin Ho, A. G.-P. (2010). *Employee Attrition in the Malaysian Service Industry: Push and Pull Factors*. IUP Journal of Organizational Behavior.

J.H. & Callanan, G.A. (1994). Career Management. The Dryden Press.

Mehdi, A., Raju, R. M., & Mukherji, A. (2012, July). Abusive supervision and employee attrition: A study of executives in the Indian high technology sector. In *Competition Forum* (Vol. 10, No. 2, p. 42). American Society for Competitiveness.

Morgan, C. K., & Tam, M. (1999). Unravelling the complexities of distance education student attrition. *Distance Education*, *20*(1), 96–108. doi:10.1080/0158791990200108

Nappinnai, M. V., & Premavathy, N. (2013). Employee attrition and retention in a global competitive scenario. *International Journal of Research in Business Management, 1*(6), 11-14.

Palan, R. (2007). Does employee training lead to attrition? *Performance Improvement*, *46*(4), 5–8. doi:10.1002/pfi.118

Planning Commission. (2015, July 8). *Sector-wise contribution of GDP of India*. Retrieved from Statistics Times: http://statisticstimes.com/economy/sectorwise-gdp-contribution-of-india.php

Samson, S. M. (2013). Attrition issues and retention challenges of employees. *Asia Pacific Journal of Research in Business Management, 4*(7).

Shoaib, M., Noor, A., Tirmizi, S. R., & Bashir, S. (2009). Determinants of employee retention in telecom sector of Pakistan. *Proceedings of the 2nd CBRC, 14*.

Shoaib, M. A. (2009). Determinants of employee retention in telecom sector of Pakistan. *Proceedings of the 2nd CBRC, 14*.

Singh, H. P. (2015, October 30). *Sector-wise contribution of GDP of India*. Jagran Josh.

Steel, R. P., & Ovalle, N. K. (1984). *A review and meta-analysis of research on the relationship between behavioral intentions and employee turnover*. Academic Press.

Subramony, M., & Holtom, B. C. (2012). The long-term influence of service employee attrition on customer outcomes and profits. *Journal of Service Research, 15*(4), 460–473. doi:10.1177/1094670512452792

Related References

To continue our tradition of advancing academic research, we compiled a list of recommended IGI Global readings. These references will provide additional information and guidance to further enrich your knowledge and assist you with your own research and future publications.

Abdullah, M., Ahmad, R., Peck, L. S., Kasirun, Z. M., & Alshammari, F. (2014). Benefits of CMM and CMMI-based software process improvement. In *Software design and development: Concepts, methodologies, tools, and applications* (pp. 1385–1400). Hershey, PA: IGI Global. doi:10.4018/978-1-4666-4301-7.ch067

Abu-Shanab, E., & Ghaleb, O. (2012). Adoption of mobile commerce technology: An involvement of trust and risk concerns. *International Journal of Technology Diffusion*, *3*(2), 36–49. doi:10.4018/jtd.2012040104

Adapa, S. (2013). Electronic retailing of prepared food in Australia. In K. Tarnay, S. Imre, & L. Xu (Eds.), *Research and development in e-business through service-oriented solutions* (pp. 280–292). Hershey, PA: IGI Global. doi:10.4018/978-1-4666-4181-5.ch014

Aklouf, Y., & Drias, H. (2011). An adaptive e-commerce architecture for enterprise information exchange. In *Enterprise information systems: Concepts, methodologies, tools and applications* (pp. 329–345). Hershey, PA: IGI Global. doi:10.4018/978-1-61692-852-0.ch202

Al-Nawayseh, M. K., Alnabhan, M. M., Al-Debei, M. M., & Balachandran, W. (2013). An adaptive decision support system for last mile logistics in e-commerce: A study on online grocery shopping. *International Journal of Decision Support System Technology*, *5*(1), 40–65. doi:10.4018/jdsst.2013010103

Al-Somali, S. A., Clegg, B., & Gholami, R. (2013). An investigation into the adoption and implementation of electronic commerce in Saudi Arabian small and medium enterprises. In *Small and medium enterprises: Concepts, methodologies, tools, and applications* (pp. 816–839). Hershey, PA: IGI Global. doi:10.4018/978-1-4666-3886-0.ch040

Al-Somali, S. A., Gholami, R., & Clegg, B. (2013). An investigation into the adoption of electronic commerce among Saudi Arabian SMEs. In M. Khosrow-Pour (Ed.), *E-commerce for organizational development and competitive advantage* (pp. 126–150). Hershey, PA: IGI Global. doi:10.4018/978-1-4666-3622-4.ch007

Alavi, S. (2013). Collaborative customer relationship management-co-creation and collaboration through online communities. *International Journal of Virtual Communities and Social Networking*, *5*(1), 1–18. doi:10.4018/jvcsn.2013010101

Alavi, S., & Ahuja, V. (2013). E-commerce in a web 2.0 world: Using online business communities to impact consumer price sensitivity. *International Journal of Online Marketing*, *3*(2), 38–55. doi:10.4018/ijom.2013040103

Alawneh, A., Al-Refai, H., & Batiha, K. (2011). E-business adoption by Jordanian banks: An exploratory study of the key factors and performance indicators. In A. Tatnall (Ed.), *Actor-network theory and technology innovation: Advancements and new concepts* (pp. 113–128). Hershey, PA: IGI Global. doi:10.4018/978-1-60960-197-3.ch008

Albuquerque, S. L., & Gondim, P. R. (2012). Applying continuous authentication to protect electronic transactions. In T. Chou (Ed.), *Information assurance and security technologies for risk assessment and threat management: Advances* (pp. 134–161). Hershey, PA: IGI Global. doi:10.4018/978-1-61350-507-6.ch005

Alfahl, H., Sanzogni, L., & Houghton, L. (2012). Mobile commerce adoption in organizations: A literature review and future research directions. *Journal of Electronic Commerce in Organizations*, *10*(2), 61–78. doi:10.4018/jeco.2012040104

Aloini, D., Dulmin, R., & Mininno, V. (2013). E-procurement: What really matters in B2B e-reverse auctions. In P. Ordóñez de Pablos, J. Lovelle, J. Gayo, & R. Tennyson (Eds.), *E-procurement management for successful electronic government systems* (pp. 87–113). Hershey, PA: IGI Global. doi:10.4018/978-1-4666-2119-0.ch006

Amer, M., & Gómez, J. M. (2010). Measuring B2C quality of electronic service: Towards a common consensus. In I. Lee (Ed.), *Encyclopedia of e-business development and management in the global economy* (pp. 135–143). Hershey, PA: IGI Global. doi:10.4018/978-1-61520-611-7.ch014

Amer, M., & Gómez, J. M. (2012). Measuring quality of electronic services: Moving from business-to-consumer into business-to-business marketplace. In E. Kajan, F. Dorloff, & I. Bedini (Eds.), *Handbook of research on e-business standards and protocols: Documents, data and advanced web technologies* (pp. 637–654). Hershey, PA: IGI Global. doi:10.4018/978-1-4666-0146-8.ch029

Andriole, S. J. (2010). Business technology strategy for an energy information company. *Journal of Information Technology Research, 3*(3), 19–42. doi:10.4018/jitr.2010070103

Andriole, S. J. (2010). Templates for the development of business technology strategies. *Journal of Information Technology Research, 3*(3), 1–10. doi:10.4018/jitr.2010070101

Archer, N. (2010). Electronic marketplace support for B2B business transactions. In *Electronic services: Concepts, methodologies, tools and applications* (pp. 85–93). Hershey, PA: IGI Global. doi:10.4018/978-1-61520-967-5.ch007

Archer, N. (2010). Management considerations for B2B online exchanges. In *Business information systems: Concepts, methodologies, tools and applications* (pp. 1740–1747). Hershey, PA: IGI Global. doi:10.4018/978-1-61520-969-9.ch105

Arduini, D., Nascia, L., & Zanfei, A. (2012). Complementary approaches to the diffusion of innovation: Empirical evidence on e-services adoption in Italy. *International Journal of E-Services and Mobile Applications, 4*(3), 42–64. doi:10.4018/jesma.2012070103

Arh, T., Dimovski, V., & Blažic, B. J. (2011). ICT and web 2.0 technologies as a determinant of business performance. In M. Al-Mutairi & L. Mohammed (Eds.), *Cases on ICT utilization, practice and solutions: Tools for managing day-to-day issues* (pp. 59–77). Hershey, PA: IGI Global. doi:10.4018/978-1-60960-015-0.ch005

Arikpo, I., Osofisan, A., & Eteng, I. E. (2012). Enhancing trust in e-commerce in developing IT environments: A feedback-based perspective. In A. Usoro, G. Majewski, P. Ifinedo, & I. Arikpo (Eds.), *Leveraging developing economies with the use of information technology: Trends and tools* (pp. 193–203). Hershey, PA: IGI Global. doi:10.4018/978-1-4666-1637-0.ch011

Aryanto, V. D., & Chrismastuti, A. A. (2013). Model for digital economy in Indonesia. In I. Oncioiu (Ed.), *Business innovation, development, and advancement in the digital economy* (pp. 60–77). Hershey, PA: IGI Global. doi:10.4018/978-1-4666-2934-9.ch005

Asim, M., & Petkovic, M. (2012). Fundamental building blocks for security interoperability in e-business. In E. Kajan, F. Dorloff, & I. Bedini (Eds.), *Handbook of research on e-business standards and protocols: documents, data and advanced web technologies* (pp. 269–292). Hershey, PA: IGI Global. doi:10.4018/978-1-4666-0146-8.ch013

Askool, S., Jacobs, A., & Nakata, K. (2013). A method of analysing the use of social networking sites in business. In *IT policy and ethics: Concepts, methodologies, tools, and applications* (pp. 794–813). Hershey, PA: IGI Global. doi:10.4018/978-1-4666-2919-6.ch036

Association, I. R. (2013). *Enterprise resource planning: Concepts, methodologies, tools, and applications* (Vols. 1–3). Hershey, PA: IGI Global. doi:10.4018/978-1-4666-4153-2

Azab, N., & Khalifa, N. (2013). Web 2.0 and opportunities for entrepreneurs: How Egyptian entrepreneurs perceive and exploit web 2.0 technologies. In N. Azab (Ed.), *Cases on web 2.0 in developing countries: Studies on implementation, application, and use* (pp. 1–32). Hershey, PA: IGI Global. doi:10.4018/978-1-4666-2515-0.ch001

Azevedo, S. G., & Carvalho, H. (2012). RFID technology in the fashion supply chain: An exploratory analysis. In T. Choi (Ed.), *Fashion supply chain management: Industry and business analysis* (pp. 303–326). Hershey, PA: IGI Global. doi:10.4018/978-1-60960-756-2.ch017

Baporikar, N. (2013). ICT challenge for ebusiness in SMEs. *International Journal of Strategic Information Technology and Applications*, *4*(1), 15–26. doi:10.4018/jsita.2013010102

Barbin Laurindo, F. J., Monteiro de Carvalho, M., & Shimizu, T. (2010). Strategic alignment between business and information technology. In M. Hunter (Ed.), *Strategic information systems: Concepts, methodologies, tools, and applications* (pp. 20–28). Hershey, PA: IGI Global. doi:10.4018/978-1-60566-677-8.ch002

Barjis, J. (2012). Software engineering security based on business process modeling. In K. Khan (Ed.), *Security-aware systems applications and software development methods* (pp. 52–68). Hershey, PA: IGI Global. doi:10.4018/978-1-4666-1580-9.ch004

Barnes, D., & Hinton, M. (2011). The benefits of an e-business performance measurement system. In N. Shi & G. Silvius (Eds.), *Enterprise IT governance, business value and performance measurement* (pp. 158–169). Hershey, PA: IGI Global. doi:10.4018/978-1-60566-346-3.ch011

Bask, A., Lipponen, M., & Tinnilä, M. (2012). E-commerce logistics: A literature research review and topics for future research. *International Journal of E-Services and Mobile Applications*, *4*(3), 1–22. doi:10.4018/jesma.2012070101

Bask, A., & Tinnilä, M. (2013). Impact of product characteristics on supply chains: An analytical literature review. *International Journal of Applied Logistics*, *4*(1), 35–59. doi:10.4018/jal.2013010103

Basu, S. (2012). Direct taxation and e-commerce: Possibility and desirability. In E. Druicã (Ed.), *Digital economy innovations and impacts on society* (pp. 26–48). Hershey, PA: IGI Global. doi:10.4018/978-1-4666-1556-4.ch003

Beckinsale, M. (2010). E-business among ethnic minority businesses: The case of ethnic entrepreneurs. In B. Thomas & G. Simmons (Eds.), *E-commerce adoption and small business in the global marketplace: Tools for optimization* (pp. 187–207). Hershey, PA: IGI Global. doi:10.4018/978-1-60566-998-4.ch010

Beckinsale, M. (2011). eBusiness among ethnic minority businesses: Ethnic entrepreneurs' ICT adoption and readiness. In S. Sharma (Ed.), E-adoption and socio-economic impacts: Emerging infrastructural effects (pp. 168-189). Hershey, PA: IGI Global. doi:10.4018/978-1-60960-597-1.ch009

Bedini, I., Gardarin, G., & Nguyen, B. (2011). Semantic technologies and e-business. In E. Kajan (Ed.), *Electronic business interoperability: Concepts, opportunities and challenges* (pp. 243–278). Hershey, PA: IGI Global. doi:10.4018/978-1-60960-485-1.ch011

Beedle, J., & Wang, S. (2013). Roles of a technology leader. In S. Wang & T. Hartsell (Eds.), *Technology integration and foundations for effective leadership* (pp. 228–241). Hershey, PA: IGI Global. doi:10.4018/978-1-4666-2656-0.ch013

Belhajjame, K., & Brambilla, M. (2013). Ontological description and similarity-based discovery of business process models. In J. Krogstie (Ed.), *Frameworks for developing efficient information systems: Models, theory, and practice* (pp. 30–50). Hershey, PA: IGI Global. doi:10.4018/978-1-4666-4161-7.ch002

Benou, P., & Bitos, V. (2010). Developing mobile commerce applications. In M. Khosrow-Pour (Ed.), *E-commerce trends for organizational advancement: New applications and methods* (pp. 1–15). Hershey, PA: IGI Global. doi:10.4018/978-1-60566-964-9.ch001

Berisha-Namani, M. (2013). Information systems usage in business and management. In I. Oncioiu (Ed.), *Business innovation, development, and advancement in the digital economy* (pp. 48–59). Hershey, PA: IGI Global. doi:10.4018/978-1-4666-2934-9.ch004

Bermúdez, G. M., & Rojas, L. A. (2013). Model-driven engineering for electronic commerce. In V. Díaz, J. Lovelle, B. García-Bustelo, & O. Martínez (Eds.), *Progressions and innovations in model-driven software engineering* (pp. 196–208). Hershey, PA: IGI Global. doi:10.4018/978-1-4666-4217-1.ch007

Bernardino, J. (2013). Open business intelligence for better decision-making. *International Journal of Information Communication Technologies and Human Development*, *5*(2), 20–36. doi:10.4018/jicthd.2013040102

Berzins, M. (2012). Scams and the Australian e-business environment. In K. Mohammed Rezaul (Ed.), *Strategic and pragmatic e-business: Implications for future business practices* (pp. 156–175). Hershey, PA: IGI Global. doi:10.4018/978-1-4666-1619-6.ch007

Binsaleh, M., & Hassan, S. (2011). Systems development methodology for mobile commerce applications. *International Journal of Mobile Computing and Multimedia Communications*, *3*(4), 36–52. doi:10.4018/jmcmc.2011100103

Binsaleh, M., & Hassan, S. (2013). Systems development methodology for mobile commerce applications. In I. Khalil & E. Weippl (Eds.), *Contemporary challenges and solutions for mobile and multimedia technologies* (pp. 146–162). Hershey, PA: IGI Global. doi:10.4018/978-1-4666-2163-3.ch009

Blake, R., Gordon, S., & Shankaranarayanan, G. (2013). The role of case-based research in information technology and systems. In P. Isaias & M. Baptista Nunes (Eds.), *Information systems research and exploring social artifacts: approaches and methodologies* (pp. 200–220). Hershey, PA: IGI Global. doi:10.4018/978-1-4666-2491-7.ch011

Boateng, R., Heeks, R., Molla, A., & Hinson, R. (2013). Advancing e-commerce beyond readiness in a developing country: Experiences of Ghanaian firms. In M. Khosrow-Pour (Ed.), *E-commerce for organizational development and competitive advantage* (pp. 1–17). Hershey, PA: IGI Global. doi:10.4018/978-1-4666-3622-4.ch001

Bonfatti, F., Monari, P. D., & Martinelli, L. (2011). Business document exchange between small companies. In E. Kajan (Ed.), *Electronic business interoperability: Concepts, opportunities and challenges* (pp. 482–510). Hershey, PA: IGI Global. doi:10.4018/978-1-60960-485-1.ch020

Boucadair, M., & Binet, D. (2014). Issues with current internet architecture. In M. Boucadair & D. Binet (Eds.), *Solutions for sustaining scalability in internet growth* (pp. 1–16). Hershey, PA: IGI Global. doi:10.4018/978-1-4666-4305-5.ch001

Bouras, A., Gouvas, P., & Mentzas, G. (2009). A semantic service-oriented architecture for business process fusion. In I. Lee (Ed.), *Electronic business: Concepts, methodologies, tools, and applications* (pp. 504–532). Hershey, PA: IGI Global. doi:10.4018/978-1-60566-056-1.ch032

Braun, P. (2011). Advancing women in the digital economy: eLearning opportunities for meta-competency skilling. In *Global business: Concepts, methodologies, tools and applications* (pp. 1978–1990). Hershey, PA: IGI Global. doi:10.4018/978-1-60960-587-2.ch708

Brown, M., & Garson, G. (2013). Organization behavior and organization theory. In *Public information management and e-government: Policy and issues* (pp. 160–195). Hershey, PA: IGI Global. doi:10.4018/978-1-4666-3003-1.ch007

Brown, M., & Garson, G. (2013). The information technology business model. In *Public information management and e-government: Policy and issues* (pp. 76–98). Hershey, PA: IGI Global. doi:10.4018/978-1-4666-3003-1.ch004

Burete, R., Badica, A., Badica, C., & Moraru, F. (2011). Enhanced reputation model with forgiveness for e-business agents. *International Journal of Agent Technologies and Systems, 3*(1), 11–26. doi:10.4018/jats.2011010102

Business Research and Case Center. (2011). *Cases on business and management in the MENA region: New trends and opportunities*. Hershey, PA: IGI Global. doi:10.4018/978-1-60960-583-4

Bwalya, K. J. (2011). E-commerce penetration in the SADC region: Consolidating and moving forward. In M. Cruz-Cunha & J. Varajão (Eds.), *E-business managerial aspects, solutions and case studies* (pp. 235–253). Hershey, PA: IGI Global. doi:10.4018/978-1-60960-463-9.ch014

Charbaji, R., Rebeiz, K., & Sidani, Y. (2010). Antecedents and consequences of the risk taking behavior of mobile commerce adoption in Lebanon. In H. Rahman (Ed.), *Handbook of research on e-government readiness for information and service exchange: Utilizing progressive information communication technologies* (pp. 354–380). Hershey, PA: IGI Global. doi:10.4018/978-1-60566-671-6.ch018

Chaturvedi, N. (2013). Collaborative web for natural resources industries. In *Supply chain management: Concepts, methodologies, tools, and applications* (pp. 601–614). Hershey, PA: IGI Global. doi:10.4018/978-1-4666-2625-6.ch035

Chen, C., & Yang, S. C. (2008). E-commerce and mobile commerce application adoptions. In A. Becker (Ed.), *Electronic commerce: Concepts, methodologies, tools, and applications* (pp. 826–836). Hershey, PA: IGI Global. doi:10.4018/978-1-59904-943-4.ch068

Chen, Q., & Zhang, N. (2013). IT-supported business performance and e-commerce application in SMEs. *Journal of Electronic Commerce in Organizations*, *11*(2), 41–52. doi:10.4018/jeco.2013040104

Chen, T. F. (2011). Emerging business models: Value drivers in e-business 2.0 and towards enterprise 2.0. In T. Chen (Ed.), *Implementing new business models in for-profit and non-profit organizations: Technologies and applications* (pp. 1–28). Hershey, PA: IGI Global. doi:10.4018/978-1-60960-129-4.ch001

Chen, T. F. (2011). The critical success factors and integrated model for implementing e-business in Taiwan's SMEs. In *Global business: Concepts, methodologies, tools and applications* (pp. 1109–1133). Hershey, PA: IGI Global. doi:10.4018/978-1-60960-587-2.ch416

Chew, E., & Gottschalk, P. (2013). Critical success factors of IT strategy. In *Knowledge driven service innovation and management: IT strategies for business alignment and value creation* (pp. 185–220). Hershey, PA: IGI Global. doi:10.4018/978-1-4666-2512-9.ch006

Chew, E., & Gottschalk, P. (2013). Strategic alignment and IT-enabled value creation. In *Knowledge driven service innovation and management: IT strategies for business alignment and value creation* (pp. 141–184). Hershey, PA: IGI Global. doi:10.4018/978-1-4666-2512-9.ch005

Chew, E., & Gottschalk, P. (2013). Theories and models of service-oriented firms. In *Knowledge driven service innovation and management: IT strategies for business alignment and value creation* (pp. 1–34). Hershey, PA: IGI Global. doi:10.4018/978-1-4666-2512-9.ch001

Chiang, L. (2010). Digital confidence in business: A perspective of information ethics. In M. Pankowska (Ed.), *Infonomics for distributed business and decision-making environments: Creating information system ecology* (pp. 288–300). Hershey, PA: IGI Global. doi:10.4018/978-1-60566-890-1.ch017

Chugh, R., & Gupta, P. (2011). A unified view of enablers, barriers, and readiness of small to medium enterprises for e-business adoption. In M. Cruz-Cunha & J. Varajão (Eds.), *E-business issues, challenges and opportunities for SMEs: Driving competitiveness* (pp. 291–312). Hershey, PA: IGI Global. doi:10.4018/978-1-61692-880-3.ch017

Clear, F., Woods, A., & Dickson, K. (2013). SME adoption and use of ICT for networked trading purposes: The influence of sector, size and age of firm. In *Small and medium enterprises: Concepts, methodologies, tools, and applications* (pp. 774–791). Hershey, PA: IGI Global. doi:10.4018/978-1-4666-3886-0.ch038

Connolly, R. (2013). eCommerce trust beliefs: Examining the role of national culture. In P. Isaias & M. Baptista Nunes (Eds.), Information systems research and exploring social artifacts: Approaches and methodologies (pp. 20-42). Hershey, PA: IGI Global. doi:10.4018/978-1-4666-2491-7.ch002

Cormican, K. (2013). Collaborative networks: Challenges for SMEs. In *Small and medium enterprises: Concepts, methodologies, tools, and applications* (pp. 1638–1653). Hershey, PA: IGI Global. doi:10.4018/978-1-4666-3886-0.ch083

Costante, E., Petkovic, M., & den Hartog, J. (2013). Trust management and user's trust perception in e-business. In *IT policy and ethics: Concepts, methodologies, tools, and applications* (pp. 64–83). Hershey, PA: IGI Global. doi:10.4018/978-1-4666-2919-6.ch004

Costin, Y. (2012). Adopting ICT in the mompreneurs business: A strategy for growth? In C. Romm Livermore (Ed.), *Gender and social computing: Interactions, differences and relationships* (pp. 17–34). Hershey, PA: IGI Global. doi:10.4018/978-1-60960-759-3.ch002

Cox, S. (2013). E-business planning in morphing organizations: Maturity models of business transformation. In E. Li, S. Loh, C. Evans, & F. Lorenzi (Eds.), *Organizations and social networking: Utilizing social media to engage consumers* (pp. 286–312). Hershey, PA: IGI Global. doi:10.4018/978-1-4666-4026-9.ch015

Cruz-Cunha, M. M., Moreira, F., & Varajão, J. (2014). *Handbook of research on enterprise 2.0: Technological, social, and organizational dimensions*. Hershey, PA: IGI Global. doi:10.4018/978-1-4666-4373-4

D'Aubeterre, F., Iyer, L. S., Ehrhardt, R., & Singh, R. (2011). Discovery process in a B2B emarketplace: A semantic matchmaking approach. In V. Sugumaran (Ed.), *Intelligent, adaptive and reasoning technologies: New developments and applications* (pp. 80–103). Hershey, PA: IGI Global. doi:10.4018/978-1-60960-595-7.ch005

Dabbagh, R. A. (2011). E-business: Concepts and context with illustrative examples of e-business and e-commerce in education. In A. Al Ajeeli & Y. Al-Bastaki (Eds.), *Handbook of research on e-services in the public sector: E-government strategies and advancements* (pp. 450–462). Hershey, PA: IGI Global. doi:10.4018/978-1-61520-789-3.ch033

Demirkan, H., & Spohrer, J. C. (2012). Servitized enterprises for distributed collaborative commerce. In S. Galup (Ed.), *Technological applications and advancements in service science, management, and engineering* (pp. 70–83). Hershey, PA: IGI Global. doi:10.4018/978-1-4666-1583-0.ch005

Denno, P. (2013). Trade collaboration systems. In *Supply chain management: Concepts, methodologies, tools, and applications* (pp. 615–633). Hershey, PA: IGI Global. doi:10.4018/978-1-4666-2625-6.ch036

Djoleto, W. (2011). E-business efficacious consequences the etiquettes and the business decision making. In O. Bak & N. Stair (Eds.), *Impact of e-business technologies on public and private organizations: Industry comparisons and perspectives* (pp. 278–295). Hershey, PA: IGI Global. doi:10.4018/978-1-60960-501-8.ch017

Djoleto, W. (2013). Information technology and organisational leadership. In *Electronic commerce and organizational leadership: Perspectives and methodologies*. Hershey, PA: IGI Global. doi:10.4018/978-1-4666-2982-0.ch003

Djoleto, W. (2013). Cloud computing and ecommerce or ebusiness: "The now it way" – An overview. In *Electronic commerce and organizational leadership: Perspectives and methodologies* (pp. 239–254). Hershey, PA: IGI Global. doi:10.4018/978-1-4666-2982-0.ch010

Djoleto, W. (2013). eCommerce and organisational leadership. In Electronic commerce and organizational leadership: Perspectives and methodologies (pp. 99-121). Hershey, PA: IGI Global. doi:10.4018/978-1-4666-2982-0.ch005

Djoleto, W. (2013). eCommerce: An overview. In Electronic commerce and organizational leadership: Perspectives and methodologies (pp. 74-98). Hershey, PA: IGI Global. doi:10.4018/978-1-4666-2982-0.ch004

Djoleto, W. (2013). Empirical analyses of ecommerce: The findings – A mixed methodology perspective. In *Electronic commerce and organizational leadership: Perspectives and methodologies* (pp. 150–189). Hershey, PA: IGI Global. doi:10.4018/978-1-4666-2982-0.ch007

Djoleto, W. (2013). Future endeavours. In *Electronic commerce and organizational leadership: Perspectives and methodologies* (pp. 269–280). Hershey, PA: IGI Global. doi:10.4018/978-1-4666-2982-0.ch012

Djoleto, W. (2013). Information technology: The journey. In *Electronic commerce and organizational leadership: Perspectives and methodologies* (pp. 32–54). Hershey, PA: IGI Global. doi:10.4018/978-1-4666-2982-0.ch002

Doolin, B., & Ali, E. I. (2012). Mobile technology adoption in the supply chain. In *Wireless technologies: Concepts, methodologies, tools and applications* (pp. 1553–1573). Hershey, PA: IGI Global. doi:10.4018/978-1-61350-101-6.ch603

Duin, H., & Thoben, K. (2011). Enhancing the preparedness of SMEs for e-business opportunities by collaborative networks. In M. Cruz-Cunha & J. Varajão (Eds.), *E-business issues, challenges and opportunities for SMEs: Driving competitiveness* (pp. 30–45). Hershey, PA: IGI Global. doi:10.4018/978-1-61692-880-3.ch003

Dulai, T., Jaskó, S., & Tarnay, K. (2013). IOTP and payments protocols. In K. Tarnay, S. Imre, & L. Xu (Eds.), *Research and development in e-business through service-oriented solutions* (pp. 20–56). Hershey, PA: IGI Global. doi:10.4018/978-1-4666-4181-5.ch002

Dza, M., Fisher, R., & Gapp, R. (2013). Service-dominant logic and supply network management: An efficient business mix? In N. Ndubisi & S. Nwankwo (Eds.), *Enterprise development in SMEs and entrepreneurial firms: Dynamic processes* (pp. 376–389). Hershey, PA: IGI Global. doi:10.4018/978-1-4666-2952-3.ch021

Ehsani, E. (2011). Defining e-novation in action. In H. Pattinson & D. Low (Eds.), *E-novation for competitive advantage in collaborative globalization: Technologies for emerging e-business strategies* (pp. 58–74). Hershey, PA: IGI Global. doi:10.4018/978-1-60566-394-4.ch005

Ekong, U. O., Ifinedo, P., Ayo, C. K., & Ifinedo, A. (2013). E-commerce adoption in Nigerian businesses: An analysis using the technology-organization-environmental framework. In *Small and medium enterprises: Concepts, methodologies, tools, and applications* (pp. 840–861). Hershey, PA: IGI Global. doi:10.4018/978-1-4666-3886-0.ch041

Emens, S. (2010). The new paradigm of business on the internet and its ethical implications. In D. Palmer (Ed.), *Ethical issues in e-business: Models and frameworks* (pp. 15–27). Hershey, PA: IGI Global. doi:10.4018/978-1-61520-615-5.ch002

Eriksson, P., Henttonen, E., & Meriläinen, S. (2011). Managing client contacts of small KIBS companies: Turning technology into business. *International Journal of Innovation in the Digital Economy, 2*(3), 1–10. doi:10.4018/jide.2011070101

Escofet, E., Rodríguez-Fórtiz, M. J., Garrido, J. L., & Chung, L. (2012). Strategic e-business/ IT alignment for SME competitiveness. In *Computer engineering: Concepts, methodologies, tools and applications* (pp. 1427–1445). Hershey, PA: IGI Global. doi:10.4018/978-1-61350-456-7.ch604

Eze, U. C., & Poong, Y. S. (2013). Consumers' intention to use mobile commerce and the moderating roles of gender and income. In I. Lee (Ed.), *Strategy, adoption, and competitive advantage of mobile services in the global economy* (pp. 127–148). Hershey, PA: IGI Global. doi:10.4018/978-1-4666-1939-5.ch007

Eze, U. C., & Poong, Y. S. (2013). The moderating roles of income and age in mobile commerce application. *Journal of Electronic Commerce in Organizations, 11*(3), 46–67. doi:10.4018/jeco.2013070103

Fehér, P. (2012). Integrating and measuring business and technology services in the context of enterprise architecture. In V. Shankararaman, J. Zhao, & J. Lee (Eds.), *Business enterprise, process, and technology management: Models and applications* (pp. 148–163). Hershey, PA: IGI Global. doi:10.4018/978-1-4666-0249-6.ch008

Feja, S., Witt, S., & Speck, A. (2014). Tool based integration of requirements modeling and validation into business process modeling. In *Software design and development: Concepts, methodologies, tools, and applications* (pp. 285–309). Hershey, PA: IGI Global. doi:10.4018/978-1-4666-4301-7.ch016

Fengel, J. (2012). Semantic alignment of e-business standards and legacy models. In E. Kajan, F. Dorloff, & I. Bedini (Eds.), *Handbook of research on e-business standards and protocols: Documents, data and advanced web technologies* (pp. 676–704). Hershey, PA: IGI Global. doi:10.4018/978-1-4666-0146-8.ch031

Ferreira, M. P. (2013). SMEs and e-business: Implementation, strategies and policy. In *Small and medium enterprises: Concepts, methodologies, tools, and applications* (pp. 97–117). Hershey, PA: IGI Global. doi:10.4018/978-1-4666-3886-0.ch006

Fluvià, M., & Rigall-I-Torrent, R. (2013). Public sector transformation and the design of public policies for electronic commerce and the new economy: Tax and antitrust policies. In N. Pomazalová (Ed.), *Public sector transformation processes and internet public procurement: Decision support systems* (pp. 32–57). Hershey, PA: IGI Global. doi:10.4018/978-1-4666-2665-2.ch003

Franquesa, J., & Brandyberry, A. (2011). Organizational slack and information technology innovation adoption in SMEs. In I. Lee (Ed.), *E-business applications for product development and competitive growth: emerging technologies* (pp. 25–48). Hershey, PA: IGI Global. doi:10.4018/978-1-60960-132-4.ch002

Fries, T. P. (2014). Reengineering structured legacy system documentation to UML object-oriented artifacts. In *Software design and development: Concepts, methodologies, tools, and applications* (pp. 749–771). Hershey, PA: IGI Global. doi:10.4018/978-1-4666-4301-7.ch036

Galinski, C., & Beckmann, H. (2014). Concepts for enhancing content quality and eaccessibility: In general and in the field of eprocurement. In *Assistive technologies: Concepts, methodologies, tools, and applications* (pp. 180–197). Hershey, PA: IGI Global. doi:10.4018/978-1-4666-4422-9.ch010

Gan, J., & Gutiérrez, J. A. (2011). Viable business models for m-commerce: The key components. In M. Cruz-Cunha & F. Moreira (Eds.), *Handbook of research on mobility and computing: Evolving technologies and ubiquitous impacts* (pp. 837–852). Hershey, PA: IGI Global. doi:10.4018/978-1-60960-042-6.ch052

Garito, M. (2012). Mobile business and mobile TV: Available technologies, future opportunities and new marketing trends. In E-marketing: Concepts, methodologies, tools, and applications (pp. 1240-1251). Hershey, PA: IGI Global. doi:10.4018/978-1-4666-1598-4.ch072

Ghobakhloo, M., & Zulkifli, N. (2013). Adoption of mobile commerce: The impact of end user satisfaction on system acceptance. *International Journal of E-Services and Mobile Applications*, *5*(1), 26–50. doi:10.4018/jesma.2013010102

Gill, A. Q., & Bunker, D. (2014). SaaS requirements engineering for agile development. In *Software design and development: Concepts, methodologies, tools, and applications* (pp. 351–380). Hershey, PA: IGI Global. doi:10.4018/978-1-4666-4301-7.ch019

Gimenez, J. (2014). Reflections of professional practice: Using electronic discourse analysis networks (EDANs) to examine embedded business emails. In H. Lim & F. Sudweeks (Eds.), *Innovative methods and technologies for electronic discourse analysis* (pp. 327–345). Hershey, PA: IGI Global. doi:10.4018/978-1-4666-4426-7.ch015

Gionis, G. A., Schroth, C., & Janner, T. (2011). Advancing interoperability for agile cross-organisational collaboration: A rule-based approach. In Y. Charalabidis (Ed.), *Interoperability in digital public services and administration: Bridging e-government and e-business* (pp. 238–253). Hershey, PA: IGI Global. doi:10.4018/978-1-61520-887-6.ch013

Gnoni, M. G., & Rollo, A. (2011). A content analysis for evaluating RFID applications in supply network management. In I. Mahdavi, S. Mohebbi, & N. Cho (Eds.), *Electronic supply network coordination in intelligent and dynamic environments: Modeling and implementation* (pp. 93–112). Hershey, PA: IGI Global. doi:10.4018/978-1-60566-808-6.ch004

Gonçalves, A., Serra, N., Serra, J., & Sousa, P. (2011). How to use information technology effectively to achieve business objectives. In M. Cruz-Cunha & J. Varajao (Eds.), *Enterprise information systems design, implementation and management: Organizational applications* (pp. 21–37). Hershey, PA: IGI Global. doi:10.4018/978-1-61692-020-3.ch002

Gordini, N., & Veglio, V. (2014). Customer relationship management and data mining: A classification decision tree to predict customer purchasing behavior in global market. In P. Vasant (Ed.), *Handbook of research on novel soft computing intelligent algorithms: Theory and practical applications* (pp. 1–40). Hershey, PA: IGI Global. doi:10.4018/978-1-4666-4450-2.ch001

Gottschalk, P. (2007). The CIO developing e-business. In P. Gottschalk (Ed.), *CIO and corporate strategic management: Changing role of CIO to CEO* (pp. 148–185). Hershey, PA: Idea Group Publishing. doi:10.4018/978-1-59904-423-1.ch007

Goutam, S. (2010). Analysis of speedy uptake of electronic and digital signatures in digital economy with special reference to India. In E. Adomi (Ed.), *Frameworks for ICT policy: Government, social and legal issues* (pp. 76–88). Hershey, PA: IGI Global. doi:10.4018/978-1-61692-012-8.ch005

Grieger, M., Hartmann, E., & Kotzab, H. (2011). E-markets as meta-enterprise information e systems. In *Enterprise information systems: Concepts, methodologies, tools and applications* (pp. 638–647). Hershey, PA: IGI Global. doi:10.4018/978-1-61692-852-0.ch306

grzonkowski, s., ensor, b. d., & mcdaniel, b. (2013). applied cryptography in Electronic Commerce. In *IT policy and ethics: Concepts, methodologies, tools, and applications* (pp. 368-388). Hershey, PA: IGI Global. doi:10.4018/978-1-4666-2919-6.ch017

Ha, H. (2012). Online security and consumer protection in ecommerce an Australian case. In K. Mohammed Rezaul (Ed.), *Strategic and pragmatic e-business: Implications for future business practices* (pp. 217–243). Hershey, PA: IGI Global. doi:10.4018/978-1-4666-1619-6.ch010

Ha, H., Coghill, K., & Maharaj, E. A. (2012). Current measures to protect e-consumers' privacy in Australia. In *Cyber crime: Concepts, methodologies, tools and applications* (pp. 1728–1755). Hershey, PA: IGI Global. doi:10.4018/978-1-61350-323-2.ch806

Halas, H., & Klobucar, T. (2011). Business models and organizational processes changes. In *Global business: Concepts, methodologies, tools and applications* (pp. 192–205). Hershey, PA: IGI Global. doi:10.4018/978-1-60960-587-2.ch113

Han, B. (2012). I play, I pay? An investigation of the user's willingness to pay on hedonic social network sites. *International Journal of Virtual Communities and Social Networking*, *4*(1), 19–31. doi:10.4018/jvcsn.2012010102

Harnesk, D. (2011). Convergence of information security in B2B networks. In E. Kajan (Ed.), *Electronic business interoperability: Concepts, opportunities and challenges* (pp. 571–595). Hershey, PA: IGI Global. doi:10.4018/978-1-60960-485-1.ch023

Harwood, T. (2012). Emergence of gamified commerce: Turning virtual to real. *Journal of Electronic Commerce in Organizations*, *10*(2), 16–39. doi:10.4018/jeco.2012040102

Heravi, B. R., & Lycett, M. (2012). Semantically enriched e-business standards development: The case of ebXML business process specification schema. In E. Kajan, F. Dorloff, & I. Bedini (Eds.), *Handbook of research on e-business standards and protocols: Documents, data and advanced web technologies* (pp. 655–675). Hershey, PA: IGI Global. doi:10.4018/978-1-4666-0146-8.ch030

Hill, D. S. (2012). An examination of standardized product identification and business benefit. In E. Kajan, F. Dorloff, & I. Bedini (Eds.), *Handbook of research on e-business standards and protocols: Documents, data and advanced web technologies* (pp. 387–411). Hershey, PA: IGI Global. doi:10.4018/978-1-4666-0146-8.ch018

Hoops, D. S. (2011). Legal issues in the virtual world and e-commerce. In B. Ciaramitaro (Ed.), *Virtual worlds and e-commerce: Technologies and applications for building customer relationships* (pp. 186–204). Hershey, PA: IGI Global. doi:10.4018/978-1-61692-808-7.ch010

Hu, W., Zuo, Y., Kaabouch, N., & Chen, L. (2010). A technological perspective of mobile and electronic commerce systems. In M. Khosrow-Pour (Ed.), *E-commerce trends for organizational advancement: New applications and methods* (pp. 16–35). Hershey, PA: IGI Global. doi:10.4018/978-1-60566-964-9.ch002

Hua, G. B. (2013). *Implementing IT business strategy in the construction industry*. Hershey, PA: IGI Global. doi:10.4018/978-1-4666-4185-3

Hua, S. C., Rajesh, M. J., & Theng, L. B. (2011). Determinants of e-commerce adoption among small and medium-sized enterprises in Malaysia. In S. Sharma (Ed.), *E-adoption and socio-economic impacts: Emerging infrastructural effects* (pp. 71–89). Hershey, PA: IGI Global. doi:10.4018/978-1-60960-597-1.ch005

Huang, J., & Dang, J. (2011). Context-sensitive ontology matching in electronic business. In E. Kajan (Ed.), *Electronic business interoperability: Concepts, opportunities and challenges* (pp. 279–301). Hershey, PA: IGI Global. doi:10.4018/978-1-60960-485-1.ch012

Hunaiti, Z., Tairo, D., Sedoyeka, E., & Elgazzar, S. (2010). Factors facing mobile commerce deployment in United Kingdom. In W. Hu & Y. Zuo (Eds.), *Handheld computing for mobile commerce: Applications, concepts and technologies* (pp. 109–123). Hershey, PA: IGI Global. doi:10.4018/978-1-61520-761-9.ch007

Hung, W. J., Tsai, C., Hung, S., McQueen, R., & Jou, J. (2011). Evaluating web site support capabilities in sell-side B2B transaction processes: A longitudinal study of two industries in New Zealand and Taiwan. *Journal of Global Information Management, 19*(1), 51–79. doi:10.4018/jgim.2011010103

Hunter, M. G. (2013). The duality of information technology roles: A case study. In C. Howard (Ed.), *Strategic adoption of technological innovations* (pp. 38–49). Hershey, PA: IGI Global. doi:10.4018/978-1-4666-2782-6.ch003

Huq, N., Shah, S. M., & Mihailescu, D. (2012). Why select an open source ERP over proprietary ERP? A focus on SMEs and supplier's perspective. In R. Atem de Carvalho & B. Johansson (Eds.), *Free and open source enterprise resource planning: Systems and strategies* (pp. 33–55). Hershey, PA: IGI Global. doi:10.4018/978-1-61350-486-4.ch003

Ingvaldsen, J., & Gulla, J. (2010). Semantic business process mining of SAP transactions. In M. Wang & Z. Sun (Eds.), *Handbook of research on complex dynamic process management: Techniques for adaptability in turbulent environments* (pp. 416–429). Hershey, PA: IGI Global. doi:10.4018/978-1-60566-669-3.ch017

Ingvaldsen, J., & Gulla, J. (2011). Semantic business process mining of SAP transactions. In *Enterprise information systems: Concepts, methodologies, tools and applications* (pp. 866–878). Hershey, PA: IGI Global. doi:10.4018/978-1-61692-852-0.ch320

Ioannou, M. (2013). Customer relationship management (CRM): A one-size-fits-all philosophy? In H. Kaufmann & M. Panni (Eds.), *Customer-centric marketing strategies: Tools for building organizational performance* (pp. 150–170). Hershey, PA: IGI Global. doi:10.4018/978-1-4666-2524-2.ch008

Islam, M. S., & Scupola, A. (2013). E-service research trends in the domain of e-government: A contemporary study. In A. Scupola (Ed.), *Mobile opportunities and applications for e-service innovations* (pp. 152–169). Hershey, PA: IGI Global. doi:10.4018/978-1-4666-2654-6.ch009

Jailani, N., Patel, A., Mukhtar, M., Abdullah, S., & Yahya, Y. (2010). Concept of an agent-based electronic marketplace. In I. Lee (Ed.), *Encyclopedia of e-business development and management in the global economy* (pp. 239–251). Hershey, PA: IGI Global. doi:10.4018/978-1-61520-611-7.ch024

Johns, R. (2011). Technology, trust and B2B relationships: A banking perspective. In O. Bak & N. Stair (Eds.), *Impact of e-business technologies on public and private organizations: Industry comparisons and perspectives* (pp. 79–96). Hershey, PA: IGI Global. doi:10.4018/978-1-60960-501-8.ch005

Joshi, S. (2013). E-supply chain collaboration and integration: Implementation issues and challenges. In D. Graham, I. Manikas, & D. Folinas (Eds.), *E-logistics and e-supply chain management: Applications for evolving business* (pp. 9–26). Hershey, PA: IGI Global. doi:10.4018/978-1-4666-3914-0.ch002

Kamal, M., Qureshil, S., & Wolcott, P. (2013). Promoting competitive advantage in micro-enterprises through information technology interventions. In *Small and medium enterprises: Concepts, methodologies, tools, and applications* (pp. 581–606). Hershey, PA: IGI Global. doi:10.4018/978-1-4666-3886-0.ch030

Kamel, S. (2012). Electronic commerce prospects in emerging economies: Lessons from Egypt. In *Regional development: Concepts, methodologies, tools, and applications* (pp. 1104–1115). Hershey, PA: IGI Global. doi:10.4018/978-1-4666-0882-5.ch604

Kamoun, F., & Halaweh, M. (2012). User interface design and e-commerce security perception: An empirical study. *International Journal of E-Business Research, 8*(2), 15–32. doi:10.4018/jebr.2012040102

Karakaya, F. (2012). Business-to-consumers ecommerce: How companies use the internet in marketing products and services to consumers. In N. Delener (Ed.), *Service science research, strategy and innovation: Dynamic knowledge management methods* (pp. 227–244). Hershey, PA: Business Science. doi:10.4018/978-1-4666-0077-5.ch014

Karakaya, F. (2013). B2B ecommerce: Current practices. In *Supply chain management: Concepts, methodologies, tools, and applications* (pp. 497–510). Hershey, PA: IGI Global. doi:10.4018/978-1-4666-2625-6.ch029

Karimov, F. P. (2013). Factors influencing e-commerce growth: A comparative study of central Asian transition economies. In S. Sharma (Ed.), *Adoption of virtual technologies for business, educational, and governmental advancements* (pp. 1–17). Hershey, PA: IGI Global. doi:10.4018/978-1-4666-2053-7.ch001

Kart, F., Moser, L. E., & Melliar-Smith, P. M. (2010). An automated supply chain management system and its performance evaluation. *International Journal of Information Systems and Supply Chain Management*, *3*(2), 84–107. doi:10.4018/jisscm.2010040105

Kelarev, A. V., Brown, S., Watters, P., Wu, X., & Dazeley, R. (2011). Establishing reasoning communities of security experts for internet commerce security. In J. Yearwood & A. Stranieri (Eds.), *Technologies for supporting reasoning communities and collaborative decision making: Cooperative approaches* (pp. 380–396). Hershey, PA: IGI Global. doi:10.4018/978-1-60960-091-4.ch020

Kerr, D., Gammack, J. G., & Boddington, R. (2011). Overview of digital business security issues. In D. Kerr, J. Gammack, & K. Bryant (Eds.), *Digital business security development: Management technologies* (pp. 1–36). Hershey, PA: IGI Global. doi:10.4018/978-1-60566-806-2.ch001

Kerr, D., Gammack, J. G., & Bryant, K. (2011). *Digital business security development: Management technologies*. Hershey, PA: IGI Global. doi:10.4018/978-1-60566-806-2

Kett, H. (2013). A business model approach for service engineering in the internet of services. In P. Ordóñez de Pablos & R. Tennyson (Eds.), *Best practices and new perspectives in service science and management* (pp. 228–236). Hershey, PA: IGI Global. doi:10.4018/978-1-4666-3894-5.ch013

Khurana, R., & Aggarwal, R. (2013). *Interdisciplinary perspectives on business convergence, computing, and legality*. Hershey, PA: IGI Global. doi:10.4018/978-1-4666-4209-6

Kim, G., & Suh, Y. (2012). Building semantic business process space for agile and efficient business processes management: Ontology-based approach. In V. Shankararaman, J. Zhao, & J. Lee (Eds.), *Business enterprise, process, and technology management: Models and applications* (pp. 51–73). Hershey, PA: IGI Global. doi:10.4018/978-1-4666-0249-6.ch004

King, K. P., & Foley, J. J. (2012). 21st century learning opportunities for SME success: Maximizing technology tools and lifelong learning for innovation and impact. In *Human resources management: Concepts, methodologies, tools, and applications* (pp. 731–752). Hershey, PA: IGI Global. doi:10.4018/978-1-4666-1601-1.ch045

Kipp, A., & Schubert, L. (2011). E-business interoperability and collaboration. In E. Kajan (Ed.), *Electronic business interoperability: Concepts, opportunities and challenges* (pp. 153–184). Hershey, PA: IGI Global. doi:10.4018/978-1-60960-485-1.ch008

Klink, S., & Weiß, P. (2011). Social impact of collaborative services to maintain electronic business relationships. In *Virtual communities: Concepts, methodologies, tools and applications* (pp. 2011–2040). Hershey, PA: IGI Global. doi:10.4018/978-1-60960-100-3.ch609

Koumpis, A., & Protogeros, N. (2010). Doing business on the globalised networked economy: Technology and business challenges for accounting information systems. In M. Cruz-Cunha (Ed.), *Social, managerial, and organizational dimensions of enterprise information systems* (pp. 81–92). Hershey, PA: IGI Global. doi:10.4018/978-1-60566-856-7.ch004

Kritchanchai, D., Tan, A. W., & Hosie, P. (2010). An empirical investigation of third party logistics providers in Thailand: Barriers, motivation and usage of information technologies. *International Journal of Information Systems and Supply Chain Management, 3*(2), 68–83. doi:10.4018/jisscm.2010040104

Kritchanchai, D., Tan, A. W., & Hosie, P. (2012). An empirical investigation of third party logistics providers in Thailand: Barriers, motivation and usage of information technologies. In J. Wang (Ed.), *Information technologies, methods, and techniques of supply chain management* (pp. 272–288). Hershey, PA: IGI Global. doi:10.4018/978-1-4666-0918-1.ch016

Kumar, M. (2011). Role of web interface in building trust in B2B e-exchanges. In S. Chhabra & H. Rahman (Eds.), *Human development and global advancements through information communication technologies: New initiatives* (pp. 63–74). Hershey, PA: IGI Global. doi:10.4018/978-1-60960-497-4.ch005

Kumar, M., & Sareen, M. (2012). Trust theories and models of e-commerce. In *Trust and technology in B2B e-commerce: Practices and strategies for assurance* (pp. 58–77). Hershey, PA: IGI Global. doi:10.4018/978-1-61350-353-9.ch003

Kumar, M., Sareen, M., & Chhabra, S. (2013). Technology related trust issues in SME B2B e-commerce. In S. Chhabra (Ed.), *ICT influences on human development, interaction, and collaboration* (pp. 243–259). Hershey, PA: IGI Global. doi:10.4018/978-1-4666-1957-9.ch015

Kung, M. T., & Zhang, Y. (2011). Creating competitive markets for small businesses with new media and e-business strategy. *International Journal of E-Business Research, 7*(4), 31–49. doi:10.4018/jebr.2011100103

Kuo, D., Wong, D., Gao, J., & Chang, L. (2013). A 2D barcode validation system for mobile commerce. In W. Hu & S. Mousavinezhad (Eds.), *Mobile and handheld computing solutions for organizations and end-users* (pp. 1–19). Hershey, PA: IGI Global. doi:10.4018/978-1-4666-2785-7.ch001

Kyobe, M. (2010). E-crime and non-compliance with government regulations on e-commerce: Barriers to e-commerce optimization in South African SMEs. In B. Thomas & G. Simmons (Eds.), *E-commerce adoption and small business in the global marketplace: Tools for optimization* (pp. 47–66). Hershey, PA: IGI Global. doi:10.4018/978-1-60566-998-4.ch003

Lawrence, J. E. (2011). The growth of e-commerce in developing countries: An exploratory study of opportunities and challenges for SMEs. *International Journal of ICT Research and Development in Africa, 2*(1), 15–28. doi:10.4018/jictrda.2011010102

Lawrence, J. E. (2013). Barriers hindering ecommerce adoption: A case study of Kurdistan region of Iraq. In A. Zolait (Ed.), *Technology diffusion and adoption: Global complexity, global innovation* (pp. 152–165). Hershey, PA: IGI Global. doi:10.4018/978-1-4666-2791-8.ch010

Lee, I. (2012). B2B e-commerce, online auction, supply chain management, and e-collaboration. In *Electronic commerce management for business activities and global enterprises: Competitive advantages* (pp. 249–299). Hershey, PA: IGI Global. doi:10.4018/978-1-4666-1800-8.ch007

Lee, I. (2012). B2C online consumer behavior. In *Electronic commerce management for business activities and global enterprises: competitive advantages* (pp. 166–201). Hershey, PA: IGI Global. doi:10.4018/978-1-4666-1800-8.ch005

Lee, I. (2012). Introduction to e-commerce in the global economy. In *Electronic commerce management for business activities and global enterprises: Competitive advantages* (pp. 1–46). Hershey, PA: IGI Global. doi:10.4018/978-1-4666-1800-8.ch001

Lee, I. (2012). Mobile commerce. In *Electronic commerce management for business activities and global enterprises: Competitive advantages* (pp. 300–338). Hershey, PA: IGI Global. doi:10.4018/978-1-4666-1800-8.ch008

Lee, I. (2012). Online payment systems. In *Electronic commerce management for business activities and global enterprises: Competitive advantages* (pp. 340–365). Hershey, PA: IGI Global. doi:10.4018/978-1-4666-1800-8.ch009

Leonard, L. N. (2010). C2C mobile commerce: Acceptance factors. In I. Lee (Ed.), *Encyclopedia of e-business development and management in the global economy* (pp. 759–767). Hershey, PA: IGI Global. doi:10.4018/978-1-61520-611-7.ch076

Lertpittayapoom, N., & Paul, S. (2010). The roles of online intermediaries in collective memory-supported electronic negotiation. In *Electronic services: Concepts, methodologies, tools and applications* (pp. 1831–1847). Hershey, PA: IGI Global. doi:10.4018/978-1-61520-967-5.ch112

Li, L., Liu, C., Zhao, X., & Wang, J. (2011). Transactional properties of complex web services. In H. Leung, D. Chiu, & P. Hung (Eds.), *Service intelligence and service science: Evolutionary technologies and challenges* (pp. 21–34). Hershey, PA: IGI Global. doi:10.4018/978-1-61520-819-7.ch002

Li, X., & Lin, J. (2011). Call u back: An agent-based infrastructure for mobile commerce. *International Journal of E-Entrepreneurship and Innovation*, *2*(2), 1–13. doi:10.4018/jeei.2011040101

Liao, Q., Luo, X., & Gurung, A. (2011). Trust restoration in electronic commerce. In S. Clarke & A. Dwivedi (Eds.), *Organizational and end-user interactions: New explorations* (pp. 72–88). Hershey, PA: IGI Global. doi:10.4018/978-1-60960-577-3.ch003

Liberato, N. A., Varajão, J. E., Correia, E. S., & Bessa, M. E. (2011). Location based e-commerce system: An architecture. In M. Cruz-Cunha & F. Moreira (Eds.), *Handbook of research on mobility and computing: Evolving technologies and ubiquitous impacts* (pp. 881–892). Hershey, PA: IGI Global. doi:10.4018/978-1-60960-042-6.ch055

Lim, S. Y., & Wong, S. F. (2012). Impact of applying aggregate query processing in mobile commerce. *International Journal of Business Data Communications and Networking*, *8*(2), 1–17. doi:10.4018/jbdcn.2012040101

Lin, C., & Jalleh, G. (2013). Key issues and challenges for managing and evaluating B2B e-commerce projects within the Australian pharmaceutical supply chain. In *Supply chain management: Concepts, methodologies, tools, and applications* (pp. 1083–1100). Hershey, PA: IGI Global. doi:10.4018/978-1-4666-2625-6.ch064

Lin, C., Jalleh, G., & Huang, Y. (2013). E-business investment evaluation and outsourcing practices in Australian and Taiwanese hospitals: A comparative study. In K. Tarnay, S. Imre, & L. Xu (Eds.), *Research and development in e-business through service-oriented solutions* (pp. 244–266). Hershey, PA: IGI Global. doi:10.4018/978-1-4666-4181-5.ch012

Lin, C., Lin, H. K., Jalleh, G., & Huang, Y. (2011). Key adoption challenges and issues of B2B e-commerce in the healthcare sector. In M. Cruz-Cunha & F. Moreira (Eds.), *Handbook of research on mobility and computing: Evolving technologies and ubiquitous impacts* (pp. 175–187). Hershey, PA: IGI Global. doi:10.4018/978-1-60960-042-6.ch011

Liyanage, J. P. (2011). Copying with dynamic change: Collaborative business interfacing for SMEs under intergated eoperations. In M. Cruz-Cunha & J. Varajão (Eds.), *E-business managerial aspects, solutions and case studies* (pp. 136–147). Hershey, PA: IGI Global. doi:10.4018/978-1-60960-463-9.ch008

Liyanage, J. P. (2012). Hybrid intelligence through business socialization and networking: Managing complexities in the digital era. In M. Cruz-Cunha, P. Gonçalves, N. Lopes, E. Miranda, & G. Putnik (Eds.), *Handbook of research on business social networking: organizational, managerial, and technological dimensions* (pp. 567–582). Hershey, PA: IGI Global. doi:10.4018/978-1-61350-168-9.ch030

Loeser, F., Erek, K., & Zarnekow, R. (2013). Green IT strategies: A conceptual framework for the alignment of information technology and corporate sustainability strategy. In P. Ordóñez de Pablos (Ed.), *Green technologies and business practices: An IT approach* (pp. 58–95). Hershey, PA: IGI Global. doi:10.4018/978-1-4666-1972-2.ch004

Maamar, Z., Faci, N., Mostéfaoui, S. K., & Akhter, F. (2011). Towards a framework for weaving social networks into mobile commerce. *International Journal of Systems and Service-Oriented Engineering*, *2*(3), 32–46. doi:10.4018/jssoe.2011070103

Mahmood, M. A., Gemoets, L., Hall, L. L., & López, F. J. (2011). Building business value in e-commerce enabled organizations: An empirical study. In *Global business: Concepts, methodologies, tools and applications* (pp. 229–253). Hershey, PA: IGI Global. doi:10.4018/978-1-60960-587-2.ch201

Mahran, A. F., & Enaba, H. M. (2013). Exploring determinants influencing the intention to use mobile payment service. In R. Eid (Ed.), *Managing customer trust, satisfaction, and loyalty through information communication technologies* (pp. 288–309). Hershey, PA: IGI Global. doi:10.4018/978-1-4666-3631-6.ch017

Marimuthu, M., Omar, A., Ramayah, T., & Mohamad, O. (2013). Readiness to adopt e-business among SMEs in Malaysia: Antecedents and consequence. In S. Sharma (Ed.), *Adoption of virtual technologies for business, educational, and governmental advancements* (pp. 18–36). Hershey, PA: IGI Global. doi:10.4018/978-1-4666-2053-7.ch002

Mayes, P. (2014). Interactive advertising: Displays of identity and stance on YouTube. In H. Lim & F. Sudweeks (Eds.), *Innovative methods and technologies for electronic discourse analysis* (pp. 260–284). Hershey, PA: IGI Global. doi:10.4018/978-1-4666-4426-7.ch012

McGrath, T. (2012). The reality of using standards for electronic business document formats. In E. Kajan, F. Dorloff, & I. Bedini (Eds.), *Handbook of research on e-business standards and protocols: Documents, data and advanced web technologies* (pp. 21–32). Hershey, PA: IGI Global. doi:10.4018/978-1-4666-0146-8.ch002

Meredith, J., & Potter, J. (2014). Conversation analysis and electronic interactions: Methodological, analytic and technical considerations. In H. Lim & F. Sudweeks (Eds.), *Innovative methods and technologies for electronic discourse analysis* (pp. 370–393). Hershey, PA: IGI Global. doi:10.4018/978-1-4666-4426-7.ch017

Millman, C., & El-Gohary, H. (2011). New digital media marketing and micro business: A UK perspective. *International Journal of Online Marketing*, *1*(1), 41–62. doi:10.4018/ijom.2011010104

Mishra, B., & Shukla, K. K. (2014). Data mining techniques for software quality prediction. In *Software design and development: Concepts, methodologies, tools, and applications* (pp. 401–428). Hershey, PA: IGI Global. doi:10.4018/978-1-4666-4301-7.ch021

Misra, H., & Rahman, H. (2013). *Managing enterprise information technology acquisitions: Assessing organizational preparedness*. Hershey, PA: IGI Global. doi:10.4018/978-1-4666-4201-0

Mohammadi, S., Golara, S., & Mousavi, N. (2012). Selecting adequate security mechanisms in e-business processes using fuzzy TOPSIS. *International Journal of Fuzzy System Applications*, *2*(1), 35–53. doi:10.4018/ijfsa.2012010103

Möhlenbruch, D., Dölling, S., & Ritschel, F. (2010). Interactive customer retention management for mobile commerce. In K. Pousttchi & D. Wiedemann (Eds.), *Handbook of research on mobile marketing management* (pp. 437–456). Hershey, PA: IGI Global. doi:10.4018/978-1-60566-074-5.ch023

Molla, A., & Peszynski, K. (2013). E-business in agribusiness: Investigating the e-readiness of Australian horticulture firms. In S. Chhabra (Ed.), *ICT influences on human development, interaction, and collaboration* (pp. 78–96). Hershey, PA: IGI Global. doi:10.4018/978-1-4666-1957-9.ch004

Monsanto, C., & Andriole, S. J. (2010). Business technology strategy for a major real estate and mortgage brokerage company. *Journal of Information Technology Research, 3*(3), 43–53. doi:10.4018/jitr.2010070104

Montes, J. A., Gutiérrez, A. C., Fernández, E. M., & Romeo, A. (2013). Reality mining, location based services, and e-business opportunities: The case of city analytics. In S. Nasir (Ed.), *Modern entrepreneurship and e-business innovations* (pp. 87–99). Hershey, PA: IGI Global. doi:10.4018/978-1-4666-2946-2.ch007

Moqbel, A., Yani-De-Soriano, M., & Yousafzai, S. (2012). Mobile commerce use among UK mobile users: An experimental approach based on a proposed mobile network utilization framework. In A. Zolait (Ed.), *Knowledge and technology adoption, diffusion, and transfer: International perspectives* (pp. 78–111). Hershey, PA: IGI Global. doi:10.4018/978-1-4666-1752-0.ch007

Movahedi, B. M., Lavassani, K. M., & Kumar, V. (2012). E-marketplace emergence: Evolution, developments and classification. *Journal of Electronic Commerce in Organizations, 10*(1), 14–32. doi:10.4018/jeco.2012010102

Mugge, R., & Schoormans, J. P. (2010). Optimizing consumer responses to mass customization. In C. Mourlas & P. Germanakos (Eds.), *Mass customization for personalized communication environments: Integrating human factors* (pp. 10–22). Hershey, PA: IGI Global. doi:10.4018/978-1-60566-260-2.ch002

Musso, F. (2012). Technology in marketing channels: Present and future drivers of innovation. *International Journal of Applied Behavioral Economics, 1*(2), 41–51. doi:10.4018/ijabe.2012040104

Mutula, S. M. (2010). Digital economy components. In S. Mutula (Ed.), *Digital economies: SMEs and e-readiness* (pp. 29–38). Hershey, PA: IGI Global. doi:10.4018/978-1-60566-420-0.ch003

Mutula, S. M. (2010). Trends and best practices in the digital economy. In S. Mutula (Ed.), *Digital economies: SMEs and e-readiness* (pp. 283–301). Hershey, PA: IGI Global. doi:10.4018/978-1-60566-420-0.ch017

Nachtigal, S. (2011). E-business: Definition and characteristics. In O. Bak & N. Stair (Eds.), *Impact of e-business technologies on public and private organizations: Industry comparisons and perspectives* (pp. 233–248). Hershey, PA: IGI Global. doi:10.4018/978-1-60960-501-8.ch014

Nah, F. F., Hong, W., Chen, L., & Lee, H. (2012). Information search patterns in e-commerce product comparison services. In K. Siau (Ed.), *Cross-disciplinary models and applications of database management: Advancing approaches* (pp. 131–145). Hershey, PA: IGI Global. doi:10.4018/978-1-61350-471-0.ch006

Nair, P. R. (2010). Benefits of information technology implementations for supply chain management: An explorative study of progressive Indian companies. In S. Parthasarathy (Ed.), *Enterprise information systems and implementing IT infrastructures: Challenges and issues* (pp. 323–343). Hershey, PA: IGI Global. doi:10.4018/978-1-61520-625-4.ch021

Ndou, V., Del Vecchio, P., Passiante, G., & Schina, L. (2013). Web-based services and future business models. In P. Papajorgji, A. Guimarães, & M. Guarracino (Eds.), *Enterprise business modeling, optimization techniques, and flexible information systems* (pp. 1–13). Hershey, PA: IGI Global. doi:10.4018/978-1-4666-3946-1.ch001

Ndou, V., & Sadguy, N. (2013). Digital marketplaces as a viable model for SME networking. In *Supply chain management: Concepts, methodologies, tools, and applications* (pp. 275–288). Hershey, PA: IGI Global. doi:10.4018/978-1-4666-2625-6.ch016

Ochara, N. M., & Krauss, K. (2012). Towards a collaborative e-business vision for Africa. In K. Mohammed Rezaul (Ed.), *Strategic and pragmatic e-business: Implications for future business practices* (pp. 396–414). Hershey, PA: IGI Global. doi:10.4018/978-1-4666-1619-6.ch018

Oncioiu, I. (2013). *Business innovation, development, and advancement in the digital economy*. Hershey, PA: IGI Global. doi:10.4018/978-1-4666-2934-9

Ondimu, K. O., Muketha, G. M., & Ondago, C. O. (2013). E-business adoption framework in the hospitality industry: The case of Kenyan coast. In K. Tarnay, S. Imre, & L. Xu (Eds.), *Research and development in e-business through service-oriented solutions* (pp. 225–243). Hershey, PA: IGI Global. doi:10.4018/978-1-4666-4181-5.ch011

Ovaskainen, M., & Tinnilä, M. (2013). Megatrends in electronic business: An analysis of the impacts on SMEs. In S. Nasir (Ed.), *Modern entrepreneurship and e-business innovations* (pp. 12–27). Hershey, PA: IGI Global. doi:10.4018/978-1-4666-2946-2.ch002

Özcan, O., & Reeves, K. A. (2011). The firm boundary decision for sustainability-focused companies. *International Journal of Applied Logistics*, *2*(2), 49–68. doi:10.4018/jal.2011040104

Öztayşi, B., & Kahraman, C. (2014). Quantification of corporate performance using fuzzy analytic network process: The case of e-commerce. In P. Vasant (Ed.), *Handbook of research on novel soft computing intelligent algorithms: Theory and practical applications* (pp. 385–413). Hershey, PA: IGI Global. doi:10.4018/978-1-4666-4450-2.ch013

Palmer, D. E. (2010). The transformative nature of e-business: Business ethics and stakeholder relations on the internet. In D. Palmer (Ed.), *Ethical issues in e-business: Models and frameworks* (pp. 1–14). Hershey, PA: IGI Global. doi:10.4018/978-1-61520-615-5.ch001

Pańkowska, M. (2014). Frameworks of IT prosumption for business development (pp. 1-347). doi:10.4018/978-1-4666-4313-0

Pelet, J. É., & Papadopoulou, P. (2013). The effect of e-commerce websites' colors on customer trust. In I. Lee (Ed.), *Mobile applications and knowledge advancements in e-business* (pp. 167–185). Hershey, PA: IGI Global. doi:10.4018/978-1-4666-1960-9.ch011

Pennington, R. (2012). Enhanced social presence through ebranding the consumer in virtual communities. In A. Kapoor & C. Kulshrestha (Eds.), *Branding and sustainable competitive advantage: Building virtual presence* (pp. 189–206). Hershey, PA: IGI Global. doi:10.4018/978-1-61350-171-9.ch012

Peslak, A. R. (2012). Industry variables affecting ERP success and status. *International Journal of Enterprise Information Systems*, *8*(3), 15–33. doi:10.4018/jeis.2012070102

Peterson, D., & Howard, C. (2012). Electronic payment systems evaluation: A case study to examine system selection criteria and impacts. *International Journal of Strategic Information Technology and Applications*, *3*(1), 66–80. doi:10.4018/jsita.2012010105

Pflügler, C. (2012). Fostering networked business operations: A framework for B2B electronic intermediary development. *International Journal of Intelligent Information Technologies*, *8*(2), 31–58. doi:10.4018/jiit.2012040103

Pillai, K., & Ozansoy, C. (2013). Web-based digital habitat ecosystems for sustainable built environments. In P. Ordóñez de Pablos (Ed.), *Green technologies and business practices: An IT approach* (pp. 185–199). Hershey, PA: IGI Global. doi:10.4018/978-1-4666-1972-2.ch011

Pinto, M., Rodrigues, A., Varajão, J., & Gonçalves, R. (2011). Model of funcionalities for the development of B2B e-commerce solutions. In M. Cruz-Cunha & J. Varajão (Eds.), *Innovations in SMEs and conducting e-business: Technologies, trends and solutions* (pp. 35–60). Hershey, PA: IGI Global. doi:10.4018/978-1-60960-765-4.ch003

Pires, J. A., & Gonçalves, R. (2011). Constrains associated to e-business evolution. In M. Cruz-Cunha & J. Varajão (Eds.), *E-business issues, challenges and opportunities for SMEs: Driving competitiveness* (pp. 335–349). Hershey, PA: IGI Global. doi:10.4018/978-1-61692-880-3.ch019

Polovina, S., & Andrews, S. (2011). A transaction-oriented architecture for structuring unstructured information in enterprise applications. In V. Sugumaran (Ed.), *Intelligent, adaptive and reasoning technologies: New developments and applications* (pp. 285–299). Hershey, PA: IGI Global. doi:10.4018/978-1-60960-595-7.ch016

Potocan, V., Nedelko, Z., & Mulej, M. (2011). What is new with organization of e-business: Organizational viewpoint of the relationships in e-business. In M. Cruz-Cunha & J. Varajão (Eds.), *E-business issues, challenges and opportunities for SMEs: Driving competitiveness* (pp. 131–148). Hershey, PA: IGI Global. doi:10.4018/978-1-61692-880-3.ch009

Potocan, V., Nedelko, Z., & Mulej, M. (2011). What is new with organization of e-business: Organizational viewpoint of the relationships in e-business. In M. Cruz-Cunha & J. Varajão (Eds.), *E-business issues, challenges and opportunities for SMEs: Driving competitiveness* (pp. 131–148). Hershey, PA: IGI Global. doi:10.4018/978-1-61692-880-3.ch009

Pucihar, A., & Lenart, G. (2011). eSME Slovenia: Initiative and action plan for the accelerated introduction of e-business in SMEs. In Global business: Concepts, methodologies, tools and applications (pp. 995-1022). Hershey, PA: IGI Global. doi:10.4018/978-1-60960-587-2.ch409

Quan, J. (2011). E-business strategy and firm performance. In *Global business: Concepts, methodologies, tools and applications* (pp. 56–66). Hershey, PA: IGI Global. doi:10.4018/978-1-60960-587-2.ch105

Quente, C. (2010). Brand driven mobile marketing: 5 theses for today and tomorrow. In K. Pousttchi & D. Wiedemann (Eds.), *Handbook of research on mobile marketing management* (pp. 468–483). Hershey, PA: IGI Global. doi:10.4018/978-1-60566-074-5.ch025

Qureshil, S., Kamal, M., & Wolcott, P. (2011). Information technology interventions for growth and competitiveness in micro-enterprises. In M. Tavana (Ed.), *Managing adaptability, intervention, and people in enterprise information systems* (pp. 106–137). Hershey, PA: IGI Global. doi:10.4018/978-1-60960-529-2.ch006

Rabaey, M. (2014). Complex adaptive systems thinking approach to enterprise architecture. In P. Saha (Ed.), *A systemic perspective to managing complexity with enterprise architecture* (pp. 99–149). Hershey, PA: IGI Global. doi:10.4018/978-1-4666-4518-9.ch003

Rahman, H., & Ramos, I. (2012). Trends of open innovation in developing nations: Contexts of SMEs. In H. Rahman & I. Ramos (Eds.), *Cases on SMEs and open innovation: Applications and investigations* (pp. 65–80). Hershey, PA: IGI Global. doi:10.4018/978-1-61350-314-0.ch004

Rahman, H., & Ramos, I. (2013). Implementation of e-commerce at the grass roots: Issues of challenges in terms of human-computer interactions. *International Journal of Information Communication Technologies and Human Development*, *5*(2), 1–19. doi:10.4018/jicthd.2013040101

Rajagopal, D. (2010). Customer value and new product retailing dynamics: An analytical construct for gaining competetive advantage. In *Business information systems: Concepts, methodologies, tools and applications* (pp. 1998–2014). Hershey, PA: IGI Global. doi:10.4018/978-1-61520-969-9.ch121

Rajagopal, D. (2010). Internet, reengineering and technology applications in retailing. In *Business information systems: Concepts, methodologies, tools and applications* (pp. 1324–1342). Hershey, PA: IGI Global. doi:10.4018/978-1-61520-969-9.ch082

Rajagopal, D. (2011). Marketing strategy, technology and modes of entry in global retailing. In *Global business: Concepts, methodologies, tools and applications* (pp. 1–27). Hershey, PA: IGI Global. doi:10.4018/978-1-60960-587-2.ch101

Rajagopal, D. (2012). Convergence marketing. In *Systems thinking and process dynamics for marketing systems: Technologies and applications for decision management* (pp. 274–290). Hershey, PA: IGI Global. doi:10.4018/978-1-4666-0969-3.ch011

Rajagopal, D. (2012). Product development and market governance. In *Systems thinking and process dynamics for marketing systems: Technologies and applications for decision management* (pp. 88–117). Hershey, PA: IGI Global. doi:10.4018/978-1-4666-0969-3.ch004

Rajagopal, D. (2012). Systems thinking and cognitive process in marketing. In *Systems thinking and process dynamics for marketing systems: technologies and applications for decision management* (pp. 170–197). Hershey, PA: IGI Global. doi:10.4018/978-1-4666-0969-3.ch007

Rajagopal, D. (2013). Pricing for new products. In *Marketing decision making and the management of pricing: Successful business tools* (pp. 56–74). Hershey, PA: IGI Global. doi:10.4018/978-1-4666-4094-8.ch003

Ramayah, T., Popa, S., & Suki, N. M. (2013). Key dimensions on B2C e-business: An empirical study in Malaysia. *International Journal of Human Capital and Information Technology Professionals*, *4*(2), 43–55. doi:10.4018/jhcitp.2013040104

Rambo, K., & Liu, K. (2011). Culture-sensitive virtual e-commerce design with reference to female consumers in Saudi Arabia. In B. Ciaramitaro (Ed.), *Virtual worlds and e-commerce: Technologies and applications for building customer relationships* (pp. 267–289). Hershey, PA: IGI Global. doi:10.4018/978-1-61692-808-7.ch016

Ratnasingam, P. (2010). The evolution of online relationships in business to consumer e-commerce. In M. Khosrow-Pour (Ed.), *E-commerce trends for organizational advancement: New applications and methods* (pp. 167–176). Hershey, PA: IGI Global. doi:10.4018/978-1-60566-964-9.ch010

Ratnasingam, P. (2010). The impact of e-commerce customer relationship management in business-to-consumer e-commerce. In M. Hunter (Ed.), *Strategic information systems: Concepts, methodologies, tools, and applications* (pp. 2099–2111). Hershey, PA: IGI Global. doi:10.4018/978-1-60566-677-8.ch132

Razavi, A. R., Krause, P., & Moschoyiannis, S. (2010). Digital ecosystems: Challenges and proposed solutions. In N. Antonopoulos, G. Exarchakos, M. Li, & A. Liotta (Eds.), Handbook of research on P2P and grid systems for service-oriented computing: Models, methodologies and applications (pp. 1003-1031). Hershey, PA: IGI Global. doi:10.4018/978-1-61520-686-5.ch043

Regazzi, J. J. (2014). *Infonomics and the business of free: Modern value creation for information services*. Hershey, PA: IGI Global. doi:10.4018/978-1-4666-4454-0

Riaz, N., & Rehman, M. (2013). Negotiation by software agents in electronic business: An example of hybrid negotiation. In E. Li, S. Loh, C. Evans, & F. Lorenzi (Eds.), *Organizations and social networking: Utilizing social media to engage consumers* (pp. 327–349). Hershey, PA: IGI Global. doi:10.4018/978-1-4666-4026-9.ch017

Roberti, G., & Marinelli, A. (2012). Branding identity: Facebook, brands and self construction. In F. Comunello (Ed.), *Networked sociability and individualism: Technology for personal and professional relationships* (pp. 147–168). Hershey, PA: IGI Global. doi:10.4018/978-1-61350-338-6.ch008

Rodrigues, D. E. (2012). Cyberethics of business social networking. In M. Cruz-Cunha, P. Gonçalves, N. Lopes, E. Miranda, & G. Putnik (Eds.), *Handbook of research on business social networking: Organizational, managerial, and technological dimensions* (pp. 314–338). Hershey, PA: IGI Global. doi:10.4018/978-1-61350-168-9.ch016

Roos, G. (2013). The role of intellectual capital in business model innovation: An empirical study. In P. Ordóñez de Pablos, R. Tennyson, & J. Zhao (Eds.), *Intellectual capital strategy management for knowledge-based organizations* (pp. 76–121). Hershey, PA: IGI Global. doi:10.4018/978-1-4666-3655-2.ch006

Rowley, J., & Edmundson-Bird, D. (2013). Brand presence in digital space. *Journal of Electronic Commerce in Organizations, 11*(1), 63–78. doi:10.4018/jeco.2013010104

Rusko, R. (2013). The redefined role of consumer as a prosumer: Value co-creation, coopetition, and crowdsourcing of information goods. In P. Renna (Ed.), *Production and manufacturing system management: Coordination approaches and multi-site planning* (pp. 162–174). Hershey, PA: IGI Global. doi:10.4018/978-1-4666-2098-8.ch009

Sahi, G., & Madan, S. (2013). Developing a website usability framework for B2C e-commerce success. *International Journal of Information Communication Technologies and Human Development, 5*(1), 1–19. doi:10.4018/jicthd.2013010101

Sainz de Abajo, B., de la Torre Díez, I., & López-Coronado, M. (2010). Analysis of benefits and risks of e-commerce: Practical study of Spanish SME. In I. Portela & M. Cruz-Cunha (Eds.), *Information communication technology law, protection and access rights: Global approaches and issues* (pp. 214–239). Hershey, PA: IGI Global. doi:10.4018/978-1-61520-975-0.ch014

Samanta, I., & Kyriazopoulos, P. (2011). Can global environment influence B2B relationships? In P. Ordóñez de Pablos, M. Lytras, W. Karwowski, & R. Lee (Eds.), *Electronic globalized business and sustainable development through IT management: Strategies and perspectives* (pp. 54–69). Hershey, PA: IGI Global. doi:10.4018/978-1-61520-623-0.ch004

Sambhanthan, A., & Good, A. (2012). Implications for improving accessibility to e-commerce websites in developing countries: A study of hotel websites. *International Journal of Knowledge-Based Organizations, 2*(2), 1–20. doi:10.4018/ijkbo.2012040101

Sampaio, L., & Figueiredo, J. (2011). E-sourcing electronic platforms in real business. In M. Cruz-Cunha & J. Varajão (Eds.), *E-business managerial aspects, solutions and case studies* (pp. 185–205). Hershey, PA: IGI Global. doi:10.4018/978-1-60960-463-9.ch011

Seetharaman, A., & Raj, J. R. (2011). Evolution, development and growth of electronic money. In S. Sharma (Ed.), *E-adoption and socio-economic impacts: Emerging infrastructural effects* (pp. 249–268). Hershey, PA: IGI Global. doi:10.4018/978-1-60960-597-1.ch013

Sengupta, A., & Glavin, S. E. (2013). Predicting volatile consumer markets using multi-agent methods: Theory and validation. In B. Alexandrova-Kabadjova, S. Martinez-Jaramillo, A. Garcia-Almanza, & E. Tsang (Eds.), *Simulation in computational finance and economics: Tools and emerging applications* (pp. 339–358). Hershey, PA: IGI Global. doi:10.4018/978-1-4666-2011-7.ch016

Serpico, E., Aquilani, B., Ruggieri, A., & Silvestri, C. (2013). Customer centric marketing strategies: The importance and measurement of customer satisfaction – Offline vs. online. In H. Kaufmann & M. Panni (Eds.), *Customer-centric marketing strategies: Tools for building organizational performance* (pp. 315–357). Hershey, PA: IGI Global. doi:10.4018/978-1-4666-2524-2.ch016

Shareef, M. A., & Kumar, V. (2012). Prevent/control identity theft: Impact on trust and consumers' purchase intention in B2C EC. *Information Resources Management Journal, 25*(3), 30–60. doi:10.4018/irmj.2012070102

Sherringham, K., & Unhelkar, B. (2011). Business driven enterprise architecture and applications to support mobile business. In *Enterprise information systems: Concepts, methodologies, tools and applications* (pp. 805–816). Hershey, PA: IGI Global. doi:10.4018/978-1-61692-852-0.ch316

Shin, N. (2011). Information technology and diversification: How their relationship affects firm performance. In N. Kock (Ed.), *E-collaboration technologies and organizational performance: Current and future trends* (pp. 65–79). Hershey, PA: IGI Global. doi:10.4018/978-1-60960-466-0.ch005

Sidnal, N., & Manvi, S. S. (2010). Service discovery techniques in mobile e-commerce. In I. Lee (Ed.), *Encyclopedia of e-business development and management in the global economy* (pp. 812–823). Hershey, PA: IGI Global. doi:10.4018/978-1-61520-611-7.ch081

Sidnal, N., & Manvi, S. S. (2013). English auction issues in mobile e-commerce. In K. Tarnay, S. Imre, & L. Xu (Eds.), *Research and development in e-business through service-oriented solutions* (pp. 208–223). Hershey, PA: IGI Global. doi:10.4018/978-1-4666-4181-5.ch010

Singh, S. (2010). Usability techniques for interactive software and their application in e-commerce. In T. Spiliotopoulos, P. Papadopoulou, D. Martakos, & G. Kouroupetroglou (Eds.), *Integrating usability engineering for designing the web experience: Methodologies and principles* (pp. 81–102). Hershey, PA: IGI Global. doi:10.4018/978-1-60566-896-3.ch005

Söderström, E. (2010). Guidelines for managing B2B standards implementation. In E. Alkhalifa (Ed.), *E-strategies for resource management systems: Planning and implementation* (pp. 86–105). Hershey, PA: IGI Global. doi:10.4018/978-1-61692-016-6.ch005

Sood, S. (2012). The death of social media in start-up companies and the rise of s-commerce: Convergence of e-commerce, complexity and social media. *Journal of Electronic Commerce in Organizations*, *10*(2), 1–15. doi:10.4018/jeco.2012040101

Soto-Acosta, P. (2010). E-business and the resource-based view: Towards a research agenda. In I. Lee (Ed.), *Encyclopedia of e-business development and management in the global economy* (pp. 336–346). Hershey, PA: IGI Global. doi:10.4018/978-1-61520-611-7.ch033

Sourouni, A. M., Mouzakitis, S., Kourlimpini, G., Askounis, D., & Psarras, J. (2010). Ontology-based registries: An e-business transactions' registry. In E. Alkhalifa (Ed.), *E-strategies for resource management systems: Planning and implementation* (pp. 106–117). Hershey, PA: IGI Global. doi:10.4018/978-1-61692-016-6.ch006

Srinivasan, S., & Barker, R. (2012). Global analysis of security and trust perceptions in web design for e-commerce. *International Journal of Information Security and Privacy*, *6*(1), 1–13. doi:10.4018/jisp.2012010101

Su, Q., & Adams, C. (2012). Consumers' attitudes toward mobile commerce: A model to capture the cultural and environment influences. In A. Scupola (Ed.), *Innovative mobile platform developments for electronic services design and delivery* (pp. 1–20). Hershey, PA: IGI Global. doi:10.4018/978-1-4666-1568-7.ch001

Swilley, E., Hofacker, C. F., & Lamont, B. T. (2012). The evolution from e-commerce to m-commerce: Pressures, firm capabilities and competitive advantage in strategic decision making. *International Journal of E-Business Research, 8*(1), 1–16. doi:10.4018/jebr.2012010101

Swimm, N., & Andriole, S. J. (2010). Business technology strategy for an energy management company. *Journal of Information Technology Research, 3*(3), 54–65. doi:10.4018/jitr.2010070105

Tadjouddine, E. M. (2011). E-commerce systems for software agents: Challenges and opportunities. In M. Cruz-Cunha & J. Varajão (Eds.), *E-business issues, challenges and opportunities for SMEs: Driving competitiveness* (pp. 20–29). Hershey, PA: IGI Global. doi:10.4018/978-1-61692-880-3.ch002

Taylor, P. R. (2014). Enterprise architecture's identity crisis: New approaches to complexity for a maturing discipline. In P. Saha (Ed.), *A systemic perspective to managing complexity with enterprise architecture* (pp. 433–453). Hershey, PA: IGI Global. doi:10.4018/978-1-4666-4518-9.ch013

Tella, A. (2012). Determinants of e-payment systems success: A user's satisfaction perspective. *International Journal of E-Adoption, 4*(3), 15–38. doi:10.4018/jea.2012070102

Terjesen, A. (2010). Anonymity and trust: The ethical challenges of e-business transactions. In D. Palmer (Ed.), *Ethical issues in e-business: Models and frameworks* (pp. 40–57). Hershey, PA: IGI Global. doi:10.4018/978-1-61520-615-5.ch004

Tijsen, R., Spruit, M., van de Ridder, M., & van Raaij, B. (2011). BI-FIT: Aligning business intelligence end-users, tasks and technologies. In M. Cruz-Cunha & J. Varajao (Eds.), *Enterprise information systems design, implementation and management: Organizational applications* (pp. 162–177). Hershey, PA: IGI Global. doi:10.4018/978-1-61692-020-3.ch011

Toka, A., Aivazidou, E., Antoniou, A., & Arvanitopoulos-Darginis, K. (2013). Cloud computing in supply chain management: An overview. In D. Graham, I. Manikas, & D. Folinas (Eds.), *E-logistics and e-supply chain management: Applications for evolving business* (pp. 218–231). Hershey, PA: IGI Global. doi:10.4018/978-1-4666-3914-0.ch012

Tran, Q., Huang, D., & Zhang, C. (2013). An assessment method of the integrated e-commerce readiness for construction organizations in developing countries. *International Journal of E-Adoption, 5*(1), 37–51. doi:10.4018/jea.2013010103

Tung, H., Kung, H., Lawless, D. S., Sofge, D. A., & Lawless, W. F. (2011). Conservation of information and e-business success and challenges: A case study. In M. Cruz-Cunha & J. Varajão (Eds.), *E-business managerial aspects, solutions and case studies* (pp. 254–269). Hershey, PA: IGI Global. doi:10.4018/978-1-60960-463-9.ch015

Unhelkar, B. (2011). *Handbook of research on green ICT: Technology, business and social perspectives*. Hershey, PA: IGI Global. doi:10.4018/978-1-61692-834-6

Unhelkar, B., Ghanbary, A., & Younessi, H. (2010). Collaborative business process engineering (CBPE) model. In B. Unhelkar, A. Ghanbary, & H. Younessi (Eds.), *Collaborative business process engineering and global organizations: Frameworks for service integration* (pp. 98–120). Hershey, PA: IGI Global. doi:10.4018/978-1-60566-689-1.ch004

Unhelkar, B., Ghanbary, A., & Younessi, H. (2010). Emerging technologies for business collaboration. In B. Unhelkar, A. Ghanbary, & H. Younessi (Eds.), *Collaborative business process engineering and global organizations: Frameworks for service integration* (pp. 37–64). Hershey, PA: IGI Global. doi:10.4018/978-1-60566-689-1.ch002

Unhelkar, B., Ghanbary, A., & Younessi, H. (2010). Fundamentals of collaborative business. In B. Unhelkar, A. Ghanbary, & H. Younessi (Eds.), *Collaborative business process engineering and global organizations: Frameworks for service integration* (pp. 1–36). Hershey, PA: IGI Global. doi:10.4018/978-1-60566-689-1.ch001

Van Huy, L., Rowe, F., Truex, D., & Huynh, M. Q. (2012). An empirical study of determinants of e-commerce adoption in SMEs in Vietnam: An economy in transition. *Journal of Global Information Management*, *20*(3), 23–54. doi:10.4018/jgim.2012070102

Vannoy, S. A. (2011). A structured content analytic assessment of business services advertisements in the cloud-based web services marketplace. *International Journal of Dependable and Trustworthy Information Systems*, *2*(1), 18–49. doi:10.4018/jdtis.2011010102

Vasconcelos, V., & Campos, P. (2012). The role of social networks in distributed informal information systems for innovation. In J. Varajão, M. Cruz-Cunha, & A. Trigo (Eds.), *Organizational integration of enterprise systems and resources: Advancements and applications* (pp. 60–75). Hershey, PA: IGI Global. doi:10.4018/978-1-4666-1764-3.ch004

Venkatraman, R., Venkatraman, S., & Asaithambi, S. P. (2013). A practical cloud services implementation framework for e-businesses. In K. Tarnay, S. Imre, & L. Xu (Eds.), *Research and development in e-business through service-oriented solutions* (pp. 167–198). Hershey, PA: IGI Global. doi:10.4018/978-1-4666-4181-5.ch008

Verkasalo, H. (2011). Analysis of the forces reshaping the mobile internet business. In M. Bartolacci & S. Powell (Eds.), *Interdisciplinary and multidimensional perspectives in telecommunications and networking: Emerging findings* (pp. 19–45). Hershey, PA: IGI Global. doi:10.4018/978-1-60960-505-6.ch003

Verma, A. (2013). Effects of phishing on e-commerce with special reference to India. In R. Khurana & R. Aggarwal (Eds.), *Interdisciplinary perspectives on business convergence, computing, and legality* (pp. 186–197). Hershey, PA: IGI Global. doi:10.4018/978-1-4666-4209-6.ch017

Walker, B., & Posey, E. (2013). Digital El Paso: A public-private business model for community wireless networks. In A. Abdelaal (Ed.), *Social and economic effects of community wireless networks and infrastructures* (pp. 94–111). Hershey, PA: IGI Global. doi:10.4018/978-1-4666-2997-4.ch006

Wan, Y., Clegg, B., & Dey, P. K. (2013). A framework for enabling dynamic e-business strategies via new enterprise paradigms and ERP solutions. In *Enterprise resource planning: Concepts, methodologies, tools, and applications* (pp. 1561–1595). Hershey, PA: IGI Global. doi:10.4018/978-1-4666-4153-2.ch083

Wang, F., Lupton, N., Rawlinson, D., & Zhang, X. (2012). EBDMSS: A web-based decision making support system for strategic e-business management. In P. Zaraté (Ed.), *Integrated and strategic advancements in decision making support systems* (pp. 265–284). Hershey, PA: IGI Global. doi:10.4018/978-1-4666-1746-9.ch019

Wenyin, L., Liu, A., Li, Q., & Huang, L. (2011). Business models for insurance of business web services. In H. Leung, D. Chiu, & P. Hung (Eds.), *Service intelligence and service science: Evolutionary technologies and challenges* (pp. 261–272). Hershey, PA: IGI Global. doi:10.4018/978-1-61520-819-7.ch014

Wiedmann, K., Reeh, M., & Schumacher, H. (2010). Employment and acceptance of near field communication in mobile marketing. In K. Pousttchi & D. Wiedemann (Eds.), *Handbook of research on mobile marketing management* (pp. 190–212). Hershey, PA: IGI Global. doi:10.4018/978-1-60566-074-5.ch011

Williams, J. G., & Premchaiswadi, W. (2011). On-line credit card payment processing and fraud prevention for e-business. In *Global business: Concepts, methodologies, tools and applications* (pp. 699–717). Hershey, PA: IGI Global. doi:10.4018/978-1-60960-587-2.ch312

Wilms, A., & Andriole, S. J. (2010). Business technology strategy for a specialty chemicals company. *Journal of Information Technology Research*, *3*(3), 11–18. doi:10.4018/jitr.2010070102

Winkler, U., & Gilani, W. (2012). Business continuity management of business driven IT landscapes. In S. Reiff-Marganiec & M. Tilly (Eds.), *Handbook of research on service-oriented systems and non-functional properties: Future directions* (pp. 381–399). Hershey, PA: IGI Global. doi:10.4018/978-1-61350-432-1.ch017

Wollenberg, A. (2013). Optimizing international joint venture (IJV) ownership structures: A technology and knowledge transfer-linked productivity growth perspective. In B. Christiansen, E. Turkina, & N. Williams (Eds.), *Cultural and technological influences on global business* (pp. 142–164). Hershey, PA: IGI Global. doi:10.4018/978-1-4666-3966-9.ch009

Wood, A. M., Moultrie, J., & Eckert, C. (2010). Product form evolution. In A. Silva & R. Simoes (Eds.), *Handbook of research on trends in product design and development: Technological and organizational perspectives* (pp. 499–512). Hershey, PA: IGI Global. doi:10.4018/978-1-61520-617-9.ch027

Wresch, W., & Fraser, S. (2011). Persistent barriers to e-commerce in developing countries: A longitudinal study of efforts by Caribbean companies. *Journal of Global Information Management*, *19*(3), 30–44. doi:10.4018/jgim.2011070102

Wresch, W., & Fraser, S. (2013). Persistent barriers to e-commerce in developing countries: A longitudinal study of efforts by Caribbean companies. In F. Tan (Ed.), *Global diffusion and adoption of technologies for knowledge and information sharing* (pp. 205–220). Hershey, PA: IGI Global. doi:10.4018/978-1-4666-2142-8.ch009

Xiao, X., Liu, Y., & Zhang, Z. (2012). The analysis of the logistics mode decision to e-commerce. *Journal of Electronic Commerce in Organizations*, *10*(4), 57–70. doi:10.4018/jeco.2012100105

Xu, L. (2010). Outsourcing and multi-party business collaborations modeling. In K. St.Amant (Ed.), *IT outsourcing: Concepts, methodologies, tools, and applications* (pp. 558–577). Hershey, PA: IGI Global. doi:10.4018/978-1-60566-770-6.ch033

Xu, M., Rohatgi, R., & Duan, Y. (2010). Engaging SMEs in e-business: Insights from an empirical study. In *Business information systems: Concepts, methodologies, tools and applications* (pp. 115–134). Hershey, PA: IGI Global. doi:10.4018/978-1-61520-969-9.ch009

Yermish, I., Miori, V., Yi, J., Malhotra, R., & Klimberg, R. (2010). Business plus intelligence plus technology equals business intelligence. *International Journal of Business Intelligence Research, 1*(1), 48–63. doi:10.4018/jbir.2010071704

Yeung, W. L. (2013). Specifying business-level protocols for web services based collaborative processes. In A. Loo (Ed.), *Distributed computing innovations for business, engineering, and science* (pp. 137–154). Hershey, PA: IGI Global. doi:10.4018/978-1-4666-2533-4.ch007

Z arour, M., Abran, A., & Desharnais, J. (2014). Software process improvement for small and very small enterprises. In *Software design and development: Concepts, methodologies, tools, and applications* (pp. 1363-1384). Hershey, PA: IGI Global. doi:10.4018/978-1-4666-4301-7.ch066

Zerenler, M., & Gözlü, S. (2012). Issues influencing electronic commerce activities of SMEs: A study of the Turkish automotive supplier industry. In *Human resources management: Concepts, methodologies, tools, and applications* (pp. 1035–1055). Hershey, PA: IGI Global. doi:10.4018/978-1-4666-1601-1.ch064

Compilation of References

Adhikari, A. (2009). Factors affecting employee attrition: A multiple regression approach. *IUP Journal of Management Research*, *8*(5), 38.

Agarwal, R. N., & Mehta, A. (2014). Impact of performance appraisal and working environment on the job satisfaction and attrition problem in the Indian IT industry. *Paradigm*, *18*(1), 73–85.

Ahearne, M., Mathieu, J., & Rapp, A. (2005). To empower or not to empower your sales force? An empirical examination of the influence of leadership empowerment behavior on customer satisfaction and performance. *The Journal of Applied Psychology*, *90*(5), 945–955. doi:10.1037/0021-9010.90.5.945 PMID:16162066

Akerlof, G. A., Rose, A. K., Yellen, J. L., Ball, L., & Hall, R. E. (1988). Job switching and job satisfaction in the U.S. labor market. *Brookings Papers on Economic Activity*, *0*(2), 495–582. doi:10.2307/2534536

Akgunduz, Y., & Sanli, S. C. (2017). The effect of employee advocacy and perceived organizational support on job embeddedness and turnover intention in hotels. *Journal of Hospitality and Tourism Management*, *31*, 118–125. doi:10.1016/j.jhtm.2016.12.002

Albeanu, M., Hunter, I., & Radford, J. (2012). *Six Sigma in HR Transformation*. Surrey, UK: Gower Publishing.

Albrecht, S. L., & Andreetta, M. (2011). The influence of empowering leadership, empowerment and engagement on affective commitment and turnover intentions in community health service workers: Test of a model. *Leadership in Health Services*, *24*(3), 228–237. doi:10.1108/17511871111151126

Alderfer, C. P. (1969). An empirical test of a new theory of human needs. *Organizational Behavior and Human Performance*, *4*(2), 142–175. doi:10.1016/0030-5073(69)90004-X

Allen, T. D., Eby, L. T., Poteet, M. L., Lentz, E., & Lima, L. (2004). *Career benefits associated with mentoring for protégés: A meta-analysis*. Academic Press.

Alshamaila, Y., Papagiannidis, S., & Li, F. (2013). Cloud computing adoption by SMEs in the north east of England: A multi-perspective framework. *Journal of Enterprise Information Management*, *26*(3), 250–275. doi:10.1108/17410391311325225

Al-Somali, S. A., Gholami, R., & Clegg, B. (2015). A stage-oriented model (SOM) for Ecommerce adoption: A study of Saudi Arabian organisations. *Journal of Manufacturing Technology Management, 26*(1), 2–35. doi:10.1108/JMTM-03-2013-0019

Álvarez Llorente, G. (2004). Análisis empírico de los determinantes de la satisfacción laboral en España. *Revista de Economía y Empresa, 21*(52-53), 105–118.

Amabile, T. M. (1989). *Growing up creative: Nurturing a lifetime of creativity*. Crown House Publishing Limited.

Amernic, J., Craig, R., & Tourish, D. (2007). The transformational leader as pedagogue, physician, architect, commander, and saint: Five root metaphors in Jack Welch's letters to stockholders of General Electric. *Human Relations, 60*(12), 1839–1872. doi:10.1177/0018726707084916

Anbari, F. T. (2002). Six Sigma Method and Its Applications in Project Management. In *Proceedings of the Project Management Institute Annual Seminars and Symposium*. San Antonio, TX: Project Management Institute.

Anchor, K. N. (1974). *Personality integration and successful outcome in individual psychotherapy*. Academic Press.

Anderson, C. M., & Martin, M. M. (1995). Why employees speak to coworkers and bosses: Motives, gender, and organizational satisfaction. *The Journal of Business Communication, 32*(3), 249-265.

Anderson, J. C., & Gerbing, D. W. (1988). Structural equation modeling in practice: A review and recommended two-step approach. *Psychological Bulletin, 103*(3), 411–423. doi:10.1037/0033-2909.103.3.411

Andresen, M., Domsch, M., & Cascorbi, A. (2007). Working unusual hours and its relationship to job satisfaction: A study of European maritime pilots. *Journal of Labor Research, 28*(4), 714–734. doi:10.1007/s12122-007-9010-5

Anthony, L. V. L. (1994). *The relationship between transformational and transactional leadership and organizational culture, employee performance, and employee attrition* (Doctoral dissertation). University of Miami.

Arbuckle, J. L. (2011). *AMOS 20*. Meadville, PA: SPSS.

Argyle, M. (1987). *The Psychology of Happiness*. London: Routledge.

Argyle, M., Martin, M., & Crossland, J. (1989). Happiness as a Function of Personality and Social Encounters. In J. P. Forgas & J. M. Innes (Eds.), *Recent Advances in Social Psychology: An International Perspective* (pp. 189–203). Elsevier.

Ariyabuddhiphongs, V., & Kahn, S. I. (2017). Transformational leadership and turnover intention: The mediating effects of trust and job performance on café employees in Thailand. *Journal of Human Resources in Hospitality & Tourism, 16*(2), 215–233. doi:10.1080/15332845.2016.1202730

Arnold, J. A., Arad, S., Rhoades, J. A., & Drasgow, F. (2000). The empowering leadership questionnaire: The construction and validation of a new scale for measuring leader behaviors. *Journal of Organizational Behavior*, *21*(3), 249–269. doi:10.1002/(SICI)1099-1379(200005)21:3<249::AID-JOB10>3.0.CO;2-#

Arnold, K. A., Turner, N., Barling, J., Kelloway, E. K., & McKee, M. C. (2007). Transformational leadership and psychological well-being: The mediating role of meaningful work. *Journal of Occupational Health Psychology*, *12*(3), 193–203. doi:10.1037/1076-8998.12.3.193 PMID:17638487

Aron, A., Aron, E. N., & Smollan, D. (1992). Inclusion of Other in the Self Scale and the structure of interpersonal closeness. *Journal of Personality and Social Psychology*, *63*(4), 596–612. doi:10.1037/0022-3514.63.4.596

Arora, R., & Rangnekar, S. (2015). The joint effects of personality and supervisory career mentoring in predicting occupational commitment. *Career Development International*, *20*(1), 63–80. doi:10.1108/CDI-12-2014-0156

Arpan, L. M., & Roskos-Ewoldsen, D. R. (2005). Stealing thunder: Analysis of the effects of proactive disclosure of crisis information. *Public Relations Review*, *31*(3), 425–433. doi:10.1016/j.pubrev.2005.05.003

Ashforth, B. E., & Mael, F. (1989). Social identity theory and the organization. *Academy of Management Review*, *14*(1), 20–39.

Ashmos, D. P., & Duchon, D. (2000). Spirituality at work: A conceptualization and measure. *Journal of Management Inquiry*, *9*(2), 134–145. doi:10.1177/105649260092008

ASQ. (2017, April 12). *Six Sigma Belts, Executives and Champions – What does it all mean?* Retrieved September 28, 2017, from American Society for Quality: http://asq.org/learn-about-quality/six-sigma/overview/belts-executives-champions.html

Aswathappa, K. (1999). *Human Resource and Personnel Management* (2nd ed.). New Delhi: Tata McGraw-Hill Publishing Company Limited.

Averill, J. R., & More, T. A. (2000). Happiness. In M. Lewis & J. M. Jones (Eds.), *Handbook of Emotions* (pp. 663–676). New York: The Guilford Press.

Avolio, B. J. (1999). *Full leadership development: Building the vital forces in organizations*. Thousand Oaks, CA: Sage.

Avolio, B., Zhu, W., Koh, W., & Bhatia, P. (2004). Empowering leadership and organizational commitment: Mediating role of psychological empowerment and moderating role of structural distance. *Journal of Organizational Behavior*, *25*(8), 951–968. doi:10.1002/job.283

Awa, H. O., Ukoha, O., & Emecheta, B. C. (2016). Using TOE theoretical framework to study the adoption of ERP solution. *Cogent Business and Management*, *3*(1), 1196571. doi:10.1080/23311975.2016.1196571

Bagozzi, R. P., & Yi, Y. (1988). On the Evaluation of Structural Equation Models. *Journal of the Academy of Marketing Science*, *16*(1), 74–94. doi:10.1007/BF02723327

Baker, W., & Dutton, J. E. (2007). *Enabling Positive Social Capital in Organizations*. Academic Press.

Bakker, A. B., & Oerlemans, G. M. (2012). Subjective well-being in organisations. In K. S. Cameron & G. M. Spreitzer (Eds.), The Oxford handbook of positive organisational scholarship (pp. 178–189). New York: Oxford.

Bakker, A. B., Demerouti, E., & Schaufeli, W. B. (2003). Dual processes at work in a call centre: An application of the job demands-resources model. *European Journal of Work and Organizational Psychology*, *12*(4), 393–417. doi:10.1080/13594320344000165

Bakker, A. B., Demerouti, E., & Verbeke, W. (2004). Using the job demands-resources model to predict burnout and performance. *Human Resource Management*, *43*(1), 83–104. doi:10.1002/hrm.20004

Bakker, A. B., & Oerlemans, W. G. M. (2010). Subjective well-being in organisations. In K. Cameron & G. Spreitzer (Eds.), *Handbook of Positive Organisational Scholarship* (p. 8). Oxford University Press.

Balfour, D. L., & Neff, D. M. (1993). Predicting and managing turnover in human service agencies: A case study of an organization in crisis. *The Personnel Administrator*, *22*(3), 473–486. doi:10.1177/009102609302200310

Balkan, M. O., Serin, A. E., & Soran, S. (2014). The relationship between trust, turnover intentions and emotions: An application. *European Scientific Journal*, *10*(2).

Banerjee, S., & Guha, S. (2010, January). Employee Attrition in Engineering Firms: Case Study of DCIPS Pvt. Ltd, India. *Proceedings of the 2010 International Conference on Industrial Engineering and Operations Management*, 9-10.

Barnett, R. C., & Hall, D. T. (2001). How to use Reduced Hours to win the War for Talent. *Organizational Dynamics*, *29*(3), 192–210. doi:10.1016/S0090-2616(01)00024-9

Baron, R. M., & Kenny, D. A. (1986). The moderator–mediator variable distinction in social psychological research: Conceptual, strategic, and statistical considerations. *Journal of Personality and Social Psychology*, *51*(6), 1173–1182. doi:10.1037/0022-3514.51.6.1173 PMID:3806354

Bartram, T., & Casimir, G. (2007). The relationship between leadership and follower in-role performance and satisfaction with the leader: The mediating effects of empowerment and trust in the leader. *Leadership and Organization Development Journal*, *28*(1), 4–19. doi:10.1108/01437730710718218

Baumeister, R. F., Campbell, J. D., Krueger, J. I., & Vohs, K. D. (2003). Does high self-esteem cause better performance, interpersonal success, happiness, or healthier lifestyles? *Psychological Science in the Public Interest*, *4*(1), 1–44. doi:10.1111/1529-1006.01431 PMID:26151640

Baumeister, R. F., & Leary, M. R. (1995). The need to belong: Desire for interpersonal attachments as a fundamental human motivation. *Psychological Bulletin*, *117*(3), 497–529. doi:10.1037/0033-2909.117.3.497 PMID:7777651

Bellah, R., Madsen, R., Sullivan, W., Swidler, A., & Tipton, S. (1985). *Habits of the heart: Individualism and commitment in American life*. Berkeley, CA: University of California Press.

Benassi, V. A., Sweeney, P. D., & Dufour, C. L. (1988). Is there a relation between LoC orientation and depression? *Journal of Abnormal Psychology*, *97*(3), 357–367. doi:10.1037/0021-843X.97.3.357 PMID:3057032

Bennett, N., Blum, T. C., Long, R. G., & Roman, P. M. (1993). A firm-level analysis of employee attrition. *Group & Organization Management*, *18*(4), 482–499. doi:10.1177/1059601193184006

Benton, F. W., Rosen, E. D., & Peters, J. L. (1982). *National survey of correctional institution employee attrition*. National Center for Public Productivity, John Jay College of Criminal Justice, CUNY.

Benton, A., Gelber, E., Kelley, H., & Liebling, B. (1969). Reactions to various degrees of deceit in a mixed-motive relationship. *Journal of Personality and Social Psychology*, *12*(2), 170–180. doi:10.1037/h0027570 PMID:5778349

Berman, E. M., West, J. P., & Richter, M. N. Jr. (2002). Workplace relations: Friendship patterns and consequences (according to managers). *Public Administration Review*, *62*(2), 217–230. doi:10.1111/0033-3352.00172

Bernstein, B. (2003). *Class, codes and control: Applied studies towards a sociology of language* (Vol. 2). Psychology Press.

Bhatnagar, J. (2007). Talent management strategy of employee engagement in Indian ITES employees: Key to retention. *Employee Relations*, *29*(6), 640–663. doi:10.1108/01425450710826122

Bhawuk, D. P. S. (2011). *Spirituality and Indian Psychology: Lessons from the Bhagavad-Gita*. New York: Springer. doi:10.1007/978-1-4419-8110-3

Bies, R. J., Moag, J. F., Lewicki, R. J., Sheppard, B. H., & Bazerman, M. H. (1986). *Research on negotiations in organizations*. Academic Press.

Bisht, N. S., & Singh, L. K. (2012). Understanding antecedents to attrition for employees with varying levels of experience in Indian software industry professionals. *Global Business and Management Research*, *4*(1), 99.

Blau, P. M. (1964). *Exchange and Power in Social Life*. New York: Wiley.

Bobbio, A., Bellan, M., & Manganelli, A. M. (2012). Empowering leadership, perceived organizational support, trust, and job burnout for nurses: A study in an Italian general hospital. *Health Care Management Review*, *37*(1), 77–87. doi:10.1097/HMR.0b013e31822242b2 PMID:21743337

Boehm, J. K., & Lyubomirsky, S. (2008). Does happiness promote career success? *Journal of Career Assessment, 16*(1), 101–116. doi:10.1177/1069072707308140

Bohlander, G., & Snell, S. (2005). *Managing Human Resources* (13th ed.). Mason, OH: Thomson South-Western Publishing.

Bono, J. E., & Judge, T. A. (2003). Self-concordance at work: Toward understanding the motivational effects of transformational leaders. *Academy of Management Journal, 46*(5), 554–571. doi:10.2307/30040649

Bowlby, J. (1969). *Attachment and loss* (Vol. 3). Random House.

Bowles, S., & Wright, L. (1970). Personality integration in preadolescent males. *Developmental Psychology, 2*(1), 151. doi:10.1037/h0028612

Bowling, N. A., Eschleman, K. J., & Wang, Q. (2010). A meta-analytic examination of the relationship between job satisfaction and subjective well-being. *Journal of Occupational and Organizational Psychology, 84*(4), 915–934. doi:10.1348/096317909X478557

Box, G. E. P., Hunter, J., & Hunter, S. (1978). *Statistics For Experimenters*. New York, NY: John Wiley & Sons.

Bradburn, N. (1969). *The Structure of Psychological Well-being*. Chicago: Aldine.

Braun, S., Peus, C., Weisweiler, S., & Frey, D. (2013). Transformational leadership, job satisfaction, and team performance: A multilevel mediation model of trust. *The Leadership Quarterly, 24*(1), 270–283. doi:10.1016/j.leaqua.2012.11.006

Brickman, P., & Campbell, D. T. (1971). Hedonic Relativism and Planning the Good Society. In M. H. Appley (Ed.), *Adaptation Level Theory: A Symposium.* New York: Academic Press.

Brief, A. P., & Weiss, H. M. (2002). Organisational behaviour: Affect in the workplace'. *Annual Review of Psychology, 53*(1), 279–307. doi:10.1146/annurev.psych.53.100901.135156 PMID:11752487

Brill, M., Weidemann, S., Olsen, J., & Keable, B. O. S. T. I. (2001). *The Buffalo Organization for Social & Technological Innovation.* Associates.

Brockway, J., & Njus, D. (1999). Perceptions of competence and LoC for positive and negative outcomes. *Personality and Individual Differences, 26*, 531–548. doi:10.1016/S0191-8869(98)00169-X

Brown, S., McHardy, J., McNabb, R., & Taylor, K. (2011). Workplace performance, worker commitment, and loyalty. *Journal of Economics & Management Strategy, 20*(3), 925–955. doi:10.1111/j.1530-9134.2011.00306.x

Brue, G. (2005). *Six Sigma for Managers*. New Delhi: Tata McGraw Hill Publishing Company Ltd.

Bryer, J., Peterson-Graziose, V., & Nikolaidou, M. (2015). Self-esteem and self-efficacy as predictors of attrition in RN-BS completion students: A descriptive correlational study. *Teaching and Learning in Nursing*, *10*(1), 30–34. doi:10.1016/j.teln.2014.08.004

Burchill, S. L., & Stiles, W. B. (1988). Interactions of depressed college students with their roommates: Not necessarily negative. *Journal of Personality and Social Psychology*, *55*(3), 410–419. doi:10.1037/0022-3514.55.3.410 PMID:3171913

Butler, J. K. Jr, Cantrell, R. S., & Flick, R. J. (1999). Transformation leadership behaviors, upward trust, and satisfaction in self-managed work teams. *Organization Development Journal*, *17*, 13–28.

Buunk, B. P., & Van Yperen, N. W. (1991). Referential comparisons, relational comparisons, and exchange orientation: Their relation to marital satisfaction. *Personality and Social Psychology Bulletin*, *17*(6), 709–717. doi:10.1177/0146167291176015

Cabrera, A., Collins, W. C., & Salgado, J. F. (2006). Determinants of individual engagement in knowledge sharing. *International Journal of Human Resource Management*, *17*(2), 245–264. doi:10.1080/09585190500404614

Cameron, K. S., Dutton, J., & Quinn, R. (2003). Foundations of positive organisational scholarship. In K. S. Cameron, J. E. Dutton, & R. E. Quinn (Eds.), *Positive organisational scholarship* (pp. 1–10). San Francisco, CA: Berrett-Koehler.

Campbell, J. P., Dunnette, M. D., Lawler, E. E., & Weick, K. E. (1970). *Managerial behavior, performance, and effectiveness*. New York: McGraw-Hill.

Carmeli, A., & Weisberg, J. (2006). Exploring turnover intentions among three professional groups of employees. *Human Resource Development International*, *9*(2), 191–206. doi:10.1080/13678860600616305

Carson, A. D., & Lowman, R. L. (2002). Individual-level variables in organisational consultation. In R. L. Lowman (Ed.), *Handbook of organisational consulting psychology*. San Francisco, CA: Jossey-Bass.

Carson, J. B., Tesluk, P. E., & Marrone, J. A. (2007). Shared leadership in teams: An investigation of antecedent conditions and performance. *Academy of Management Journal*, *50*(5), 1217–1234. doi:10.2307/20159921

Carter, D., & Baghurst, T. (2014). The influence of servant leadership on restaurant employee engagement. *Journal of Business Ethics*, *124*(3), 453–464. doi:10.1007/s10551-013-1882-0

Castro, M. G. A., Padilla, J. M. C., & Ramírez, S. M. (2009). Grado de satisfacción laboral y condiciones de trabajo: Una exploración cualitativa. *Enseñanza e Investigación en Psicología*, *14*(1), 105–118.

Chakrabarti, D. (2009). Well-being of the elderly residing in old age home vs. those in family setting in Tripura. *Nursing Journal of India*, *C*(10). Retrieved from http://www.tnaionline.org/oct-09/4.htm PMID:20358676

Chamikutty, P. (2013). *Problems facing the Indian artifacts sector*. Retrieved February 2, 2017. From https://social.yourstory.com/2013/06/crafting-a-livelihood-a-snapshot-of-the-indian-artifacts-sector-2/

Chao, G. T., Walz, P., & Gardner, P. D. (1992). Formal and informal mentorships: A comparison on mentoring functions and contrast with nonmentored counterparts. *Personnel Psychology, 45*(3), 619–636. doi:10.1111/j.1744-6570.1992.tb00863.x

Charmaz, K. (1991). *Good days, bad days: The self in chronic illness and time*. Rutgers University Press.

Chatman, J. A. (1989, August). Matching people and organizations: Selection and socialization in public accounting firms. In Academy of Management proceedings (Vol. 1989, No. 1, pp. 199-203). Academy of Management.

Chattopadhyay, P., George, E., & Shulman, A. D. (2008). The asymmetrical influence of sex dissimilarity in distributive vs. colocated work groups. *Organization Science, 19*(4), 581–593. doi:10.1287/orsc.1070.0324

Chattopadhyay, P., Tluchowska, M., & George, E. (2004). Identifying the ingroup: A closer look at the influence of demographic dissimilarity on employee social identity. *Academy of Management Review, 29*(2), 180–202.

Cheng, J. H. (2011). Inter-organizational relationships and knowledge sharing in green supply chains—Moderating by relational benefits and guanxi. *Transportation Research Part E, Logistics and Transportation Review, 47*(6), 837–849. doi:10.1016/j.tre.2010.12.008

Cherniss, C. (1991). Career commitment in human service professionals: A biographical study. *Human Relations, 44*(5), 419–437. doi:10.1177/001872679104400501

Cheung, C. (2000). Commitment to the organization in exchange for support from the organization. *Social Behavior and Personality, 28*(2), 125–140. doi:10.2224/sbp.2000.28.2.125

Chew, J. (2004). *The impact of HRM practices on retention of core employees of Australian Organizations: An Empirical Study*. Greenhaus.

Chiang, M. M., & Ojeda, J. F. (2013). Estudio de la relación entre satisfacción laboral y el desempeño de los trabajadores de las ferias libres. *Contaduría y Administración, 58*(2), 39–60.

Chien, M.H. (n.d.). *A study to improve Organisational citizenship behaviours*. Academic Press.

Chiu, Y. J., Chen, H. C., Tzeng, G. H., & Shyu, J. Z. (2006). Marketing strategy based on customer behaviour for the LCD-TV. *International Journal of Management and Decision Making, 7*(2-3), 143-165.

Cho, J. (2007). *Psychological processes underlying the relationship between transformational leadership and multi-foci organizational citizenship behaviors: a multi-level approach* (PhD dissertation). The State University of New York, Buffalo, NY.

Choi, I. S., Son, Y. E., & Shin, K. A. (2015). *Statistical Yearbook of Social Worker*. Seoul: Korea Association of Social Worker.

Cho, Y. J., & Ringquist, E. J. (2011). Managerial trustworthiness and organizational outcomes. *Journal of Public Administration: Research and Theory*, *21*(1), 53–86. doi:10.1093/jopart/muq015

Christopher, A. N., Saliba, L., & Deadmarsh, E. J. (2009). Materialism and well-being: The mediating effect of LoC. *Personality and Individual Differences*, *46*(7), 682–686. doi:10.1016/j.paid.2009.01.003

Clark, A. E., Layard, R., & Senik, C. (2012). The causes of happiness and misery. *UN World Happiness Report*, 59-89.

Clark, E. R., & Dubovec, J. (1994). *U.S. Patent No. 5,296,805*. Washington, DC: U.S. Patent and Trademark Office.

Clarke, D. (2004). Neuroticism: Moderator or mediator in the relation between LoC and depression? *Personality and Individual Differences*, *37*(2), 245–258. doi:10.1016/j.paid.2003.08.015

Clegg, C. V. (1983). Psychology of employee lateness, absence and turnover: A methodological critical and an empirical study. *The Journal of Applied Psychology*, *68*(1), 88–101. doi:10.1037/0021-9010.68.1.88

Coelho, P. S., & Henseler, J. (2012). Creating customer loyalty through service customization. *European Journal of Marketing*, *46*(3/4), 331–356. doi:10.1108/03090561211202503

Coetzee, M., & Bergh, Z. (2009). Psychological career resources and subjective work experiences of working adults: An exploratory study. *Southern African Business Review*, *13*(2), 1–31.

Coetzer, C. F., & Rothmann, S. (2007). Job demands, job resources, and work engagement of employees in a manufacturing organisation. *Southern African Business Review*, *11*(3), 17–32.

Cohen, S., & Wills, T. A. (1985). Stress, social support, and the buffering hypothesis. *Psychological Bulletin*, *98*(2), 310–357. doi:10.1037/0033-2909.98.2.310 PMID:3901065

Colbert, B. A. (2004). The complex resource-based view: Implications for theory and practice in strategic human resource management. *Academy of Management Review*, *29*(3), 341–358.

Collins, N. L., & Miller, L. C. (1994). Self-disclosure and liking: A meta-analytic review. *Psychological Bulletin*, *116*(3), 457–475. doi:10.1037/0033-2909.116.3.457 PMID:7809308

Cooley, R. S., & Seeman, J. (1979). Personality integration and social schemata. *Journal of Personality*, *47*(2), 288–304. doi:10.1111/j.1467-6494.1979.tb00203.x

Cornelis, I., Van Hiel, A., & De Cremer, D. (2006). Effects of procedural fairness and leader support on interpersonal relationships among group members. *Group Dynamics*, *10*(4), 309–328. doi:10.1037/1089-2699.10.4.309

Cortese, C. G., Gatti, P., & Ghislieri, C. (2013). Job demands, meaningful work, and turnover intention among nurses. *La Medicina del Lavoro*, *105*(1), 37–47. PMID:24552093

Cotton, J. L., & Tuttle, J. M. (1986). Employee turnover: A meta-analysis and review with implications for research. *Academy of Management Review*, *11*(1), 55–70.

Cozby, P. C. (1972). Self-disclosure, reciprocity and liking. *Sociometry*, *35*(1), 151–160. doi:10.2307/2786555 PMID:5011335

Cropanzano, R., & Mitchell, M. S. (2005). Social exchange theory: An interdisciplinary review. *Journal of Management*, *31*(6), 874–900. doi:10.1177/0149206305279602

Csikszentmihalyi, M. (1990). *Flow: The Psychology of Optimal Experience*. New York: Harper and Row.

Dalai Lama, H. H. (1998). The Art of Happiness. London: Coronet Books.

Dalal, A. K., & Misra, G. (2006). Psychology of health and well-Being: Some emerging perspectives. *Psychological Studies*, *2*(2-3).

Dalal, A. K., & Misra, G. (2011). Advances in psychology of health and well-being. In G. Misra (Ed.), *Handbook of Psychology in India*. New Delhi: Oxford University Press.

Dalton, D. R., Todor, W. D., & Krackhardt, D. M. (1982). Turnover overstated: The functional taxonomy. *Academy of Management Review*, *7*(1), 117–123.

Dave, R., Tripathi, K. N., Singh, P., & Udainiya, R. (2011). Subjective well-being, locus of control and general self-efficacy among university students. *Amity Journal of Applied Psychology*, *2*(1), 151–155.

De Cooman, R., De Gieter, S., Pepermans, R., Hermans, S., Du Bois, C., Caers, R., & Jegers, M. (2009). Person–organization fit: Testing socialization and attraction–selection–attrition hypotheses. *Journal of Vocational Behavior*, *74*(1), 102–107. doi:10.1016/j.jvb.2008.10.010

De Vos, A., & Meganck, A. (2008). What HR managers do versus what employees value: Exploring both parties' views on retention management from a psychological contract perspective. *Personnel Review*, *38*(1), 45–60. doi:10.1108/00483480910920705

DeConinck, J. B. (2011). The effects of ethical climate on organizational identification, supervisory trust, and turnover among salespeople. *Journal of Business Research*, *64*(6), 617–624. doi:10.1016/j.jbusres.2010.06.014

DeFeo, J. A. (2000, Summer). Six Sigma: New Opportunities for HR, New Career Growth for Employees. *Employment Relations Today*, *27*(Summer), 1–6. doi:10.1002/ert.3910270202

DeNeve, K. M., & Cooper, H. (1998). The happy personality: A meta-analysis of 137 personality traits and subjective well-being. *Psychological Bulletin*, *124*(2), 197–229. doi:10.1037/0033-2909.124.2.197 PMID:9747186

Deutsch, F. M., & Yao, B. (2014). Gender differences in faculty attrition in the USA. *Community Work & Family*, *17*(4), 392–408. doi:10.1080/13668803.2014.885880

Devarajan, R. (2011, April 12). *Emerging trends in HR management, Chennai.* Retrieved 12 12, 2012, from The Hindu: http://www.thehindu.com/books/emerging-trends-in-hr-management/article1691138.ece

Development Dimensions International. (1999, August). Good HR practice going unrecognised at the top. *Works Management, 52*(8), 9.

Dewettinck, K., & Van Ameijde, M. (2011). Linking leadership empowerment behavior to employee attitudes and behavioral intentions: Testing the mediating role of psychological empowerment. *Personnel Review, 40*(3), 284–305. doi:10.1108/00483481111118621

Diener, E., Lucas, R. E., & Oishi, S. (2005). The science of happiness and life satisfaction. In C. R. Snyder & S. J. Lopez (Eds.), Handbook of positive psychology (pp. 63–73). New York: Oxford.

Diener, E. (1984). Subjective Well Being. *Psychological Bulletin, 95*(3), 542–575. doi:10.1037/0033-2909.95.3.542 PMID:6399758

Diener, E. (2000). Subjective well-being: The science of happiness and a proposal for a national index. *The American Psychologist, 55*(1), 34–43. doi:10.1037/0003-066X.55.1.34 PMID:11392863

Diener, E. D., Sandvik, E. D., & Pavot, W. (1999). Happiness is the frequency not the intensity of positive versus negative affect. *Psychological Science*, 119–139.

Diener, E., Kesebir, P., & Lucas, R. (2008). Benefits of accounts of well-being - For societies and for psychological science. *Applied Psychology: An International Journal, 57*(s1), 37–53. doi:10.1111/j.1464-0597.2008.00353.x

Diener, E., Lucas, R. E., & Scollon, C. N. (2006). Beyond hedonic adaptation: Revising the adaptation theory of well-being. *The American Psychologist, 61*(4), 305–314. doi:10.1037/0003-066X.61.4.305 PMID:16719675

Diener, E., Lucas, R., & Oishi, S. (2002). Subjective well-being: The science of happiness and life satisfaction. In C. R. Snyder & S. J. Lopez (Eds.), *The Handbook of Positive Psychology* (pp. 63–73). New York: Oxford University Press.

Diener, E., Nickerson, C., Lucas, R. E., & Sandvik, E. (2002). Dispositional affect and job outcomes. *Social Indicators Research, 59*(3), 229–259. doi:10.1023/A:1019672513984

Diener, E., & Suh, E. (1997). Measuring quality of life: Economic, social and subjective indicators. *Social Indicators Research, 40*(1/2), 189–216. doi:10.1023/A:1006859511756

Diener, E., Suh, E. M., Lucas, R. E., & Smith, H. L. (1999). Subjective well-being: Three decades of progress. *Psychological Bulletin, 125*(2), 276–302. doi:10.1037/0033-2909.125.2.276

Dirks, K. T., & Ferrin, D. L. (2001). The role of trust in organizational settings. *Organization Science, 12*(4), 450–467. doi:10.1287/orsc.12.4.450.10640

Dirks, K., & Ferrin, D. (2002). Trust in leadership: Metaanalytic findings and implications for research and practice. *The Journal of Applied Psychology*, *87*(4), 611–628. doi:10.1037/0021-9010.87.4.611 PMID:12184567

Doyne, S. E. (1969). *Effects of a sensitivity training laboratory experience on self-disclosure, self-esteem, and social desirability* (Doctoral dissertation). George Peabody College for Teachers.

Duncan, C. B. (1966). A reputation test of personality integrations. *Journal of Personality and Social Psychology*, *3*(5), 516–524. doi:10.1037/h0023297 PMID:5939600

Dutton, J. E., & Heaphy, E. D. (2003). The power of high-quality connections. *Positive Organizational Scholarship: Foundations of a New Discipline, 3*, 263-278.

Dutton, J. E., & Glynn, M. A. (2008). The SAGE handbook of organizational behavior: Vol. 1. *Positive organizational scholarship*. SAGE.

Dyer, J. H., & Chu, W. (2003). The role of trustworthiness in reducing transaction costs and improving performance: Empirical evidence from the United States, Japan, and Korea. *Organization Science*, *14*(1), 57–68. doi:10.1287/orsc.14.1.57.12806

Eby, L. T., Freeman, D. M., Rush, M. C., & Lance, C. E. (1999). Motivational bases of affective commitment: A partial test of an integrative theoretical model. *Journal of Occupational and Organizational Psychology*, *72*(4), 463–483. doi:10.1348/096317999166798

Eden, D., & Aviram, A. (1993). Self-efficacy training to speed reemployment: Helping people to help themselves. *The Journal of Applied Psychology*, *78*(3), 352–360. doi:10.1037/0021-9010.78.3.352

Edwards, M. R., & Peccei, R. (2007). Organizational identification: Development and testing of a conceptually grounded measure. *European Journal of Work and Organizational Psychology*, *16*(1), 25–57. doi:10.1080/13594320601088195

Eisenbeiss, S. A., van Knippenberg, D., & Boerner, S. (2008). Transformational leadership and team innovation: Integrating team climate principles. *The Journal of Applied Psychology*, *93*(6), 1438–1446. doi:10.1037/a0012716 PMID:19025260

Eisenberger, R., Armeli, S., Rexwinkel, B., Lynch, P. D., & Rhoades, L. (2001). Reciprocation of perceived organizational support. *The Journal of Applied Psychology*, *86*(1), 42–51. doi:10.1037/0021-9010.86.1.42 PMID:11302232

Eisenberger, R., Fasolo, P., & Davis-LaMastro, V. (1990). Perceived organizational support and employee diligence, commitment, and innovation. *The Journal of Applied Psychology*, *75*(1), 51–59. doi:10.1037/0021-9010.75.1.51

Elger, C., & Smith, T. (1999). Good enough production' and the shaping of worker cooperation, compliance and non-compliance in Japanese transplants. In *International Labour Process Conference*. Royal Holloway University of London.

Ellett, A. J., Ellis, J. I., Westbrook, T. M., & Dews, D. (2007). A qualitative study of 369 child welfare professionals' perspectives about factors contributing to employee retention and turnover. *Children and Youth Services Review*, *29*(2), 264–281. doi:10.1016/j.childyouth.2006.07.005

Ellingwood, S. (2002). *The collective advantage*. Academic Press.

Elliott, K. M. (2001). Key factors influencing student satisfaction related to recruitment and retention. *Journal of Marketing for Higher Education*, 10.

Employee attrition and retention. (n.d.). *Shodhganga*. Retrieved from http://shodhganga.inflibnet.ac.in/bitstream/10603/15957/10/10_chapter%202.pdf

Erikson, E. H. (1959). Identity and the life cycle: Selected papers. *Psychological Issues*.

Ertürk, A. (2014). Influences of HR practices, social exchange, and trust on turnover intentions of public IT professionals. *Public Personnel Management*, *43*(1), 140–175. doi:10.1177/0091026013517875

Estrada, L., Dupoux, E., & Wolman, C. (2006). The relationship between LoC and personal-emotional adjustment and social adjustment to college life in students with and without learning disabilities. *College Student Journal*, *40*(1), 43–54.

Fairbrother, K., & Warn, J. (2003). Workplace dimensions, stress and job satisfaction. *Journal of Managerial Psychology*, *18*(1), 8–21. doi:10.1108/02683940310459565

Falk, D. R., & Wagner, P. N. (1985). Intimacy of self-disclosure and response processes as factors affecting the development of interpersonal relationships. *The Journal of Social Psychology*, *125*(5), 557–570. doi:10.1080/00224545.1985.9712029

Feeley, T. H., Hwang, J., & Barnett, G. A. (2008). Predicting employee turnover from friendship networks. *Journal of Applied Communication Research*, *36*(1), 56–73. doi:10.1080/00909880701799790

Feldman, D. C., & Arnold, H. J. (1995). Personality types and career patterns: Some empirical evidence on Holland's Model. *Canadian Journal of Administrative Sciences*, *35*(2), 192–210.

Ferreira, N. (2012). Hardiness in relation to organisational commitment in the human resource management field. *Journal of Human Resource Management*, *10*(2), 418–428.

Festinger, L. (1954). A theory of social comparison processes. *Human Relations*, *7*(2), 117–140. doi:10.1177/001872675400700202

Field, L., & Buitendach, J. H. (2011). Happiness, work engagement and organisational commitment of support staff at a tertiary education institution in South Africa. *SA Journal of Industrial Psychology*, *37*(1), 1–10. doi:10.4102/sajip.v37i1.946

Financial Express. (2016). Retrieved February 2, 2017. From http://www.financialexpress.com/industry/companies/Ecommerce-in-india-why-ishippo-com-is-eyeing-space-shunned-by-amazon-flipkart-snapdeal/290251/

Fisher, C. D. (2003). Why do lay people believe that satisfaction and performance are correlated? Possible sources of common sense theory. *Journal of Organizational Behavior*, *24*(6), 753–777. doi:10.1002/job.219

Fisher, C. D. (2010). Happiness at work. *International Journal of Management Reviews*, *12*(4), 384–412. doi:10.1111/j.1468-2370.2009.00270.x

Fleming, J. H., Coffman, C., & Harter, J. K. (2005, July - August). Manage your Human Sigma. *Harvard Business Review*, 106–114. PMID:16028821

Flynn, F. J. (2005). Identity orientations and forms of social exchange in organizations. *Academy of Management Review*, *30*(4), 737–750. doi:10.5465/AMR.2005.18378875

Folger, R., & Konovsky, M. A. (1989). Effects of procedural and distributive justice on reactions to pay raise decisions. *Academy of Management Journal*, *32*(1), 115–130. doi:10.2307/256422

Forgas, J. P. (2011). Affective influences on self-disclosure: Mood effects on the intimacy and reciprocity of disclosing personal information. *Journal of Personality and Social Psychology*, *100*(3), 449–461. doi:10.1037/a0021129 PMID:21171788

Fosam, E. G., Grimsley, M. F. J., & Wisher, S. J. (1998). Exploring models for employee satisfaction with particular reference to a police force. *Total Quality Management*, *9*(2/3), 235–247. doi:10.1080/0954412989090

Fredrickson, B. L. (1998). What good are positive emotions? *Review of General Psychology*, *2*(3), 300–319. doi:10.1037/1089-2680.2.3.300 PMID:21850154

Fredrickson, B. L. (2001). The role of positive emotions in positive psychology: The broaden-and build theory of positive emotions. *The American Psychologist*, *56*(3), 218–226. doi:10.1037/0003-066X.56.3.218 PMID:11315248

Fredrickson, B. L. (2003). Positive emotions and upward spirals in organisational settings. In K. Cameron, J. Dutton, & R. Quinn (Eds.), *Positive Organisational Scholarship*. San Francisco: Berrettkoehler.

Fredrickson, B. L., & Brangian, C. (2005). Positive emotions broaden the scope of attention and thought action repertories. *Cognition and Emotion*, *79*(3), 313–332. doi:10.1080/02699930441000238 PMID:21852891

Furman, W., & Buhrmester, D. (2009). Methods and measures: The network of relationships inventory: Behavioral systems version. *International Journal of Behavioral Development*, *33*, 470–478.

Galinha, I. C., & Pais-Ribeiro, J. L. (2011). Cognitive, affective and contextual predictors of subjective wellbeing. *International Journal of Wellbeing*, *2*(1), 34–53. doi:10.5502/ijw.v2i1.3

Gamero, C. (2003). La satisfacción laboral como variable económica. In C. Gamero (Ed.), *PhD thesis: Análisis económico de la satisfacción laboral* (pp. 7–70). Málaga: Retrieved from http://www.eumed.net/tesis-doctorales/cgb/c1.pdf

Gangwar, H., Date, H., & Ramaswamy, R. (2015). Understanding determinants of cloud computing adoption using an integrated TAM-TOE model. *Journal of Enterprise Information Management, 28*(1), 107–130. doi:10.1108/JEIM-08-2013-0065

Garvin, D. A. (1988). *Managing quality: The strategic and competitive edge*. Simon and Schuster.

Gavin, J. H., & Mason, R. O. (2004). The Virtuous Organisation: The Value of Happiness in the Workplace. *Organizational Dynamics, 33*(4), 379–392. doi:10.1016/j.orgdyn.2004.09.005

George, J. M., & Bettenhausen, K. (1990). Understanding prosocial behavior, sales performance, and turnover: A group-level analysis in a service context. *The Journal of Applied Psychology, 75*(6), 698–709. doi:10.1037/0021-9010.75.6.698

Gibbs, J. L., & Kraemer, K. L. (2004). A cross-country investigation of the determinants of scope of e-commerce use: An institutional approach. *Electronic Markets, 14*(2), 124–137. doi:10.1080/10196780410001675077

Gilstrap, J. B., & Collins, B. J. (2012). The importance of being trustworthy: Trust as a mediator of the relationship between leader behaviors and employee job satisfaction. *Journal of Leadership & Organizational Studies, 19*(2), 152–163. doi:10.1177/1548051811431827

Giyar, M. R. (2011). A-*Study of Ecommerce Related Practices in Selected Small Scale Wooden Handicraft Enterprises*. Available at SSRN 1948146.

Gofton, K. (1999). Call-centers widen their field of vision. *Marketing, 22*, 20–32.

Goodwin, V. L., Whittington, J. L., Murray, B., & Nichols, T. (2011). Moderator or mediator? examining the role of trust in the transformational leadership paradigm. *Journal of Managerial Issues*, 409–425.

Graham, C., Eggers, A., & Sukhtankar, S. (2004). Does happiness pay? An exploration bases on panel data from Russia. *Journal of Economic Behavior & Organization, 55*, 319–342.

Green, P. E., & Krieger, A. M. (1991). Segmenting markets with conjoint analysis; IN. *Journal of Marketing, 55*(4), 20–31. doi:10.2307/1251954

Greiner, L. (2002). Steve Kerr and His Years with Jack Welch at GE. *Journal of Management Inquiry, 11*(4), 343–350. doi:10.1177/1056492602238840

Griffeth, R. W., Hom, P. W., & Gaertner, S. (2000). A meta-analysis of antecedents and correlates of employee turnover: Update, moderator tests, and research implications for the next millennium. *Journal of Management, 26*(3), 463–488. doi:10.1177/014920630002600305

Griffiths, J. (2005). Global consensus on top HR issues. *People Management, 11*(16), 10.

Grover, S. L., & Crooker, K. J. (1995). Who appreciates family-responsive human resource policies: The impact of family-friendly policies on the organizational attachment of parents and non-parents. *Personnel Psychology, 48*(2), 271–288. doi:10.1111/j.1744-6570.1995.tb01757.x

Guide Review of managing people. (n.d.). Available in: http://www.centrosdeexcelencia.com/dotnetnuke/Portals/0/Guia_cex_personas_def.pdf

Gupta, S. S. (2011). *Employee Attrition and Retention: Exploring the Dimensions in the urban centric BPO Industry* (Doctoral dissertation). Jaypee Institute of Information Technology, Noida, India.

Gupta, P. (2005). *Six Sigma in Human Resources.* Quality Digest.

Gupta, S. D., & Kumar, D. (2010). Psychological correlates of happiness. *Indian Journal of Social Science Researches*, *7*(1), 60–64.

Guthrie, J. P. (2001). High-involvement work practices, turnover, and productivity: Evidence from New Zealand. *Academy of Management Journal*, *44*(1), 180–190. doi:10.2307/3069345

Hackman, J. R., & Oldham, G. R. (1975). Development of the job diagnostic survey. *The Journal of Applied Psychology*, *60*(2), 159–170. doi:10.1037/h0076546

Hair, J. F., Anderson, R. E., Babin, B. J., & Black, W. C. (2010). *Multivariate data analysis: A global perspective* (Vol. 7). Upper Saddle River, NJ: Pearson.

Hair, J. F., Black, W. C., Babin, B. J., & Anderson, R. E. (2010). *Multivariate Data Analysis: A Global Perspective.* Pearson Education International.

Hair, J., Anderson, R., Tathaman, R., & Black, W. (1999). *Análisis Multivariante. 5ª edición.* Madrid: Prentice Hall.

Hakanen, J. J., Schaufeli, W. B., & Ahola, K. (2008). The job demands-resources model: A three-year cross-lagged study of burnout, depression, commitment, and work engagement. *Work and Stress*, *22*(3), 224–241. doi:10.1080/02678370802379432

Hall, D. T., & Moss, J. E. (1998). The new protean career contract: Helping organizations and employees adapt. *Organizational Dynamics*, *26*(3), 22–37. doi:10.1016/S0090-2616(98)90012-2

Halvorsen, A. (2005). Incorporating critical thinking skills development into/EFL courses. *The 76 Internet TESL Journal, 12*(3). Retrieved from http://iteslj.org/

Hamid, P. N. (1994). Self-monitoring, LoC, and social encounters of Chinese and New Zealand students. *Journal of Cross-Cultural Psychology*, *25*(3), 353–368. doi:10.1177/0022022194253004

Hammer, A. L., & Schnell, E. R. (2000). *FIRO-B® Technical Guide.* Mountain View, CA: CPP, Inc.

Han, S. J., Bonn, M. A., & Cho, M. (2016). The relationship between customer incivility, restaurant frontline service employee burnout and turnover intention. *International Journal of Hospitality Management*, *52*, 97–106. doi:10.1016/j.ijhm.2015.10.002

Haring, R., Alte, D., Völzke, H., Sauer, S., Wallaschofski, H., John, U., & Schmidt, C. O. (2009). Extended recruitment efforts minimize attrition but not necessarily bias. *Journal of Clinical Epidemiology*, *62*(3), 252–260. doi:10.1016/j.jclinepi.2008.06.010 PMID:18834716

Harpaz, I. (1983). *Job satisfaction: theoretical perspectives and longitudinal analysis*. Libra.

Harrison, B., Kelley, M. R., & Gant, J. (1996). Innovative firm behavior and local milieu: Exploring the intersection of agglomeration, firm effects, and technological change. *Economic Geography*, *72*(3), 233–258. doi:10.2307/144400

Harris, S. M., Dersch, C. A., & Mittal, M. (1999). Look who's talking: Measuring self-disclosure in MFT. *Contemporary Family Therapy*, *21*(3), 405–415. doi:10.1023/A:1021968517320

Harter, J. K., Schmidt, F. L., & Hayes, T. L. (2002). Business-unit-level relationship between employee satisfaction, employee engagement and business outcomes: A meta-analysis. *The Journal of Applied Psychology*, *87*(2), 268–279. doi:10.1037/0021-9010.87.2.268 PMID:12002955

Hartline, M. D., & Ferrell, O. C. (1996). The management of customer–contact service employees: An empirical investigation. *Journal of Marketing*, *60*(4), 52–70. doi:10.2307/1251901

Haskins, W. A. (1996). Freedom of speech: construct for creating a culture which empowers organizational members. *The Journal of Business Communication, 33*(1), 85-97.

Hassan, A., & Ahmed, F. (2011). Authentic leadership, trust and work engagement. *International Journal of Humanities and Social Science*, *6*(3), 164–170.

Hayes, A. F. (2013). *Introduction to mediation, moderation, and conditional process analysis: A regression-based approach*. Guilford Press.

Heaphy, E. D., & Dutton, J. E. (2008). Positive social interactions and the human body at work: Linking organizations and physiology. *Academy of Management Review*, *33*(1), 137–162. doi:10.5465/AMR.2008.27749365

Hearn, C. B., Jr. (1968). *Personality integration and person perception in college males* (Doctoral dissertation). ProQuest Information & Learning.

Herzberg, F., & Mausner, B. S. (1978). BB 1959. The Motivation to work. New York: Academic Press.

Herzberg, F., Mausner, B., & Snyderman, B. B. (1959). *The Motivation to Work* (2nd ed.). New York, NY: Wiley.

Heskett, J. L., Jones, T. O., Loveman, G. W., Sasser, W. E. Jr, & Schlesinger, L. (1994). Putting the service–profit chain to work. *Harvard Business Review*, *72*(2), 164–174.

Heuring, L. (2004, March). Six Sigma in Sight. *HR Magazine*, 76-80.

Hills, P., & Argyle, M. (2002). The Oxford happiness questionnaire: A compact scale for the measurement of psychological well-being. *Personality and Individual Differences*, *33*(7), 1073–1082. doi:10.1016/S0191-8869(01)00213-6

Hofstede, G. (1984). Cultural dimensions in management and planning. *Asia Pacific Journal of Management*, *1*(2), 81–99. doi:10.1007/BF01733682

Ho, J. S. Y., Downe, A. G., & Loke, S. P. (2010). Employee attrition in the Malaysian service industry: Push and pull factors. *The IUP Journal of Organizational Behavior*, *9*(1), 16–31.

Holtbrügge, D., Friedmann, C. B., & Puck, J. F. (2010). Recruitment and retention in foreign firms in India: A resource-based view. *Human Resource Management*, *49*(3), 439–455. doi:10.1002/hrm.20353

Holtom, B. C., Mitchell, T. R., Lee, T. W., & Eberly, M. B. (2008). 5 Turnover and Retention Research: A Glance at the Past, a Closer Review of the Present, and a Venture into the Future. *The Academy of Management Annals*, *2*(1), 231–274. doi:10.1080/19416520802211552

Horner, K. L. (1996). LoC, neuroticism, and stressors: Combined influences on reported physical illness. *Personality and Individual Differences*, *21*(2), 195–204. doi:10.1016/0191-8869(96)00067-0

Hsieh, P. C., & Su, H. F. (2007). Retention and attrition of certified care assistants in the long-term care industry from the Taipei area: An interview survey. *International Journal of Nursing Studies*, *44*(1), 93–104. doi:10.1016/j.ijnurstu.2005.11.024 PMID:16413554

Hsu, M. K., Jiang, J. J., Klein, G., & Tang, Z. (2003). Perceived career incentives and intent to leave. *Information & Management*, *40*(5), 361–369. doi:10.1016/S0378-7206(02)00018-6

Hsu, M. L., & Fan, H. L. (2010). Organizational innovation climate and creative outcomes: Exploring the moderating effect of time pressure. *Creativity Research Journal*, *22*(4), 378–386. doi:10.1080/10400419.2010.523400

Huang, Y. H., Lee, J., McFadden, A. C., Murphy, L. A., Robertson, M. M., Cheung, J. H., & Zohar, D. (2016). Beyond safety outcomes: An investigation of the impact of safety climate on job satisfaction, employee engagement and turnover using social exchange theory as the theoretical framework. *Applied Ergonomics*, *55*, 248–257. doi:10.1016/j.apergo.2015.10.007 PMID:26611987

Hunt, D. M., & Michael, C. (1983). Mentorship: A career training and development tool. *Academy of Management Review*, *8*(3), 475–485.

Huta, V., & Ryan, R. M. (2010). Pursuing pleasure or virtue: The differential and overlapping well-being benefits of hedonic and eudaimonic motives. *Journal of Happiness Studies*, *11*(6), 735–762. doi:10.1007/s10902-009-9171-4

Iacovou, C. L., Benbasat, I., & Dexter, A. S. (1995). Electronic data interchange and small organizations: Adoption and impact of technology. *Management Information Systems Quarterly*, *19*(4), 465–485. doi:10.2307/249629

Ignatius, E., & Kokkonen, M. (2007). Factors contributing to verbal self-disclosure. *Nordic Psychology*, *59*(4), 362–391. doi:10.1027/1901-2276.59.4.362

Ingersoll, R. M. (2002). The teacher shortage: A case of wrong diagnosis and wrong prescription. *NASSP Bulletin*, *86*(631), 16–31. doi:10.1177/019263650208663103

Ironson, G. H., Smith, P. C., Brannick, M. T., Gibson, W. M., & Paul, K. B. (1989). Construction of a Job in General scale: A comparison of global, composite, and specific measures. *The Journal of Applied Psychology, 74*(2), 193–200. doi:10.1037/0021-9010.74.2.193

Ivancevich, J. M., & Glueck, W. G. (1989). *Foundations of Personnel/Human Resource Management*. Business Publications.

Ivanov, M. (2010). Communication via a strategic mediator. *Journal of Economic Theory, 145*(2), 869–884. doi:10.1016/j.jet.2009.08.001

J.H. & Callanan, G.A. (1994). Career Management. The Dryden Press.

Jahoda, M. (1958). *Current conceptions of positive mental health*. New York: Basic Books. doi:10.1037/11258-000

Jahoda, M. (1982). *Employment and unemployment: A social-psychological analysis* (Vol. 1). CUP Archive.

Jain, M. (2013). Employee attrition-causes and remedies. *Journal of Social Welfare and Management, 5*(2), 69–74.

Jaiswal, N. K., & Dhar, R. L. (2015). Transformational leadership, innovation climate, creative self-efficacy and employee creativity: A multilevel study. *International Journal of Hospitality Management, 51*, 30–41. doi:10.1016/j.ijhm.2015.07.002

James, M. J., & Faisal, U. (2013). *Empirical study on addressing high employee attrition in BPO industry focusing on employee salary and other factors in Karnataka and Kerala states of India*. Research Journal of Management Sciences.

Jessica Sze-Yin Ho, A. G.-P. (2010). *Employee Attrition in the Malaysian Service Industry: Push and Pull Factors*. IUP Journal of Organizational Behavior.

Jha, P. K., & Kumari, U. (2009). Happiness as a function of marital status, locale and caste groups. *Behavioural Scientist, 10*(2), 91–95.

Johns, G., Xie, J. L., & Fang, Y. (1992). Mediating and moderating effects in job design. *Journal of Management, 18*(4), 657–676. doi:10.1177/014920639201800404

Johnson, S. J., Batey, M., & Holdsworth, L. (2009). Personality and health: The mediating role of trait emotional intelligence and work LoC. *Personality and Individual Differences, 47*(5), 470–475. doi:10.1016/j.paid.2009.04.025

Jourard, S. M. (1971). *Self-disclosure: An experimental analysis of the transparent self*. Academic Press.

Judge, T. A., & Bono, J. E. (2001). Relationship of core self-evaluations traits—self-esteem, generalized self-efficacy, LoC, and emotional stability—with job satisfaction and job performance: A meta-analysis. *The Journal of Applied Psychology, 86*(1), 80–92. doi:10.1037/0021-9010.86.1.80 PMID:11302235

Judge, T. A., & Zapata, C. P. (2015). The person-situation debate revisited: Effect of situation strength and trait activation on the validity of the Big Five personality traits in predicting job performance. *Academy of Management Journal*, *58*(4), 1149–1179. doi:10.5465/amj.2010.0837

Jung, D., & Avolio, B. (2000). Opening the black box: An experimental investigation of the mediating effects of trust and value congruence on empowering and transactional leadership. *Journal of Organizational Behavior*, *21*(8), 949–964. doi:10.1002/1099-1379(200012)21:8<949::AID-JOB64>3.0.CO;2-F

Kahn, R. L., & Juster, T. F. (2002). Well-being: Concepts and measures. *The Journal of Social Issues*, *58*(4), 627–644. doi:10.1111/1540-4560.00281

Kahn, W. A. (1990). Psychological conditions of personal engagement and disengagement at work. *Academy of Management Journal*, *33*(4), 692–724. doi:10.2307/256287

Kahn, W. A. (1992). ‗To be fully there: Psychological presence at work'. *Human Relations*, *45*(4), 321–349. doi:10.1177/001872679204500402

Kampa-Kokesch, S. (2001). *Executive coaching as an individually tailored consultation intervention: Does it increase leadership?* (Unpublished doctoral dissertation). Western Michigan University.

Karatepe, O. M. (2011). Procedural justice, work engagement, and job outcomes: Evidence from Nigeria. *Journal of Hospitality Marketing & Management*, *20*(8), 855–878. doi:10.1080/19368623.2011.577688

Kark, R., & Shamir, B. (2002). The dual effect of transformational leadership: priming relational and collective selves and further effects on followers. In B. J. Avolio & F. J. Yammarino (Eds.), *Transformational and charismatic leadership: The road ahead* (Vol. 2, pp. 67–91). Oxford, U.K.: Elsevier Science.

Kashdan, T. B., Biswas-Diener, R., & King, L. A. (2008). Reconsidering happiness: The costs of distinguishing between hedonics and eudaimonia. *The Journal of Positive Psychology*, *3*(4), 219–233. doi:10.1080/17439760802303044

Kashyap, V., & Rangnekar, S. (2016). The mediating role of trust: Investigating the relationships among employer brand perception and turnover intentions. *Global Business Review*, *17*(3), 64–75. doi:10.1177/0972150916631083

Keyes, C. L. M., & Magyar-Moe, J. L. (2003). The measurement and utility of adult subjective well-being. In S. J. Lopez & C. R. Snyder (Eds.), *Positive psychological assessment: A handbook of models and measures* (p. 420). Washington, DC: American Psychological Association. doi:10.1037/10612-026

Khanna, S., & Pathak, K. (2016, September). Reliance Jio sends a message to rivals: It's war. *Live Mint*. Retrieved March 2017, from http://www.livemint.com/Companies/D4leWGTopPio6OYUQg2CEP/Mukesh-Ambani-kicks-off-Reliance-Jio-services-at-company-AGM.html

Khatri, N., Halbesleben, J. R., Petroski, G. F., & Meyer, W. (2007). Relationship between management philosophy and clinical outcomes. *Health Care Management Review*, *32*(2), 128–139. doi:10.1097/01.HMR.0000267789.17309.18 PMID:17438396

Kim, H., & Lee, S. Y. (2009). Supervisory communication, burnout, and turnover intention among social workers in health care settings. *Social Work in Health Care*, *48*(4), 364–385. doi:10.1080/00981380802598499 PMID:19396707

King, L. A., Eells, J. E., & Burton, C. M. (2004). The good life, broadly and narrowly considered. In P. A. Linley & S. Joseph (Eds.), *Positive psychology in practice* (pp. 35–52). Hoboken, NJ: Wiley. doi:10.1002/9780470939338.ch3

Kiran Kumar, S. K. (2003). An Indian conception of well being. In J. Henry (Ed.), *European Positive Psychology Proceedings 2002*. Leicester, UK: British Psychological Society.

Kiran Kumar, S. K. (2004). Perspectives on Well-Being in the Indian Tradition. *Journal of Indian Psychology*, *22*(2), 63–72.

Kiran Kumar, S. K. (2008). Indian Thought and Tradition: A Psychohistorical Perspective. In K. R. Rao, A. C. Paranjpe, & A. K. Dalal (Eds.), *Handbook of Indian Psychology*. New Delhi: Foundation Books. doi:10.1017/UPO9788175968448.003

Klemmer, E. T., & Snyder, F. W. (1972). Measurement of time spent communicating. *Journal of Communication*, *22*(2), 142–158. doi:10.1111/j.1460-2466.1972.tb00141.x

Konovsky, M. A., & Cropanzano, R. (1991). Perceived fairness of employee drug testing as a predictor of employee attitudes and job performance. *The Journal of Applied Psychology*, *76*(5), 698–707. doi:10.1037/0021-9010.76.5.698 PMID:1960142

Kostova, T., & Roth, K. (2003). Social capital in multinational corporations and a micro-macro model of its formation. *Academy of Management Review*, *28*(2), 297–317.

Kozma, A., Stones, M. J., & McNeil, J. K. (1991). *Psychological Well-Being in Later Life*. Toronto: Butterworths.

Kraimer, M. L., Seibert, S. E., & Liden, R. C. (1999). Psychological empowerment as a multi-dimensional construct: A construct validity test. *Educational and Psychological Measurement*, *59*(1), 127–142. doi:10.1177/00131644995910

Kramer, R. M. (1991). Intergroup Relations and Organizational Dilemmas-The role of categorization processes. *Research in Organizational Behavior*, *13*, 191–228.

Kraut, R. (1979). Two conceptions of happiness. *The Philosophical Review*, *88*(2), 167–197. doi:10.2307/2184505

Krishnamohan, K. (2001). Spirituality and well-being: an overview. In M. Cornelissen (Ed.), *Consciousness and Its Transformation*. Pondicherry: SAICE.

Kristof-Brown, A. L., Zimmerman, R. D., & Johnson, E. C. (2005). Consequences of individuals' fit at work: A meta-analysis of person–job, person–organization, person–group, and person–supervisor fit. *Personnel Psychology*, *58*(2), 281–342. doi:10.1111/j.1744-6570.2005.00672.x

Krosgaard, M. A., Brodt, S. E., & Whitener, E. M. (2002). Trust in the face of conflict: The role of managerial trustworthy behavior and organizational context. *The Journal of Applied Psychology*, *87*(2), 312–324. doi:10.1037/0021-9010.87.2.312 PMID:12002959

Kulshrestha, U., & Sen, C. (2006). Subjective well being in relation to emotional intelligence and locus of control among executives. *Journal of the Indian Academy of Applied Psychology*, *32*(2), 129–134.

Kumar, D., & Rajeev, P. V. (2014). Marketing challenges of handicraft retailers in changing environment. *ZENITH International Journal of Business Economics and Management Research*, *4*(10), 22–33.

Kumar, N., & Yakhlef, A. (2016). Managing business-to-business relationships under conditions of employee attrition: A transparency approach. *Industrial Marketing Management*, *56*, 143–155. doi:10.1016/j.indmarman.2016.01.002

Lal, R. (2004). Demographic correlates of happiness: A study of adolescents. *Indian Journal of Community Psychology*, *1*(2), 267–277.

Lapointe, É., & Vandenberghe, C. (2017). Supervisory mentoring and employee affective commitment and turnover: The critical role of contextual factors. *Journal of Vocational Behavior*, *98*, 98–107. doi:10.1016/j.jvb.2016.10.004

Laschinger, H. K. S., Finegan, J., Shamian, J., & Casier, S. (2000). Organizational trust and empowerment in restructured healthcare settings: Effects on staff nurse commitment. *The Journal of Nursing Administration*, *30*(9), 413–425. doi:10.1097/00005110-200009000-00008 PMID:11006783

Laschinger, H., Finegan, J., & Shamian, J. (2001). The impact of workplace empowerment and organizational trust on staff nurses' work satisfaction and organizational commitment. *Health Care Management Review*, *26*(3), 7–23. doi:10.1097/00004010-200107000-00002 PMID:11482178

Latha, K. L. (2013). A study on employee attrition and retention in manufacturing industries. *BVIMSR's Journal of Management Research*, *5*(1), 1–23.

Lee, Y., & Chang, H. (2008). Relations between team work and innovation in organizations and the job satisfaction of employees: A factor analytic study. *International Journal of Management*, *25*(3), 732–739.

Levinger, G. (1979). A social exchange view on the dissolution of pair relationships. *Social Exchange in Developing Relationships, 3*, 169-193.

Li, Y. H. (2008). An empirical investigation on the determinants of e-procurement adoption in Chinese manufacturing enterprises. In *2008 International Conference on Management Science and Engineering 15th Annual Conference Proceedings* (pp. 32-37). IEEE. doi:10.1109/ICMSE.2008.4668890

Liden, R. C., Wayne, S. J., & Sparrowe, R. T. (2000). An examination of the mediating role of psychological empowerment on the relations between the job, interpersonal relationships, and work outcomes. *The Journal of Applied Psychology*, *85*(3), 407–416. doi:10.1037/0021-9010.85.3.407 PMID:10900815

Li, J. J., Kim, W. G., & Zhao, X. R. (2017). Multilevel model of management support and casino employee turnover intention. *Tourism Management*, *59*, 193–204. doi:10.1016/j.tourman.2016.08.006

Lin, C. L., & Tzeng, G. H. (2009). A value-created system of science (technology) park by using DEMATEL. *Expert Systems with Applications*, *36*(6), 9683–9697. doi:10.1016/j.eswa.2008.11.040

Lin, H. F. (2006). Interorganizational and organizational determinants of planning effectiveness for Internet-based interorganizational systems. *Information & Management*, *43*(4), 423–433. doi:10.1016/j.im.2005.10.004

Lips-Wiersma, M., & Wright, S. (2012). Measuring the meaning of meaningful work: Development and validation of the Comprehensive Meaningful Work Scale (CMWS). *Group & Organization Management*, *37*(5), 655–685. doi:10.1177/1059601112461578

Locke, E. A. (1976). The nature and causes of job satisfaction. Handbook of Industrial and Organizational Psychology, 1, 1297-1343.

Lok, P., & Crawford, J. (2004). The effect of organizational culture and leadership style on job satisfaction and organizational commitment: A cross-national comparison. *Journal of Management Development*, *23*(4), 321–338. doi:10.1108/02621710410529785

Lopes Branco Bonfada, P., Henn Bonfada, M. R., Alén Gonzalez, M. E., & Gonçalves Gândara, J. M. (2011). El turismo de salud y el uso terapéutico del agua. *Estudios y Perspectivas en Turismo*, *20*(2), 462–477.

Loveman, G. W. (1998). Employee satisfaction, customer loyalty, and financial performance: An empirical examination of the service profit chain in retail banking. *Journal of Service Research*, *1*(1), 18–31. doi:10.1177/109467059800100103

Luce, R. D., & Tukey, J. W. (1964). Conjoint analysis: A new form of fundamental measurement; IN. *Journal of Mathematical Psychology*, *1*, 1–36. doi:10.1016/0022-2496(64)90015-X

Lu, L., Gilmour, R., & Kao, S. (2001). Cultural values and happiness: An East-West dialogue. *The Journal of Social Psychology*, *141*(4), 477–493. doi:10.1080/00224540109600566 PMID:11577847

Lu, L., & Lin, Y. Y. (1998). Family roles and happiness in adulthood. *Personality and Individual Differences*, *25*(2), 195–207. doi:10.1016/S0191-8869(98)00009-9

M.Sias, P., & Jablin, F. M. (1995, September). Differential Superior-Subordinate Relations, Perceptions of Fairness, and Coworker Communication. *Human Communication Research*, *22*(1), 5–38 doi:10.1111/j.1468-2958.1995.tb00360.x

Macdonald, D. (1999). Teacher attrition: A review of literature. *Teaching and Teacher Education*, *15*(8), 835–848. doi:10.1016/S0742-051X(99)00031-1

Macintosh, G. (2009). Examining the antecedents of trust and rapport in services: Discovering new interrelationships. *Journal of Retailing and Consumer Services*, *16*(4), 298–305. doi:10.1016/j.jretconser.2009.02.001

Madi, M. Y. A. (2013). *Communication, Job Satisfaction and Employees Turnover in Multinational Engineering Organizations in the United Arab Emirates* (Doctoral dissertation). The British University in Dubai.

Maertz, C. P., Griffeth, R. W., Campbell, N. S., & Allen, D. G. (2007). The effects of perceived organizational support and perceived supervisor support on employee turnover. *Journal of Organizational Behavior*, *28*(8), 1059–1075. doi:10.1002/job.472

Mangione, T. W., & Quinn, R. P. (1975). Job satisfaction, counterproductive behaviour and drug use at work. *The Journal of Applied Psychology*, *60*(1), 114–116. doi:10.1037/h0076355 PMID:1110252

Maslow, A. H. (1943). A theory of human motivation. *Psychological Review*, *50*(4), 370–396. doi:10.1037/h0054346

Maslow, A. H. (1954). *Motivation and Personality*. Harper & Row.

Mast, J. D. (2006). Six Sigma and Competitive Advantage. *Total Quality Management*, *17*(4), 455–464. doi:10.1080/14783360500528221

Matchette, D. R. (2006, July-August). Six Sigma for the DoD. *Defense AT, L*, 19–21.

May, D., Gilson, R., & Harter, L. (2004). The psychological conditions of meaningfulness, safety and availability and the engagement of the human spirit at work. *Journal of Occupational and Organizational Psychology*, *77*(1), 11–37. doi:10.1348/096317904322915892

Mayer, R. C., Davis, J. H., & Schoorman, F. D. (1995). An integrative model of organizational trust. *Academy of Management Review*, *20*(3), 709–734.

Mayer, R. C., & Gavin, M. B. (2005). Trust in management and performance: Who minds the shop while the employees watch the boss? *Academy of Management Journal*, *48*(5), 874–888. doi:10.5465/AMJ.2005.18803928

McClelland, D. C. (1961). *The Achieving Society*. Van Nostrand Reinhold. doi:10.1037/14359-000

McEvoy, G. M., & Cascio, W. F. (1985). Strategies for reducing employee turnover: A meta-analysis. *The Journal of Applied Psychology*, *70*(2), 342–353. doi:10.1037/0021-9010.70.2.342

McMahon, D. M. (2006). *Happiness: A history*. New York, NY: Grove Press.

Meeberg, G. A. (1993). Quality of life: A concept analysis. *Journal of Advanced Nursing, 18*(1), 32–38. doi:10.1046/j.1365-2648.1993.18010032.x PMID:8429165

Mehdi, A., Raju, R. M., & Mukherji, A. (2012, July). Abusive supervision and employee attrition: A study of executives in the Indian high technology sector. In *Competition Forum* (Vol. 10, No. 2, p. 42). American Society for Competitiveness.

Meliá, J. L., & Peiró, J. M. (1989). The measurement of job satisfaction in organizational settings: The S20/23 Job Satisfaction Questionnaire. *Psicologemas, 5*, 59–74.

Meliá, J. L., Peiró, J. M., & Calatayud, C. (1986). El Cuestionario General de Satisfacción en Organizaciones Laborales: Estudios factoriales, fiabilidad y validez [presentación del Cuestionario S4/82]. *Revista de Filosofía. Psicología y Ciencias de la Educación, 11*, 43–78.

Merriam-Webster. (2008). *Online Dictionary*. Springfield, MA: Merriam-Webster.

Meyer, J. P., Stanley, D. J., Herscovitch, L., & Topolnytsky, L. (2002). Affective, continuance, and normative commitment to the organization: A meta-analysis of antecedents, correlates, and consequences. *Journal of Vocational Behavior, 61*(1), 20–52. doi:10.1006/jvbe.2001.1842

Mikulincer, M., & Segal, J. (1991). Loneliness and the desire for intimacy: The intervening role of LoC. *Personality and Individual Differences, 12*(8), 801–809. doi:10.1016/0191-8869(91)90146-3

Mishra, J., & Morrissey, M. A. (1990). Trust in employee/employer relationships: A survey of West Michigan managers. *Public Personnel Management, 19*(4), 443–486. doi:10.1177/009102609001900408

Misra, G. (2013). Happiness. In K. D. Keith (Ed.), *The Encyclopedia of Cross-Cultural Psychology*. John Wiley & Sons, Inc. doi:10.1002/9781118339893.wbeccp259

Mitchell, T. R., Holtom, B. C., & Lee, T. W. (2001). How to keep your best employees: Developing an effective retention policy. *The Academy of Management Executive, 15*(4), 96–108. doi:10.5465/AME.2001.5897929

Molla, A., & Licker, P. S. (2005a). Ecommerce adoption in developing countries: A model and instrument. *Information & Management, 42*(6), 877–899. doi:10.1016/j.im.2004.09.002

Molla, A., & Licker, P. S. (2005b). Perceived e-readiness factors in ecommerce adoption: An empirical investigation in a developing country. *International Journal of Electronic Commerce, 10*(1), 83–110.

Moneta, G. B., & Csikszentmihalyi, M. (1996). The effect of perceived challenges and skills on the quality of subjective experience. *Journal of Personality, 64*(2), 275–310. doi:10.1111/j.1467-6494.1996.tb00512.x PMID:8656320

Money, K., Hillebrand, C., & Da Camara, N. (2008). Putting positive psychology to work in organisations. *Journal of General Management, 34*(2), 21–36.

Morgan, C. K., & Tam, M. (1999). Unravelling the complexities of distance education student attrition. *Distance Education*, *20*(1), 96–108. doi:10.1080/0158791990200108

Morgan, D. E., & Zeffane, R. (2003). Employee involvement, organizational change and trust in management. *International Journal of Human Resource Management*, *14*(1), 55–75. doi:10.1080/09585190210158510

Morrison, K. A. (1997). Personality correlates of the Five-Factor Model for a sample of business owners/managers: Associations with scores on self-monitoring, Type A behavior, LoC, and subjective well-being. *Psychological Reports*, *80*(1), 255–272. doi:10.2466/pr0.1997.80.1.255 PMID:9122336

Morrison, R. L. (2009). Are women tending and befriending in the workplace? Gender differences in the relationship between workplace friendships and organizational outcomes. *Sex Roles*, *60*(1-2), 1–13. doi:10.1007/s11199-008-9513-4

Moskowitz, H.R., & Gofman, A. (2004). *System and method for performing conjoint analysis.* Academic Press.

Moskowitz, H. R., Gofman, A., Itty, B., Katz, R., Machaiah, M., & Ma, Z. (2001). Rapid, inexpensive, actionable concept generation and optimization – the use and promise of self-authoring conjoint analysis for the foodservice industry. *Food Service Technology*, *1*(3-4), 149–16. doi:10.1046/j.1471-5740.2001.00021.x

Moskowitz, H. R., Porretta, S., & Silcher, M. (2005). *Concept Research in Food Product Design & Development*. Ames, IA: Blackwell Publishing Professional. doi:10.1002/9780470290132

Mowday, R. T., Porter, L. W., & Steers, R. M. (1982). *Employee-organization linkage. The psychology of commitment absenteeism, and turn over*. London: Academic Press Inc.

Mowday, R. T., Steers, R. M., & Porter, L. W. (1979). The measurement of organizational commitmen. *Journal of Vocational Behavior*, *14*(2), 224–247. doi:10.1016/0001-8791(79)90072-1

Mueller, C. W., & McCloskey, J. C. (1990). Nurses' job satisfaction: A proposed measure. *Nursing Research*, *39*(2), 113–116. doi:10.1097/00006199-199003000-00014 PMID:2315065

Mutsuddi, I. (2011). *Essentials of Human Resource Management.* New Delhi: New Age International Publishers.

Myer, D. G., & Diener, E. (1995). Who is happy? *Psychological Science*, *6*(1), 10–19. doi:10.1111/j.1467-9280.1995.tb00298.x

Naim, M. F., & Lenka, U. (2016). Knowledge sharing as an intervention for Gen Y employees' intention to stay. *Industrial and Commercial Training*, *48*(3), 142–148. doi:10.1108/ICT-01-2015-0011

Naim, M. F., & Lenka, U. (2017a). Talent management: A burgeoning strategic focus in Indian IT industry. *Industrial and Commercial Training*, *49*(3), 183–188. doi:10.1108/ICT-12-2016-0084

Naim, M. F., & Lenka, U. (2017b). Investigating the impact of social media on Gen Y employees' engagement: An empirical investigation. *International Journal of Human Capital and Information Technology Professionals*, *8*(3), 29–48. doi:10.4018/IJHCITP.2017070103

Nappinnai, M. V., & Premavathy, N. (2013). Employee attrition and retention in a global competitive scenario. *International Journal of Research in Business Management, 1*(6), 11-14.

Natvig, G. K., Albrektsen, G., & Qvarnstrom, U. (2003). Associations between psychosocial factors and happiness among school adolescents. *International Journal of Nursing Practice*, *9*(3), 166–175. doi:10.1046/j.1440-172X.2003.00419.x PMID:12801248

Nave, D. (2002, March). How to Compare Six Sigma, Lean and the Theory of Constraints. *Quality Progress*, 73-78.

Nehra, N. S., & Rangnekar, S. (2018). Linking the emotional maturity factors and self-disclosure: A study of Indian organizations. *International Journal of Organizational Analysis, 26*(2).

Nehra, N. S., & Rangnekar, S. (2016). Relationship understanding between social adjustment and self-disclosure-results from the Indian power sector. *16th Global Conference on Flexible Systems and Flexibility*, 256-266.

Nehra, N. S., & Rangnekar, S. (2017). Relationship understanding between emotional stability, self-disclosure, and social adjustment. *Journal of Intercultural Communication Research*, *46*(6), 558–578. doi:10.1080/17475759.2017.1387165

Nehra, N. S., & Rangnekar, S. (in press). Does emotional stability mediates the relationship between self-disclosure, personality integration, social adjustment. *International Journal of Business Excellence.*

Nicholls, A. R., Levy, A. R., & Perry, J. L. (2015). Emotional maturity, dispositional coping, and coping effectiveness among adolescent athletes. *Psychology of Sport and Exercise*, *17*, 32–39. doi:10.1016/j.psychsport.2014.11.004

Nielsen, K., & Munir, F. (2009). How do transformational leaders influence followers' affective well-being? Exploring the mediating role of self-efficacy. *Work and Stress*, *23*(4), 313–329. doi:10.1080/02678370903385106

Norman, S. M. (2006). *The role of trust: Implications for psychological capital and authentic leadership* (Unpublished doctoral dissertation). University of Nebraska.

Norton, D. L. (1976). *Personal Destinies: A Philosophy of Ethical Individualism.* Princeton University Press.

Nunnally, J. (1979). *Psychometric Theory*. New York: McGraw-Hill.

Nunnally, J. C. (1978). *Psychometric theory* (2nd ed.). New York: McGraw-Hill.

Nurosis, M. J. (1993). *SPSS. Statistical Data Análisis*. SPSS Inc.

Nyhan, R. C. (1999). Increasing Affective Organizational Commitment in Public Organizations The Key Role of Interpersonal Trust. *Review of Public Personnel Administration*, *19*(3), 58–70. doi:10.1177/0734371X9901900305

Nyhan, R. C., & Marlowe, H. A. Jr. (1997). Development and psychometric properties of the organizational trust inventory. *Evaluation Review*, *21*(5), 614–635. doi:10.1177/0193841X9702100505

O'malley, E., & O'gorman, C. (2001). Competitive advantage in the Irish indigenous software industry and the role of inward foreign direct investment. *European Planning Studies*, *9*(3), 303–321. doi:10.1080/713666484

Oakland, J. S. (1995). *Total quality management: Text with cases*. London, U.K.: Butterworth–Heinemann.

Odom, M. L., Seeman, J., & Newbrough, J. R. (1971). A study of family communication patterns and personality integration in children. *Child Psychiatry and Human Development*, *1*(4), 275–285. doi:10.1007/BF01441090 PMID:5163304

Oishi, S., Graham, J., Kesebir, S., & Galinha, I. C. (2013). Concepts of happiness across time and cultures. *Personality and Social Psychology Bulletin*, *39*(5), 559–577. doi:10.1177/0146167213480042 PMID:23599280

Oke, A., Prajogo, D. I., & Jayaram, J. (2013). Strengthening the innovation chain: The role of internal innovation climate and strategic relationships with supply chain partners. *The Journal of Supply Chain Management*, *49*(4), 43–58. doi:10.1111/jscm.12031

Oliveira, T., & Martins, M. F. (2010a). Firms patterns of e-business adoption: Evidence for the European Union-27. *The Electronic Journal Information Systems Evaluation*, *13*(1), 47–56.

Oliveira, T., Thomas, M., & Espadanal, M. (2014). Assessing the determinants of cloud computing adoption: An analysis of the manufacturing and services sectors. *Information & Management*, *51*(5), 497–510. doi:10.1016/j.im.2014.03.006

Organ, D. W. (1977). A reappraisal and reinterpretation of the satisfaction- causes-performance hypothesis. *Academy of Management Review*, *2*(1), 46–53.

Osakidetza/ Servicio Vasco de Salud. (2001). *Manual de evaluación y mejora de la satisfacción de las personas en las organizaciones de servicios*. Available in: http://www.osakidetza.euskadi.net/r850319/es/contenidos/informacion/organizacion_gestion_osk/es_og/adjuntos/satisfaccion/evaluacion.pdf

Padmanabhan, G. (2010, January 17). An enigma called happiness. *The Hindu*, p. 1.

Palan, R. (2007). Does employee training lead to attrition? *Performance Improvement*, *46*(4), 5–8. doi:10.1002/pfi.118

Pande, P. S., Neuman, R. P., & Cavanage, R. R. (2004). *The Six Sigma Way*. New Delhi: Tata McGraw Hill Company Limited.

Paranjpe, A. C. (1996). Some Basic Psychological Concepts from the Intellectual Tradition of India. *Psychology and Developing Societies*, *8*(1), 7–27. doi:10.1177/097133369600800102

Pareek, U., & Purohit, S. (2011). *Training Instruments in HRD and OD*. McGraw Hill.

Park, N., & Huebner, E. S. (2005). A cross-cultural study of the levels and correlates of life satisfaction among adolescents. *Journal of Cross-Cultural Psychology*, *36*(4), 444–456. doi:10.1177/0022022105275961

Park, N., Peterson, C., & Ruch, W. (2009). Orientations to happiness and life satisfaction in twenty-seven nations. *The Journal of Positive Psychology*, *4*(4), 273–279. doi:10.1080/17439760902933690

Pattanayak, B. (2005). *Human Resource Management* (3rd ed.). New Delhi: Printice Hall of India.

Pearce, C. L., Sims, H. P. Jr, Cox, J. F., Ball, G., Schnell, K. A., Smith, K. A., & Trevino, L. (2003). Transactors, transformers and beyond: A multi-method development of a theoretical typology of leadership. *Journal of Management Development*, *22*(4), 273–307. doi:10.1108/02621710310467587

Perlow, R., & Latham, L. L. (1993). Relationship of client abuse with LoC and gender: A longitudinal study in mental retardation facilities. *The Journal of Applied Psychology*, *78*(5), 831–834. doi:10.1037/0021-9010.78.5.831 PMID:8253634

Peterson, C., Park, N., & Seligman, M. E. P. (2005). Orientations to happiness and life satisfaction: The full life versus the empty life. *Journal of Happiness Studies*, *6*(1), 25–41. doi:10.1007/s10902-004-1278-z

PIB, Press Information Bureau. (2014). *Initiatives of the New Government in the Textile Sector, Govt of India, Ministry of Textiles*. Retrieved February 2, 2017. From http://pib.nic.in/newsite/PrintRelease.aspx?relid=110128

Planning Commission. (2015, July 8). *Sector-wise contribution of GDP of India*. Retrieved from Statistics Times: http://statisticstimes.com/economy/sectorwise-gdp-contribution-of-india.php

Podsakoff, P. M., Mackenzie, S. B., Moorman, R. H., & Fetter, R. (1990). Empowering leader behaviors and their effects on followers' trust in leader, satisfaction, and organizational citizenship behaviors. *The Leadership Quarterly*, *1*(2), 107–142. doi:10.1016/1048-9843(90)90009-7

Podsakoff, P. M., MacKenzie, S. B., & Podsakoff, N. P. (2012). Sources of method bias in social science research and recommendations on how to control it. *Annual Review of Psychology*, *63*(1), 539–569. doi:10.1146/annurev-psych-120710-100452 PMID:21838546

Podsakoff, P. M., & Organ, D. W. (1986). Self-reports in organizational research: Problems and prospects. *Journal of Management*, *12*(4), 531–544. doi:10.1177/014920638601200408

Porter, M. E., & Millar, V. E. (1985). *How information gives you competitive advantage*. Academic Press.

Porter, L. W., & Steers, R. M. (1973). Organizational, work, and personal factors in employee turnover and absenteeism. *Psychological Bulletin, 80*(2), 151–176. doi:10.1037/h0034829

Porter, M. E. (1990). The competitive advantage of nations. *Harvard Business Review, 68*(2), 73–93.

Posey, C., Lowry, P. B., Roberts, T. L., & Ellis, T. S. (2010). Proposing the online community self-disclosure model: The case of working professionals in France and the UK who use online communities. *European Journal of Information Systems, 19*(2), 181–195. doi:10.1057/ejis.2010.15

Postmes, T., Tanis, M., & De Wit, B. (2001). Communication and commitment in organizations: A social identity approach. *Group Processes & Intergroup Relations, 4*(3), 227–246. doi:10.1177/1368430201004003004

Pratt, M. G., & Ashforth, B. E. (2003). Fostering meaningfulness in working and at work. *Positive Organizational Scholarship: Foundations of a new discipline*, 309-327.

Provisional patent application, 60/538,787, filed January 23, 2004.

Ramdani, B., & Kawalek, P. (2007), SME adoption of enterprise systems in the Northwest of England. In *IFIP International Working Conference on Organizational Dynamics of Technology-Based Innovation* (pp. 409-429). Springer US. doi:10.1007/978-0-387-72804-9_27

Randel, A. E., & Ranft, A. L. (2007). Motivations to maintain social ties with coworkers the moderating role of turnover intentions on information exchange. *Group & Organization Management, 32*(2), 208–232. doi:10.1177/1059601106286778

Rangaswami, K. (1994). Spirituality and psychotherapy. *Indian Journal of Clinical Psychology, 21*, 1–2.

Rao, P. S. (2004). *Personal and Human Resource Management – Text and Cases*. Mumbai: Himalaya Publishing House.

Rao, V. S. P. (2002). *Human Resource Management – Text and Cases*. New Delhi: Excel Books.

Rastogi, M. R. (2005). Triguna and psychological well Being. *Indian Journal of Community Psychology, 1*(2), 115–124.

Ratna, R., & Chawla, S. (2012). Key factors of retention and retention strategies in telecom sector. *Global Management Review, 6*(3).

Rebeťák, M., & Farkašová, V. (2015). Managing High–Potential Employees. *Procedia Economics and Finance, 23*, 867–871. doi:10.1016/S2212-5671(15)00437-2

Rego, A., Ribeiro, N., & Cuhna, M.P. (n.d.). *Perceptions of organisational virtuousness and happiness as predictors of organisational citizenship behaviours*. Academic Press.

Rego, A., & Cunha, M. P. (2008). Authentizotic climates and employee happiness: Pathways to individual performance. *Journal of Business Research, 61*(7), 739–752. doi:10.1016/j.jbusres.2007.08.003

Renn, R. W., & Vandenberg, R. J. (1995). The critical psychological states: An under-represented component in job characteristics model research. *Journal of Management*, *21*(2), 279–304. doi:10.1177/014920639502100206

Riach, K., & Wilson, F. (2007). Don't screw the crew: Exploring the rules of engagement in organizational romance. *British Journal of Management*, *18*(1), 79–92. doi:10.1111/j.1467-8551.2006.00503.x

Rich, G. A. (1997). The sales manager as a role model: Effects on trust, job satisfaction, and performance of salespeople. *Journal of the Academy of Marketing Science*, *25*(4), 319–328. doi:10.1177/0092070397254004

Riordan, C. M., & Griffeth, R. W. (1995). The opportunity for friendship in the workplace: An underexplored construct. *Journal of Business and Psychology*, *10*(2), 141–154. doi:10.1007/BF02249575

Ritchie, J. (1993). Strategies for human resource management: Challenges in smaller and entrepreneurial organisations. *Human Resource Management*, 111–135.

Robbins, S. (2004). *Comportamiento Organizacional*. Pearson Educación.

Robinson, S. L., & Greenberg, J. (1998). Employees behaving badly: Dimensions, determinants and dilemmas in the study of workplace deviance. *Journal of Organizational Behavior (1986-1998)*, 1.

Robles-García, M., Dierssen-Sotos, T., Martínez-Ochoa, E., Herrera-Carral, P., Díaz-Mendi, A., & Llorca-Díaz, J. (2005). Variables relacionadas con la satisfacción laboral: Un estudio transversal a partir del modelo EFQM. *Gaceta Sanitaria*, *19*(2), 127–134. doi:10.1157/13074368 PMID:15860161

Rogers, J. D., Clow, K. E., & Kash, T. J. (1994). Increasing job satisfaction of service personnel. *Journal of Service Management*, *8*, 14–26.

Rothmann, S., & Joubert, J. H. M. (2007). Job demands, job resources, burnout and work engagement of managers at a platinum mine in the North West Province. *South African Journal of Business Management*, *38*(3), 49–61.

Rotter, J. B. (1966). Generalized expectancies for internal versus external control of reinforcement. *Psychological Monographs*, *80*(1), 1–28. doi:10.1037/h0092976 PMID:5340840

Rousseau, D. M. (1998). The'problem'of the psychological contract considered. *Journal of Organizational Behavior*, *19*(S1), 665–671. doi:10.1002/(SICI)1099-1379(1998)19:1+<665::AID-JOB972>3.0.CO;2-X

Rousseau, D., Sitkin, S., Burt, R., & Camerer, C. (1998). Not so different after all: A cross-discipline view of trust. *Academy of Management Review*, *23*(3), 393–404. doi:10.5465/AMR.1998.926617

Rubinstein, E. A. (1954). Personality integration and the perceptual process. *Journal of Clinical Psychology*, *10*(1), 23–29. doi:10.1002/1097-4679(195401)10:1<23::AID-JCLP2270100105>3.0.CO;2-X PMID:13117975

Ryan, R. M., & Deci, E. L. (2000). Self-determination theory and the facilitation of intrinsic motivation, social development, and well-being. *The American Psychologist, 55*(1), 68–78. doi:10.1037/0003-066X.55.1.68 PMID:11392867

Ryan, R. M., & Deci, E. L. (2001). On happiness and human potentials: A review of research on hedonic and eudemonic well-being. *Annual Review of Psychology, 52*(1), 141–166. doi:10.1146/annurev.psych.52.1.141 PMID:11148302

Ryckman, R. M., Sherman, M. F., & Burgess, G. D. (1973). LoC and self-disclosure of public and private information by college men and women: A brief note. *The Journal of Psychology, 84*(2), 317–318. doi:10.1080/00223980.1973.9923845 PMID:4717162

Ryff, C. D. (1989). Happiness is everything, or is it? Explorations on the meaning of psychological well-being. *Journal of Personality and Social Psychology, 57*(6), 1069–1081. doi:10.1037/0022-3514.57.6.1069

Sahay, V. (2017, March). War of attrition in India's telecom space. *Herald Goa*. Retrieved March 2017, from http://www.heraldgoa.in/Business/In-Business/War-of-attrition-in-India%E2%80%99s-telecom-space/112623.html

Şahin, N. H., Basım, H. N., & Çetin, F. (2009). LoC and self-concept in interpersonal conflict resolution approaches. *Türk Psikiyatri Dergisi, 20*, 153–163. PMID:19504366

Samson, S. M. (2013). Attrition issues and retention challenges of employees. *Asia Pacific Journal of Research in Business Management, 4*(7).

Sandhya, K. K., & Kumar, D. (2011). Employee retention by motivation. *Indian Journal of Science and Technology, 4*(12), 1778–1782.

Sarrasin, O., Mayor, E., & Faniko, K. (2014). Gender traits and cognitive appraisal in young adults: The mediating role of LoC. *Sex Roles, 70*(3-4), 122–133. doi:10.1007/s11199-013-0336-6

Satiani, B., Williams, T. E., Brod, H., Way, D. P., & Ellison, E. C. (2013). A review of trends in attrition rates for surgical faculty: A case for a sustainable retention strategy to cope with demographic and economic realities. *Journal of the American College of Surgeons, 216*(5), 944–953. doi:10.1016/j.jamcollsurg.2012.12.052 PMID:23522787

Scandura, T. A. (1992). Mentorship and career mobility: An empirical investigation. *Journal of Organizational Behavior, 13*(2), 169–174. doi:10.1002/job.4030130206

Schaffer, H. R. (1996). *Social development*. Blackwell Publishing.

Schlesinger, L. A., & Zornitsky, J. (1991). Job satisfaction, service capability and customer satisfaction: An examination of linkages and management implications. *Human Resource Planning, 14*(2), 141–149.

Schneider, B., Macey, W. H., Barbera, K. M., & Martin, N. (2009). Driving customer satisfaction and financial success through employee engagement. *People and Strategy, 32*(2), 22–34.

Schneider, B., & Reichers, A. E. (1983). On the etiology of climates. *Personnel Psychology, 36*(1), 19–39. doi:10.1111/j.1744-6570.1983.tb00500.x

Schueller, S. M., & Seligman, M. E. P. (2010). Pursuit of pleasure, engagement, and meaning: Relationships to subjective and objective measures of well-being. *The Journal of Positive Psychology, 5*(4), 253–263. doi:10.1080/17439761003794130

Schutz, W. C. (1958). *FIRO: A three-dimensional theory of interpersonal behavior*. Academic Press.

Schutz, W. (1977). *FIRO Awareness Scales*. Consulting Psychologists Press.

Schutz, W. (1992). Beyond FIRO-B—Three new theory-derived measures—Element B: Behavior, Element F: Feelings, Element S: Self. *Psychological Reports, 70*(3), 915–937. doi:10.2466/pr0.1992.70.3.915 PMID:1620783

Schutz, W. C. (1955). What makes groups productive? *Human Relations, 8*(4), 429–465. doi:10.1177/001872675500800404

Schuurman, N. (2013). Tweet me your talk: Geographical learning and knowledge production 2.0. *The Professional Geographer, 65*(3), 369–377. doi:10.1080/00330124.2012.693873

Schwepker, C. H. Jr. (2001). Ethical climate's relationship to job satisfaction, organizational commitment, and turnover intention in the salesforce. *Journal of Business Research, 54*(1), 39–52. doi:10.1016/S0148-2963(00)00125-9

Scott, M., Roberts, I., Holroyd, G., & Sawbridge, D. (1989). *Management and Industrial Relations in Small Firms.* Department of Employment Research Paper No. 70.

Scroggins, W. A. (2008). Antecedents and outcomes of experienced meaningful work: A person-job fit perspective. *Journal of Business Inquiry, 7*(1), 68–78.

Seeman, J. (1959). Toward a concept of personality integration. *The American Psychologist, 14*(10), 633–637. doi:10.1037/h0042986

Seeman, J. (1963). Teacher judgments of high and low adjustment. *The Journal of Educational Research, 57*(4), 213–216. doi:10.1080/00220671.1963.10883064

Seeman, J., Barry, E., & Ellinwood, C. (1963). Personality integration as a criterion of therapy outcome. *Psychotherapy (Chicago, Ill.), 1*(1), 14–16. doi:10.1037/h0088566

Seibert, S. E., Wang, G., & Courtright, S. H. (2011). *Antecedents and consequences of psychological and team empowerment in organizations: a meta-analytic review*. Academic Press.

Seligman, M. E. P. (2002). *Authentic happiness*. New York: Free Press.

Seligman, M. E. P. (2002). *Authentic happiness: Using the new positive psychology to realize your potential for lasting fulfillment*. New York: Free Press.

Seligman, M. E. P. (2008). Positive health. *Applied Psychology, 57*(s1), 3–18. doi:10.1111/j.1464-0597.2008.00351.x

Seligman, M. E., & Csikszentmihalyi, M. (2000). Positive psychology: An introduction. *The American Psychologist, 55*(1), 5–14. doi:10.1037/0003-066X.55.1.5 PMID:11392865

Shahnawaz, M. G., & Goswami, K. (2011). Effect of psychological contract violation on organizational commitment, trust and turnover intention in private and public sector Indian organizations. *Vision: The Journal of Business Perspective, 15*(3), 209–217. doi:10.1177/097226291101500301

Shamir, B. (1991). Meaning, self and motivation in organizations. *Organization Studies, 12*(3), 405–424. doi:10.1177/017084069101200304

Sharma, A. (2011). Subjective well-being of retired teachers: The role of psycho-Social factors. *International Journal of Psychological Studies, 3*(1), 36–42. doi:10.5539/ijps.v3n1p36

Sharma, N. (2014). Managing Talent for Sustainable Competitive Differentiation. *Parikalpana: KIIT Journal of Management, 10*(1), 9–22.

Sharma, R. (2003). *The Monk who sold his Ferrari*. Jaico Publishing House.

Shastri, R. K. (2008). A strategic action plan for managing non government with special reference of India definition of NGOs. *International NGO Journal, 3*(3), 74–76.

Sherif, M., Harvey, O. J., White, B. J., & Hood, W. R. (1961). *The robber's cave experiment: Intergroup conflict and cooperation*. Academic Press.

Shih, T. H., & Fan, X. (2007). Response rates and mode preferences in web-mail mixed-mode surveys: A meta-analysis. *International Journal of Internet Science, 2*(1), 59–82.

Shin, J., Suh, E. M., Eom, K., & Kim, H. S. (2017). Article. *Journal of Happiness Studies*, 1–14.

Shoaib, M., Noor, A., Tirmizi, S. R., & Bashir, S. (2009). Determinants of employee retention in telecom sector of Pakistan. *Proceedings of the 2nd CBRC, 14*.

Shouksmith, G., Pajo, K., & Jepsen, A. (1990). Construction of a multidimensional scale of job satisfaction. *Psychological Reports, 67*(2), 355–364. doi:10.2466/pr0.1990.67.2.355 PMID:2263682

Silvestro, R., & Cross, S. (2000). Applying the service-profit chain in a retail environment: Challenging the satisfaction mirror. *International Journal of Service Industry Management, 11*(3), 244–268. doi:10.1108/09564230010340760

Simons, T. (2002). The high cost of lost trust. *Harvard Business Review, 80*(9), 18–19. PMID:12389455

Simpson, M. R. (2008). Engagement at work: A review of the literature. *International Journal of Nursing Studies, 1*, 1–13. PMID:18701104

Singh, H. P. (2015, October 30). *Sector-wise contribution of GDP of India*. Jagran Josh.

Singh, Y., & Bhargava, M. (1990). Manual for Emotional Maturity Scale. National Psychological Corporation.

Singh, N., & Rangnekar, S. (2016). Relationship between meaningful work and organizational trust: A study of techno-managers in the Indian power sector. *Proceedings of GLOGIFT, 16*, 247–255.

Smith, P. C., Kendall, L. M., & Hulin, C. L. (1969). *The measurement of satisfaction in work and retirement*. Chicago: Rand McNally.

Snee, R. D. (1999, September). Why should statisticians pay attention to Six Sigma? Quality Progress, 100-103.

Snipes, R. L., Oswald, S. L., LaTour, M., & Armenakis, A. A. (2005). The effects of specific job satisfaction facets on customer perceptions of service quality: An employee-level analysis. *Journal of Business Research, 58*(10), 1330–1339. doi:10.1016/j.jbusres.2004.03.007

Snyder, C. R., & Lopez, S. J. (Eds.). (2002). Handbook of Positive Psychology. New York: Oxford University Press.

Snyder, C. R., & Lopez, S. J. (2007). *Positive Psychology: The Scientific and Practical Explorations of Human Strengths*. Sage.

Soliman, K. S., & Janz, B. D. (2004). An exploratory study to identify the critical factors affecting the decision to establish Internet-based interorganizational information systems. *Information & Management, 41*(6), 697–706. doi:10.1016/j.im.2003.06.001

Song, J. H., Kim, H. M., & Kolb, J. A. (2009). The effect of learning organization culture on the relationship between interpersonal trust and organizational commitment. *Human Resource Development Quarterly, 20*(2), 147–167. doi:10.1002/hrdq.20013

Song, S. H., & Olshfski, D. (2008). Friends at Work A Comparative Study of Work Attitudes in Seoul City Government and New Jersey State Government. *Administration & Society, 40*(2), 147–169. doi:10.1177/0095399707312827

Spector, P. E. (1982). Behavior in organizations as a function of employee's LoC. *Psychological Bulletin, 91*(3), 482–497. doi:10.1037/0033-2909.91.3.482

Spreitzer, G. M. (2008). Taking stock: A review of more than twenty years of research on empowerment at work. Handbook of Organizational Behavior, 54-72.

Spreitzer, G. M. (1995). Psychological empowerment in the workplace: Dimensions, measurement, and validation. *Academy of Management Journal, 38*(5), 1442–1465. doi:10.2307/256865

Srivastava, A. K., & Misra, G. (2011). Happiness and Well Being: An Indian Perspective. In G. Misra (Ed.), *Handbook of Psychology in India*. New Delhi: Oxford University Press.

Srivastava, A. P., & Dhar, R. L. (2016). Authentic leadership for teacher's academic optimism: Moderating effect of training comprehensiveness. *European Journal of Training and Development, 40*(5), 321–344.

Srivastava, A., Bartol, K. M., & Locke, E. A. (2006). Empowering leadership in management teams: Effects on knowledge sharing, efficacy, and performance. *Academy of Management Journal, 49*(6), 1239–1251. doi:10.5465/AMJ.2006.23478718

Steel, R. P., & Ovalle, N. K. (1984). *A review and meta-analysis of research on the relationship between behavioral intentions and employee turnover*. Academic Press.

Steel, R. P., & Ovalle, N. K. (1984). A review and meta-analysis of research on the relationship between behavioral intentions and employee turnover. *The Journal of Applied Psychology, 69*(4), 673–686. doi:10.1037/0021-9010.69.4.673

Stiles, W. B. (1987). I have to talk to somebody. In Self-disclosure (pp. 257-282). Springer US.

Stiles, W. B., Shuster, P. L., & Harrigan, J. A. (1992). Disclosure and anxiety: A test of the fever model. *Journal of Personality and Social Psychology, 63*(6), 980–988. doi:10.1037/0022-3514.63.6.980 PMID:1460564

Stuart, H. (1999). Towards a definitive model of the corporate identity management process. *Corporate Communications, 4*(4), 200–207. doi:10.1108/13563289910299328

Subramony, M., & Holtom, B. C. (2012). The long-term influence of service employee attrition on customer outcomes and profits. *Journal of Service Research, 15*(4), 460–473. doi:10.1177/1094670512452792

Suls, J., & Wheeler, L. (2000). *Handbook of social comparison*. New York: Kluwer.

Sveningsson, S., & Alvesson, M. (2003). Managing managerial identities: Organizational fragmentation, discourse and identity struggle. *Human Relations, 56*(10), 1163–1193. doi:10.1177/00187267035610001

Szeliski, V., & Paradiso, L. J. (1936). Demand for Boots and Shoes as Affected by Price Levels and National Income. *Econometrica, 4*, 338–355.

Tajfel, H., & Turner, J. C. (1979). An integrative theory of intergroup conflict. *The Social Psychology of Intergroup Relations, 33*(47), 74.

Taneja, M. (2017, February). Bharti Airtel to acquire Telenor India as Jio threat grows. *VC Circle*. Retrieved March 2017, from http://www.vccircle.com/news/telecom/2017/02/23/bharti-airtel-acquire-telenor-india

Tasnim, Z. (2016). Happiness at Workplace: *Building a Conceptual Framework. World. Journal of social Sciences, 6*(2), 62–70.

Tatarkiewicz, W. (1976). *Analysis of happiness*. The Hague, The Netherlands: Martinus Nijhoff. doi:10.1007/978-94-010-1380-2

Taylor, C. C. W. (1998). Eudaimonia. In E. Craig (Ed.), *Routledge Encyclopedia of Philosophy* (Vol. 3, pp. 450–452). New York: Routledge.

Thau, S., Aquino, K., & Poortvliet, P. M. (2007). Self-defeating behaviors in organizations: The relationship between thwarted belonging and interpersonal work behaviors. *The Journal of Applied Psychology*, *92*(3), 840–847. doi:10.1037/0021-9010.92.3.840 PMID:17484563

The Times of India. (2014). *India's ITeS sector sees double-digit attrition rate*. Accessed 1 February, 2016 http://timesofindia.indiatimes.com/tech/jobs/Indias-ITeS-sector-sees-double-digit-attrition-rate/articleshow/37067873.cms

Thomas, G. F., Zolin, R., & Hartman, J. L. (2009). The central role of communication in developing trust and its effects on employee involvement. *Journal of Business Communication*, *46*(3), 287–310. doi:10.1177/0021943609333522

Thomas, K. W., & Velthouse, B. A. (1990). Cognitive elements of empowerment: An 'interpretive' model of intrinsic task motivation. *Academy of Management Review*, *15*(4), 666–681.

Thomas, M., & Seeman, J. (1971). Criterion measures for therapy outcome: A study in personality integration. *Psychotherapy (Chicago, Ill.)*, *8*(1), 26–30. doi:10.1037/h0086619

Tirelli, A., & Goh, S. C. (2015). The relationship between trust, learning capability, affective organisational commitment and turnover intentions. *International Journal of Human Resources Development and Management*, *15*(1), 54–68. doi:10.1504/IJHRDM.2015.069971

Tiwari, B., & Lenka, U. (2015). Building and branding talent hub: An outlook. *Industrial and Commercial Training*, *47*(4), 208–213. doi:10.1108/ICT-11-2014-0077

Tiwari, B., & Lenka, U. (2016). Building psychological safety for employee engagement in post-recession. *Development and Learning in Organizations: An International Journal*, *30*(1), 19–22.

Tornatzky, L. G., Fleischer, M., & Chakrabarti, A. K. (1990). *Processes of technological innovation*. Lexington Books.

Tseng, M. L. (2009). A causal and effect decision making model of service quality expectation using grey-fuzzy DEMATEL approach. *Expert Systems with Applications*, *36*(4), 7738–7748. doi:10.1016/j.eswa.2008.09.011

Turner, N., Barling, J., & Zacharatos, A. (2002). Positive psychology at work. Handbook of Positive Psychology, 52, 715-728.

Tyler, T. R., & Lind, E. A. (1992). A relational model of authority in groups. *Advances in Experimental Social Psychology*, *25*, 115–191. doi:10.1016/S0065-2601(08)60283-X

Uchida, Y., Norasakkunkit, V., & Kitayama, S. (2004). Cultural Constructions of Happiness: Theory and Empirical Evidence. *Journal of Happiness Studies*, *5*(3), 223–239. doi:10.1007/s10902-004-8785-9

Ulrich, D. (1997). *Human Resource Champions - The next agenda for adding value and delivering results*. Boston: Harvard Business School Press.

Urwin, S., Stanley, R., Jones, M., Gallagher, A., Wainwright, P., & Perkins, A. (2010). Understanding student nurse attrition: Learning from the literature. *Nurse Education Today*, *30*(2), 202–207. doi:10.1016/j.nedt.2009.07.014 PMID:19910083

Van den Heuvel, S., van den Heuvel, S., Freese, C., Freese, C., Schalk, R., Schalk, R., & van Assen, M. (2017). How change information influences attitudes toward change and turnover intention: The role of engagement, psychological contract fulfillment, and trust. *Leadership and Organization Development Journal*, *38*(3), 398–418. doi:10.1108/LODJ-03-2015-0052

Van Schalkwyk, L., & Rothmann, S. (2010). Job satisfaction in a chemical factory. *Southern African Business Review*, *14*(3), 108–130.

VanZyl, L. E., Deacon, E., & Rothmann, S. (2010). Towards happiness: Experiences of work-role fit, meaningfulness, and work engagement of industrial/organisational psychologists in South Africa. *SA Journal of Industrial Psychology*, *36*(1), 1–10.

Varma, A., Srinivas, E. S., & Stroh, L. K. (2005). A comparative study of the impact of leader-member exchange in US and Indian samples. *Cross Cultural Management*, *12*(1), 84–95. doi:10.1108/13527600510797971

Veenhoven, R. (2015). *Size of the Collections*. World Database of Happiness, Erasmus University of Rotterdam. Accessed on 11-02-2016 at: http://worlddatabaseofhappiness.eur.nl

Veenhoven, R. (1984). *Conditions of Happiness*. Dordrecht, The Netherlands: Reidel. doi:10.1007/978-94-009-6432-7

Veenhoven, R. (1991). Is happiness relative? *Social Indicators Research*, *24*(1), 1–34. doi:10.1007/BF00292648

Veenhoven, R. (2003). Happiness. *The Psychologist*, *16*(3), 128–129.

Veenhoven, R. (2017). Co-development of Happiness Research-Addition to "Fifty Years After the Social Indicator Movement". *Social Indicators Research*, 1–7.

Verquer, M. L., Beehr, T. A., & Wagner, S. H. (2003). A meta-analysis of relations between person–organization fit and work attitudes. *Journal of Vocational Behavior*, *63*(3), 473–489. doi:10.1016/S0001-8791(02)00036-2

Vittersø, J. (2003). Flow versus life satisfaction: A projective use of cartoons to illustrate the difference between the evaluation approach and the intrinsic motivation approach to subjective quality of life. *Journal of Happiness Studies*, *4*(2), 141–167. doi:10.1023/A:1024413112234

Wallace, J. C., Edwards, B. D., Arnold, T., Frazier, M. L., & Finch, D. M. (2009). Work stressors, role-based performance, and the moderating influence of organizational support. *The Journal of Applied Psychology*, *94*(1), 254–262. doi:10.1037/a0013090 PMID:19186910

Walumbwa, F. O., & Lawler, J. J. (2003). Building effective organizations: Transformational leadership, collectivist orientation, work-related attitudes, and withdrawal behaviors in three emerging economies. *International Journal of Human Resource Management*, *14*(7), 1083–1101. doi:10.1080/0958519032000114219

Warr, P. (2009). Work, happiness, and unhappiness. *Cognitive Behavioural Therapy Book Reviews, 5*(5), 1-3.

Warr, P., Cook, J., & Wall, T. (1979). Scales for the measurement of some work attitudes and aspects of psychological well-being. *Journal of Occupational Psychology*, *52*(2), 129–148. doi:10.1111/j.2044-8325.1979.tb00448.x

Waterman, A. S. (1990). The relevance of Aristotle's conception of eudaimonia for the psychological study of happiness. *Theoretical and Philosophical Psychology*, *10*(1), 39–44. doi:10.1037/h0091489

Watson, D., Clark, L. A., & Tellegen, A. (1988). Development and validation of Brief Measures of Positive and Negative Affect: The PANAS Scales. *Journal of Personality and Social Psychology*, *54*(6), 1063–1070. doi:10.1037/0022-3514.54.6.1063 PMID:3397865

Wayne, S. J., Shore, L. M., & Linden, R. C. (1997). Perceived organizational support and leader-member exchange: A social Exchange perspective. *Academy of Management Journal*, *40*(1), 82–111. doi:10.2307/257021

WebTeam D. N. (2017, March). Beyond price and data war: There are other nightmares Reliance Jio could create for its competition. *Daily News and Analysis*. Retrieved March 2017, from http://www.dnaindia.com/money/report-beyond-price-and-data-war-there-are-other-nightmares-reliance-jio-could-create-for-its-competition-2345309

Weiss, D. J., Dawis, R. V., England, G. W., & Lofquist, L. H. (1967). *Manual for the Minnesota Satisfaction Questionnaire*. Minneapolis, MN: University of Minnesota, Industrial Relation Center.

Weiss, H., & Sherman, J. (1973). Internal-external control as a predictor of task effort and satisfaction subsequent to failure. *The Journal of Applied Psychology*, *57*(2), 132–136. doi:10.1037/h0037054 PMID:4784756

Weitz, K. (2011). *Positivity (happiness) in the workplace and organisational change*. Retrieved from http://libraryofprofessionalcoaching.com/tools/executive-presence/positivity-happiness-in-the-workplace-and-organisational-change/10/

Welch, J., & Byrne, J. A. (2001). *JACK: Straight from the Gut*. New York: Warner Books Inc.

West, S. G., Finch, J. F., & Curran, P. J. (1995). *Structural equation models with nonnormal variables: Problems and remedies*. Academic Press.

Wheeless, L. R., & Grotz, J. (1977). The measurement of trust and its relationship to self-disclosure. *Human Communication Research*, *3*(3), 250–257. doi:10.1111/j.1468-2958.1977.tb00523.x

Whitener, E. M., Brodt, S. E., Korsgaard, M. A., & Werner, J. M. (1998). Managers as initiators of trust: An exchange relationship framework for understanding managerial trustworthy behavior. *Academy of Management Review*, *23*(3), 513–530.

Wikipedia. (2017, September 30). *Human resource management.* Retrieved October 2, 2017, from Wikipedia: https://en.wikipedia.org/wiki/Human_resource_management

Williams, H. M., Parker, S. K., & Turner, N. (2007). Perceived dissimilarity and perspective taking within work teams. *Group & Organization Management*, *32*(5), 569–597. doi:10.1177/1059601106293769

Winstead, B. A., Derlega, V. J., Montgomery, M. J., & Pilkington, C. (1995). The quality of friendships at work and job satisfaction. *Journal of Social and Personal Relationships*, *12*(2), 199–215. doi:10.1177/0265407595122003

Wittink, D. R., & Cattin, P. (1989). Commercial use of conjoint analysis: An update; IN. *Journal of Marketing*, *53*(3), 91–96. doi:10.2307/1251345

Witt, L. A., & Nye, L. G. (1992). Gender and the relationship between perceived fairness of pay or promotion and job satisfaction. *The Journal of Applied Psychology*, *77*(6), 910–917. doi:10.1037/0021-9010.77.6.910 PMID:1468995

Witt, U. (1998). Imagination and leadership–the neglected dimension of an evolutionary theory of the firm. *Journal of Economic Behavior & Organization*, *35*(2), 161–177. doi:10.1016/S0167-2681(98)00058-4

Wright, R. A., & Brehm, J. W. (1984). The impact of task difficulty upon perceptions of arousal and goal attractiveness in an avoidance paradigm. *Motivation and Emotion*, *8*(2), 171–181. doi:10.1007/BF00993072

Wright, T. A., & Bonett, D. G. (2007). Job satisfaction and psychological well-being as non- additive predictors of workplace turnover. *Journal of Management*, *33*(2), 141–152. doi:10.1177/0149206306297582

Wrzesniewski, A., & Dutton, J. E. (2001). Crafting a job: Revisioning employees as active crafters of their work. *Academy of Management Review*, *26*(2), 179–201.

Wu, W. W., & Lee, Y. T. (2007). Developing global managers' competencies using the fuzzy DEMATEL method. *Expert Systems with Applications*, *32*(2), 499–507. doi:10.1016/j.eswa.2005.12.005

Wyper, B., & Harrison, A. (2000). Deployment of Six Sigma methodology in Human Resource function: A case study. *Total Quality Management*, *11*(4 & 5), S720. doi:10.1080/09544120050008129

Xue, Y., Bradley, J., & Liang, H. (2011). Team climate, empowering leadership, and knowledge sharing. *Journal of Knowledge Management*, *15*(2), 299–312. doi:10.1108/13673271111119709

Xu, S., Martinez, L. R., & Lv, Q. (2017). Explaining the link between emotional labor and turnover intentions: The role of in-depth communication. *International Journal of Hospitality & Tourism Administration*, 1–19. doi:10.1080/15256480.2017.1324339

Yadav, R., & Mahara, T. (2016). An exploratory study to investigate value chain of Saharanpur wooden carving handicraft cluster. *International Journal of System Assurance Engineering and Management*, 1-8.

Yağışan, N., Sünbül, A. M., & Yücalan, Ö. B. (2007). Müzik bölümü öğrencilerinin benlik imgeleri ve denetim odaklarının incelenmesi. *Erciyes Üniversitesi Sosyal Bilimler Enstitüsü Dergisi*, *1*(22), 243–262.

Yamaguchi, I. (2006). Multiple group factor analysis of organizational communications for sending the outcome of decision making in Japan–US companies. *Human Communication Studies*, *34*, 35–51.

Yamaguchi, I. (2009). Influences of organizational communication tactics on trust with procedural justice effects: A cross-cultural study between Japanese and American workers. *International Journal of Intercultural Relations*, *33*(1), 21–31. doi:10.1016/j.ijintrel.2009.01.002

Yang, J. (2005). *The Role of Trust in Organizations: Do Foci and Bases Matter?* (Doctoral dissertation). Nanjing University, China.

Yee, R. W., Yeung, A. C., & Cheng, T. C. (2008). The impact of employee satisfaction on quality and profitability in high-contact service industries. *Journal of Operations Management*, *26*(5), 651–668. doi:10.1016/j.jom.2008.01.001

Yoo, G. J., Aviv, C., Levine, E. G., Ewing, C., & Au, A. (2010). Emotion work: Disclosing cancer. *Supportive Care in Cancer*, *18*(2), 205–215. doi:10.1007/s00520-009-0646-y PMID:19434430

Yoon, M. H., Beatty, S. E., & Suh, J. (2001). The effect of work climate on critical employee and customer outcomes: An employee-level analysis. *International Journal of Service Industry Management*, *12*(5), 500–521. doi:10.1108/EUM0000000006095

Yukl, G. (2006). *Leadership in organizations* (6th ed.). Upper Saddle River, NJ: Pearson-Prentice Hall.

Zagenczyk, T. J., Scott, K. D., Gibney, R., Murrell, A. J., & Thatcher, J. B. (2010). Social influence and perceived organizational support: A social networks analysis. *Organizational Behavior and Human Decision Processes*, *111*(2), 127–138. doi:10.1016/j.obhdp.2009.11.004

Zeithaml, V.A., & Bitner, M.J. (2000). *Services Marketing*. McGraw-Hill.

Index

I

J

K

L

M

O

P

Q

R

S

Purchase Print, E-Book, or Print + E-Book

IGI Global books can now be purchased from three unique pricing formats: Print Only, E-Book Only, or Print + E-Book. Shipping fees apply.

www.igi-global.com

Recommended Reference Books

ISBN: 978-1-4666-8745-5
© 2016; 410 pp.
List Price: $220

ISBN: 978-1-4666-9604-4
© 2016; 378 pp.
List Price: $205

ISBN: 978-1-4666-9624-2
© 2016; 2,266 pp.
List Price: $2,200

ISBN: 978-1-4666-8468-3
© 2015; 1,704 pp.
List Price: $2,395

ISBN: 978-1-4666-9484-2
© 2016; 514 pp.
List Price: $265

ISBN: 978-1-4666-8353-2
© 2015; 438 pp.
List Price: $310

Looking for free content, product updates, news, and special offers?

Join IGI Global's mailing list today and start enjoying exclusive perks sent only to IGI Global members. Add your name to the list at **www.igi-global.com/newsletters.**

Publishing Information Science and Technology Research Since 1988

IGI Global DISSEMINATOR OF KNOWLEDGE

www.igi-global.com Sign up at www.igi-global.com/newsletters facebook.com/igiglobal twitter.com/igiglobal

Stay Current on the Latest Emerging Research Developments

Become an IGI Global Reviewer for Authored Book Projects

The overall success of an authored book project is dependent on quality and timely reviews.

In this competitive age of scholarly publishing, constructive and timely feedback significantly decreases the turnaround time of manuscripts from submission to acceptance, allowing the publication and discovery of progressive research at a much more expeditious rate. Several IGI Global authored book projects are currently seeking highly qualified experts in the field to fill vacancies on their respective editorial review boards:

Applications may be sent to:
development@igi-global.com

Applicants must have a doctorate (or an equivalent degree) as well as publishing and reviewing experience. Reviewers are asked to write reviews in a timely, collegial, and constructive manner. All reviewers will begin their role on an ad-hoc basis for a period of one year, and upon successful completion of this term can be considered for full editorial review board status, with the potential for a subsequent promotion to Associate Editor.

If you have a colleague that may be interested in this opportunity, we encourage you to share this information with them.

www.igi-global.com

InfoSci®-Books

A Database for Information Science and Technology Research

Maximize Your Library's Book Collection!

Invest in IGI Global's InfoSci®-Books database and gain access to hundreds of reference books at a fraction of their individual list price.

The InfoSci®-Books database offers unlimited simultaneous users the ability to precisely return search results through more than 80,000 full-text chapters from nearly 3,900 reference books in the following academic research areas:

Business & Management Information Science & Technology • Computer Science & Information Technology
Educational Science & Technology • Engineering Science & Technology • Environmental Science & Technology
Government Science & Technology • Library Information Science & Technology • Media & Communication Science & Technology
Medical, Healthcare & Life Science & Technology • Security & Forensic Science & Technology • Social Sciences & Online Behavior

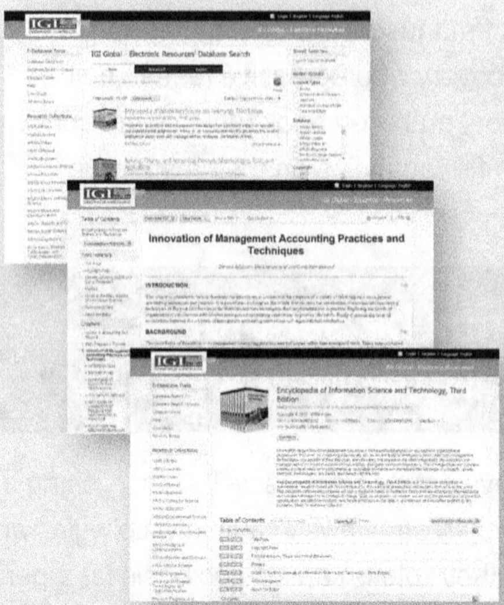

Peer-Reviewed Content:
- Cutting-edge research
- No embargoes
- Scholarly and professional
- Interdisciplinary

Award-Winning Platform:
- Unlimited simultaneous users
- Full-text in XML and PDF
- Advanced search engine
- No DRM

Librarian-Friendly:
- Free MARC records
- Discovery services
- COUNTER4/SUSHI compliant
- Training available

To find out more or request a free trial, visit: www.igi-global.com/eresources

IGI Global DISSEMINATOR OF KNOWLEDGE
www.igi-global.com

IGI Global
DISSEMINATOR OF KNOWLEDGE
www.igi-global.com

IGI Global Proudly Partners with

eContent Pro International

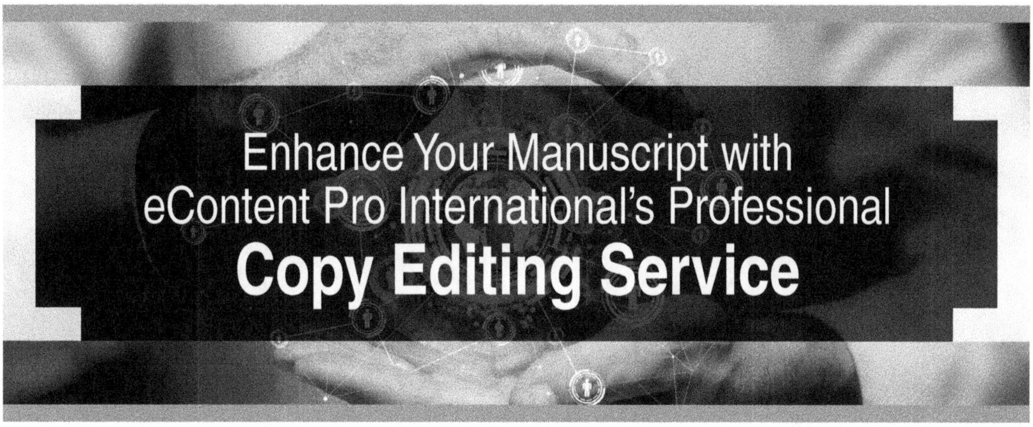

Expert Copy Editing

eContent Pro International copy editors, with over 70 years of combined experience, will provide complete and comprehensive care for your document by resolving all issues with spelling, punctuation, grammar, terminology, jargon, semantics, syntax, consistency, flow, and more. In addition, they will format your document to the style you specify (APA, Chicago, etc.). All edits will be performed using Microsoft Word's Track Changes feature, which allows for fast and simple review and management of edits.

Additional Services

eContent Pro International also offers fast and affordable proofreading to enhance the readability of your document, professional translation in over 100 languages, and market localization services to help businesses and organizations localize their content and grow into new markets around the globe.

IGI Global Authors Save 25% on eContent Pro International's Services!

Scan the QR Code to Receive Your 25% Discount

The 25% discount is applied directly to your eContent Pro International shopping cart when placing an order through IGI Global's referral link. Use the QR code to access this referral link. eContent Pro International has the right to end or modify any promotion at any time.

Email: customerservice@econtentpro.com

econtentpro.com

www.ingramcontent.com/pod-product-compliance
Lightning Source LLC
LaVergne TN
LVHW080340011026
849161LV00009B/2130
9781522540380